Archeological Region of Oaxaca

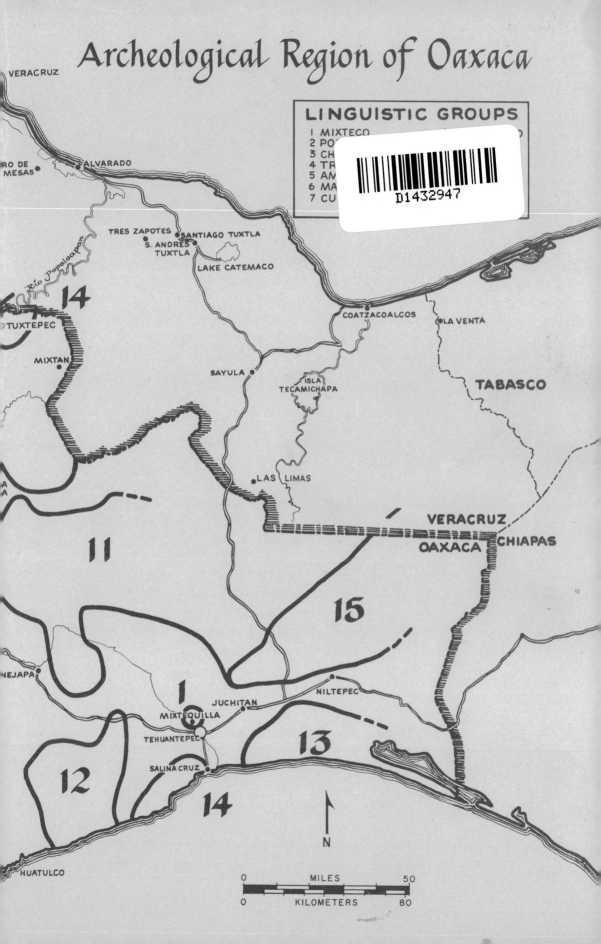

VERACRUZ

RO DE
MESAS

ALVARADO

Río Papaloapan

TRES ZAPOTES
S. ANDRES
TUXTLA

SANTIAGO TUXTLA

LAKE CATEMACO

14

TUXTEPEC

MIXTAN

SAYULA

ISLA
TECAMICHAPA

COATZACOALCOS

LA VENTA

TABASCO

LAS LIMAS

VERACRUZ

OAXACA

CHIAPAS

11

15

NEJAPA

1

JUCHITAN

NILTEPEC

MIXTEQUILLA

TEHUANTEPEC

13

SALINA CRUZ

12

14

N

HUATULCO

0	MILES	50
0	KILOMETERS	80

Ancient Oaxaca

Edited by John Paddock

With contributions by

Ignacio Bernal
Alfonso Caso
Robert Chadwick
Howard F. Cline
Wigberto Jiménez Moreno
Howard Leigh
John Paddock
Donald Robertson
Charles R. Wicke

Ancient Oaxaca

Discoveries in Mexican Archeology and History

Stanford University Press, Stanford, California

Part I was originally published in Spanish, in somewhat different form, as pp. 1019–1108 of Volume II of *Esplendor del México antiguo*, ed. Carmen Cook de Leonard (México, 1959), under the title "Síntesis de la historia pretolteca de Mesoamérica." The line drawings were first published in the Spanish edition.

The last six papers in Part III were originally published in Spanish, in somewhat different form, in the *Actas y Memorias del XXXV Congreso Internacional de Americanistas, México, 1962* (México, 1964). Part II, the Chadwick and Leigh papers of Part III, and all the photographs in Parts II and III, except as indicated on p. x, are published here for the first time.

For this second printing, minor corrections have been made throughout the book and a new Postscript to Part II has been supplied by the Editor.

To the memory of
Robert Hayward Barlow
1918–1951

Preface

Most of those who take up this book will not have known the name of Robert Hayward Barlow, to whose memory it is dedicated by all the authors. Quite possibly no such book would exist but for his work in Mexico. Although Wigberto Jiménez Moreno and Pedro Bosch-Gimpera were formally the co-founders of the Department of Anthropology at Mexico City College in 1947, Barlow was the first person to give his full-time attention to it, and he followed them as Chairman. Research in the archeology, ethnohistory, and ethnology of Mesoamerica began under Barlow's direction in 1947. Ignacio Bernal, who succeeded Barlow, naturally turned this research toward the area in which he himself had specialized as a student of Alfonso Caso, the founder of Oaxaca archeology. As Bernal's student and finally his successor in the chairmanship, I have continued that orientation.

The contributors to this book are former teachers or former students of Barlow in some cases; in others, beneficiaries of a tradition to which he almost literally gave his life. As Bernal said in an obituary, "Only rarely does a historian's passion for his theme fail to sweep him into a blind admiration of it. In fact, the Aztec militarists [Barlow's special field of study] were deeply disagreeable to him, and his sympathies were always with the other peoples who, although perhaps more cultivated, were always conquered." But, "as Alfred L. Kroeber once observed, 'Barlow is a born historian'; when he died, January 1, 1951, at 32 years of age, he had already accomplished a lifework of which an elderly man might be proud." Certain other friends must be mentioned for their crucial roles in encouraging Barlow's work and the work that grew from it: the late Lorna Lavery Stafford, founder and dean of the Graduate School at Mexico City College, now University of the Americas, and Paul V. Murray, who as Vice President and President insisted that even a struggling small college, less an institution than a mere strong conviction in those early days, could and should sponsor research.

Publication in English of the Oaxaca symposium papers of Part III was the idea of J. G. Bell, Editor of the Stanford University Press. He and his staff, in particular Muriel Davison and Pauline Wickham, have extended their efforts far beyond the usual requirements of their demanding profession during the long and unpredictable creation of the book. Their courage, care, skill, and patience are apparently inexhaustible. Maudie Bullington has given much to the archeology of several regions of Mesoamerica, and she has not often been thanked for her intelligently expressed good will. Let it be noted here that in addition to her senior collaboration on the translation of Part I, she contributed financial support to the explorations at Yagul and Zaachila. A group of American tourists in 1960 dipped into their travel funds to make possible the important radiocarbon date on the Yagul brazier of Monte Albán Ic.

Since Bernal first took some Mexico City College students (briefly, but decisively for me, I was there) to Oaxaca in 1952, many students have contributed to our work. Their tuition has financed nearly all our field work, and their labors in and after the excavations have been little acknowledged. The questions they ask are an invaluable guide and stimulus in the preparation of such a book as this one. A grant to me from a cultivated American couple who wish to remain anonymous has greatly eased work in the last stages of production of the book, freeing me temporarily of teaching duties.

Carmen Cook de Leonard, whose name appears more than once in the pages to follow, kindly allowed our use of the English translation of Jiménez Moreno's study as Part I of this book, even though she had hoped to bring it out some day in an English version of the fine collection of essays she edited in Spanish as *Esplendor del México antiguo*. Santiago Genovés and Lauro José Zavala ably edited the three large volumes of *Actas y memorias del XXXV Congreso Internacional de Americanistas, México, 1962*, and were most cooperative in allowing me to provide Spanish versions for the *Actas* of the three English-language papers in the Oaxaca symposium. The symposium thus appeared entirely in Spanish in the *Actas*, and Part III is its first publication in English.

Like the text, the illustrations are the work of many. Illustration credits will be found on p. x. Ross Parmenter's drawings from an engraved Mixtec bone, still unpublished in complete form, appear on the title page and at the ends of Parts I and II. We are indebted to Nancy Fouquet, David Pauly, and Jacinto Quirarte for the maps, tables, and drawings.

Directed by Darío Quero and Eligio Martínez Sr., the staff of the Museo Frissell de Arte Zapoteca in Mitla has served, befriended, and taught many of us in the house where its predecessors did the same for generations of earlier students, beginning well over a century ago. These gracious people have been deservedly thanked in many a book's preface, as they are sincerely in the present one. Modern Oaxacans, descendants of the Cloud People, make working and staying among them so agreeable that, like most of my colleagues, I would live here if I could. After twelve years of intermittent work in and around Tlacolula and Mitla, I can only thank their people collectively, for they include many and good friends. All of us who have participated in or benefited from this research are deeply indebted to them.

Ever since the end—well over twenty years ago—of the Monte Albán excavations, there has been no such thing as a full-time Oaxaca archeologist. A tiny group of specialists has been the uncomfortable but helpless possessor of a near monopoly on detailed knowledge of ancient Oaxaca. Every one of us in Mexico is a Oaxaca archeologist only in time snatched from other occupations, and these are in every case both multiple and exigent. Classroom teaching is an example: it has allowed us to unburden ourselves very slightly of our monopoly, but at the same time it has made wider publication more difficult. This book is intended to help end the unwelcome secrecy, and to make ancient Oaxaca more accessible to more interested people.

J.P.

Mitla, March 1966

Preface to the Second Printing

On pp. 241–42 I have sketched very generally what kind of new understanding is coming from current work in Oaxaca archeology. Preliminary reports with further detail may be found occasionally in *Science, American Antiquity* (especially its "Current Research: Western Mesoamerica"), the *Boletín* of Mexico's Instituto Nacional de Antropología e Historia, and other journals.

The cultural ecology of the entire Valley of Oaxaca from its first habitation to Monte Albán I times is the theme of a project directed by Kent V. Flannery. Ignacio Bernal is exploring Dainzú. Excavations in the Mixteca Alta are directed by Ronald Spores. The Miahuatlan work and the study of the Pacific coast are projects of Donald L. Brockington. Small-scale excavations have been done by Matthew Wallrath in the Isthmus of Tehuantepec and by Shirley Gorenstein at Tepexi in southern Puebla, within the Mixteca Baja. The Oaxaca "neighborhood" at Teotihuacan, a tomb at Huajuapan, the Lambityeco site, and late times at Mitla have been studied under my direction.

The unfailingly helpful attitude of Mexican officials has done much to make our work easier, and the continuing support of individuals and small private foundations in the United States has made it possible.

J.P.

Instituto de Estudios Oaxaqueños, Mitla
November 1969

Illustration Credits

PART I. Fig. 41, MNA; 42, University of Oklahoma Press.

PART II. Figs. 5, 10–13, 15, 16, 22, 28–30, 44, 60–62, 64–66, 69–72, 74, 82, 86, 88, 90, 96, 100, 101, 106, 107, 109, 122, 124, 126, 127, 129, 132, 140, 141, 178–81, 184, 189, 190, 191, 232a, 232b, 244–46, 263, 278, 290, photos by Eric Schwarz, courtesy MNA. Figs. 2a, 2b, Román Piña Chán; 33, 36a, 36h, 47, Marilu Pease; 134, 236–40, 256, ADV; 142, Howard Brunson, courtesy Paddock; 150, 174, Rivas, Oaxaca; 166, adapted from Bernal, *Official Guide to Monte Albán,* courtesy INAH; 182b, Caso & Bernal, *Urnas de Oaxaca,* courtesy INAH; 203; Chris L. Moser, 216–219a, 222, CRW; 224a–d, Walter Wakefield, courtesy Paddock; 231a, 231b, BM; 243, 286–89, Thomas MacDougall, courtesy University of the Americas; 273, Marjorie Cordley Rouillion. Map 2 inset, courtesy Aerotécnica de México, S.A., and Cecil R. Welte. Fig. 255 (Paddock photo) was published in *Mesoamerican Notes* No. 4 (1955).

PART III. *Chadwick paper.* Figs. 2, 3a, CRW. *Robertson paper:* 1–3, BM; 4, 5, ADV; 6, 7, Vatican Library. *Caso paper:* 1–7, 11–14, 25–35, INAH (17, 18, 25, photos by Roberto Gallegos); 8–10, BM. *Wicke paper:* 3, 9, 10, CRW; 9, BM. *Bernal paper:* 6, 8, 10–12, 17, 19, adapted from the *Actas;* 14, INAH. The following Part III photographs have been published previously: *Cline paper,* Figs. 3, 4, in the *Actas; Wicke paper,* 4 (Paddock photo), in *Mesoamerican Notes* No. 4 (1955); *Bernal paper,* 14, in the *Actas.*

Color section. Plate 5, ADV; 6–8, Bodleian Library, Oxford; 9, Liverpool Free Public Museum; 10–12, BM; 13, 14, 18–40, INAH.

KEY: *Actas, Actas y Memorias del XXXV Congreso Internacional de Americanistas, México, 1962* (México, 1964); ADV, Akademische Druck– u. Verlagsanstalt, Graz, Austria; BM, British Museum; CRW, Charles R. Wicke; INAH, Instituto Nacional de Antropología e Historia; MNA, Museo Nacional de Antropología.

Plates 1–4 and 15–17 and all black-and-white photographs not otherwise credited here are by John Paddock.

Contents

Major Maps, Plans, and Chronological Charts

Contributors

IGNACIO BERNAL, one of Alfonso Caso's principal collaborators in the Monte Albán excavations, is Director of Mexico's Museo Nacional de Antropología and of the government's major archeological project at Teotihuacan. In 1962 he presided over the XXXV International Congress of Americanists, at which most of the papers in Part III of this volume were presented. His publications include *Compendio de arte mesoamericano* (1950); *Monte Albán–Mitla, Guía oficial* (1957); *Exploraciones en Cuilapan de Guerrero, 1902–1954* (1958); *Mexico: Prehispanic Paintings* (1958); *Bibliografía de arqueología y etnografía* (1962); and three articles on Oaxaca in the *Handbook of Middle American Indians*, Volume III (1965).

ALFONSO CASO was the founder of the Sociedad Mexicana de Antropología and of the Instituto Nacional Indigenista, which he directs. As director of the first scientific explorations at Monte Albán, beginning in 1930, he is virtually the founder too of Oaxaca archeology. He has been a Cabinet minister and Rector of the National University. He is the author of a series of reports on the Monte Albán excavations; many articles on Mesoamerican calendars, writing, and codices, soon to be issued in a two-volume collection, as well as longer studies from *Las estelas zapotecas* (1928) to *Interpretation of the Codex Selden* (1964) and a study of Codex Colombino (in press); *Urnas de Oaxaca* (with Bernal, 1952); *The Aztecs, People of the Sun* (1959); a book on Monte Albán ceramics (with Bernal and Jorge R. Acosta, in press); and five articles on Oaxaca in Volume III of the *Handbook of Middle American Indians* (1965).

ROBERT CHADWICK teaches archeology at the University of Alberta in Calgary. He participated in excavations at Yagul as a graduate student at the University of the Americas, and later served as an archeologist on the Tehuacan Archaeological-Botanical Project and as staff archeologist on the Teotihuacan project of the Mexican government.

HOWARD F. CLINE is Director of the Hispanic Foundation of the Library of Congress. He is the author of *Mexico: From Revolution to Evolution* (1962); of *The United States and Mexico* (rev. ed., 1963); and of numerous articles on the Atlantic slope of the Oaxaca region.

WIGBERTO JIMÉNEZ MORENO, a documentary historian, achieved fame in the 1930's by demonstrating that Tula—not Teotihuacan, as everyone since the Aztecs had supposed—was the Toltec capital. He now heads the Department of Historical Research of Mexico's Instituto Nacional de Antropología e Historia, and teaches Nahuatl at the Escuela Nacional de Antropología and ancient history of Mexico at the University ot the Americas. He has been a Visiting Professor of History at the Universities of Illinois and Wisconsin. He is the author, with Salvador Mateos Higuera, of *Códice de Yanhuitlan* (1940); *Estudios de historia colonial* (1958); and *Estudios mixtecos* (1962).

HOWARD LEIGH is a painter, a resident of Mitla, and a longtime student of the Zapotec language and writing system. He played an active role in the founding of the Museo Frissell de Arte Zapoteca in Mitla, and serves on the Executive Council of the Museo.

JOHN PADDOCK is Co-Chairman of the Department of Anthropology at the University of the Americas and President of the Executive Council of the Museo Frissell. He has directed excavations at Mitla and Yagul, and served as technical adviser for the Oaxaca room at the Museo Nacional de Antropología.

DONALD ROBERTSON is Professor of the History of Art at Sophie Newcomb College, Tulane University. He is the author of *Mexican Manuscript Painting of the Early Colonial Period* (1959) and *Pre-Columbian Architecture* (1963).

CHARLES R. WICKE is Co-Chairman of the Department of Anthropology at the University of the Americas. He has worked as an archeologist in Peru and the Maya region, as well as in Oaxaca. He is the author of *Olmec: An Early Art Style of Precolumbian Mexico* (in press).

Mesoamerica Before the Toltecs

It may seem curious that the following study by Jiménez Moreno, in which the Aztec period is barely mentioned and the Maya people are given much less than the customary attention, should have been chosen to serve here as a general introduction to ancient Mesoamerican civilization, of which Oaxaca was a major part. Further, it appears to be a rather dismayingly technical essay, in which the author has assumed, for example, that the reader already knows who Ixtlilxóchitl and Veytia were, and what Xochipilli presided over. For all these idiosyncrasies, however, "Mesoamerica Before the Toltecs" remains an outstandingly creative effort to present the general outlines of this fascinating civilization's development.

In the late 1930's Jiménez Moreno, as a fledgling scholar, dramatically proposed that if the archeologists (he is himself a documentary historian) would dig at Tula, Hidalgo, they would find that it and not Teotihuacan had been the capital of the Toltecs of the early traditions. Although almost everyone since the Aztecs had believed with them that Teotihuacan was the only central Mexican ruin impressive enough to fit the Toltec legends, excavation soon proved Jiménez correct.

Turning then to the "Olmec" problem, Jiménez quickly separated the "Olmecs" of late times, often mentioned in the traditional histories, from the early and purely archeological "Olmecs" of La Venta, a people he now proposes calling the Tenocelome. The opinion held by Caso, Covarrubias, and Jiménez Moreno about the Gulf coast "Olmecs" was vigorously opposed by North Americans until the 1960's, when radiocarbon dating and new excavations made it clear that the Mexicans were right.

During the 1940's and early 1950's, Jiménez continued his work in the baffling morass of apparent and real contradictions that constitutes the documentary heritage of ancient Mexico. He succeeded in synthesizing out of this material a plausible chronicle of the years from about A.D. *900 to the Spanish conquest, especially in the Valley of Mexico (1945, 1953, 1956). Beginning in about 1956, he became interested in what few hints his sources gave about the history of earlier times. As he notes, he held a long series of conferences with Ignacio Bernal, Alfonso Caso, and Eduardo Noguera on archeological possibilities. The result is the present essay, written during 1958 for publication in* Esplendor del México antiguo *(1959).*

One of the most fundamental changes proposed by Jiménez in our way of thinking about ancient Mesoamerica is his clear statement of what we might call a non-monolithic Classic horizon. Since I published a similar idea at about the same time (Paddock 1959), I should like to point out here that we both believe we came upon the idea and wrote it out quite independently. Naturally we both were affected by the same developments, and in some earlier publications (for example, Caso 1953) the seed of the proposal may be found. I have developed it much further in Part II.

As for the Aztecs and the Mayas, they are here omitted for very sound reasons. Of the approximately forty centuries of Mesoamerican development from the appearance of pottery to the Spanish conquest, the Aztecs participated only in the last one. And the last was far from the best: as Jiménez points out, the Europeans (if they had been capable of crossing the Atlantic) would have found a more brilliant culture in A.D. *519 than they found in 1519. In the development of Mesoamerican culture, then, Aztec innovations are of necessity neither fundamental nor numerous.*

The Mayas are de-emphasized for different reasons. They were intensely creative, and they lived their greatest days during the period covered in the Jiménez synthesis. However, they have been very adequately described, notably by Morley and Brainerd (1956) and Thompson (1954), while their contemporaries have been unjustifiably neglected. Further, despite their impressive achievements, their geographical remoteness was so extreme that they seem to have had very little effect on the course of cultural development in the remainder of Mesoamerica.

The Oaxaca peoples, by contrast, were again and again at the center of critical developments in Mesoamerican history, as we shall see in detail in Part II. Here again Jiménez has been ahead of his time. Indeed, though he might disclaim the honor, he has been a kind of prophet for Oaxaca just as he was for the Toltecs and the "Olmecs."

The translation, made for this edition, is a fairly free one, and the 1959 text has been further modified for the present audience by minor style editing and the addition of new notes and of references to material published since 1959. The 1959 drawings, though imperfect, have been retained. The maps were redrawn for the present edition, and the two photographs are new.

Mesoamerica Before the Toltecs

WIGBERTO JIMÉNEZ MORENO

Translated by Maudie Bullington and Charles R. Wicke

My purpose in this study is to trace the cultural development of prehispanic Mexico from the earliest beginnings of pottery manufacture in about 1500 B.C. (or two or three centuries earlier if we accept Canby's stratigraphy for Yarumela in Honduras) right up to the foundation of the Toltec empire in about A.D. 1000.[1] In 1500 B.C., important technical innovations in the art of war were enabling the Egyptians to build a large empire, under the leadership of Thutmose I (1530–20) and Thutmose III (1504–1450); evidence appears of the beginning of the use of iron among the Hittites and in Crete; the Mycenaean culture was beginning to flower in southern Greece; and the Bronze Age was starting in China under the Shang dynasty. Thus our Mexican high cultures entered upon their course quite late, and at the time the Europeans arrived, Mexico had not advanced technologically beyond the Chalcolithic Age. Because of this, the Mexica of Moctezuma II had to hurdle several stages in order to assimilate the Renaissance culture that Cortés and his Spaniards brought with them. The success of the cultural blending of Spaniard and Indian is accordingly all the more remarkable.

To help me in my attempted reconstruction I have consulted works by Caso (1953), Armillas (1948, 1951, 1956, 1957), and Bernal (1950, 1953); Palerm's compendium (1955) and the recent study by Willey and Phillips (1958); and the contributions of two symposiums, one held in New York in 1947 (Bennett 1948), and the other in Tucson in 1953 (Steward 1955). I have

---

[1] The panorama here presented is conjectural, and, like any attempt at historical reconstruction, subject to corrections occasioned by new investigations. I wish to thank Alfonso Caso, Ignacio Bernal, and Eduardo Noguera for the generous help and valuable suggestions they gave me when I showed them this work, which is a more comprehensive effort than the article I wrote in 1942, "El Enigma de los olmecas." I am indebted to the Instituto Nacional de Antropología e Historia for the facilities put at my disposal, and to Raúl Noriega and Carmen Cook de Leonard for their constant assistance.

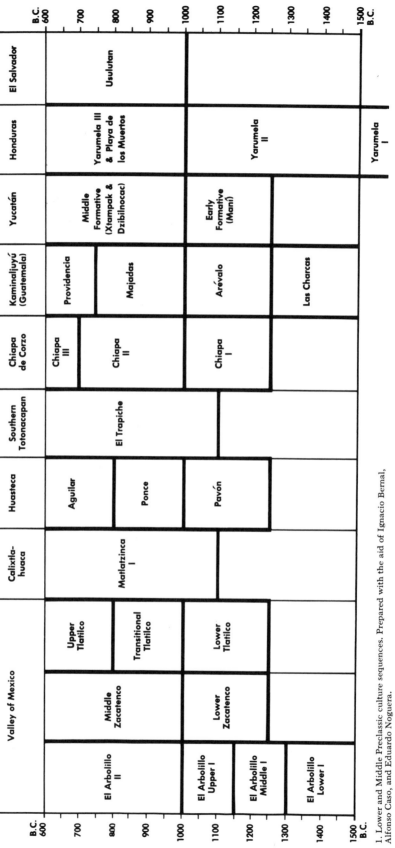

1. Lower and Middle Preclassic culture sequences. Prepared with the aid of Ignacio Bernal, Alfonso Caso, and Eduardo Noguera.

taken into consideration, but used only in small part, the excellent material they contain. I have consulted, in addition, works on prehispanic Mexico of a general nature, such as those by Marquina (1951) and Krickeberg (1956), and particularly the recent study by Covarrubias (1957). The newest radiocarbon dates have been taken into account (Wauchope 1955); a few of them, the ones obtained from the Tikal lintel on which the Maya inscription 9.15.10.0.0 is deciphered, seem to agree with the Spinden correlation (Libby 1955).[2] Since in some cases, for example at Teotihuacan,[3] a carbon 14 date turned out to be unacceptable, I believe it would be premature to discard the Goodman-Martínez-Thompson correlation on the basis of the dating of only one of the Maya sites that contain inscriptions. Until new and better arguments force us to abandon it, I believe that this correlation, set midway between those of Spinden and Escalona Ramos, still accords best with the available data, and I shall therefore continue to accept it.

The long lapse of three thousand years, stretching from the appearance of pottery in Mexico to the arrival of the Spaniards, is usually divided into three horizons: Preclassic, Classic, and Postclassic. These in turn are subdivided into the following periods: Lower, Middle, and Upper for the Preclassic; Early and Late, and perhaps Middle or Full, for the Classic; Toltec and Post-Toltec for the Postclassic. I shall adopt this system with slight modifications. In considering the first horizon, we shall be guided by the recent contributions of Piña Chán (1955b, 1958b: 112–20).

THE LOWER PRECLASSIC

In the Lower Preclassic, the earliest cultural centers appear in the Valley of Mexico (El Arbolillo I, followed by Lower Tlatilco and Lower Zacatenco), in the Guatemala highlands (the Las Charcas and Arévalo phases of Kaminaljuyú), and in Honduras, where, according to Canby (1951), the Yarumela II phase precedes the appearance of Usulutan pottery, which would place Yarumela II within the Lower Preclassic. Canby believes that there is an earlier local phase, Yarumela I. If he is right, and not everyone agrees with him,

[2] Libby (p. 132) says that the date obtained was A.D. 481 ± 120 years. From other samples belonging to this same Maya inscription were obtained the following figures: A.D. 469 ± 120, and 433 ± 170. In the Spinden correlation this inscription would correspond to A.D. 481, and in the Goodman-Martínez-Thompson correlation to A.D. 741. [A thorough re-examination of this question, involving 50 runs on carbon samples of lintel and vault beams from Tikal, appears to support the Goodman-Martínez-Thompson correlation. See Satterthwaite and Ralph (1960).—Translators.] [An apparently definitive word in favor of the same correlation, based on new and exhaustive studies, is given in Ralph (1965).—Editor.]

[3] From wood of a pillar excavated in 1921 in the "Citadel" or Temple of Quetzalcóatl at Teotihuacan, the age 3,424 ± 230 was obtained, corresponding to 1470 ± 230 B.C.; this turns out to be absurd. [Since this enormous piling was a tree trunk that may well have been very old when installed in the building, the age determined may in fact be rather accurate. It is the application of the age of the wood to the much later building that is mistaken. See also Ignacio Bernal (1965).—Editor.]

Yarumela I pottery would date back to approximately 1800 B.C., making it the first in Mesoamerica.[4] Apart from Yarumela I, these early cultures could be placed between 1500 and 1000 B.C.

According to García Payón (1950), the beginning of El Trapiche, Veracruz, belongs in part to this first period; so, it seems, does the oldest stratum of Tecáxic-Calixtlahuaca in the Valley of Toluca (García Payón 1941); and in addition perhaps we should include Chiapa de Corzo I (Lowe 1957: 16), the so-called Early Formative of Yucatán (Brainerd 1951), and what Mac-Neish (1954) terms the Pavón phase in the Huasteca. (See Figure 1.)

As to the Valley of Mexico, Armillas has emphasized that "the reason for its importance lies in [its] lacustrine character," and he points out that it offered an "abundance of game and fish," and "ideal conditions . . . for the *chinampa* system of agriculture and easy communication by water." As early as the Preclassic, subsistence in the Basin of Mexico was based upon agriculture, which, it seems, was carried out by a system of seasonally flooding areas for growing corn. Hunting and fishing filled out the diet. Textiles were certainly known in this period, as evidenced by Vaillant's discovery of pieces of cloth associated with a skeleton belonging to his Early Zacatenco; the cloth may have wrapped the skeleton (Vaillant 1930: 188). Nevertheless, to judge by the general nudity of figurine types C1, C2, C3, C4, and early F of this first period, clothing was not worn. Face and body painting, however, was extremely popular, and the women, the only sex represented in the clay figurines, adorned themselves with nose and ear plugs, and wore complicated turbans. This exclusive representation of women suggests to Piña Chán (1955b: 39) the possibility that women were dominant in the society, and that there were matrilineal clans. On the other hand, it has been thought that these nude figurines, which at this time rarely appear in funerary offerings, indicate the existence of a fertility cult. If we consider all these inferences justified, perhaps we could say of the Valley of Mexico, "In the beginning was the woman, the mother: the Mother Earth and the fruitful earth." In fact, in the Post-Toltec period ethnic groups of low cultural level, such as the Chichimecs of Xólotl, limited their religion to the worship of the "Sun Father" and the "Earth Mother." I suggest that in doing so, they were retaining forms of primitive stages of religious development. In other words, the Earth Goddess was of ancient origin, and her importance seems to have lasted until the Spanish conquest, when the Virgin of Guadalupe took her place. Thus, already at this time it appears that Mexico was incubating in the valley of its name under the symbol of the mother.

The people who inhabited the Basin of Mexico in the Lower Preclassic lived in villages set along river banks or on the shores of the lake. The houses

---

[4] The Purrón complex, recently discovered by MacNeish in the Tehuacan area, which dates between 2500 and 1900 B.C., is characterized by crude pottery (MacNeish 1962; 1964a; 1964c).—Translators.

in these villages were scattered, as they still are in Indian settlements. In their initial phases, El Arbolillo, Zacatenco, and Tlatilco must have been like this. Piña Chán estimates that at most these centers would have had a population of some 200 each. Referring to their funerary customs, he says, "Burials are made directly in the earth, in an extended position and accompanied by poor offerings; cemeteries, in the strict sense, do not exist." In conclusion, it is evident that these ancient inhabitants of the Valley did not live on a truly primitive cultural level, and that they had fully developed pottery as well as numerous stone and bone implements. Similar conditions appear to have existed in the Guatemala highlands in the Las Charcas and perhaps Arévalo phases of Kaminaljuyú (Piña Chán 1958b: 112; 1955b: 25).

THE MIDDLE PRECLASSIC

By the beginning of the Middle Preclassic, i.e. about 1000 B.C., the known occupied sites have multiplied. Piña Chán lists El Arbolillo II, Upper Tlatilco, Middle Zacatenco, Copilco, and the initial phase of Tlapacoyan in the Valley of Mexico; Atlihuayan, Gualupita I, Tlayacapan, the beginning of Chalcatzingo, Xochimilcatzingo, and Olintepec I in Morelos; in the Huasteca the Ponce and Aguilar phases that preceded Pánuco I; El Trapiche and Lower Tres Zapotes in Veracruz; and El Opeño in Michoacan. I would add a probable early occupation of Jiquilpan, suggested by a type of figurine resembling the C4 of Zacatenco and the figurines of El Opeño. Unfortunately the Jiquilpan figurines were not found in stratigraphic excavations, so that they could be much more recent. Also in this period are the Mamóm phase of Uaxactún in the Petén; perhaps the whole of the Majadas stratum, and probably, in my view, part of the Providencia in Kaminaljuyú in the Guatemala highlands. I would include, too, Chiapa de Corzo II, the Middle Formative of Yucatán, Yarumela III and Playa de los Muertos in Honduras, and Usulutan in El Salvador (Piña Chán 1955b: 105; 1958b: 119; 1955a: 25–27; Müller 1948; Canby 1951; Brainerd 1951; Covarrubias 1957; Lowe 1957; Noguera 1944; Shook and Kidder 1952).

La Venta at the end of the Middle Preclassic, as I see it, was beginning the long ascent that culminated in the Upper Preclassic, in which period I would also place Monte Albán I. In the Valley of Mexico, according to Piña Chán, the figurines characteristic of this epoch are types B, F, K, C5, and C9, as well as D1, D2, D3, A1, and "baby face" and "Olmecoid." This last tradition can be explained as the result of the arrival in the Valley of Mexico of a people undoubtedly related culturally to La Venta, a people whom many archeologists persist in calling "Olmec." However, this nomenclature confuses these earlier people, established for the most part in central and southern Veracruz and western Tabasco, with the late Olmecs of the traditional histories, who in my opinion transmitted Cholulteca I culture, as I have suggested in another study (1942). To avoid this confusion, I shall call the "Olmec" people the "Tenocelome," meaning "those of the tiger mouth."

The people of the culture that began in the Lower Preclassic at El Arbo-lillo, Zacatenco, and Tlatilco in the Valley of Mexico continued to develop their cultural heritage in these first two sites, where now, during the Middle Preclassic, El Arbolillo II and Zacatenco II emerged. This group thus preserved their own tradition and continued their ancient village life. At Tlatilco, however, new immigrants established themselves, people who came perhaps from settlements of Tenocelome affiliation in the Morelos region, such as Chalcatzingo and Atlihuayan. They brought with them major innovations, and converted Tlatilco into a settlement larger than a village but smaller than a city, so that it has been characterized as a "town." Incipient urbanization can be inferred. Some of the original inhabitants of Tlatilco, perhaps dispossessed of their lands by the colonists or simply wanting to continue their own cultural tradition without accepting the foreign one, went to settle in the nearby site of Atoto, where no evidence of Tenocelome innovations has been found. Tlatilco represents not only a great step in the direction of urbanization, but according to Palerm, "an advance toward a secure agricultural economy as opposed to the precarious economy of Zacatenco." Piña Chán believes that although seasonally flooded areas were still used for agriculture, the *milpa* or slash-and-burn system of cultivation was beginning.

In the Tlatilco figurines we find the use of textiles in the form of "skirts, breechclouts, coats, turbans, hats"; "head-shaving and cranial deformation, tattooing, tooth mutilation" appear; and facial and body painting is "applied by means of stamps or clay seals" according to Piña Chán. He points out, too, that in this period the figurines include "representations of male personages such as dwarfs, dancers, acrobats, wizards, musicians, and ball players."

Several of these features had been noted previously by Miguel Covarrubias in 1943 and 1950. Covarrubias showed further (1957: 19–32) that the inhabitants of Tlatilco "were stocky and rather small, went naked for the most part, and had peculiar ways of decorating themselves, painting their faces and bodies, and wearing elaborate headdresses. They were essentially agriculturists, peasants, not unlike Indians in remote parts of tropical America today. They cultivated maize, which they ground with milling stones to make pancakes. They also cultivated squashes and chili peppers, but there is no evidence that they grew beans. Meat was provided by fattening and raising a special breed of dog, or by hunting deer, rabbits, ducks, and other waterfowl with javelins propelled by spear-throwers. They also caught fish and shrimp in the lakes. They probably lived in small huts of woven branches, daubed with mud and roofed with thatch, [and] grouped into autonomous, communalistic villages. Their household articles were of the simplest sort: ropes, mats, baskets, stools, and four-footed beds. It is presumed that they used calabash bowls and bottles, the shapes of which they sometimes copied in pottery, as well as wooden and stone bowls. For tools they used sharp axes, celts of hard, polished greenstone hafted onto wooden handles; knives, drills, and scrapers of flaked obsidian and flint; awls and needles of bone; and flaking tools of deer's horn.

"For cooking, eating, and storing food they made excellent pottery of amazing variety, from the coarse plain storage jars of thick brown clay to little pots, bottles with long necks, stirrup-neck bottles, bowls, cups, shallow dishes, and vases of all sorts. The finest pottery they made was reserved for offerings to be buried with the dead. It had an infinite variety of shapes and was formed of various fine clays. . . . They also modeled remarkable effigy-vessels in the shapes of men, monkeys, peccaries, rabbits, raccoons, ducks, other birds, and fish. There are notable examples from Tlatilco of such effigy-vessels: acrobats, fat fishes, charming ducks, and a strange quadruped wearing a human mask and ingeniously made so that when liquid was poured out of the funnel-shaped tail the animal's ears whistled softly in a double gurgling note.

"The most important contribution of Tlatilco is the unprecedented wealth of artistic material it has yielded, giving us a new insight into the mentality and technology of the Early period. The Tlatilcans were essentially ceramists; their stone sculpture is negligible, and if they ever carved wood intensively, we shall probably never know it, there being little chance that any has survived. Besides the pottery already mentioned, the principal artistic activity was the making of charming, [expressive] figurines of clay, large and small, freely and ably modeled by hand in the gingerbread technique—the features and ornaments made by filleting, punching, gouging, and incising the fresh clay with a little stick, with a directness and feeling for form later lost when the arts became more formalized and more subjected to the limitations of less emotional, more intellectual religious symbolism. Their artistic mentality was radically different from that of the artists of the later Classic cultures. Their art was simple and unassuming, but gay and sensitive, free of religious themes. This is evident in the effigy-vessels, in the clay figurines, some as large as a baby, finely modeled and highly polished, which must have required considerable skill in the potter's art, and particularly in the small, solid figurines, even if, to judge by their uniformity and large numbers, they were made by mass-production methods.

"Hundreds of complete figurines and thousands of fragments have come out of the earth at Tlatilco in a most varied range of styles; most of them are of women with small breasts, short arms, slim waists, and large, bulbous legs; some are standing, some seated, others carrying babies on their hips or caressing a small dog held in their arms. The figures of women are invariably naked, and it seems that feminine coquetry was limited to painting the face and body and wearing elaborate headdresses, of which there is an unlimited variety. Occasionally they wear abbreviated garments, such as turbans and short skirts, which seem to have been made of grass in some cases, of cloth in others, worn low at the hips. Figurines of exceptionally fat women wearing such skirts are shown in dance poses, and it is possible that these skirts were worn for dancing. The feminine figures generally show the hair shaved off in patches or worn bobbed in the back, with a long lock on each side reaching down to the waist in front. Another lock of hair was worn over the forehead, held in place by a band or garland decorated with leaves or tassels and placed at a jaunty angle like a modern lady's hat. The hair is usually painted red, suggesting that they dyed their hair, perhaps bleaching it with lime as among the Melanesians or tinting it with red *achiote (Bixa orellana)* seeds, as is still done by the Colorado Indians of Ecuador."

With regard to their religion, Covarrubias points out that "a pair of figurines found in a Tlatilco burial perhaps represent shamans: each is accompanied by a dwarf, and each of the shamans wears a small mask." He adds, "The Tlatilcans were apparently little concerned with religious symbolism, though the figurines must have served a ceremonial purpose; the motifs on their pottery and clay stamps were purely decorative, and little in their art could be called representations of deities. However, a rather unusual and fascinating concept is found in certain feminine figurines with two heads or, stranger still, two sets of features on a single head: two noses, two mouths, and three eyes, reminiscent of certain paintings of Picasso, perhaps connected with the idea of twins. There are also figurines of jaguar-like beings or persons wearing jaguar masks; old crouched men, probably representations of the fire god; and strange masks of clay, one of which shows a face of which half is contorted with a hanging tongue and the other half is a human skull, perhaps representing the idea of life and death; there are also half-human, half-jaguar faces that have a strange counterpart in the probably contemporary Chavín culture of faraway Peru. . . .

"A careful study of the clay figurines of the florescent Middle Zacatenco period reveals a number of significant factors. One is an apparent lack of concern with the representation of personified deities and religious symbols, showing that religion had not yet attained the highly intellectualized, esoteric concepts typical of the cultures of the Classic period. Beyond the fact that these figurines were made to be buried with the dead, their purpose remains a mystery. It has been suggested that they represent a feminine fertility deity because some of them have greatly exaggerated hips and legs, but this is true of only a few types. There are also masculine figures that seem to represent ordinary human beings. I feel it more likely that they were meant to represent company—perhaps symbolical attendants—for the dead, particularly as some burials at Tlatilco showed evidences of human sacrifices of children and adults, and others had been equipped with as many as one hundred figurines."

As for social structure, Covarrubias sees in this Middle Preclassic period "two opposed tendencies, [which] probably represent the coexistence of two different peoples or, rather, of two conflicting social classes: one, the founder of the early Zacatenco culture, the peasants who had developed in centuries past the agricultural techniques and ceramic arts; the other, more urban and aristocratic, perhaps the carriers of the 'Olmec' culture, probably a powerful elite of artists and magicians with a more complex culture that eventually became a dominant influence among the peasants by its superiority, laying in time the foundations of the theocratic system."

Finally, according to Covarrubias, Tlatilco extended its contacts "to the north as far as the Ohio River Valley (Hopewell Culture), others in the opposite direction, such as La Venta in Tabasco, Tres Zapotes in Veracruz, Monte Albán in Oaxaca, Miraflores in Guatemala, Playa de los Muertos in Honduras, and from there as far south as the north coast of Peru in the Cupisnique and Chavín cultures, with which Tlatilco has startling similarities." (See Coe 1962, 1963b; Lanning 1963; Tello 1953.)

Armillas (1958: 43) sums up the fundamental features of the Middle Preclassic in the Valley of Mexico and neighboring regions in these words: "Toward 1000 B.C. there appear in central Mexico clear indications of the differentiation of an elite, attested to by the concentration of wealth and the refinement of funeral offerings in the great cemetery of Tlatilco. The hieratic symbolism of the stylized jaguar utilized as a decorative motive in the art of that culture (compare with Chavín) indicates the roots of religious ideas which crystallize later in the formal religion of the 'Classic' epoch."

As we have noted, we find within this period (going from north to south through the length of the present state of Veracruz) the Ponce and Aguilar stages in the Huasteca, and El Trapiche, Lower Remojadas, and Lower Tres Zapotes in the center and south. At this time, too, La Venta in Tabasco may have begun its brilliant development, which in my opinion fits for the most part into the Upper Preclassic. Also it appears to be in the Middle Preclassic that the Mamóm phase in the Petén, the Playa de los Muertos and Yarumela III phases in Honduras, and the Usulutan in El Salvador begin. I have already mentioned what was taking place in Kaminaljuyú in the Guatemala highlands. In fact, during this period and the following there are so many similarities between the pottery and figurines from Pánuco and those from the sites in Guatemala, El Salvador, and Honduras that a cultural continuum appears to have existed from the Huasteca to northern Central America (see Figures 1–3).

According to García Payón's reports (1950), the culture he found in El Trapiche, near Cempoala, is related to Early Zacatenco, and therefore dates back to the Lower Preclassic. However, in view of the abundance of type D figurines, it seems that the full flowering of El Trapiche must fall within the Middle Preclassic, thus coinciding with Piña Chán's Transitional and Upper Tlatilco. Furthermore, the El Trapiche culture, which according to García Payón extended along the coast northward to Misantla, turns out to be in large part the same culture as that found in Tres Zapotes in the Los Tuxtlas region and in La Venta in the swamps of Tabasco. Up to now, the earliest

2. Prehispanic culture sequences in Mesoamerica (I). Prepared with the aid of Ignacio Bernal, Alfonso Caso, José García Payón, Alfonso Medellín Z., and Eduardo Noguera; some data are taken from the chart in Román Piña Chán (1958b).

Chart contents (regions with their culture sequences, listed latest to earliest):

Cholula	Cholulteca III; Cholulteca II; Cholulteca I (Historic Olmecs); "Azter" I; Teotihuacan IV; Teotihuacan III (?); Teotihuacan II; Teotihuacan I; Ticoman & Cuicuilco
Valley of Mexico	"Aztec" IV; "Aztec" III; "Aztec" II; Toltec Complex; Teotihuacan IV; Teotihuacan III; Teotihuacan II; Teotihuacan I; Ticoman & Cuicuilco; Copilco; Upper Tlatilco; Transitional Tlatilco
Morelos	"Aztec" III; "Tlalhuica"; Toltec Complex (Xochicalco IV); Xochicalco III; Xochicalco II; Xochicalco I; Gualupita II; Gualupita I
The Mixteca	Mexica Conquest; Coixtlahuaca / Ñuiñe; ?; Yucuñudahui; Yatachio; ?; Tilltepec & Huamelulpan; Monte Negro
The Zapoteca	Monte Albán V; Monte Albán IV; Monte Albán IIIb; Transition IIIa–IIIb; Monte Albán IIIa; Transition II–III; Monte Albán II; Monte Albán I
Santa Lucía Cozumalcapan, & El Salvador	San Juan Plumbate & Tiquizate; San Juan Pre-Plumbate; San Francisco
Guatemala Highlands	Amatle & Magdalena; Esperanza; Santa Clara; Arenal; Miraflores; Providencia; Majadas
Petén	Tepeu; Tzakol; Matzanel (Holmul I); Chicanel; Mamom
Campeche & Yucatán	Disintegration; Toltec Influence II; Toltec Influence I (X Fine Orange); Puuc (Z Fine Orange); Old Petén Style (Oxkintok, etc.); Late Formative (Yaxuná); Middle Formative (Xtampak & Dzibilnocac)
Coatzacoalco	La Venta
Los Tuxtlas	Upper Tres Zapotes; Middle Tres Zapotes; Lower Tres Zapotes
Cerro de las Mesas	Upper Cerro de las Mesas II; Upper Cerro de las Mesas I; Lower Cerro de las Mesas II; Lower Cerro de las Mesas I
Central Veracruz	Quiahuiztlan; Cerro Montoso; Isla de Sacrificios; Upper Remojadas II; Upper Remojadas I (Rancho de las Ánimas); Lower Remojadas
Totonacapan	Cempoala; El Tajín III; El Tajín II; El Tajín I
The Huasteca	Pánuco VI (Pánuco); Pánuco V (Las Flores); Pánuco IV (Zaquil); Pánuco III (Pithayas); Pánuco II (El Prisco); Pánuco I (Chila); Aguilar; Ponce

Time scale (A.D. / B.C.): 1500, 1400, 1300, 1200, 1100, 1000, 900, 800, 700, 600, 500, 400, 300, 200, 100, A.D./0/B.C., 100, 200, 300, 400, 500, 600, 700, 800, 900, 1000

3. Prehispanic culture sequences in Mesoamerica (II). Prepared with the aid of Ignacio Bernal, Alfonso Caso, Eduardo Noguera, and Daniel F. Rubín de la Borbolla; some data are taken from charts in Isabel Kelly (1949).

Beginning of the Postclassic Horizon

Beginning of the Classic Horizon

known center in all this vast zone, which seems to have stretched along the Gulf coast from around the Nauhtla River in the north to near the Grijalva in the south, is El Trapiche; but the real nucleus of the area seems to have been in the Los Tuxtlas region, which, with the exception of Tres Zapotes, has not yet been systematically investigated. It is possible that archeological remains as old as those of El Trapiche may be found there.

It is important for us to find an explanation of whence and how this energetic group of Tenocelome immigrants, who brought so many highly important innovations, could arrive at Tlatilco at such an early date, perhaps 1000 B.C. Their probable origin from other sites of the same cultural affiliation in the Morelos Valley, such as Chalcatzingo and Atlihuayan, has been noted. These sites are near tributaries of the Mexcala and Balsas Rivers, which connect them with the Guerrero region, where according to Covarrubias there flourished an early phase of the culture ambiguously designated as "Olmec." The easternmost of these sites, Chalcatzingo, in the vicinity of Jonacatepec, is near a route which from time immemorial has connected this region with that of Itzocan (present-day Matamoros Izúcar), a zone linked in the precolonial era with old Cuauhquechollan in Atlixco. (See Coe 1965.)

Ancient Itzocan, in turn, is located near the basin of the Atoyac River, which was inhabited in former times by the late historic Olmecs. From Itzocan, by way of Tejaluca, a trail leads to Huehuetlan and on to Molcaxac. At Molcaxac are two possible points of departure: one in the direction of Tecali, Tepeaca, and Tecamachalco, and the other toward Tlacotepec and Tehuacan. Another early route joins Itzocan with Tepeji and Ixcaquiztla, Atéxcal, Zapotitlan, and Tehuacan. Still another route, which follows the path of prehispanic travelers, goes from Itzocan to Tehuitzingo, passes near Piaztla, and soon touches Acatlan and Petlatzingo, Chila, and Huajuapan. From Huajuapan, which is the terminus of the Mixteca Baja, as well as from Petlatzingo, there are roads to Tehuacan. Lastly, then as today, as dictated by the topography, Atlixco, at the foot of the spurs of Popocatépetl, and Tehuacan, near the coastal gateway of Acultzingo, were and are connected via Cholula, Tepeaca, Tecamachalco, and Tlacotepec. Similarly, we should not forget that from Tepeaca, Acatzingo, and Quechólac on the north, and from Tehuacan on the south, the route goes to Orizaba and there bifurcates, one branch leading to El Trapiche in the region of Cempoala, and the other to La Mixtequilla and Los Tuxtlas, where Cerro de las Mesas and Tres Zapotes are located.

To summarize, the Tenocelome people, whether coming from Cempoala or from the direction of La Mixtequilla and Los Tuxtlas, probably had to pass into the high plateau through Orizaba, going from there toward Tehuacan or Tepeaca, where different routes could have led them to that part of the Balsas basin which extends between Atlixco and Huajuapan and is the passageway to Chalcatzingo. From there, via Cuauhtla, Amecameca, and Chalco, they could arrive at the lakeshore in the Valley of Mexico. It is up to geographers as well as archeologists to confirm or refute this hypothesis.

THE CHRONOLOGICAL PLACEMENT OF LA VENTA

To establish the chronological location of the great La Venta culture is a very difficult task. Drucker, who carried out the stratigraphic investigation, says that La Venta corresponds to the Middle Tres Zapotes period, which, in turn, he estimates to be contemporary with phase III, and in part phase II, of Teotihuacan (1943b: 87; 1952). He considers Upper Tres Zapotes contemporary with Lower Cerro de las Mesas II, and correlates both with Teotihuacan IV–V and the "yoke–*hacha*–laughing-face" complex. Finally, he asserts that Upper I, the immediately following phase of Cerro de las Mesas, which corresponds to Noguera's Cholulteca I, is characterized in large part by a strong Cholula influence. We shall see how these data can be reinterpreted so as to produce a result more compatible with the cultural sequences of other archeological provinces. (See Coe 1966a, 1966b.)

I have suggested elsewhere (1956: 224) that we should place the beginning of Cholulteca I at about A.D. 800 because, as I explained in my article "El enigma de los olmecas" (1942),[5] I am sure that the bearers of this phase in Cholula should be identified with the historic Olmecs. According to Torquemada, Olmec domination in Cholula lasted 500 years, ending in the year 1 Flint, which has usually been correlated with 1168, but which in my opinion actually corresponds to 1292, as I have shown in another work (1953). The date 800, or a little later, would correspond to the end of the period Lower Cerro de las Mesas II and its contemporary Upper Tres Zapotes.

There is no doubt that in their last parts, i.e. from A.D. 650 to 800, these phases show a strong Teotihuacan IV influence, and that the diffusion in this zone of the "yoke–*hacha*–laughing-face" complex must be assigned to this time. But I wish to make the point that Teotihuacan influence is already present earlier in these phases, and that their initial stages, i.e. between A.D. 300 and 600, coincide with Teotihuacan III. Even if the main Teotihuacan influence dates from late Teotihuacan III and especially from IV (as Drucker maintains, on the assumption that roads hitherto closed were only then opened to communication), this does not rule out the possibility that these phases of Cerro de las Mesas and Tres Zapotes *began* at the peak of Teotihuacan (phase III), with close contacts developing later. There are certainly clear indications of Teotihuacan III influence in both La Mixtequilla and Los Tuxtlas. Kidder, Jennings, and Shook have already expressed a similar view (1946).

Accordingly, we can place the end of Middle Tres Zapotes at about A.D. 300. For although Drucker, in his stratigraphic table of Cerro de las Mesas and in the text of his work, correlates it with part of Teotihuacan II and with all or the greater part of Teotihuacan III, I believe that the correct equation would be with Teotihuacan I and II. For one thing, Drucker himself esti-

[5] Quoted at length in English in Covarrubias (1946: 122–39).

mates that at least the greater part of Middle Tres Zapotes coincides with Strebel's Ranchito de las Ánimas (1885–89), whose culture corresponds to that of Upper Remojadas I, for which Medellín (1955) discovered a complete sequence, and which turns out to be contemporaneous with the first two phases of Teotihuacan. If this is accepted, then Upper Remojadas I as well as Middle Tres Zapotes could be dated as starting in about 300 B.C. and lasting to A.D. 300, a span of 600 years. For this and other reasons, I would suggest a date of between 900 B.C. and 300 B.C. for Lower Tres Zapotes.

We can now return to the problem of locating in time the great flowering of the famous island of La Venta—an island lost today in the swamps of Tabasco but once the most representative site of Tenocelome culture. One is immediately confronted by two irreconcilable positions. For Drucker, La Venta belongs to the Middle Tres Zapotes phase, which he is inclined to correlate with the Tzakol period in the Petén area. But Tzakol, according to a recent study by Smith (1955), probably falls between a Maya date equivalent to A.D. 277 and one a little before A.D. 600 in the Goodman-Martínez-Thompson system. Thus La Venta would be contemporary with Teotihuacan III, which appears to be impossible. Drucker agrees, however, that "La Venta could scarcely be earlier than the upper phases of Chicanel"; and he admits the possibility that "we shall eventually find that Olmec art in plastic media especially attained its full bloom stylistically in the Lower Tres Zapotes period." In addition, for the most part the types of figurines found at La Venta correspond to the Middle Tres Zapotes phase.

If it is agreed that the dates 300 B.C. to A.D. 300 that we have proposed for the Middle Tres Zapotes ceramic level are acceptable, then the development of La Venta should be placed within this chronological framework. Therefore, it would coincide with the second half of Chicanel and with Matzanel (equivalent to Holmul I), which I would put between the beginning of our era and the year A.D. 250. This chronological position of La Venta would, I believe, be basically in accord with Drucker's point of view. But the dates that Drucker, Heizer, and Squier (1959: 260–67) obtained for the Tenocelome metropolis, using radioactive carbon, extend from 1154 B.C. ± 300 years to 174 B.C. ± 300 years. Even if we subtract the figure 300 to obtain the latest possible dating, we are still left with the span 854 B.C. to A.D. 126, a long period of 980 years, of which the greater part falls before 300 B.C., the date I have proposed for the beginning of Middle Tres Zapotes. Using the carbon 14 figures, Heizer and his colleagues seem to favor a date between 800 B.C. and 400 B.C. for the construction of the architectural complex that they explored at La Venta in 1955, and that afforded the samples they analyzed. Such a dating would of course be incompatible with the date I have ventured to assign to Middle Tres Zapotes, the phase to which, according to Drucker, La Venta belongs; but it would agree better with the seeming necessity of placing La Venta not too far from Tlatilco in the chronological scale. Although the material from the two sites is not precisely identical, it is in many cases analogous, and if the Tlatilco stage belonging to the Middle Preclassic has been set at between 1000 B.C. and 600 B.C., the start of cultural development at La Venta at about 800 B.C. would be plausible.

Nevertheless, I have the impression that this great cultural center of La Venta attained a higher degree of artistic development than Tlatilco, where, for example, important stone sculpture seems not to have been produced. Because of this I am inclined to place La Venta just at the end of Tlatilco, at about 600 B.C., when the Middle Preclassic ends and the Upper Preclassic begins. At this time, too, period I of Monte Albán was starting. As is known, there are quite clear indications of contact between the La Venta culture and that of Monte Albán I, indications that are striking enough to suggest that the two centers were just then the most highly evolved of all; and probably for this very reason they acted more or less in unison as the guiding forces of the cultural development, a sort of La Venta–Monte Albán civilizing axis.

Unlike Monte Albán, the La Venta metropolis, which at this time represented the highest flowering of the Tenocelome style, does not appear to have had a system of calendrical glyphs until a relatively late date, 31 B.C., which corresponds in the Goodman-Martínez-Thompson correlation to the inscription on Stela C of Tres Zapotes, where the Maya Long Count system was already in use. It is well known that the oldest inscriptions so far found in the Maya area do not antedate A.D. 320.[6] Therefore, the inscriptions at Tres Zapotes as well as those on the Tuxtla Statuette are earlier, the latter being dated A.D. 162. However, it is quite possible that the Maya carved on stelae that have not yet been discovered, or, as Bernal has suggested, on wooden ones now lost—in other words, that their earliest inscriptions, dating from at least as early as the Chicanel phase (which, according to my hypothesis, began sometime between 500 and 400 B.C.), are still unknown.

During this phase there is evident in the Petén an important influence that certainly came from La Venta, which is expressed in the style of the large masks on the pyramid E-VII-sub of Uaxactún (Figure 42). The island of La Venta, which was perhaps the great cultural capital of the Tenocelome, sent out radiations to places as far off as Piedra Parada in Guatemala and Chalchuapa in El Salvador, to Monte Albán and the Oaxaca coast, to the Balsas River basin, and elsewhere. To a limited degree we can assume that La Venta played the role that Teotihuacan was to play later. The Tenocelome opened the great routes that were later followed in commercial relations as well as in the migrations of the civilizing elite. And at the end of La Venta's glorious career, at a date that I would put before the Christian era, a dispersal of part

[6] Stela 29 of Tikal, discovered by Shook in May 1959, is now the oldest dated Maya monument, with a reading of 8.12.14.8.15 or A.D. 292 in the Goodman-Martínez-Thompson correlation (Shook 1960).—Translators.

4. Wooden mask; Cañón de la Mano, Guerrero.

5. Stone mask; Zumpango del Río, Guerrero.

6. Figurine; Iguala, Guerrero.

7. Statuette; San Jerónimo, Guerrero.

8. Jadeite alligator.

9. Jadeite plaque; Olinalan, Guerrero.

10. The Kunz "axe"; said to be from Oaxaca.

11. Jaguar; from the Mixteca

12. Carved stone; Tlacotepec, Guerrero.

13. Jadeite pebble; Niltepec, Oaxaca.

of its inhabitants must have prefigured the Teotihuacan diaspora of about A.D. 650, and the Toltec diasporas of the times of Topiltzin-Quetzalcóatl and Huémac.

At any rate, heretical though it may seem, I suggest that we should regard the inscription of Stela C at Tres Zapotes, which corresponds to 31 B.C., as representing the testament of the La Venta culture. It is true that on this stone there is a stylized face with the classic "tiger mouth" of unmistakable Tenocelome tradition; but it seems to me that by this time a people coming from the Maya area, who I assume used the Long Count, had already reached the Los Tuxtlas region, where Tres Zapotes is located, after having traveled through the La Venta zone. The La Venta culture, which appears to have lacked calendric glyphs for so many centuries, now came to adopt them at the end of its long course.

Everything combines to suggest that what Stela C represents is not the culmination of a development that had taken place within the Tenocelome cultural province, but rather the assimilation of a knowledge that was lacking there and came from outside. I assume that it originated in the Maya area, but since up to now no inscriptions older than that at Tres Zapotes have been discovered in this zone, my hypothesis does not have a solid base. Indeed the opposite opinion may turn out to be more feasible: that it was in the Los Tuxtlas region that this knowledge originated, and that from Los Tuxtlas it was carried to the Maya area. I cannot believe that this whole system of complex calendric glyphs possessed by the Maya, and perhaps linked with their language, appeared suddenly, rather than developing gradually throughout the centuries in conformity with the geographic environment of the Yucatán Peninsula. Furthermore, Caso has detected possible cultural influences from the Maya area at Monte Albán at the beginning of its phase II, i.e. in about 200 B.C., which probably came from Chiapas and the Petén;[7] and connections have been noted with the Chicanel and Matzanel levels (the latter being equivalent to Holmul I). Similarly, Noguera (1945, 1947, 1958) thinks one can isolate strong Maya influences at Xochicalco at the beginning of phase I, influences that originated in the southern part of the Maya area and possibly came to Morelos by way of the Chiapas, Oaxaca, and Guerrero coasts, from there moving northward to reach Xochicalco.

The recent exploration of De Cicco and Brockington (1956) on the Oaxaca coast has brought to light ancient Maya influences that Noguera took into consideration when he formulated his hypothesis. Thus, as Covarrubias has suggested (1957: 77), we might well discover that La Venta had been smothered by a vigorous expansion of Maya groups, perhaps around the same date of 200 B.C. or a bit later, unless its undeniable strength had managed to resist this perhaps more than cultural invasion. At any rate, if by 31 B.C. a stela

[7] For a different interpretation, see Part II of this volume, p. 120.

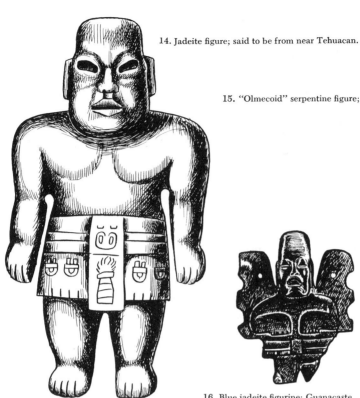

14. Jadeite figure; said to be from near Tehuacan.

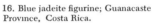

15. "Olmecoid" serpentine figure; Teotihuacan.

16. Blue jadeite figurine; Guanacaste Province, Costa Rica.

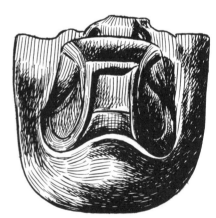

17. Green serpentine mask; Teotihuacan.

18. Fragment of serpentine mask; Apoala, Oaxaca.

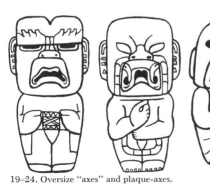

19–24. Oversize "axes" and plaque-axes.

with a Long Count inscription was carved in Los Tuxtlas, this probably happened because peoples whose integrating nucleus was in the Petén had found an unobstructed road that took them to Tres Zapotes by way of La Venta, a road that was open for the good reason that La Venta no longer existed or was dying.

To sum up on the basis of all the preceding theories, some quite solid and others rather fragile, I am inclined to believe that the flowering of La Venta most probably occurred between 600 and 200 B.C., that is, contemporaneously with Monte Albán I. However, I am willing to admit the possibility that the development of the island had begun as early as 800, and also that it lasted until just before the beginning of our era. In any case, I think it unlikely that La Venta continued to function after the birth of Christ as the cultural capital it had been. There remains, though, a problem that has not been solved: whether it was exclusively in the Middle Tres Zapotes phase that this great ceremonial center flourished. Only in small part do the dates I have suggested fit with those I proposed for the evolution of the Middle Tres Zapotes ceramic stratum of Los Tuxtlas. We are left, therefore, with the following alternatives: (1) a different date for La Venta; (2) a different date for Middle Tres Zapotes; (3) the possibility that in new excavations at La Venta a ceramic stratum may be found corresponding to Lower Tres Zapotes. The last certainly would reconcile almost all the present discrepancies.

At any rate, I agree with Covarrubias that the Tenocelome culture must have lasted a millennium or slightly more. As a matter of fact, in El Trapiche it seems contemporaneous in its beginnings with the end of Early Zacatenco, and this phase of the Valley of Mexico ends in about 1000 B.C. On the other hand, the final stage of the Tenocelome culture seems to have been that of Middle Tres Zapotes, which I have suggested lasted from 300 B.C. to A.D. 300. In the La Venta region, however, this culture had already perished, perhaps just before the beginning of the Christian era, that is to say at the end of Teotihuacan I, when the Preclassic horizon comes to an end in the Valley of Mexico. In contrast, in the Los Tuxtlas region, which includes Tres Zapotes, the Tenocelome culture was able to prolong its life with some vigor for about three centuries more until the end of Middle Tres Zapotes, and to persist, though definitely decadent, all through the following phase, Upper Tres Zapotes, in the face of an increasingly strong avalanche of influences from Teotihuacan III and IV and El Tajín II. But now in this Upper Tres Zapotes stage, which was contemporaneous with Lower Cerro de las Mesas II (A.D. 300–800), the true cultural center appears to have been the metropolis of La Mixtequilla, which must have functioned as an intermediary between Teotihuacan and the Maya area.

To recapitulate, it seems that the disintegration of the Tenocelome culture had started in the La Venta region a little before the beginning of our era as a result of Maya cultural influences coming from nearby Chiapa de Corzo

25. Greenish serpentine mask;
Tuxtla Gutiérrez, Chiapas.

26. Jadeite mask; Tabasco.

27. "Olmec" type jade figurine;
Cerro de las Mesas.

28. Serpentine figurine; Tlatilco.

30. Serpentine figurine;
La Venta, Tabasco.

29. "Olmec" or Tenocelome carving;
Monument 19, La Venta.

31. Serpentine statuette;
Papantla, Veracruz.

32. Mask; Cárdenas, Tabasco.

33. Black serpentine figurine;
Orizaba, Veracruz.

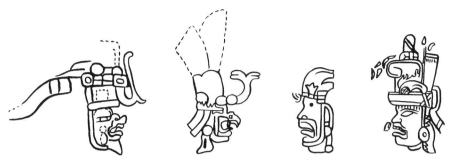

34–37. Carvings: 34, San Isidro Piedra Parada, Quetzaltenango, Guatemala; 35, Jonacatepec, Morelos; 36, palette from Palenque; 37, "axe" from Tapijulapa, Tabasco.

and the more distant Petén. But in the Los Tuxtlas region the Tenocelome culture remained strong, until at the start of phase III of Teotihuacan (the phase of the Teotihuacan apogee) that northern Tenocelome redoubt also gradually succumbed, although leaving a good part of its heritage to the new center, formerly peripheral, of Cerro de las Mesas, in its Lower II phase. At the same time that impulses were coming from the Maya area and perhaps from Monte Albán, the Tenocelome legacy in Cerro de las Mesas merged with a strong Teotihuacan influence, and later, between A.D. 650 and 800, there is evidence of a sweeping influence from Teotihuacan IV and El Tajín II.

To conclude this discussion of chronology, I should like to add that we do not know to which precise period the objects of Tenocelome culture found in Guerrero should be attributed, since almost none of them have been found in stratigraphic excavations. Some might be very old, dating from the Preclassic horizon;[8] others could perhaps be the result of the dispersion we have postulated, in which case they would date from a little before or after the beginning of the Christian era. Finally, two problems have still not been solved: that of the origin of the great Tenocelome culture, and that of the maximum extension of its radiations. With regard to the first, there are three points of view: (1) the most generally accepted, according to which it originated on the Gulf coast, either in northern or in southern Veracruz; (2) Piña Chán's, according to which its form crystallized in the region where the boundaries of Morelos, Puebla, and Guerrero converge; and (3) that of Covarrubias and Escalona Ramos, according to which its origin should be sought on the Pacific coast, probably in Guerrero, although a larger zone that includes Oaxaca is not ruled out.

As to the second problem, Covarrubias himself was of the opinion that the Tenocelome cultural sphere reached as far north as the Ohio Valley of the United States, and as far south as the region where the Chavín culture flour-

[8] Recent study of "Olmec" materials by Wicke (1965) results in a proposed sequence of development of "Olmec" traits, and in a conclusion that the Guerrero materials do include much that is at the beginning of the developmental sequence.—Editor.

ished in northern Peru. I do not propose to tackle this question here (nor indeed is there sufficient information at present); Figures 4–37, however, give some idea of how widespread this culture was.

THE UPPER PRECLASSIC AND THE PROTOCLASSIC

I shall not try to summarize the most important cultural traits of La Venta because this gap can easily be filled by reading the pertinent chapter in Covarrubias's magnificent work *Indian Art of Mexico and Central America* (1957). For the same reason I do not intend to attempt a characterization of Monte Albán I or Monte Negro; the omission can be remedied by consulting Bernal's recent articles (1958a, 1958b).[9] But I do want to comment on the architecture of these three places, which testifies to great advances in this period (see Figures 38–39, and Figure 8, Part II, this volume). At La Venta, a huge pyramid was erected, and a tumulus built to cover a room formed out of great natural basalt columns. At the same time in the Mixteca at Monte Negro, a building was constructed with patios and columns, while in phase I at Monte Albán temples were being placed on top of pyramids, and the construction of subterranean chambers to be used as tombs began.

In the Valley of Mexico, throughout the Upper Preclassic, three principal centers flourished: Cerro del Tepalcate near Tlatilco, Cuicuilco, and Tlapacoyan (Figures 40–41). In Cerro del Tepalcate, perhaps at a very early time, a temple was constructed upon a platform. In Cuicuilco, an important monument of truncated conical form was built in four superimposed layers, probably no later than 300 to 200 B.C. The lowest layer was covered by lava from the volcano Xictli, which erupted at about this time—the lava that formed the rocky area known as the "Pedregal de San Ángel." At Tlapacoyan (Barba de Piña Chán 1956) a pyramid-shaped base, erected during three distinct periods, is considered the most obvious antecedent of the Teotihuacan pyramids. It seems likely that the truncated cone of Cuicuilco was built before the pyramidal base of Tlapacoyan, since Cuicuilco was engulfed by the lava sea erupted by Xictli, whereas Tlapacoyan appears to have lasted until the beginning of the second phase at Monte Albán, that is until 200 B.C. The Teotihuacan culture, too, began its swift rise within the Upper Preclassic, but in the second half. From humble beginnings, evident in the findings at El Tepalcate near Chimalhuacan, Teotihuacan progressed at the end of the first phase and the beginning of the second to the building of its colossal pyramids—truly the work of giants. The appearance of such constructions clearly shows that Teotihuacan was advancing to a new stage: the Early Classic.

In Kaminaljuyú in the Maya area, to quote Armillas (1957: 47–48), "a goodly number of pyramidal mounds correspond to the same epoch. One of

---

[9] And Paddock's description in Part II of this volume, pp. 91–99.—Editor.

them (mound E-III-3) began with a small platform-altar of packed clay, which, by superposition of constructions of the same material, reached the height of 16 meters at about the date with which we are dealing—it was made higher later—in the form of a pyramid of stepped sides. In the interior there were two tombs of personages buried with a considerable store of objects indicative of wealth; the construction represents successive enlargements of the monument."

This mound has been dated by carbon 14 at about 550 B.C. $\pm$ 300 and corresponds to the Miraflores phase (formerly Verbena subphase), which could date between 500 and 250 B.C. According to Armillas, "In Yucatán there exist monumental constructions in Santa Rosa Xtampak that are attributable to the intermediate Formative period, and in Yaxuná ones that may belong to the late Formative period, but their absolute age is unknown. All that we can say is that they antedate the beginning of the Classic epoch, and can be dated in the Yucatán region after the beginning of the Christian era."

I am also inclined to place pyramid E-VII-sub at Uaxactún in the Upper Preclassic, unless clear evidence be found that its construction preceded only slightly the erection of the stela that according to the Goodman-Martínez-Thompson correlation bears the date A.D. 328. It has been said that pyramid E-VII-sub (Figure 42) belongs to the Chicanel phase, which I would date between the year 400 B.C. and the beginning of our era, and for this reason I suggest Upper Preclassic for its chronological position. Finally, in an archeological zone explored in 1957 in Chiapa de Corzo, Chiapas, investigation revealed "abundant architectural platforms" corresponding to the Chiapa IV phase (Lowe 1957: 16), which can be correlated with Chicanel.

In addition to the sites just referred to, Upper (or Late) Zacatenco and Ticoman in the Valley of Mexico belong to the Upper Preclassic, as perhaps in Western Mexico do the Curútaran phase in the Zamora area, and the Potrero de la Isla in the Zacapu archeological zone. Most certainly the Chupícuaro culture, which was contemporaneous with Teotihuacan I and II and extended over a wide area of the Middle Lerma River drainage, is of this period.

Chupícuaro culture sent forth influences eastward to Tepeji del Río, to the Cerro del Tepalcate near Tlatilco, to Cuanalan, to Teotihuacan, and on to Tulancingo. On the north it seems to have spread to encompass a large part of El Bajío, between San Juan del Río and León. Vessels of this culture were found in La Quemada, according to Batres. To the south, Chupícuaro culture spread from the Valley of Mexico and the northern part of the state of Mexico to Maravatio, Zinapécuaro, Zacapu, and finally Purépero and Jacona near Zamora. This culture, which must have flourished between 300 B.C. and A.D. 300, seems to have played a role in Western Mexico comparable to that of the Tenocelome or "Olmec" culture in the rest of Mexican Mesoamerica.

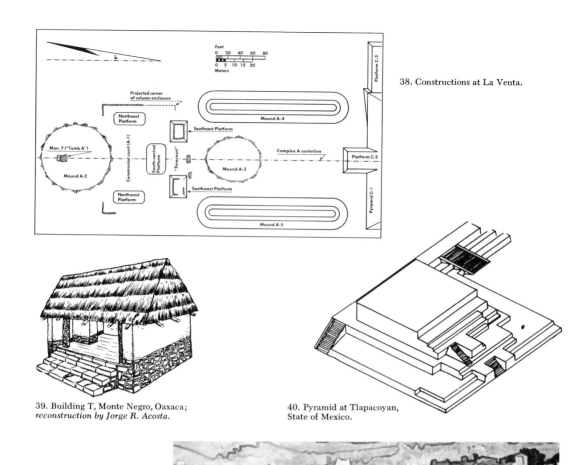

38. Constructions at La Venta.

39. Building T, Monte Negro, Oaxaca; *reconstruction by Jorge R. Acosta.*

40. Pyramid at Tlapacoyan, State of Mexico.

41. Main buildings, Cuicuilco; *reconstruction painting by Alfredo Zalce, MNA.*

42. Mound E-VII-sub, Uaxactún; *reconstruction drawing by Tatiana Proskouriakoff.*

Chupícuaro polychrome ceramics seem ancestral to the other polychrome wares in this vast area (Vaillant 1931, Noguera 1931, Caso 1929, Porter 1956, Rubín de la Borbolla 1947b, Batres 1903).[10]

Other centers of the Upper Preclassic are Gualupita II, Upper Chalcatzingo, Olintepec II, and the Mazatepec I phase of Chimalacatlan, all in the Valley of Morelos. In Veracruz in this period, Pánuco I, Lower Remojadas, and Lower Tres Zapotes are succeeded respectively by Pánuco II, Upper Remojadas I, and Middle Tres Zapotes, the last being contemporaneous with Lower Cerro de las Mesas I. Also in this period, we go from Monte Albán I to Monte Albán II in Oaxaca. In the Maya area the Chiapa IV and Chiapa V phases flourish in the region of Chiapa de Corzo; the Miraflores, Arenal, and Santa Clara in Kaminaljuyú; the Chicanel and Matzanel in the Petén; and lastly the Late Formative in Yucatán (Piña Chán 1958a, 1958b, Müller 1948, Ekholm 1944, Medellín 1955, Drucker 1943a, 1943b, Bernal 1958b, Lowe 1957, Shook and Kidder 1952, Smith 1955, Brainerd 1951).

We must remember that it is difficult to separate the end of the Preclassic horizon from the beginning of the Classic. In the Valley of Mexico, the Upper Preclassic appears to end with Teotihuacan I, and the Early Classic to start with Teotihuacan II at the beginning of our era. In the Valley of Oaxaca, it is estimated that the Classic horizon starts with the Monte Albán II–III transitional phase, which must have begun in about A.D. 200.[11] In the Maya area, the Tzakol phase is referred to as Early Classic. I would place the beginning of Tzakol at about A.D. 250, a date that I would assign also to the beginning of Esperanza at Kaminaljuyú and to phase VI at Chiapa de Corzo. I believe that the southern half of the state of Veracruz entered the Classic horizon in about A.D. 300 with the Upper Remojadas II, Lower Cerro de las Mesas II, and Upper Tres Zapotes phases. Meanwhile, at the same date, the northern half of the state was entering the Classic horizon with the Pánuco III phase, in which Teotihuacan influences appear and the technique of making molded figurines is introduced, even though technological survivals from the Preclassic continue. The Huastec culture does not appear to adopt a "Classic" aspect until Pánuco IV, which is contemporaneous with El Tajín II, i.e. about A.D. 650. However, El Tajín must have reached the Classic horizon at the beginning of phase I, i.e. in about A.D. 200. Lastly, Western Mexico seems to have remained comparatively static just as did the Huastec region. Following Corona Núñez, I would place the beginning of a Classic horizon in Western Mexico a little after A.D. 300, when contacts with Teotihuacan III appear. Nevertheless, it should be emphasized that, in among other elements, the figurines (Figures 43–56) retain a Preclassic appearance, many being com-

---

[10] See Porter (1956) for a bibliography. According to data supplied me by Carmen Cook de Leonard for Tepeji, Hidalgo, and by César Lizardi Ramos for Tulancingo, Hidalgo, Chupícuaro pottery is found at both places.

[11] An alternative judgment of both the beginning of the "Classic" and the time of Transición II-III is given in Part II of this volume, pp. 111–27.—Editor.

43. Figurine fragment;
Chiametla, Sinaloa.

44 and 45. Figurines; Apatzingan,
Michoacán.

46. Figurine; found near
Tepalcatepec, Michoacán.

47. Figurine of woman;
Huetamo, Michoacán.

48. Figurine; Pátzcuaro,
Michoacán.

49. Figurine; Colima.

50. Figurine; La Quemada,
Zacatecas.

51. Teotihuacan II figurine;
Teotihuacan.

52 and 53. Teotihuacan I figurine heads;
Teotihuacan.

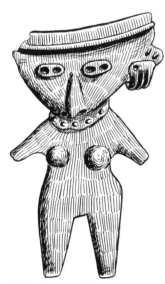

54. Teotihuacanoid figurine;
western Mexico.

55. Head (fragment of vessel);
Huetamo, Michoacán.

56. Figurine; Jiquilpan,
Michoacán.

parable to types of Teotihuacan I, or at the latest phase II.[12] Although some
of Isabel Kelly's stratigraphic excavations and other data oblige me to agree
that these figures are contemporary with Teotihuacan III or IV, I still believe
that an important Teotihuacan influence may have reached the west as early
as phase I, transmitted perhaps by the Chupícuaro culture (Ekholm 1944;
Corona Núñez and Noguera 1955; Kelly 1944, 1947a, 1949).

Clearly, some Upper Preclassic centers, such as La Venta, Monte Albán I,
and Monte Negro, could be considered "Protoclassic" as early as about 600
B.C., as could some of the other centers I have mentioned.[13] But for the Maya
area the term Protoclassic is not used until Chiapa de Corzo V and the Matzanel phase in the Petén. It must be remembered that at this time some communities remained completely Preclassic; in fact, some of them remained
so even after the beginning of the true Classic horizon. For a full discussion
of this subject, the reader may profitably consult Wauchope's study (1951);
this important contribution lists the elements, mainly ceramic, belonging to
what Wauchope called Village Formative, Urban Formative, and Protoclassic. (The various archeological sites within each of these three stages in cultural evolution are not always coeval, of course.)

All this should be taken into account in reading the following section, in
which I try to catalog the distinguishing characteristics of the Upper Preclassic. We should remember that although in the Valley of Mexico the period
ends at the beginning of the Christian era, in the Maya area and in regions
like Oaxaca and Veracruz the Classic horizon seems not to begin until about
A.D. 200 or 300.

CHARACTERISTICS OF THE UPPER PRECLASSIC

The construction of temples on top of stepped platforms and the appearance
of "planned ceremonial centers," in some cases associated with a necropolis,
are among the characteristics of the Upper Preclassic that are isolated by
Armillas, Caso, and Bernal, and summed up by Palerm. Such centers approach the idea of a city or are cities in the true sense. Some, for instance
Monte Albán in its first period and Monte Negro, were true city-states in the
opinion of Caso, who writes: "I believe that it would have been impossible
to accomplish works like the tower of Cuicuilco or the pyramids of Teotihuacan without a territorial political structure, a large dominated population occupying an extensive area, ... and an organized religion." He mentions, too, the presence beginning about this time of an organized priesthood,
and of various gods such as the fire god, the rain god, the earth goddess,

---

[12] Similarly, at Monte Albán, figurines of Preclassic appearance occur in phases I and II,
when the culture in general seems to have moved on to the Classic.—Editor.

[13] "Protoclassic" means that part of the Upper Preclassic (or of the period just after it,
as the case may be) in which urban traits are increasingly appearing, but still not to the
point of fully developed urbanism.—Editor.

and Xipe Totec, the flayed god. Bernal points to "the appearance of the first recognizable anthropomorphic gods." Palerm notes the "absence of warrior gods" and, apparently, of human sacrifice (although this last is open to doubt); he adds that "the religion deals principally with peaceful divinities of fertility." Armillas observes that art becomes hieratic. The first evidences of the calendar and of writing date from this period.

The great advances of the Upper Preclassic seem due to the goad, or "challenge," as Toynbee would say, of a period of drought in the Valley of Mexico, which could have stimulated the development of irrigation methods. Palerm (1955) registers the objection that up to now no proof of irrigation has been found before the Postclassic horizon.[14] But he admits, at any rate, that definite "advances in the efficiency of agricultural systems" are evident, notably the type of terraced cultivation that was coming into use in Monte Negro. He goes on to say that practically all the basic cultivated plants were known at this time, and that foods of agricultural origin could be relied upon. It even appears that the cultivation of predominantly commercial plants (cotton, cacao, and others) may have begun in this period.

Palerm thinks, too, that perhaps professional merchants formed an independent class or were allied to the priestly class. He believes that this incipient specialization existed not only in commerce, but also in other activities, since "the new constructions imply, among other things, the coordination of the work of many people, the ordered division of tasks, and the planning and arrangement of buildings." There seems to be no doubt, he says, that "the planners and directors of the work were true specialists, and that certain phases of the work were entrusted to special artisans." It is thought that in the Upper Preclassic there was a general population increase, the consequence of the more dependable food supply that resulted from the intensification of agriculture. The "planned ceremonial centers" that we have already noted made their appearance now, and according to Palerm must have served both as meeting places for the surrounding population during the religious ceremonies and as commercial centers. He believes, further, that "the political and administrative functions of the governing class probably increased at this time, and its control over a considerable territory was strengthened and extended." He sees "the diversification of occupation, and the social division of labor . . . as well as the intensification of social differences," and believes that this was "a society composed of an upper class of theocratic character with diversified functions, superimposed upon an enormous mass, also with diversified functions, but in a homogeneous social situation." "We are dealing," he says, "with a theocratic, monopolistic state." Armillas, Caso, and Ber-

---

[14] In the Tehuacan area, MacNeish has found in the Palo Blanco phase, which has an estimated span of 200 B.C. to A.D. 700, "aqueducts, irrigation ditches, dams, and terraces" (MacNeish 1962). Later work reported by Woodbury shows that these waterworks in fact began in the preceding (Santa María) phase, 900–200 B.C. Richard B. Woodbury (1965).–Translators.

nal, for their part, agree that we are confronted with a "complex society" in which the "first great social differences" become perceptible.

Piña Chán (1958b) characterizes this stage as "proto-urban," mentions some of the features we have discussed, and emphasizes in great detail the changes that occur in pottery. With regard to the pottery, Caso (1953) notes that "it becomes more complex, with new technical forms, colors, and decoration; for example, the technique of painting vessels 'alfresco.'"[15] This technique, in fact, is used in Monte Albán from phase II (or perhaps from the end of phase I), which there precedes the Classic horizon; but in Teotihuacan it does not appear until the second phase, which is considered within the Classic horizon.

To Pablo Martínez del Río we owe the suggestion that the conditions we find in the Upper Preclassic and Protoclassic coincide with those found in Mesopotamia and described by Frankfort (1956) for the period he calls "Formative" or "Protoliterate," because it is then that writing appears. This is not the place to establish the parallel in detail, and consequently I shall comment only briefly that in this Near East region a theocratic regime existed; that the ziggurats, which Martínez del Río (1946) has compared with Mesoamerican pyramids, were thought of as mountains; and that "mountain" was a term charged with religious significance. The analogy with Mesoamerica is immediately apparent, for there the rain god and his attendants lived and revealed themselves on mountain tops as did Jupiter on Olympus. Furthermore, these comparisons should be extended to include the Far East, where, according to Heine-Geldern, in some regions the stepped monuments had a cosmic symbolism, and where other elements, too, are comparable with certain aspects of this period of our prehispanic cultural evolution.

THE PRECLASSIC AND THE TRANSITION TO THE CLASSIC

Before going on to examine this evolutionary process, I want to refer to the two maps in which I represent schematically some of the important developments and events of the Middle and Upper Preclassic (Maps 1 and 2), and the transition of the Upper Preclassic to the Classic horizon (Map 3). The second map shows the great expansion of the Tenocelome culture, the "Olmec" of the archeologists, which prefigures the expansion that Teotihuacan was to realize at its apogee. The radiations of the Tenocelome culture cover a wide area (see Figures 4–37), extending on the northeast at least to the Huastec region even before Pánuco I, and on the northwest through El Opeño as far as San Marcos, Jalisco, and possibly, according to Alberto Escalona Ramos, to Culiacan, Sinaloa. On the southeast, the same influences are clearly perceptible in Guatemala and El Salvador, reaching as far as Costa Rica, and they are particularly evident in the style of some of the decorative masks on pyramid E-VII-sub at Uaxactún (Figure 42).

---

[15] Not true fresco, of course. The finished vessel is covered with an unbaked white substance upon which colored paints may be applied.—Editor.

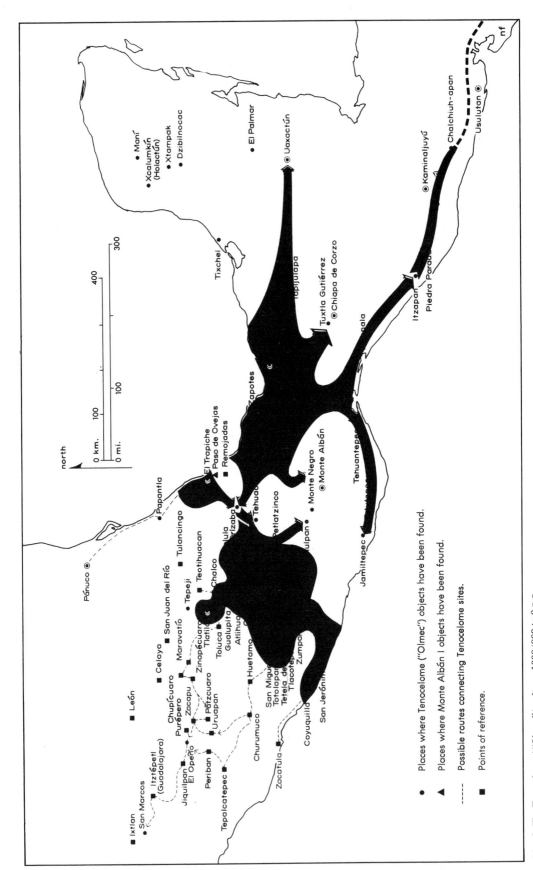

Map 1. The Tenocelome ("Olmec") culture, 1000/900 to 0 B.C.

- Places where Tenocelome ("Olmec") objects have been found.
- Places where Monte Albán I objects have been found.
- Possible routes connecting Tenocelome sites.
- Points of reference.

Ixtlan
San Marcos
Iztépetl (Guadalajara)
León
Celaya
San Juan del Río
Chupícuaro
Maravatió
Tepeji
Teotihuacan
Jiquilpan
El Openo
Purépero
Zacapu
Zinapécuaro
Tlatilco
Periban
Pátzcuaro
Toluca
Chalco
Uruapan
Gualupita
Atlihuayán
Churumuco
Huetamo
San Miguel
Totolapan
Tetela del...
Tlacotepec
Izúcar
Petlatzinco
Coyuquilla
Zumpango
Monte Negro
San Jerónimo
Zacatula
Jamiltepec
Monte Albán
Tehuantepec
Pánuco
Papantla
Tulancingo
El Trapiche
Paso de Ovejas
Remojadas
Tehuacan
Zapotes
Tuxpan
Tlapijulapa
Tuxtla Gutiérrez
Chiapa de Corzo
...gala
Itzapan
Piedra Parada
Kaminaljuyú
Chalchiuh-apan
Usulutan
Uaxactún
Maní
Xcalumkín (Holactún)
Xtampak
Dzibilnocac
El Palmar
Tixchel

north
0 km. 100 200 300 400
0 mi. 100 200 300

nf

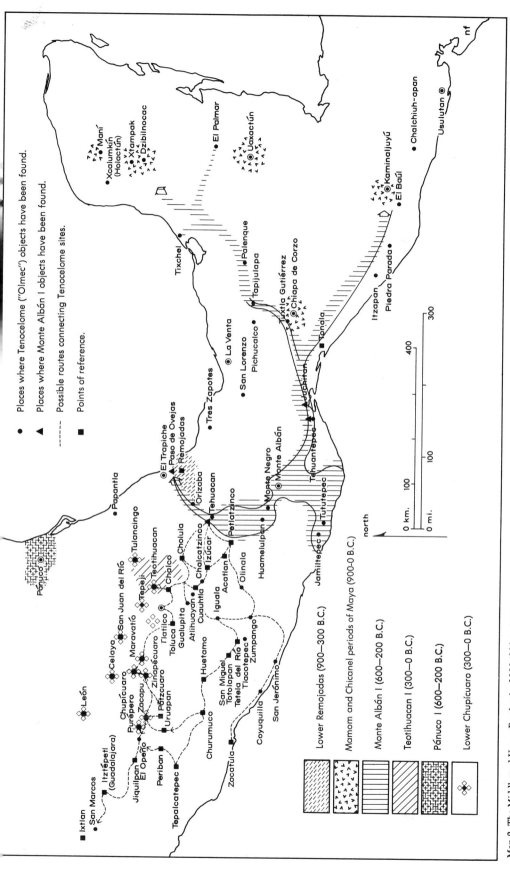

● Places where Tenocelome ("Olmec") objects have been found.

▲ Places where Monte Albán I objects have been found.

----- Possible routes connecting Tenocelome sites.

■ Points of reference.

Lower Remojadas (900–300 B.C.)

Mamom and Chicanel periods of Maya (900–0 B.C.)

Monte Albán I (600–200 B.C.)

Teotihuacan I (300–0 B.C.)

Pánuco I (600–200 B.C.)

Lower Chupícuaro (300–0 B.C.)

north

0 km. 100   100   400   300

0 mi.

Map 2. The Middle and Upper Preclassic, 1000/900 to 0 B.C.

33

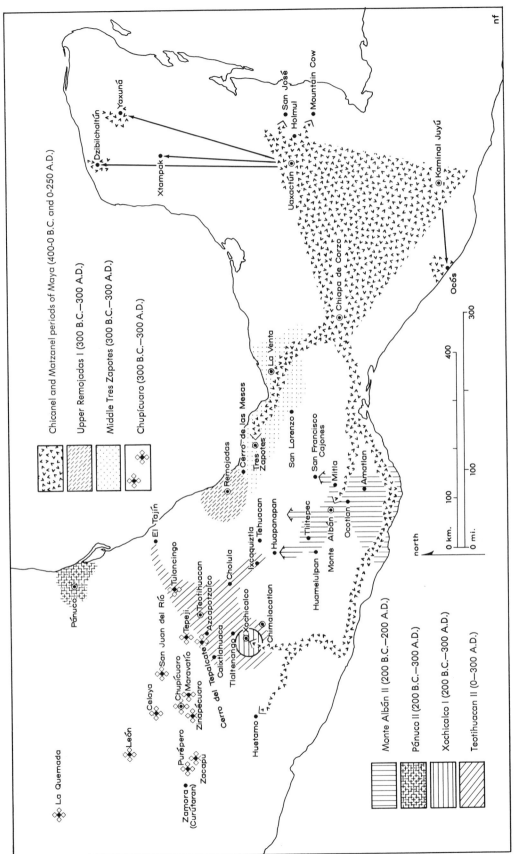

Chicanel and Matzanel periods of Maya (400-0 B.C. and 0-250 A.D.)

Upper Remojadas I (300 B.C.–300 A.D.)

Middle Tres Zapotes (300 B.C.–300 A.D.)

Chupícuaro (300 B.C.–300 A.D.)

Monte Albán II (200 B.C.–200 A.D.)

Pánuco II (200 B.C.–300 A.D.)

Xochicalco I (200 B.C.–300 A.D.)

Teotihuacan II (0–300 A.D.)

north

0 km.   100   100   400   300

0 mi.

La Quemada

Zamora
(Curútaran)   Purépero
Zacapú

León   Chupícuaro   Maravatío
       Celaya   Zinapécuaro
San Juan del Río   Tepejí   Tulancingo
       Teotihuacan
       Azcapotzalco   Cholula
Cerro del Tepalcate   Calixtlahuaca
       Tlatenango   Xochicalco
Huetamo   Chimalacatlan

El Tajín   Pánuco

Remojadas   Cerro de las Mesas
       Tres Zapotes   La Venta

San Lorenzo   San Francisco Cajones

Ixcaquixtla   Tehuacan   Huapanapan
Huamelulpan   Tliltepec   Mitla   Amatlan
Monte Albán   Ocotlan

Xtampak   Dzibilchaltún   Yaxuná
Uaxactún   San José   Holmul   Mountain Cow
Chiapa de Corzo   Kaminal Juyú
       Ocós

Map 3. The Late Preclassic and Early Classic, 400/200 B.C. to A.D. 200/300.

In order to try to define the total range of Tenocelome culture, I have taken into account the sites in which "Olmec" artifacts have been found, and have used information from a small map prepared by Covarrubias (1946: 121). Also, I have marked the probable cultural area of Monte Albán I, basing myself on Bernal (1949a). Information furnished by the exploration of Brockington and De Cicco (1956) on the Oaxaca coast, data relating to Chiapas and Guatemala, and still further data supplied by Alberto Ruz (1945) for Campeche have been added.[16] Although other cultures, such as the Zacatenco and Ticoman, flourished within the Middle and Upper Preclassic periods to which the map refers, they are not included, since my aim was to attempt a schematic rather than an exhaustive study, and to concentrate on the importance of the La Venta–Monte Albán cultural axis.

In the third map, the transition from the final Preclassic to the initial Classic is studied. It is at this time that strong cultural influences from the Maya area of the Chicanel and Matzanel phases are clearly perceptible in Monte Albán, dating from the beginning of phase II in about 200 B.C. They seem to have come, in large part, from Chiapa de Corzo, phase V or Protoclassic. At about the same date, Maya influences seem to have reached as far as Xochicalco, according to Noguera. He believes that the most likely route was along the Oaxaca coast, where Brockington and De Cicco found objects showing Maya characteristics, and from there along the coast of Guerrero, where Weitlaner found similar material. From the Guerrero coast, the route to Xochicalco must have been basically the same as that leading from Acapulco via Chilpancingo to Iguala, a route that approaches Cuernavaca from the south. Furthermore, a supposed Maya arch was found in Oztuma;[17] Moedano has pointed out other Mayoid indications in the Middle Balsas basin, and Rubín de la Borbolla has commented upon seemingly similar influences shown by some of the Huetamo stelae (Hendrichs 1940, Armillas 1945, Moedano 1947, Rubín de la Borbolla 1958, Weitlaner 1947). Finally, we can see in this map the invasion of Maya influences in the region in which the La Venta culture attained its greatest development—an invasion that left its imprint, in my somewhat unorthodox opinion, in the inscription of Stela C of Tres Zapotes, which dates from 31 B.C.

It seems, then, that in the face of the expansive force of Maya culture the great Tenocelome culture succumbed first in its southeastern part, where La Venta is situated, but that despite these pressures it managed to keep itself intact in a reduced area around Los Tuxtlas. This last Tenocelome stronghold survived until after the year A.D. 300, when Teotihuacan, then at

---

[16] Ignacio Bernal brought to my attention the evidence of Monte Albán influence found by Ruz in Campeche. [Alfonso Caso published in 1965 a provocative, though necessarily not definitive, case for the existence of a Tenocelome empire: "¿Existió un imperio olmeca?" —Editor.]

[17] Armillas cites other works on Oztuma by Lister (1941) and Moedano (1942), and believes that the arch could well be a construction of the colonial period.

its peak, invaded it culturally if not politically as well. However, survivals of Tenocelome culture continue to be evident until about A.D. 800, when the historic Olmecs, who had conquered Cholula, put an end to the cultural tradition of Cerro de las Mesas at the end of the Lower II phase and substituted their own. From the time of the irruption of Teotihuacan III culture in the Los Tuxtlas region—evidence for which has been found by Valenzuela and Ruppert as well as by Drucker—the cultural continuum that had existed along the Gulf coast from the Huasteca to the Maya area was broken. Accordingly, as Ekholm notes, a change in orientation occurred when Teotihuacan influences began in the first part of the Pánuco III phase (Valenzuela 1945a, 1945b; Ekholm 1944).

THE DELIMITATION OF THE PRECLASSIC AND THE CLASSIC

As we turn our attention to the Classic horizon, we must be careful to keep in mind what we have already noted about the difficulty of defining this horizon. If we had only to deal with Teotihuacan culture, we could use a terminology in which phase I could be called Protoclassic, phase II Early Classic, phase III Full Classic, and phase IV Epiclassic. But it would not be easy to adapt such a nomenclature to other areas. In the Maya area, for example, the Matzanel (or Holmul I) phase is known as Protoclassic, Tzakol as Early Classic, and Tepeu as Late Classic.

In view of the difficulty that scholars have had in agreeing on the criteria for determining which cultures are "Classic" and at what point they become so,[18] I decided to conform to the most generally accepted usage, and after consulting Caso, I arrived at the line drawn in Figure 2 to mark the beginning of this horizon (see p. 12). According to this reasoning, the Classic horizon began with Teotihuacan II, Xochicalco II, the transitional phase between Monte Albán II and III, Esperanza, Tzakol, Upper Tres Zapotes, Lower Cerro de las Mesas II, Upper Remojadas II, El Tajín I, and Pánuco III.

It is debatable whether a Classic horizon can be spoken of for Western Mexico, and indeed, as Bernal has pointed out, whether the cultures of this vast region can be considered Mesoamerican at all during that horizon. They seem to have lacked some of the most basic Mesoamerican characteristics, such as a knowledge of the calendar and of writing. If any cultural province of the subarea attained such knowledge, as happened in the region around Lake Pátzcuaro and in other regions conquered by the Tarascans, it was generally owing to influences from the Toltec or Mixtec-Cholultec cultures at the beginning of the Postclassic horizon, i.e. at the time of the Aztatlan complex in northwestern Mexico.

In contrast, certain cultural elements comparable to those found in Costa Rica, Colombia, Ecuador, and Peru were present in Western Mexico before the Toltec influence. One of the most notable was a particular type of tomb

---

[18] This question is treated, and a new solution proposed, in Part II of this volume, pp. 111–12.—Editor.

discovered by José Corona Núñez in El Arenal near Etzatlan, Jalisco, which enabled him and Eduardo Noguera to establish some far-reaching parallels (Corona Núñez and Noguera 1955).

These Western cultures preserved a Preclassic aspect until the end of the Teotihuacan epoch or the beginning of the Toltec. Only from that time, in the full Postclassic horizon, do clay figurines begin to be manufactured in molds. But there can be no doubt that these cultures were influenced by the great Teotihuacan culture of the Classic horizon, as is demonstrated by the architecture of Itztépete near Guadalajara, the handsome alfresco vessel from Jiquilpan, and the Thin Orange pottery associated with the Ortices phase in Colima. For this reason, in Figure 3 (p. 13) I have indicated the beginning of Teotihuacan III–IV influences by a thick dotted line, the symbol used for the beginning of the Classic horizon. However, I should warn the reader that even if in the chart I have settled on the date A.D. 300 for the beginning of the cultures subject to Teotihuacan influence, this does not preclude the possibility that such cultural diffusions could have come a little later, although most probably not later than A.D. 400.

Figures 43–56 show a series of clay figurines from Western Mexico—ranging from Michoacán to Sinaloa and Zacatecas, and including Colima, Jalisco, and Nayarit—in which Teotihuacan inspiration is apparent. It is worth noting here that although all, or nearly all, the figurines are contemporaneous with Teotihuacan III and IV, as the stratigraphic excavations of Kelly and other archeologists have proved, they are more comparable stylistically with Teotihuacan I figurines, and, as Noguera has demonstrated, only doubtfully and occasionally with those of Teotihuacan II.

I am therefore inclined to think that the strong influence of Teotihuacan culture on Western Mexico began with phase I of Teotihuacan, and that this may have been transmitted through contacts with the Chupícuaro culture, which would have served as an intermediary. As we have already noted, Chupícuaro pottery extends from Tulancingo, Hidalgo, as far as La Quemada, Zacatecas. Covarrubias (1957: 88–89) has maintained that the cultures of Western Mexico must have begun to evolve in Preclassic times not only in the Zamora region (where the great antiquity of El Opeño has been demonstrated by Noguera) and the Chupícuaro (where a chronological relationship with the beginning of Teotihuacan I has been established by Muriel Porter), but also in other zones, where, according to Isabel Kelly, the ceramic strata can be correlated with Teotihuacan III but not earlier. From information furnished by Kelly (1947), it follows that at least the Chumbícuaro phase of Apatzingan, inasmuch as it precedes the Delicias (which she estimates to be coeval with Teotihuacan III), should be considered contemporaneous with Teotihuacan II. For my part, I should like to suggest that the chronological picture could well be similar to that of Chupícuaro, where the final phase is correlated in an analogous way with Teotihuacan II, but the initial phase is definitely associated with Teotihuacan I.

Lastly, it seems reasonable to assume that if the cultures of Western Mexico retained a Preclassic aspect when the greater part of the Mesoamerican cultures were in the Full Classic horizon, if they remained backward and archaistic, it was owing to their relative isolation. They did not change until a people who probably originated in Western Mexico, the Toltec-Chichimecs, coming perhaps from the Cazcan region of northern Jalisco and Zacatecas, conquered the Valley of Mexico and the surrounding valleys, except for a while the Puebla-Tlaxcala zone. The Toltec-Chichimecs created a great empire, which sent out cultural, and possibly political, influences that spread all through Western Mexico, from Sinaloa and Durango in the northwest to Guerrero in the south of this subarea, which cannot be considered completely Mesoamerican until the great influx of Toltec or the related Mixtec-Cholula culture in the initial period of the Postclassic horizon. The radiations from Tula reached still farther, from New Mexico to Costa Rica.

ESSENTIAL FEATURES OF THE CLASSIC HORIZON

Guided by Palerm's compendium, I shall now try to sum up the characteristic features named by Armillas, Caso, and Bernal for the Classic horizon. Agriculture seems to have made constant progress: terracing was used in Monte Negro from the time of the Upper Preclassic, and I should like to add that in El Tepalcate, near Chimalhuacan, indications appeared of the existence of *chinampas* from Teotihuacan I, according to Ola Apenes. Later, in the Classic horizon, irrigation was probably known and practiced, according to Armillas, although it should be kept in mind that there is no archeological proof for this during the Classic epoch except outside of Mesoamerica, in the Colonial phase of the Hohokam culture of the southwestern United States.[19] The proofs we have of this technique, as well as data from our historical sources, do not go back further than the Postclassic horizon. I believe, nevertheless, that it would have been difficult to achieve the splendor of our Classic world without canal irrigation, for only in this way could agriculture have developed fast enough to provide the economic basis necessary to support a population that was certainly greatly enlarged.

Such a population growth can be inferred from the fact that so many grandiose monuments were constructed at the height of Mesoamerican civilization, an enterprise that demanded a considerable labor force. In this epoch, too, we find all the basic food plants, and also, as Palerm notes, an increase in plants for commercial use, among them cotton. In addition, important technological progress was achieved, which made possible something akin to mass production, presupposing the incipient industrial development and unmistakable commercial expansion that are clearly attested to by archeology.

Clay figurines began to be made in molds from Teotihuacan III; and according to Armillas, "hollow drills, no doubt of bone," were used to perforate

[19] See n. 14.

"Teotihuacan-style stone masks." He goes on to say that jade carving and the making of pyrite mirrors became widespread in response to "the new society's demands for luxury." He adds that rollers seem to have been employed to move huge weights, such as the "enormous monoliths of the monumental architecture," and that the wheel was known from this time in Pánuco III, "although used only for toys and not for practical ends."

He says that "the styles of the fine wares, made to satisfy the requirements of temple and tomb, became diversified and modified in local traditions which grew up around the principal ceremonial centers," and that from "the diffusion of the different local styles we can draw conclusions about the relationships between the different production centers." In some instances the diffusion was by imitation, notably with regard to the extremely popular "cylindrical tripod vessel with flat base and conical cover characteristic of Teotihuacan III and the Esperanza phase of Kaminaljuyú, which with varying differences is found in other zones as far as the southern limits of Mesoamerica."

He points out that the most representative commercial pottery of this phase (Teotihuacan III–Monte Albán IIIa–Esperanza–Tzakol)—the apogee of the Classic stage, when active commercial relations linked the different centers, and the interruption of trade to which the phase Teotihuacan IV–Monte Albán IIIb–Amantle Pamplona–Tepeuh attests had not yet come about—was doubtless that known as Thin Orange. This, he says, though it had "only one center of production, ... by means of trade ... reached the limits of Mesoamerica to remote Colima in the northwest and Copán in the southeast."

For my part, I shall add that in the northwest the Teotihuacan influences seem to have extended as far as Chiametla, Sinaloa (Kelly 1938), and La Quemada, Zacatecas (Batres 1903), and that the production center of Thin Orange pottery, which is known to have existed as early as Teotihuacan II, seems to have been in the Ixcaquiztla zone near Tepeji de la Seda in southern Puebla, according to the explorations of Carmen Cook de Leonard (1953). According to Palerm, the unprecedented importance of commercial relations could have led to "the formation of independent groups of merchants," or at least to the "secularization" of commerce, that is, to a progressive loss of theocratic control. In this connection, Steward seems to think that the earliest commercial mercantile operations must have taken place in ceremonial centers under the watchful eye of priests.

In the Classic horizon, urbanization reaches such an advanced level that not only do true cities exist, but there are also great metropolises, which the indigenous accounts called "Tollan." The name Tollan was perhaps first applied by the Nahua-speaking people to the city in which they lived, the great urban center of Teotihuacan. According to ancient sources, the builders of Teotihuacan, as well as those who erected the great pyramid of Cholula, were "giants."

Therefore, Palerm speaks now of "urban ceremonial centers," which have added new features to the previous types of ceremonial centers. These features are: "(1) conversion of the center into a place of large-scale manufacturing; (2) extension of city planning from the area of the ceremonial center proper to practically the whole residential zone; (3) complete transformation into an 'administrative center' or 'seat of state government.'" All this, according to him, is accompanied by "a substantial increase in the resident population and a greater internal diversification of work." At the same time, typically urban services, "such as the construction of extensive drainage systems and of a system for the domestic storage of water," made their appearance.

Armillas believes that "the settlement pattern in this epoch seems generally to have been in villages grouped around ceremonial centers of primarily religious function, permanently inhabited by a relatively small priestly nobility and their servants. The inhabitants of the villages congregated there on the occasion of great festivals.... Besides the temples of the gods, and palaces and monasteries for the ruler-priests, there was room in these ceremonial centers for the burial of important personages in sumptuous tombs built under the temple platforms or grouped in extensive necropolises, of which Monte Albán is the best example."

With respect to Teotihuacan, Bernal (1953: 48) believes that the type of settlement to which it belonged went even further than that described in the preceding quotation, and that it was "a true city." Thus it seems that Armillas's interpretation must be reconciled with the views of Bernal and Caso, who speak of cities, and with Palerm's contribution.

In the architecture of the period, several innovations appear: notably, the combination of panel and slope at the beginning of Teotihuacan II, and the effect that this architectural trait exerted on Monte Albán, where it produced a panel-and-slope type of building decoration of a special character. In the Zapotec metropolis, new types of tombs began to be constructed, some having an antechamber and others a cruciform plan. Sculpture reached great heights, although in some instances, as in Teotihuacan, it was subordinated to, and influenced by, architecture. Even though we find stelae in the Preclassic from the inception of Monte Albán I and Tenocelome sculpture is then in full splendor, it is only at the beginning of the Classic horizon in the Tzakol phase that we find magnificently carved stelae scattered all over the Maya area.

It must also have been at the start of the Classic horizon that sculpture on buildings and on individual stones began in Xochicalco II and El Tajín I, even though archeological evidences are practically unknown in the first site and are scarce in the second.[20] Mural painting flourished; there are striking

---

[20] In October 1961, César Sáenz unearthed at Xochicalco three stelae, which "are the first true stelae (with dates, sculptured on all four sides, and erected as free-standing monuments) that have been found in the center of Mexico" (Sáenz 1962a, 1962b; Caso 1963).—Translators.

examples in Teotihuacan III and in the Transición IIIa–IIIb of Monte Albán. Almost at the end of the horizon, the development of mural painting culminated in the splendid pictorial creation of Bonampak in the Maya area in about A.D. 800. The same artistic splendor touches pottery, which often is not only graceful in form, but beautifully decorated.

Certainly, as Armillas observes, it is "a hieratic, fully developed art," and the perfection of an architecture like that of Teotihuacan, which can be compared in its irreproachable geometry to some of the great Gothic masterpieces of Europe, leads one to think of the presence of a well-integrated cosmic vision, such as that of the *Summa* of Saint Thomas. There must have existed as well a religious doctrine and a very coherent and harmonious philosophy fostering the architectural, sculptural, and pictorial creations. Even such industrial arts as pottery were affected, as can be seen in Teotihuacan, in many of the Maya ceremonial centers so beautifully reconstructed in Tatiana Proskouriakoff's admirable drawings, and in Monte Albán and other centers.

Along with art, the pure as well as the applied sciences undoubtedly made astonishing progress. We know, for example, of the mathematical genius of the Maya, and of their meticulous and exact recording of eclipses and the revolutions of celestial bodies, as well as the perfection of their calendar, implicit in their "Long Count" system. All this, which had antecedents in the Upper Preclassic from Monte Albán I, now reached full culmination among the Maya. Even all the advances made in Teotihuacan appear peripheral compared with the great strides made in the Maya area, Cerro de las Mesas, and Monte Albán. Perhaps the same could be said of cultural centers as important as El Tajín and the Huasteca. Although in all these archeological provinces the calendar was known, not many calendric inscriptions have been found in them compared with the great number discovered in the Maya area, Veracruz, and Oaxaca, which must have been the true centers of astronomical knowledge.

As to religion, new gods appear, one of the most important being Quetzalcóatl, whom Caso sees in constant association with the rain god, Tláloc, and whom Armillas considers a sort of development out of Tláloc. Other deities who emerge in this period are the maize god, the butterfly god, and the fat god. The first is characteristic of Monte Albán and the Maya area, and the last two of Teotihuacan. According to Laurette Séjourné, Xochipilli (also called Macuilxóchitl or Piltzintecuhtli) seems to have been worshiped in Teotihuacan. There are slight indications there of human sacrifice, and although Armillas agrees that "nothing has been found in this horizon corresponding to the eagle-sun complex," it must be remembered that this cult was already deeply rooted in El Tajín II, which corresponds to late Classic, and that paintings apparently representing eagles were found recently in a construction of phase II at Teotihuacan. This may mean that as a religious symbol the eagle had an important significance there at the very latest from the beginning of the Classic horizon. What is still to be proved, in my opinion, is the absence of the cult of war gods in this horizon.

All the available facts seem to support Armillas's view that during the Classic horizon we are dealing with "a theocratic society whose economic base permitted a tremendous channeling of energy to the service of the gods and the dead." According to Armillas, "we must infer a theocratic form of government from the importance of the temples and the elaborate character of the representations of priests in painting and sculpture." Bernal, too, stresses "the continual representation of priests instead of warriors, as well as the probability that the civilization was the work of a small group of priest-sages." However, he adds that "this does not imply the absence of wars," and reminds us that representations of warlike scenes and warriors predominate in the Bonampak paintings. In this connection it must be remembered that the Bonampak murals date from what we shall call the Epiclassic, that is from the final period of the horizon now under study; and it was precisely in this last period that the Classic world disintegrated.

There is no doubt, then, as Armillas says, that "religion was the principal integrating force in these societies," and that "we can infer that the political power was exercised by a priestly nobility." And surely Bernal (1950: 32) is right when he asserts that "probably we are considering great theocratic organizations which, in the beginning, give a tremendous impulse to the culture and achieve marvelous works of art, but which, once triumphant, think only of conserving their gains and fossilize, thus losing their inner force and becoming ripe to fall victim to the first man of daring or to die smothered by the weight of their own works." I had also arrived at the same general idea of theocracies, an idea that I developed in my course "Ancient History of Mexico" in the Escuela Nacional de Antropología e Historia at more or less the same time that J. Alden Mason (1943: 43) described the cultures of the Classic horizon as "theocratic."

Palerm thinks that "some centers influenced by Teotihuacan could have been true commercial-religious colonies, similar to the colonies created by other civilizations in the Old World," and that such colonies "do not imply military conquest or domination of the surrounding territory and people, but rather the contrary: an essentially pacific relationship interested primarily in commerce with the local people and perhaps also in religious proselytizing." Palerm, in agreement with Caso, adds that in this same horizon we find "the first evidences of 'priest-kings' to whom divine origin is attributed." It should be added that Caso is inclined to concede the possibility that Teotihuacan constructed an empire. Lastly, there seems to be a growing social stratification, which, as Armillas observes, is reflected in the funerary customs; and perhaps there existed, as Palerm suggests, some form of servitude or slavery, to which Seler (1915), too, was inclined to give credence.[21]

21 Seler alludes to the possible existence of slaves, represented in figurines.

The Classic horizon, which marks the apogee but not the maximum expansion of prehispanic civilization in Mesoamerica, is characterized, as Caso (1953) makes clear, by "an extraordinary development of local cultures, with a very distinct personality in the art style, pottery, writing, and calendar of each, although at the same time a free cultural exchange was taking place among these thriving centers. For example, Monte Albán received influences from Teotihuacan and El Tajín; Kaminaljuyú shows ceramic features of El Tajín, Teotihuacan, and Monte Albán; and the influence of El Tajín at Teotihuacan is undeniable." This is a period of peaceful relations, when the fruitful cultural interchange that had started, at the latest, in the Middle Preclassic and increased steadily throughout the Upper Preclassic reached its maximum intensity. To quote Willey and Phillips (1958: 151), "one of the reasons that Classic cultures could be developed in Middle America was that there was a multiplicity of regional traditional antecedents. The intertwining of the many varied strands of the Formative produced the Classic. Individually, these strands would have supported nothing of greater moment than a culture like the Mississippian of the eastern United States, with its temple mounds, or the Coclé culture of Panama, with its fine pottery and metal craft. Together, they emerge as Middle American civilization. This does not mean that the Middle American Classic stage was characterized by a single, homogeneous culture or civilization. Regionalism persisted, but it was a regionalism in which the various Classic cultures had assimilated enough from each other so that all drew upon a common fund of great depth and richness."

From the Classic horizon on, according to Caso, we can begin to form conclusions about the historic peoples. There seems to be no doubt that we can attribute the magnificent constructions in the Maya area during the Tzakol and Tepeu phases (or their equivalents) to the Maya, and those of Monte Albán to the Zapotecs—with some confidence from Monte Albán IIIa through Monte Albán IV. As for Teotihuacan, it is my conjecture that if in the first and second periods the bearers of that culture were Nahua-Totonacs, in the third they were Popoloca-Mazatecs, existing side by side with Nahuas, as I have suggested in another study (1942).

The most ancient historical traditions go back to the Classic horizon. We know that the Maya chronicles narrate events of the year A.D. 435,[22] while the earliest records of occurrences and genealogical-dynastic changes of fortune in the Mixteca, according to Caso, reach back to A.D. 692. We also have accounts furnished by Sahagún's sixteenth-century Indian informants concerning the Tamoanchan epoch and the exodus of the *tlamatinime* (learned men), which must correspond to the final period of the Classic horizon. Finally, Torquemada has gathered information about the beginning of the tyranny of the historic Olmecs in Cholula, which can apparently be dated a short

---

[22] Evidence attesting to the dynastic historical nature of Maya inscriptions has recently come to light; see Proskouriakoff (1960) and Kelley (1962).—Translators.

time before or after A.D. 800, and the resulting Pipil migration toward Central America, which we shall discuss later (Barrera Vásquez and Morley 1949; Caso 1949, 1951; Torquemada 1943; Jiménez Moreno 1942, 1956).[23]

Since the Maya inscriptions deciphered up to now seem to relate only to the recording of time periods within the Long Count or to the notation of eclipses or other astronomical phenomena, one gets the impression that the refined and brilliant people who produced such detailed records were more interested in the history of the celestial bodies than in the history of the men who erected the exquisitely sculptured stelae and raised magnificent buildings to their gods. Even so, there must have been some sort of written history, at least from the Tzakol phase; otherwise it would not be easy to explain the existence of traditions that go back to the first half of the fifth century. Similarly, Caso suspects that at least as early as Teotihuacan III, when the great city reached its apogee and the wonderful murals of Tepantitla were painted, there existed pictorial codices dealing not only with ritual, but with historical matters as well. It seems to me that some earlier codex, perhaps from Teotihuacan, must have inspired the first Mixtec attempts at writing history at the close of the seventh century and the start of the eighth, because it is difficult to imagine that such a detailed genealogical history as that possessed by the Mixtecs was entirely committed to memory by successive generations. However, examples do exist of genealogies and traditions preserved exclusively by word of mouth, as, for instance, among the Arabs and the Polynesians. Despite all this, I believe that a true historiography arose only with the conditions of anguish and chaos that seem to have prevailed in Central Mexico from the end of the great Teotihuacan epoch in about A.D. 650, i.e. only when the Classic world was beginning to disintegrate.

I do not profess belief in existentialism, unless, more or less unconsciously, a Christian existentialism, but I do believe that great crises have sharpened the historical awareness of peoples, producing in some of the best men a psychic detachment that predisposes them to a sort of moral self-evaluation. At such times, in the face of the uncertainty of the surrounding chaos, the individual himself becomes the most reliable point of reference.[24]

[23] Unfortunately there are a number of typographical errors in my "Síntesis de la historia precolonial del Valle de México" (1956), and as a result certain names of persons and places, as well as some of the dates given there, make nonsense.

[24] For an invaluable outline of the most important characteristics of the Classic horizon, the reader should consult Bernal's *Compendio de Arte Mesoamericano* (1950: 25–32). This provides details of the cultural evolution of such great centers as Teotihuacan and Monte Albán, as well as informed conjectures about the artistic accomplishments of the cultures of Western Mexico. Further publications by Bernal on both the Zapotec and Mixtec regions of Oaxaca appeared in 1959 in the *Boletín de Estudios Oaxaqueños*. For the Maya area, Thompson's excellent work *The Rise and Fall of Maya Civilization* (1954) should be consulted; and for all the cultural provinces alluded to, Covarrubias's magnificent book *Indian Art of Mexico and Central America* (1957) is the best guide. Olivé's *Estructura y dinámica de Mesoamérica* (1958) contains important suggestions, and should certainly be referred to.

THE FULL CLASSIC

In Map 4, I offer a schematic configuration of the Full Classic, the epoch between A.D. 200/300 and A.D. 600/700, which has as a center of reference Teotihuacan III (A.D. 300–650), when Mesoamerica had not yet attained its maximum expansion and Teotihuacan culture dominated the northern area.[25] On the northwest at this time, Mesoamerica did not extend beyond the limits of recognized Teotihuacan influence (i.e. the regions of Chiametla and La Quemada), and on the northeast it reached no farther than the Huasteca, where the Teotihuacan impact was more perceptible than in the northwest. On the east the Pánuco III culture would include an area as far as the Valles region, from which later, in its following stage, this culture was to advance to the center of San Luis Potosí. On the north it must have extended beyond El Mante in Tamaulipas, and on the south at least to Tuxpan in Veracruz. Farther to the south, perhaps adjacent to the Huastec province, was the region of El Tajín, a center which has been considered an offshoot of Teotihuacan II, and which at the time of El Tajín I (A.D. 200–650) was in close contact with its cultural progenitor. Already at this stage, from the great center near Papantla just as from the other center of Yohualichan in the Sierra de Puebla (which according to García Payón seems to be older), the Tajín culture was to spread to Cuauhchinanco and the environs of Zacatlan on the west; and on the south, at the very least to Xiuhtetelco in the Teciuhtlan region—the point of the contact of the putative mother culture with her hypothetical offspring. We cannot speak with certainty in designating the perimeter of these and other cultural provinces because in many cases precise data are lacking. However, using the few facts available, I have undertaken the rash and dangerous task of presenting a picture of the geographical extension of the most important Mesoamerican cultures. Of course any such picture is tentative and subject to correction and amplification, and I intend it as no more than a basis for discussion.

In Map 4, I offer a representation, vague because of the scarcity of information, of the extension of the culture of Lower Cerro de las Mesas II (A.D. 300–800). I should point out, however, that the end of this phase is not presented here, since in about A.D. 650 strong influences from Teotihuacan IV and El Tajín II irrupted in the Cerro de las Mesas zone, and the province was probably conquered by the historic Olmecs in about A.D. 800. This put an end to period II and resulted in the migration of the Pipiles toward Central America, a point to which we shall return.

The extension of Monte Albán culture given in the map is basically that attributed to phase IIIa in Bernal's study (1949a). Influences from this cul-

---

[25] New radiocarbon dates in considerable numbers on Teotihuacan materials have confirmed the early dating of Teotihuacan that Jiménez Moreno ventured in this paper, and in fact Teotihuacan II and III may be even slightly earlier than he proposed. See Bernal (1965).—Editor.

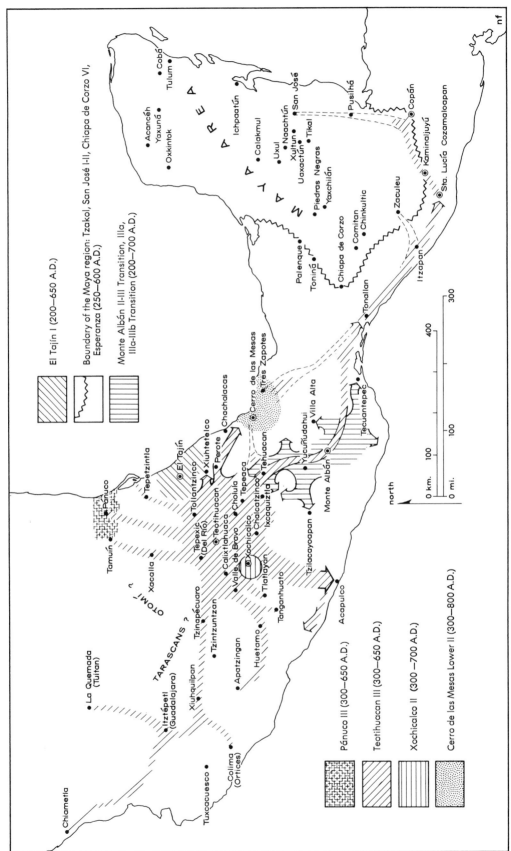

Map 4. The Full Classic, A.D. 200/300 to 600/700.

El Tajín I (200—650 A.D.)

Boundary of the Maya region: Tzakol, San José I-II, Chiapa de Corzo VI, Esperanza (250—600 A.D.)

Monte Albán II-III Transition, IIIa, IIIa-IIIb Transition (200—700 A.D.)

Pánuco III (300—650 A.D.)

Teotihuacan III (300—650 A.D.)

Xochicalco II (300 —700 A.D.)

Cerro de las Mesas Lower II (300—800 A.D.)

tural phase of the Valley of Oaxaca, together with others from Teotihuacan III and El Tajín I, extended to Kaminaljuyú, on the outskirts of Guatemala City, and then on to San José in British Honduras or Belice, probably via the Valley of Oaxaca, Tehuantepec, and the Soconusco coast, as indicated on the map. Within the same horizon, influences that are perceptible in Tonala, Chiapas, traveled from Teotihuacan III and Lower Cerro de las Mesas II (possibly side by side), and perhaps crossed the Isthmus of Tehuantepec from north to south before reaching the Chiapas coast. It seems likely that the Mixteca of eastern Guerrero, southern Puebla, and western Oaxaca was much more open than the Zapotec region to Teotihuacan influences during the apogee of the great metropolis. Nevertheless, undeniable Teotihuacan influence is found in Transición II–III, IIIa, and Transición IIIa–IIIb of Monte Albán, not only in architecture and painting but in industrial arts such as pottery. We can go so far as to say that a Teotihuacan–Monte Albán cultural axis played a role similar to that of the La Venta–Monte Albán axis in the Upper Preclassic. Of course, we must not forget the importance of the Maya civilization, which reached glorious heights at this time and was the cultural pinnacle of all America.

Since the Mixteca was much nearer Teotihuacan, it must have received powerful impulses from there, as can be seen in the Yucuñudahui phase (which coincides with Monte Albán Transición IIIa–IIIb), even though there was a close dependency on the great Zapotec ceremonial center. A little later, however, when the period we have called Epiclassic began in the Mixteca, somewhat before A.D. 700, the Mixteca ceased to be culturally subordinate to Monte Albán. It is my belief that in the Mixteca Baja, particularly around Acatlan, signs must have appeared of a new style, the Mixteca-Puebla, which did not fully materialize in Cholula until 800, at the beginning of the "Olmec tyranny" spoken of by Torquemada, which caused the Pipil exodus toward Central America.

Teotihuacan influence was very strong in Guerrero, a point that was stressed in the 1946 discussion of the IV Mesa Redonda de Antropología. Covarrubias has emphasized this, too. The same cultural current had great importance in the *tierra caliente* of Guerrero and Michoacán, in places such as Tanganhuato and Huetamo, which Armillas (1950a) refers to, and in Apatzingan, which Kelly (1947b) has studied. Rubín de la Borbolla (1947a), in his stratigraphic study of Tzintzuntzan, has spoken of "lapidary work with a Teotihuacan influence" in describing the Lower Lacustrine phase, which seemingly correlates with Teotihuacan IV. In addition, in Figure 48, I show a Teotihuacanoid figurine of known Pátzcuaro origin. The look of this figurine, the hint of the existence of a stonework style (apparent in the stone masks of Teotihuacan III if not in other objects), and Moedano's discovery (1946) in Tzinapécuaro that Tzintzuntzan derived a good part of its earliest ceramic style from the phase he called "Antigua" (contemporary with Teotihuacan III) lead me to infer that cultural infusions from the "city of the giants and the gods" could have influenced the Lake Pátzcuaro region at least from the end of Teotihuacan III.

At about the same time, cultural influences of the same origin reach Jiquilpan, the source of a lovely alfresco painted vessel and a figurine of definite "Teotihuacanoid" aspect (Noguera 1944). Perhaps from Jiquilpan, by way of Sayula, such influences reached as far as Colima, where Kelly (1938) found Ortices-phase pottery in association with Teotihuacan Thin Orange. It was perhaps from Jiquilpan, too, that these same radiations advanced to Itztépete. The radiations must have been transmitted to Itztépete at least from the time of Teotihuacan III, to judge by the figurines I remember having seen at this site near Guadalajara. I should add, however, that the architecture of Itztépete probably corresponds to Teotihuacan IV, at least in one of the several phases of its enlargement, because although it displays the unmistakable Teotihuacan style of panel and slope, the slope is excessively high, recalling in this respect the great height of the slope of the monument dating from phase III in Xochicalco, i.e. A.D. 700 to 1000, according to Gálvez (1958).

From the Guadalajara region or nearby come legends, collected more than three hundred years ago by the chronicler Tello (published in 1891), that speak of giants, who could also be identified with the people of Teotihuacan. Itztépete, then, besides being an important branch of Teotihuacan, could have been a place of passage through which Teotihuacan influences flowed to faraway Chiametla, near Mazatlan, and to La Quemada in the south of Zacatecas. To the north, there is no evidence of pottery-making in a considerable part of Sinaloa and Sonora—that is, up to the Hohokam and Mogollón area of the southwestern United States.

It is worth noting that until now the region of El Bajío has not furnished clear proof of Teotihuacan presence. Thus it appears as though there were a hiatus between the end of the Chupícuaro culture, which, as already mentioned, spread out through El Bajío between San Juan del Río and León, and the beginning in this region of a very strong Toltec influence. I have sometimes wondered whether a large part of these plains might not have been covered by water during the apogee and maximum expansion of Teotihuacan, a circumstance that would account for the complete lack of Teotihuacan influences.[26] (I imagine that geologists could tell us whether this is a likely hypothesis, and perhaps a study for the zone does in fact exist.) Another plausible explanation would be that at the time of the Teotihuacan apogee, this relatively low-lying region was occupied by nomads, perhaps Otomí or some of the Tarascans.

---

[26] When I mentioned this idea to Rubín de la Borbolla, he reminded me of the constant inundations of Acámbaro and many lowland cities; and indeed there have again been dreadful floods in this area only recently. ["Recently" refers to the time of writing, the summer rainy season of 1958.—Editor.]

By contrast, the cultures of Michoacán, Jalisco, and Colima flourished at the time of the Teotihuacan apogee, as did the Delicias phase of Apatzingan and the culture of Tuxcacuesco. We are not sure that the cultures of Ameca, Etzatlan, and Ixtlan were developing at this time, but it seems likely in view of their archaistic appearance and the fact that they were on a route to the north of Nayarit and the south of Sinaloa. Southern Sinaloa is the location of Chiametla, where the oldest stratum must have been contemporaneous with Teotihuacan III. At the same time, it should be remembered that San Marcos, also in this region, is the source of an object that is typical of Tenocelome culture, which suggests even greater antiquity. Furthermore, in the interior of Itztépete, near the juncture of Jalisco and Nayarit, some relatively old pottery has been found, which, according to Corona Núñez, would be Preclassic within what he calls the "Early Cora horizon" in this zone. Kelly is of the opinion that the zone seems to form part of a single cultural province, which, in addition to Colima, Autlan, and Tuxcacuesco, would include the Sayula region, connected with Tuxcacuesco, and the region of Zacualco, related to that of Ameca.

In western Guerrero the culture of Pláceres del Oro, reported by Spinden (1911) and described by Krickeberg (1956: 566) and Covarrubias (1957: 113) as looking "Chavinoid," must have flowered at this stage of the Full Classic in view of the notable similarities Kelly has found between the stone and shell ornaments of the Guerrero site and those in the Delicias phase in Apatzingan. Finally, in the state of Morelos, and perhaps also in part of northern Guerrero and in part of the south of the state of Mexico, there develops in this horizon, perhaps between A.D. 300 and 700, the second stage of Xochicalco. We are dependent on Noguera's ceramic studies for all we know of Xochicalco II; but there must have been important architecture at that time, if we are to judge by the perfection in the following phase of a monument that displays, in exquisite relief, the most beautiful of all representations of the god Quetzalcóatl.[27]

THE EPICLASSIC PERIOD

The final period of the Classic horizon, generally called Late Classic and termed "Epiclassic" by me, lasts from A.D. 600/700 to 900/1000. In this period, the Classic world, with its deep-rooted civilization and theocratic tradition, disintegrates, and the historic Olmec and Toltec empires, newer cultures characterized by a strong militaristic tendency, appear. A great crisis shakes Mesoamerica from end to end, and in the midst of the chaos a new world germinates. There is a profound change in cultural orientation. The ancient cultures of a thousand years suffer defeat, and people from peripheral and backward areas come into power.

[27] See Sáenz (1962a, 1962b, 1962c) and Caso (1963) for data confirming this judgment.—Editor.

Since such situations of abrupt transition are by definition unstable, the scene becomes blurred and confused when the historian tries to arrive at a well-focused image of what happened. Let me offer, in a provisional way, a hypothesis about how these profound transformations might have taken place. To do so, it will be necessary to go back to the preceding period, the Full Classic, when, according to the consensus of the specialists, each one of the prosperous regional cultures maintained peaceful relations with the others, as attested to by archeological evidence of wide commercial interchange and mutual influence.

The great Teotihuacan culture, outstanding because it exerted influences in so many directions, ultimately established patterns and opened the routes that were to last in Central Mexico for centuries. These patterns, in spite of all the profound differences, continued to be respected under the domination of Tula, and the routes were used by the Toltecs to spread their influence to distant reaches. So great was Teotihuacan, and such the force with which she imposed her culture, so unified the area dominated by her in spite of its great size, that Caso and Bernal have rightly asked if Teotihuacan were not in fact an empire. Bernal remarks on the enormous extension of the urbanized area of Teotihuacan, which apparently has no parallel in Mesoamerica. A state having a capital of such size, within an extensive territory where the other localities are of little importance, must have been quite centralized, and this in itself implies a high degree of cohesion and unification, which is surely the essential concept of empire (though empires have existed which were neither greatly unified nor very coherent). In fact, a state organization of this kind could have been produced there, although of course it must have differed in many aspects from that of Tula, while possibly coinciding in others. Perhaps we may imagine a sort of "Holy Empire," in which the ruler-priests would wield an authority analogous to that of emperors and popes. The two ruling elements, however, would be fused in one hierarchy, with the clergy having much the greater share of power.

But it seems more likely that we are dealing with a fundamentally theocratic state, governed by a high priest endowed with temporal power and imbued with great prestige, his authority perhaps deriving from the fact that he personified the god of lightning and rain, Tláloc-Quetzalcóatl. Indeed, one source tells us that Tláloc was a lord of the *quinametin*, the "giants" whom I have identified (1945) with the Teotihuacanos. This could be understood to mean that the most venerated god in the Teotihuacan culture was personified by the ruler-priest, who would appear as Tláloc's living image; being so considered, he could have his orders obeyed without debate, and in extreme cases he would be able to impose his decisions by force.

The colonies of artisans and specialists that would leave Teotihuacan to go and settle in other parts would also be propagators of the religion of Tláloc. They would certainly establish places of worship, and these would soon fall under the spiritual sway of Teotihuacan and help this holy city—a sort of combined Rome and Mecca, attracting pilgrims from afar—to develop the magnificence revealed by archeology.

Other comparisons could be made with regions like Tibet, where the Dalai Lama, the incarnation of Buddha, was at the apex of a theocratic state. Perhaps the most illuminating and relevant comparisons are those that have been established with the ruler-priests of ancient Egypt in the times of the pyramid construction, and also with the ruler-priests of Mesopotamia in the epoch before the coming of the Semites and the formation of the Akkadian empire of Sargon I and Naram-Sin (Frankfort 1948, 1956). Moreover, we have reason to believe that comparable situations may have existed in the Indic world and the Far East.

The "pontifical" Teotihuacan state almost certainly bordered to the north on the territory of peoples of low culture, who had to be held in check, perhaps by some kind of rudimentary militia. We have proof that arms were known in Teotihuacan, notably shields, the *átlatl* or spear-thrower, and spears. An unpublished work of Caso's deals with this subject. Furthermore, Laurette Séjourné has discovered pictorial representations of warriors in Teotihuacan, and Medellín has found clay figures of warriors clasping shields in the Upper Remojadas II phase, which can be correlated with Teotihuacan III and IV.

Slight Teotihuacan influences seem to have extended to the shores of Lake Cuitzeo and Lake Pátzcuaro by way of Tzinapécuaro and Tzintzuntzan. It seems likely that to the north of these lakes there were marauding groups of nomadic hunters comparable to those of the Tarascans, who still were nonsedentary in the thirteenth century, when, from Zacapu, they invaded the lake region and then went on to dominate all of Michoacán. Beyond San Juan del Río, there probably were groups of Otomí, who were nomadic except for some who may have reached a stage approaching agricultural life. Occasionally, warlike groups, inhabitants of distant regions, would have made incursions to the borders of the Teotihuacan empire. Thus near Tulancingo it would have been quite possible for swarms of Huastecs to appear, coming from beyond Huejutla, and for Teotihuacan colonies (Itztépete, near Guadalajara, for example) to suffer attacks from the Cazcanes. For the Cazcanes, although they lived in the cultural sphere of Teotihuacan influence as did the Huastecs, can be compared to the barbarians in ancient Rome, who ended up by destroying, without meaning to, the empire whose culture they emulated.[28]

The necessity of adopting means of defense must have been felt in the territory subject to Teotihuacan much earlier than in regions farther south

[28] In 1940 I delivered a lecture to the Sociedad Mexicana de Antropología entitled "La cultura teotihuacana y los chichimecas." In reference to the influence of the Roman Empire on the barbarians, see Wheeler (1954).

such as the Maya lowlands. It is therefore understandable that although Teotihuacan attained greater cohesion and greater vigor in her political organization when confronted by the barbarian menace, she was the first to succumb at the beginning of the disintegration of the Classic world. So the contrast presents itself that whereas in the Maya area a stage of full flowering and expansion endures within the Tepeu phase (A.D. 600 to 800), the great age of Teotihuacan ends in about A.D. 650. Precisely then, a probable Teotihuacan diaspora or dispersion begins toward both the southeast and the northwest of Mesoamerica.

The causes of the collapse of Teotihuacan at the end of phase III remain unidentified. Archeology has clearly shown that the metropolis was burned when that period was ending, but we do not know whom to blame. It has been thought that, at a later time, the Toltecs may have celebrated their conquest of the already abandoned Teotihuacan by burning it; but who preceded them in the destructive task, not around the year 900, but in 650? Were they by chance the barbarians of the northern borders, or were they a closer people, perhaps the Otomí?

Although the destructive wave could have come also from the south or the northeast (which is to say we must take into consideration warlike peoples such as the Mixtecs and the Huastecs), I am inclined to think it was the Otomí, a people who were considered brave warriors. It is worth noting that in the Teotihuacan mural shown in Figure 100, a warrior is represented with facial painting characteristic of the Otomí, and appears to be armed with a shield and a spear-thrower as well as with so-called "bird arrows," the weapon that gave the Otomí ethnic group their name (Jiménez Moreno 1939). The Germans were represented similarly in sculpture by the Romans.

Of course we could assume, as do Seler and Gamio, that the Otomí correspond to an old stratum of Mesomerican population that goes back to the Preclassic horizon, and that they were enslaved by peoples of Classic cultures. But it is well to remember that the Florentine Codex (1961: 170–71) classified these "shooters of bird arrows" among the Chichimecs or barbarians, whose nonchalant attitude toward agriculture—they squandered the fruits of any plentiful harvest—suggests that they did not have a very old agricultural, much less ceramic, tradition. They probably acquired both only at the end of the Teotihuacan epoch or at the start of the Toltec, when, according to the sources, many of them were living in caves. In any event, it is significant that the Otomí language was already spoken in territory very near Teotihuacan long before the coming of the Chichimecs of Xólotl. This gives us an indication of who might have occupied some of the lands in the north of the Valley of Mexico that the people of Teotihuacan left vacant when they dispersed. Further, various sources of prehispanic history mention that the Otomí occupied this valley and the neighboring region well before the arrival of the Toltecs, and that the Toltec chieftain Mixcóatl had to fight the Otomí until they submitted. He did, however, adopt some cultural features of these barbarians, which is why the accounts say that he "turned into an Otomí" (Carrasco 1950). Thus in the north of the Valley of Mexico and in the northern plains of the Valley of Toluca, the Otomí-Mazahua constituted the dominant element. They also occupied the Mezquital Valley. Perhaps the center of their dominion was in Cuahuacan, in the region the sources call Chicomóztoc, which constituted the focal area of the Otomí, and was both the starting point of their expansion and their zone of refuge. This must have been the headquarters of the nascent nomadic dynasty that later settled in Cuauhtitlan. However, according to the sources, long before the migration to Cuauhtitlan this domain of the nomadic or incipiently sedentary Otomí of Cuahuacan was one of the political nuclei that shared power with Tula.

In any event, a situation was produced comparable to that which must have prevailed many years later under the domination of Xólotl. Some of these wild and roving Otomí, who perhaps burned Teotihuacan at the end of the third phase, were acculturated from an epigonal center of Teotihuacan tradition: San Miguel Amantla in Azcapotzalco. Here the Amanteca-Teotihuacanos produced figurines with great plumed headdresses, as well as *incensarios*, large vessels decorated with figures of human beings or gods, and other traits that apparently survived from Teotihuacan III.

Thus, while the Amantecas were continuing the cultural tradition of Teotihuacan, very near them were beginning to appear coarse antecedents of the Coyotlatelco pottery that was found by Tozzer on the outskirts of Azcapotzalco. In these, according to Noguera, Teotihuacan vessel forms seem occasionally to have been copied. Coyotlatelco ceramics could perhaps have been manufactured by a group of Otomían origin, such as the Tepanecs, who formed part of the Tula empire, and who at the disintegration of Tula made Azcapotzalco the state capital.

This is the broad picture of the Valley of Mexico in Teotihuacan IV, a phase whose existence has at times been denied. Such an opinion is probably correct in the sense that phase IV is not found at Teotihuacan proper; nor indeed could it be if the city had to be abandoned after being burned. As Bernal points out, when the makers of Mazapan ceramics, the Toltecs, settled much later in the present-day ward of Xolalpan, they seem not to have known that they were living on top of previous Teotihuacan construction, a sign that at least this and other parts of the great city had remained uninhabited for a long time. The statement that phase IV never existed may be partially correct if we take it to imply that the vessel forms and decorative motifs attributed to this stratum, and even the characteristic *incensarios* and the figurines with great feather headdresses, date back to the third phase, and that consequently nothing, or almost nothing, is added in the epigonal "Teotihuacan IV" of the environs of Azcapotzalco. But there is no denying that after the fire that seems to mark the end of phase III in the great capital,

57. Monument 7, El Baúl, Guatemala.

58. Monument 3, Santa Lucía
Cozamaloapan, Guatemala.

59. Monument at Santa
Lucía Cozamaloapan,
Guatemala.

60. Monument 1, Santa Lucía
Cozamaloapan, Guatemala.

61. Monument 13, Santa Lucía Cozamaloapan, Guatemala.

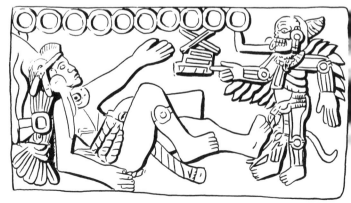

a Teotihuacan group in a city of secondary importance, Azcapotzalco, continued for more than two centuries to make a type of pottery which, in its fundamental features, existed before the great metropolis succumbed to the attack of the barbarians. This theory is confirmed by Caso's statement that features clearly of Teotihuacan style in vessels and other objects are evident not only up to the time of the Mexica empire, but even afterward, during Colonial times. Lastly, we have the support of Eduardo Pareyón, who has studied ceramics from the outskirts of Azcapotzalco and believes them to belong to Teotihuacan IV.[29]

Meanwhile, what had happened to the people of the great Teotihuacan empire? It is my opinion that although some of them remained, forming small islands in the troubled sea of Otomí invasions and other unsettling developments, many had to scatter like the Jews at the fall of Jerusalem. Small groups perhaps went toward the west, while others, more numerous, were heading southeast. Thus in Copán, one of the greatest of Maya cities and the most distant of all, a stela was carved on which appears a personage attired in a headdress with a Tláloc face and wearing sandals on which there are glyphs of undoubted Teotihuacan origin. This stela bears the date 9.12.10.0.0 in the Maya Long Count, which corresponds to the year A.D. 682 (Armillas 1950b). Clear Teotihuacan influences are evident also in Santa Lucía Cozamaloapan, Guatemala (Thompson 1948), as Figures 57–70 confirm. Possibly some of these influences, as in the case of Kaminaljuyú, go back to the end of the fifth century, but others probably correspond to the beginning of the Teotihuacan diaspora. In this connection, we shall examine later the migration of the Pipiles toward the same region and to even more remote areas in Central America.

I do not intend to mention here all the places to which the scattered emigrants from Teotihuacan might have gone (as perhaps to the Yucatán Peninsula at the beginning of the Puuc phase), but only to furnish some examples. Lastly, it must be remembered, as I have stressed in another work (1942), that not only around Azcapotzalco, but also in other sites of Central Mexico, especially in a zone that extended from Tehuacan and Cozcatlan to Teotitlan del Camino, there certainly remained Teotihuacan groups, later called Nonoalcas. Caso, in his studies of Mixtec codices, has found indications that in this region lived a high priest to whom even the Lord of Tula and the Lord 8 Deer were still rendering homage in the middle of the eleventh century. Evidence has been found that the priest lived in Teotitlan (Caso 1949; Nicholson 1955).

---

[29] As will be explained in Part II of this volume, Caso and his co-workers defined Monte Albán IV as distinct from IIIb not on the basis of any observable change in pottery and architecture, but because of the abandonment of the metropolis—a strictly parallel situation to that of Teotihuacan as set forth here.—Editor.

62. Vase; El Baúl, Guatemala.

63. Monument 1, El Baúl, Guatemala.

64. Serpent head; Sculpture 20,
El Baúl, Guatemala.

65. Cylindrical vase;
Tiquizate, Guatemala.

66. Foot of vessel;
Tiquizate, Guatemala.

67. Sculpture 15, El Baúl, Guatemala.

68. Monument 12, El Baúl, Guatemala.

69. Figurine; Tiquizate,
Guatemala.

70. *Hacha*; El Baúl, Guatemala.

THE EXPANSION OF EL TAJÍN

Meanwhile, a large part of the territory that previously came within the cultural orbit of Teotihuacan was strongly influenced by two cultures that now reached their greatest expansion: El Tajín II and Monte Albán IIIb. It is from this time that El Tajín influenced an extremely wide area stretching from Buenavista, in the center of the state of San Luis Potosí, to the Yucatán Peninsula, where the Puuc phase was flowering. The Cerro de las Mesas cultural province had received an avalanche of El Tajín influences, as can be clearly seen in the San Marcos–style figurines and the dominant Lirios pottery, which seems to correspond to the end of Upper Remojadas II. Similarly, strong Teotihuacan influences are evident in figurines and vessels whose style is usually attributed to the controversial Teotihuacan IV. Thus this culture of La Mixtequilla, which dates from about A.D. 650, little by little loses its own personality, and like that of the Los Tuxtlas zone, appears to become "Tajinized." New religious concepts, although some of them perhaps had slender roots in Teotihuacan, seem now to burst forth in full vigor at the beginning of the period I call Epiclassic. At this time the dominant culture of Mexico was probably that of El Tajín, with only one competitor of equal or greater vigor: the Maya civilization beyond the Isthmus, then at the height of its expansion and brilliant flowering.

According to verbal information from Stresser-Péan, the Huastecs have a most interesting legend in which the "old god" of fire and lightning is chained to the bottom of the sea, the young sun god having replaced him as ruler of the world. However, it is interesting to note that this indigenous Apollo has been able to come into power only with the consent of the dethroned old god; and, further, that the old god seems also to have had a solar character, though less pronounced.

It appears that what this legend recounts had occurred when certain El Tajín religious concepts became dominant. As we have seen, the eagle is believed to have been represented in very early Teotihuacan paintings, and it must already have had unquestionable importance in the great metropolis of the Valley of Mexico, especially when we take into account the representations of eagle-knights in Teotihuacan art as shown by Laurette Séjourné. Perhaps even at this early time the eagle was a symbol for the sun; but this symbolism now becomes intensified in the offshoot of Teotihuacan culture centered in the country surrounding Papantla. For example, the ceremony of the *Volador*, which is undoubtedly related to the solar cult and in which the participants disguise themselves as eagles, seems to have originated in the Papantla area. There also the eagle appears together with human sacrifice, which, although possibly practiced in Teotihuacan and perhaps as early as Tlatilco, only now attains definite popularity, as the magnificent sculptured reliefs of El Tajín show.

Also in these reliefs, a skeleton, symbolizing death, is frequently represented: one of the first clear indications of an incipient necrophilia that later became one of the chief features of Mexica art. Already in Teotihuacan we know that skulls are sculptured in stone, and that the dead, although represented as being very lively, and even happy, are portrayed in handsome murals. But the mania for representing skulls and skeletons is here not so marked as in contemporary El Tajín art, or shortly afterwards in Mixteca-Cholula and Toltec art. An expressive clay figure of a seated Mictlantecuhtli belongs to the Remojadas culture of central Veracruz; and in the Lirios pottery, within the same tradition, there are representations of fleshless men whose mask in the form of a skull can be put on and taken off.

Strangely enough, it is from this cultural area that the immense majority of so-called smiling heads come, which suggests that the Veracruz region had taken on an ambivalent attitude already in prehispanic times. It is extroverted and loves gaiety and has been capable of modeling the smile, but at the same time it seems to see death as lying in constant ambush and the gods as demanding the continual offering of human blood. Thus these smiling people at times turn grave—let us recall the contrasting personalities of two recent presidents, natives of Veracruz[30]—and at other times an imperceptible anguish hovers over the festive gaiety of the *huapango*, the *bamba*, and the tunes from Alvarado. In the El Tajín reliefs, the skeleton descending from the sky, like the Tzitzímitl or ghost of the Tenochcas, seems to be a sword of Damocles ready to cut short the lives of men.

We have noted that the solar cult, which would culminate under the Tenochcas, worshipers of Huitzilopochtli, a combination of Apollo and Mars, appears to have been important during the great expansion of El Tajín culture. It seems that in El Tajín culture the same thing occurred as among the ancient Huastecs: they came to consider the young sun god and the young maize god to be basically the same (to judge by data gathered by Stresser-Péan referring to the present-day Huastecs). Laurette Séjourné has found Teotihuacan representations of Xochipilli (also called Macuilxóchitl and identifiable with Piltzintecuhtli), and perhaps this god should be thought of as the masculine aspect of the maize deity, Centéotl, who has his feminine counterpart in Centeocíhuatl or Xochiquétzal. In some codices, the head of Piltzintecuhtli appears emerging from the beak of a pheasant, a bird associated with solar worship; many clay figurines wear pheasant headdresses from the time of Pánuco III. The popularity of the sun god, and of the bloody rites paradoxically connected with this divinity of flowers and music, seems to become extremely widespread with El Tajín culture. The bearers of this culture were probably Nahua-Totonacs, of the same extraction as those who today live in the Sierra de Puebla, and perhaps some Huastecs were incorporated with them.

---

[30] This refers to the ebullient Miguel Alemán (1946–52) and the rather austere Adolfo Ruiz Cortines (1952–58).—Translators.

According to Stresser-Péan, the present-day Huastecs have another god connected with both rain and maize, the famous Quetzalcóatl (the Plumed Serpent), who perhaps evolved, as Armillas has suggested, as a continuation of the ancient god Tláloc. Whereas Tláloc, strictly speaking, represented lightning (and therefore sometimes had the trappings of the fire god), the Plumed Serpent was the genuine symbol of rain, and even today we know that among the Nahuas in the Huastec region a heavy shower is described as a "Quetzalcóatl." Endowed with such rain symbolism, the "dragon of the waters," as he has been called, appears perhaps as early as Teotihuacan II in the magnificently sculptured temple in the Citadel, where the Plumed Serpent alternates with large masks generally thought to be representations of Tláloc. I now believe that these masks portray Xiuhcóatl, emblem of drought, and not, as in the current interpretation, "nocturnal serpents." If the suggestion is valid, this alternation of two distinct serpent heads, one of them hardly recognizable as such, could be taken to represent the succession of the wet and dry seasons.

Quetzalcóatl is of very ancient origin. Covarrubias sees antecedents of the Plumed Serpent in the Tenocelome culture, and Caso and Bernal think that effigies of him may be as early as Monte Albán I. However, it is in the Epiclassic period that he attains real popularity, not only in the Tajín II culture, where he constantly appears in the sculptured reliefs, but also in the culture of Xochicalco III. To Xochicalco III is attributed the most beautiful representation of Quetzalcóatl, masterfully carved on a high slope of the temple sometimes called the "Castle." And let us not forget that resemblances have been noted in the profiles of the architectural monuments at the ceremonial centers of both El Tajín and Xochicalco.

XOCHICALCO AND MAYA INFLUENCES

The conditions of the period we are studying will be better understood if we realize that it is the same period alluded to by Sahagún's informants when they refer to Tamoanchan. As a matter of fact, we may safely assume that the *tlamatinime*, the wise men, who the Florentine Codex says migrated toward Guatemala, were groups who scattered from Teotihuacan, leaving traces, as we have noted, in Copán and Santa Lucía Cozamaloapan, among other places. Therefore, it is understandable that in such chronicles as the *Popol Vuh* and the *Anales de los Cakchiqueles*, along with references that for the most part bear on Postclassic Tula, we find others that we believe refer to Teotihuacan. Teotihuacan was, perhaps from the time of phase III, a metropolis of Nahuas combined with Popoloca-Mazatecs, and the first city to receive the Nahua name Tollan. The name Tamoanchan, however, seems to be of Huastec origin, as I tried to show in my article "El enigma de los olmecas." I there distinguished between an older Tamoanchan, of a mythical nature, which seems to have an early relationship with the Gulf coast, and a later and protohistoric Tamoanchan, which perhaps included the Valley of Morelos, and at least the southeastern, if not all the eastern, part of the Valley of Mexico. Both the *Histoyre du Méchique* and Mendieta locate Tamoanchan in the province of Cuernavaca. Then, too, we know that one of the holy names of Amecameca was Tamoanchan Xochitlicacan. Sahagún's informants say that the calendar was invented in this region, but from the context of the narration it seems clear that nothing more than a calendric reform is intended, perhaps the one alluded to in the carvings of the Temple of Xochicalco, where there is a supposed calendric correction.

As I pointed out in "El enigma de los olmecas," the warriors represented in the reliefs of the Xochicalco sanctuary clasp square shields that are similar, though not identical, to those used by the warriors of the Maya area. Furthermore, Noguera has called to our attention certain conspicuous similarities between the architecture and pottery of Xochicalco and those of the Maya. It may be that some of these relationships not only belong to the Epiclassic, but go back to Xochicalco I, which can be dated 200 B.C. to A.D. 300. In addition, it appears that in Xochicalco a reunion of astronomers is represented that is comparable to the one carved on a huge stone in far-off Copán, a city in which we find a ball court whose contours are similar to those of the ball court at Xochicalco. The date ordinarily assigned to the Copán monument on which the assembly of astronomers is carved is A.D. 776, but in Thompson's opinion the date is A.D. 700. It is important to remember that the historian Ixtlilxóchitl, perhaps referring to the Epiclassic period, mentions the arrival in the center of Mexico of people who came from Potón-Chan, near Frontera, Tabasco, on the border of the Maya Chontal territory; so it is perfectly possible that they came from Maya territory, and perhaps from Copán itself.

All this implies that in the period we are studying, A.D. 600 to 800, the period of great Maya expansion, the Maya could have been in contact with Central Mexico. At this time, too, an advantageous interchange could have been established between the refined culture that recorded the years in the Long Count system, and the energetic, perhaps warlike, culture of El Tajín II, where the vanquished contenders in the ball game were beheaded. All this was possible because Teotihuacan, the capital of the empire that lay between the Huastec and Tajín cultures on the north, and the Cerro de las Mesas and Maya cultures on the south, had collapsed in about A.D. 650. Once Teotihuacan was fallen and abandoned, the Maya area could offer something of almost comparable greatness. This was Tikal, which at that time was the most extensive of the Maya cities, with a population, it seems, of some 100,000 (Shook *et al.* 1958).

THE EXPANSION OF MONTE ALBÁN

Extending across territories formerly under the influence of Teotihuacan culture, Monte Albán culture in its IIIb phase reached its maximum expansion in the Epiclassic period. By way of Tehuacan, Monte Albán influence was felt as far as Cholula and Huejotzingo. We must remember that Veytia, perhaps referring to this same period, mentions Zapotecs who probably lived in settlements in that part of the state of Puebla, south of the present capital, that Kirchhoff locates in a map in his article "Los Pueblos de la Historia Tolteca-Chichimeca." I have suggested in another study (1942) that the Zapotecs were perhaps "Zapotitecas" (from Zapotitlan), who spoke Chocho-Popoloca; but Bernal's map (1949a) showing the geographic extension of Monte Albán IIIb pottery now makes me think that there may indeed have been a Zapotec group or groups living in southern Puebla, as Veytia's reference implies.

Although, generally speaking, there are scarcely any evidences of an incipient militarism in Monte Albán culture, Caso has noted a method of indicating conquests of towns—namely, the use of an inverted human head beneath the place-name glyphs on the stone stelae. Granted that conquests took place, wars must have taken place, at least in the phase that Caso designates as IIIb.[31]

Did the Zapotecs use as mercenaries their Mixteca Alta neighbors, who up to that time were still well within the Zapotec culture orbit, and did the Mixtecs later serve their own ends, as the Mexicas did in relation to the Tepanecas? It is not possible at present to answer this question. It is clear, however, thanks to Caso's painstaking investigations (1949), that the Mixtec codices, which record events going back to before A.D. 692, register a series of wars that these inhabitants of poor eroded lands started to wage in A.D. 720, the year, to all appearances, in which the principality of Tilantongo was founded. Father Antonio de los Reyes, in the beginning of his *Arte en lengua mixteca* (1593), refers to traditions according to which this dynasty originally came from Apoala, whence a few lords, certainly foreigners, embarked on the domination of the "true Mixtecs." Since the cradle of the dynasties that ruled the Mixtecs was situated at the source of a river that flows down to the Tomellín Canyon, where Cuicatlan and Quiotépec are located, we can conjecture that the founders of these dynasties were perhaps Cuicatecs, and therefore related linguistically to the people whom they enslaved. Cuicatlan and Quiotépec at this time must have been a cultural crossroads, since in Cuicatlan a yoke of Tajín affiliation was found, and in Quiotépec, a construction corresponding to Monte Albán IIIb. This was not the only place in which cultural influences from Monte Albán and El Tajín confronted each other. The same thing occurred in Tuxtepec.

Another possibility worth considering (and for me certainly a preferable hypothesis) is that the non-Mixtec chieftains, who established themselves in Apoala and later founded the Tilantongo kingdom, came from the region of Teotitlan del Camino, where probably an important redoubt of Teotihuacan

[31] The use of inverted heads with place glyphs occurs on carved stones of Monte Albán II; in III there are scenes on stelae (see Part II, this volume) that seem to show conquest and prisoners, but use other symbolic devices for the purpose.—Editor.

culture still existed, maintaining the theocratic character that it preserved in some degree up to the Spanish conquest (Nicholson 1955). I have mentioned the dependence, at least spiritual, of the Lord of Tula and his Mixtec colleague, the Lord 8 Deer, on the priest of a place that Caso says must have been Tehuacan or Teotitlan, and that I have reason to believe was definitely Teotitlan. Scholars from Seler to Nicholson have all recognized the importance of the area of Teotitlan and Cozcatlan, in which traces survive not only of the Teotihuacan culture, but of the Toltec as well (Dahlgren 1954).

The inhabitants of the region, according to the *Relaciones geográficas* of the sixteenth century, were Nahuas and Mazatecs, i.e. precisely the ethnic elements that I suspect to have been the principal bearers of Teotihuacan culture from the beginning of Teotihuacan III. But other Mazatec groups, too, may have played an important part in the Cerro de las Mesas culture. The region of Teotitlan is very near the convergence of the natural routes that connect the Tomellín Canyon with the Mixtequilla, along the Santo Domingo River, and also with Tehuacan and Cholula, this last having been for many centuries a densely populated area whose inhabitants are of Teotihuacan origin.

I mention all this to show that an elite, who, setting out from Teotitlan, went into the Mixteca Alta, could have brought with them elements derived from the Cerro de las Mesas culture as well as from that of Teotihuacan. There are indications that Teotihuacan culture may have influenced Mixtec culture long before the arrival of the Toltecs. The appearance of the Ichcatec language, closely related to Mazatec, as an enclave surrounded by Mixtec in a region west of Apoala, makes this hypothesis all the more tenable.

Once the principality of Tilantongo was established in about A.D. 720, the Mixtecs won a series of wars culminating in the conquest of Cholula. They certainly participated in this conquest as an integral part of the historic Olmec group, which was probably tri-ethnic, consisting of Nahua, Mixtec, and Chocho-Popoloca. Archeologists can look for origins of the Olmec group in the Mixteca Baja, from Huajuapan and Tzilacayoapan to Izúcar and Huehuetlan, and even to the area of Atlixco, where ancient Cuauhquechollan was situated. Certainly peoples who spoke Nahua, Chocho-Popoloca, and Mixtec lived intermingled in southern Puebla in the sixteenth century, particularly in the zone of Matamoros Itzocan, Acatlan, and Tepeji. Mixtec is still spoken today as far north as Chigmecatitlan. I believe that the situation of four centuries ago indicates the composition of the group that created the Mixteca-Cholula cultural tradition in Cholula.

Acatlan, where María Antonieta Espejo believes that she has found antecedents of the Aztec I ceramic tradition, must have been an important center. Of course, it is possible that the Mixteca-Cholula culture was formed within a short time in Cholula itself, and that except for isolated traits antecedents will not be found. It is perhaps a case similar to the Toltec, although Toltec culture is even more eclectic.

The name of this ceremonial center in Mixtec is significant. According to the *Arte en lengua mixteca* by Father Antonio de los Reyes, the Mixtec name is *Ñundiyo*, which means "stair" or "stairway." This indicates that Mixtec-speaking people knew the pyramid of Cholula before it was covered by the last great structure (which perhaps they themselves built), and that the stairways constructed by the Teotihuacanos on this impressive monument could still be seen. For this reason I wonder if the place-name glyph in Mixtec codices that Caso has provisionally designated "Place of the Skull," showing a pyramid with its stairway, could not perhaps mean Cholula, an idea that is supported by the similarity in Mixtec between the word for "dead" and the word for "stairway."

THE HISTORIC OLMECS AND THE PIPIL MIGRATIONS

In trying to date the Olmec conquest of Cholula, we must remember that according to Torquemada the Olmecs ruled Cholula for 500 years, and that the "tyranny" ended when Toltec immigrants, who had taken refuge there after the ruin of their Tula empire and been enslaved by the Olmecs, took possession of the city and drove out their former masters. In the annals known as the *Historia Tolteca-Chichimeca*, the expulsion of the Olmecs took place in the year 1 Flint, which is usually correlated with 1168, but should in my opinion be corrected to 1292.[32] I am willing to admit that this date could have been 52 years earlier, A.D. 1240, but no earlier than that. Consequently, I place the beginning of the 500 years of Olmec tyranny at A.D. 792, or at the earliest 740. Since at the moment I favor the date A.D. 1292, I put the conquest of Cholula in round numbers at A.D. 800.

In the stratigraphic excavations that Noguera carried out in this sacred city (1954) he found proof that it was occupied until the Teotihuacan IV phase by people from Teotihuacan. I suggest that this could be interpreted to mean that the traditional Teotihuacan culture lasted a century or a century and a half longer in Cholula than in Teotihuacan (A.D. 650–740 or 650–792), and that consequently the Olmecs dislodged the "giants" or *quinametin*, which is exactly what some of the sources affirm. This displacement of Teotihuacan groups was so widespread that it not only affected those living in the Valley of Mexico, but reached as far as the peoples who dwelt in the Puebla-Tlaxcala region.

There are indications that something similar occurred in the Valley of Morelos at about the same time. The *Relación de Tepoztlan* speaks of people, surely Nahuas, who lived in that region and emigrated to Veracruz. The emigrants, who had left Morelos and whom I take to have been Teotihuacanos, were not able to remain in their new refuge, which must have been in the

---

[32] I gave my reasons for this dating at the meeting of the Mesa Redonda de Antropología in Jalapa in 1951. The published proceedings of this conference (Bernal and Dávalos 1953) contain a table that I worked out for the sequence of events recorded in the *Historia Tolteca-Chichimeca*, giving them their correct positions.

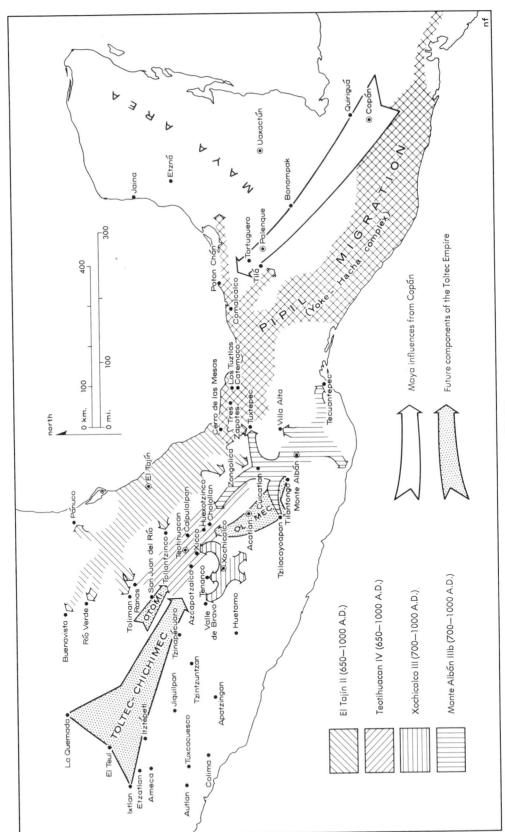

Map 5. The Epiclassic (A.D. 650–1000), shown before the Olmec and Toltec invasions of A.D. 800–900. [The author's Olmec arrow from Tilantongo to Cholollan is a prophetic indication of the subsequently discovered Ñuiñe culture, described in Part II of this volume.—Editor.]

Legend:
- El Tajín II (650–1000 A.D.)
- Teotihuacan IV (650–1000 A.D.)
- Xochicalco III (700–1000 A.D.)
- Monte Albán IIIb (700–1000 A.D.)

Maya influences from Copán

Future components of the Toltec Empire

MAYA AREA

north
0 km. 100 200 300 400
0 mi. 100 300

nf

PIPIL MIGRATION (Yoke–Hacha complex)

TOLTEC-CHICHIMEC.

OTOMÍ

OLMEC

Mixtequilla and Los Tuxtlas. Similarly, emigrants from Cholula, who must have left for the same zone and for the region between Tehuacan and Teotitlan, could not take root there because the new masters of Cholula, the sacred city from which Puebla has inherited its importance and significance, very quickly extended their sphere of influence to the center of Veracruz, where at this time Cerro Montoso pottery was being made and the real Cempoala cultural tradition began. Very soon, around A.D. 800 (or at the earliest 750), the cultural province of Cerro de las Mesas and the neighboring region of Los Tuxtlas fell before the pressure of Cholula. The Nahua inhabitants of Teotihuacan tradition who had begun to settle there, particularly since the fall of Teotihuacan in A.D. 650, and who were strongly influenced by El Tajín from then on, had no sooner given asylum to the most recent Teotihuacan fugitives, those just expelled from Cholula, than they were again displaced.

A mass migration began: that of the Pipiles, the "nobles" or "princes" who left and established themselves in Xolotan (i.e. the Soconusco coast), and from there went on to settle in Guatemala, El Salvador, Honduras, and Nicaragua, and also, though in small numbers, in Costa Rica and Panama. Further, it is probable that from Costa Rica and Panama, using a sea route, groups of Pipiles reached the southwest coast of Colombia, according to the finds of Cubillos in Tumaco (1955), the coast of the province of Esmeraldas in Ecuador, and even Túmbez, at the extreme north of the Peruvian coast. Thus these exiles whose early home was in the great twin centers of Teotihuacan and Cholula, which like a two-headed eagle dominated the cultural evolution of Central Mexico, came into contact, from the periphery of the Maya area to as far south as Peru, with peoples who practiced metallurgy. A find of metal objects in Tazumal goes back to the year A.D. 751, and another in Copán dates from 782 (Thompson 1948). More than a century later a group of Pipiles, coming perhaps from distant Tlapallan in Honduras, or at least from nearer Huehuetlapallan (which is located by Melgarejo in the region of Coatzacoalco), began a migratory movement. The migration is described in detail by Ixtlilxóchitl, who designates the group as Toltec because after passing by places such as Quiahuiztlan, Huejutla, and Tulancingo, they arrived at Tula, where, under the name of Nonoalca, they collaborated with the Toltec-Chichimecs who formed the Tula empire in about A.D. 900.

Torquemada has preserved for us the tradition that the Pipil-Nicaraos were forced to emigrate from a region which, according to Lehmann, was south of Cholula and probably north of Tehuacan. They reached Los Tuxtlas, and from there the Soconusco wastelands. Ever pursued by the Olmecs, they went farther, to the territories they finally occupied in Central America. Although Torquemada's chronicle did not appear until 1615, it had been written for some time, since there is evidence that he had begun it by 1590. He probably obtained his data on the Pipil-Nicaraos at the time the *Rela-*

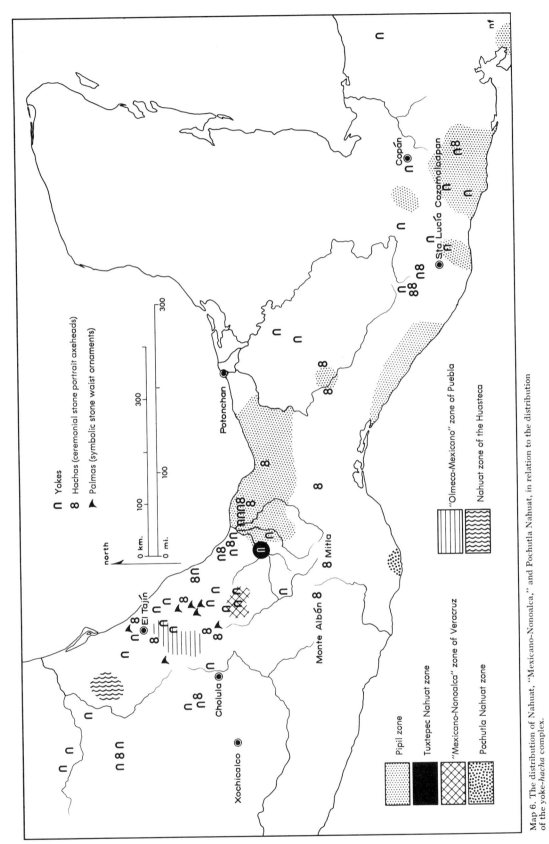

Map 6. The distribution of Nahuat, "Mexicano-Nonoalca," and Pochutla Nahuat, in relation to the distribution of the yoke-*hacha* complex.

Yokes

Hachas (ceremonial stone portrait axeheads)

Palmas (symbolic stone waist ornaments)

"Olmeca-Mexicano" zone of Puebla

Nahuat zone of the Huasteca

Pipil zone

Tuxtepec Nahuat zone

"Mexicano-Nonoalca" zone of Veracruz

Pochutla Nahuat zone

north

0 km.   100   100   300   300

0 mi.   100   300

Xochicalco

Cholula

El Tajín

Potonchan

Copán

Sta. Lucía Cozamalgapan

Monte Albán

Mitla

nf

ciones geográficas were compiled, i.e. in about 1580, basing himself on Question 14 of that work, in which the prehispanic history and ethnography of each locality are discussed. According to Torquemada's account, this migration toward Central America took place "seven or eight lives ago," the lives being described as those of "very old men," the kind one has to carry out into the sun and keep wrapped in cotton. Evidently what is meant are the 104-year periods called *huehuetiliztli*. It follows that if this tradition was set down in A.D. 1580, it would have to go back 728 or 832 years before that, i.e. to A.D. 852 or 748. The average between the two is 800, and I would therefore place the Pipil migration near this date, which coincides with the date I suggested earlier for the beginning of the Olmec tyranny in Cholula.

In Map 6, I have represented the extension of the Pipil dialect as being from the Papaloapan River in southern Veracruz to the frontier of Costa Rica with Panama. Tradition seems to indicate that the Pipiles came by a land route to Nombre de Dios on the Panamanian coast of the Caribbean. In the same figure, I show most of the places where yokes and *hachas* have been found, and although I by no means claim to have made an exhaustive study of these objects, it can be seen that their distribution coincides approximately with the extension of the Pipil dialect. The correspondence would be even more apparent if I had given an idea of the expanse of the area in which toponyms of Náhuat origin occur, because they attest to the presence of the Pipiles in many regions not mentioned by known historical documents; in such places their language survives only in nahuatizations incorporated into the local Spanish. Thus we have place names like Tegucigalpa (previously Taguzgalpa, equivalent in classic Náhuatl to Tlacochcalpan), Matagalpa, and many others that prove that the Pipil expansion went considerably beyond the limits usually assigned to it.

Consequently, I believe that the distribution of the yoke-*hacha* complex, from Veracruz as far as Nicaragua, is associated with the migration of the Pipiles through the lands that lie between the two zones. It is clear that such an extensive region would have a tendency to produce a number of distinct cultures, whose traits would vary according to the cultural substrata on which the new culture was built and the degree of its exposure to the influences of neighboring cultures. Thus, at El Baúl and Santa Lucía Cozamaloapan in Guatemala, a style developed that could not be mistaken for that of the Nicarao, although we can refer to a more or less homogeneous Pipil-Nicarao migration. I believe, furthermore, that certain ceramics, such as San Juan Plumbate and Tiquizate, both from the Pacific slopes of Guatemala and El Salvador, could be ascribed to the Pipiles; and that also associated with these descendants of Teotihuacan culture, who had been Tajinized and were known in the sources as Nonoalcas, are the Z Fine Orange vessels characteristic of the Puuc phase in the Yucatán Peninsula, while X Fine Orange vessels correspond to the era of the Tula empire, of which these same Nonoalcas came to be an integral part.

71. Stela 3, Cerro de las Mesas.

72. Stela 6, Cerro de las Mesas.

73. Stela 8, Cerro de las Mesas.

74. Monument 5, Cerro de las Mesas.

75. Stela 9, Cerro de las Mesas.

76. Stela 4, Cerro de las Mesas.

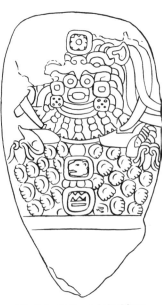

77. Stela 15, Cerro de las Mesas.

68

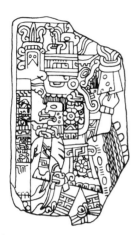

78. Stela of San Miguel Chapultepec.   79. Stela 5, Cerro de las Mesas.

SOUTHERN INFLUENCES OF CERRO DE LAS MESAS
AND TEOTIHUACAN

I should have liked to refer in detail to Cerro de las Mesas culture, and to
have shown that some of its elements seem to have reached along the coast
of Chiapas as far as Santa Lucía Cozamaloapan. However, for present purposes, pictorial presentation will have to suffice.

In Figures 71–79, I have assembled several stelae, and a stone representing
a duck-billed man with the sex organ visible, which correspond to the Cerro
de las Mesas culture of La Mixtequilla in Veracruz. In Caso's opinion, the
stela of Figure 75 should be assigned to a time perhaps earlier than the others
because of its Tenocelome traits and less rigid posture. In this stela and in
that of Figure 71 there appears a sort of tail, which ends in a glyph resembling a flower. The stela in Figure 78 is said to come from San Miguel Chapultepec, but is very similar to the one in Figure 79, which is from Cerro de
las Mesas. Those in Figures 72 and 73 have inscriptions in the Maya Long
Count corresponding to the years A.D. 468 and 533 respectively. In the stela
of Figure 73 a headdress displays something that could represent the claws
of a crab, an animal that is extremely abundant in La Mixtequilla and Los
Tuxtlas, and of course in other parts of the Gulf coast. Furthermore, in Santa
Lucía Cozamaloapan the crab god seems to have been very important (Figures 60 and 61; in the latter a personage making a sacrifice wears a headdress
showing a crab).

Although of quite different styles, in both Cerro de las Mesas and Santa
Lucía personages are represented seated, perhaps on a throne (Figures 59
and 76). The piece from Cerro de las Mesas reproduced in Figure 77 strikes

80. Stela, coastal Veracruz.

81. Stela of Tepatlachco, Veracruz.

82. Stela of Alvarado, Veracruz.

83. Stela of El Mesón, Veracruz.

84. Stela of Nopiloa, Veracruz.

me as being relatively late because of its style. On it a personage appears, perhaps a deity or priest, wearing a tiger headpiece or helmet, and with a face recalling the god Tláloc; there is a hieroglyph, perhaps also of a tiger, with the number 4 below it, as well as another glyph that I cannot identify. In Figures 80–84, I reproduce stelae from central and southern Veracruz. Figure 83 seems to retain, in an underset glyph, something of the Cerro de las Mesas style and could be from the seventh century. Figure 80, in another glyph in the same position, shows Tajín influence and is perhaps from the eighth century. Figure 81 shows similarities to Figure 80, but the personage is standing above a symbol that is the same as the lower one in Figure 82, which could be of Olmec origin. Therefore, the stelae of Figures 81 and 82 may be considered later than A.D. 800. Figure 84 seems to show unique features, which I cannot attempt to classify.

In Figures 57–70, I have reproduced pieces from the area of El Baúl and Santa Lucía Cozamaloapan; Figures 64, 65, 66, and 69, and perhaps 62, seem to show the mark of Teotihuacan. Influence from this culture or from the Toltec appears in the representation of Tláloc in Figure 67. These Teotihuacan cultural radiations may have reached El Baúl and Santa Lucía at the apogee of the huge metropolis, when, toward the end of the fifth century, it seemed to have an offshoot in Kaminaljuyú; alternatively, they could correspond to the time of the Teotihuacan diaspora, which seems to have occurred in about A.D. 650. *Hachas* like the one in Figure 70, as we have tentatively suggested, may be of the period of the Pipil migration, about A.D. 800 or a cycle before.

On the other hand, Figures 57, 58, 60, and 61 surely belong to the full flowering of Santa Lucía culture, which by then had a distinctive character, and probably they are not older than the ninth or tenth century; they could even be coeval with the beginning of the Toltec era. There are features here that seem to form a bridge between the Tajín and Tula cultures. Perhaps in Santa Lucía we are dealing with the Pipil group which, in my opinion, returned across the Isthmus and southern Veracruz to the center of Mexico, bringing metallurgical knowledge and collaborating as Nonoalcas in the cultural evolution of the Toltec empire.

Lastly, Figure 63 has an inscription which in the Maya Long Count would yield so early a date that we must question the use of the Long Count in this case. Figure 68 seems to suggest influences from Maya centers like Copán, and we do know that there were important relations between Copán and certain Pipil sites in El Salvador and Guatemala.

When we look at these examples, we have the impression of a warlike people. And indeed the Mexicas of later centuries were warlike; their sacred ball game had great ritual importance, and necrophilia was manifest in conjunction with bloody rites in which the victims were decapitated. I have already

85. Stela 9, Tonala, Chiapas.

86 and 87. Two sides of a stela formerly in the plaza at Tonala, Chiapas.

88 and 89. Two views of a stone serpent head, Tonala, Chiapas.

90. Stela 1, Izapa, Chiapas.

91. Stela 2, Izapa, Chiapas.

92. Stela 21, Izapa, Chiapas.

mentioned many of these characteristics in speaking of the great expansion of El Tajín II in the Epiclassic period.

Unfortunately, I cannot here treat the Chiapas coast in detail. In ancient times, it was a route of passage for influences from the La Venta and Monte Albán I cultures, and later from Lower Cerro de las Mesas II, Teotihuacan III, and Monte Albán IIIa; and still later from El Tajín. These influences were perhaps carried by Pipiles of Teotihuacan lineage, "Tajinized" during their stay in the Los Tuxtlas region. Figures 85–89 are from the Tonala archeological zone, and Figures 90–92 from Izapan. If we look at them carefully, it is probably possible to discern the influence of some of the other cultures.

INVADING PEOPLES AND THE FALL OF MAYA CIVILIZATION

The historical sources of Central Mexico and the Maya area have preserved the memory of the Teotihuacan diaspora in about A.D. 650 and the Pipil migration in about A.D. 800 (or 740). In Sahagún, however, the two seem to have become jumbled into one—the exodus of the *tlamatinime* or "learned men"—since, as we suggested earlier, in each instance people of Teotihuacan descent probably are dealt with. It is said that these *tlamatinime* went toward Guatemala, which seems to have been the case in both waves, and reached the sea (i.e. the Gulf of Mexico) with the historic Olmecs in hot pursuit. Presumably this harassment came to a halt for a time at the border of the Los Tuxtlas and Coatzacoalco regions, as did the later Mexica expansion. Perhaps the presence of Mixtec-speaking groups in Cozamaloapan, Veracruz, and in settlements south of the Sierra Tuxteca goes back to the time of the Olmec domination. Furthermore, pottery in the Cholultec-Mixtec tradition, which must have been made first by the historic Olmecs, is found in nearby regions such as Mixtan, near Playa Vicente, according to information given me by the late Juan Valenzuela.

In Guatemala, the recollections preserved in the *Popol Vuh* and the *Anales de los Cakchiqueles* probably go back to the days of the Teotihuacan dispersion and the arrival of the Pipiles. In the Yucatán Peninsula, the traditions in the books of *Chilam Balam* surely refer not only to the coming of the Toltecs but also to the arrival of earlier immigrants, the Nonoalcas. It appears that the chaos at the fall of Teotihuacan had awakened the historical consciousness of various Mesoamerican peoples. At least in the central Mexican region, it is only from this Epiclassic horizon that we find to a full degree what is known in the Old World as protohistory, whereas in the Maya area these traditions begin much earlier, in the Tzakol phase.

The Pipiles could have contributed to the fall of the misnamed Maya "Old Empire" because, among other things, their arrival coincided with the progressive abandonment of the cities located along routes that they probably traveled. It is significant that in both Palenque and Copán yokes are found immediately after the two cities ceased to record calendric dates in stone.

Certain figurines of the Los Tuxtlas region and small heads of a very definite style found in Jonuta seem to date from the Epiclassic period and could, perhaps, be attributed to the Pipiles. The magnificent Jaina terracottas, as beautiful as those of the Greeks, belong to the same period, but they might well be the work of skillful Maya hands. Furthermore, at the end of the eighth century, Pipil portraits seem to have been carved in stone at Copán.

The Pipiles certainly besieged the Maya groups on the eastern frontier. It must have been difficult to hold in check such combative peoples as the Pipiles, and later the Jicaques. There are indications that land formerly possessed by the civilized had to be abandoned to the barbarians.[33] On the western frontier, perhaps the presence of a new people such as the Chiapanecs, who would have arrived in the Chiapa de Corzo region probably in about A.D. 600, might have held back the thrust of the Maya expansion, which then veered away toward Tabasco. Here it certainly reached as far as Comalcalco, and small Maya groups seem to have established themselves for a time even farther north, in the Los Tuxtlas region east of the Papaloapan.

The stratigraphy found by New World Archaeological Foundation scientists in the area surrounding the old Chiapas capital ends with Chiapa VI,[34] which can be correlated with Tzakol and must have terminated in about A.D. 600 or a bit later. This could be related hypothetically to the arrival of a new people of different cultural tradition—perhaps that classed as Chorotega with reference to sculpture—since, according to Baudez, this style extends from Comitan, Chiapas, to Costa Rica, and, we think, perhaps to Panama. We know the Chorotegans had traditions of having lived in Chiapas, and that their language, sometimes called Mangue, is closely related to Chiapaneco (Lothrop 1926, Lehmann 1920, Baudez 1958).

Even though the Tepeu phase, which begins in about A.D. 600, marks the epoch of greatest splendor and maximum expansion in the Maya culture, foreign groups start to appear on the periphery of the Maya world from the initiation of this period—groups that were to force the Maya, who up to then had seemed interested only in astronomy, to lower their eyes to the ground and adopt defensive measures against their ever more numerous enemies. For a time after the fall of Teotihuacan, between A.D. 650 and 800, and par-

---

[33] We do not know how early the Jicaques are found near the Maya southeast frontier. Anne Chapman, who has studied this group, finds no data older than the sixteenth century. If the abundance of Nahua toponyms in this region to the east of the frontier is taken into account, it seems plausible to suppose that the Pipiles were the southeastern neighbors of the Maya, and that the Jicaques arrived in this zone only later. Their name—if of Nahua origin—could mean "the strong" (chicáhuac, shortened to chícac). In this way, the descendants of the Pipiles may have given a name, in their language, to these supposed intruders, whose culture has South American connections as Chapman suggests.

[34] Later publications of the New World Archaeological Foundation have presented revisions of this chronology, which is now further subdivided and also stated more confidently on the basis of radiocarbon samples. The chronological chart for Oaxaca on p. 90 of this volume provides an approximation of these recent refinements.—Editor.

ticularly in the eighth century, Maya influences seem to have had an open road toward the center of Mexico. The Maya imprint can be most clearly seen in Xochicalco.

However, the coming of the Pipiles, who, influenced by Tajín culture, lopped off human heads and, to honor the sun, performed bloody rites that were somehow associated both with the *volador* ceremony and with the sacred ball game, must have kept the Maya in a state of constant alarm. The Maya now took on a warlike attitude, as is apparent in the Bonampak frescoes, painted, we think, very close to A.D. 800. Indeed, some of the warriors represented there wear headpieces similar to those on certain of the clay figurines published by Weyerstall from the Los Tuxtlas region (Figure 94). This could mean that in about A.D. 800 there were contacts between the ancient habitat of the Pipiles and the Usumacinta region. This militarism, to which the handsomest pictorial creation of the Maya bears witness in a sort of Sistine Chapel, as the Bonampak temple has been called by Martínez del Río, must have increased during the whole century to such a degree that in about A.D. 900, or a little after, the Maya culture was completely wrecked. The Long Count system was never again used, a circumstance that justifies the assumption of a violent break in cultural tradition.

Apparently, then, for a considerable span of years there were no priests to compute the course of time in the old way. Eric Thompson (1954) has cited evidence that in the Maya city-states the members of the governing class, perhaps priests, were driven out by the rural masses whom they had ruled, and were in some instances even murdered. According to this, a true social revolution was taking place, motivated, Thompson suggests, by the "increasing demands for construction labor and food production" in a society with a constantly growing number of people who themselves produced nothing.[35] It was caused, too, I would add, by discord in the face of a chaotic situation deriving in part from the harassment of hostile peoples, and even from dissensions that could have arisen among the Maya warriors. Perhaps weakened by wealth, rivalries, and schisms, the ruler-priests were unable to remedy the critical conditions, and the masses turned against them, in some cases even destroying temples and holy images. The credibility of the scene, which has been painted for the most part by Thompson, is increased when we remember the violence of certain twentieth-century movements in Maya country: Carrillo Puerto's social radicalism and Garrido Canabal's antireligious crusade. On the basis of what seems to have occurred during the Epiclassic period in the Maya area, Julio César Olivé (1958), amplifying Thompson's diagnosis to include other Mesoamerican regions, has offered this opinion: "The breakup of the Classic world can be explained as the product of an anticlerical social revolution."

[35] Strikingly parallel events in this region, a thousand years later, are chronicled by Nelson Reed (1964).—Editor.

93. Chacmool; Quiriguá, Guatemala.

94. Head of warrior; Arroyo Guasimal, Los Tuxtlas.

95. Chacmool; Las Mercedes, Costa Rica.

96. Type C Pánuco figurine (Pánuco III).

97. Tiger knight in a Teotihuacan mural (*after Séjourné*).

98. Xochipilli, on a fresco-painted vessel, Teotihuacan (*after Séjourné*).

99. Eagle knight in a Teotihuacan mural (*after Séjourné*).

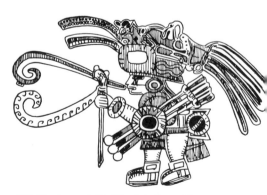

100. Warrior, probably Otomí, in the mural at Teopan-nacazco, Teotihuacan.

MILITARISM IN CENTRAL MEXICO

It is now time to turn our attention once more toward the center of Mexico and to conjecture what happened there between A.D. 800 and 900. In 800, Cholula had been conquered by the Olmec group, of which the most aggressive element must have been the Mixtecs, to judge by the wars the Mixtecs had waged from the founding of the principality of Tilantongo in about A.D. 720. The Valley of Mexico was under the control of the Otomí, nomads only then reaching a sedentary stage, and in the Valley of Morelos the Xochicalco acropolis was being built. Fortifications were constructed at Xochicalco, as well as at Xochitecatitlan in the Tlaxcala region, a center of Teotihuacan population later occupied by the Olmecs.

When and against whom did Xochicalco build these defenses? Were they perhaps raised against the Toltecs, after the year A.D. 900, to ward off the sweeping conquests of Mixcóatl, forger of an empire? Or were these parapets erected earlier, at about the time that the Olmecs from the Mixteca Baja were approaching dangerously close to Morelos by way of Itzocan, perhaps a little before or after they conquered Cholula in about A.D. 800?

Obviously archeology can furnish the answer. Meanwhile, however, we should remember that although the phases Xochicalco III and Cholulteca I were partially coexistent, there are almost no indications that the two centers had commercial relations, despite their relative proximity. I am inclined to believe that the inhabitants of Xochicalco put up the fortifications to contain a possible Olmec expansion toward their city, a great sanctuary of the god Quetzalcóatl. Xochicalco and Cholula were left face to face, perhaps struggling for the domination of the territory between them; the location of a capital in Jumiltepec (Armillas 1946, Noguera 1954, Florentine Codex 1961: 193–95) could have had this significance. Given this situation, a new and forceful element of confusion appeared with the arrival of Mixcóatl's hosts.

Since I have presented my version of how the Toltec empire was formed in a number of works (Jiménez Moreno 1941, 1942, 1945, 1956), I shall do no more than touch on the topic here. I wish only to emphasize that the great Toltec state, which ruled various ethnic groups known in legends as the sons of Iztac-Mixcóatl, was forged primarily by the Toltec-Chichimecs, who appear to have come from the lands of the Cazcanes (i.e. southern Zacatecas and northern Jalisco, the extreme northwest of the Teotihuacan sphere of influence). So, too, did the barbarians come from the confines of the Roman Empire, having constantly received influences from Rome.

Once the Toltec empire was formed, the capital, originally at Cerro de la Estrella in the Valley of Mexico, was moved to Tula for reasons already noted. Then, it seems, a group of immigrant Pipiles arrived in Tula from the region of Coatzacoalco, if not from farther away, and these people perhaps brought the knowledge of metallurgy. They were called Nonoalcas, and were

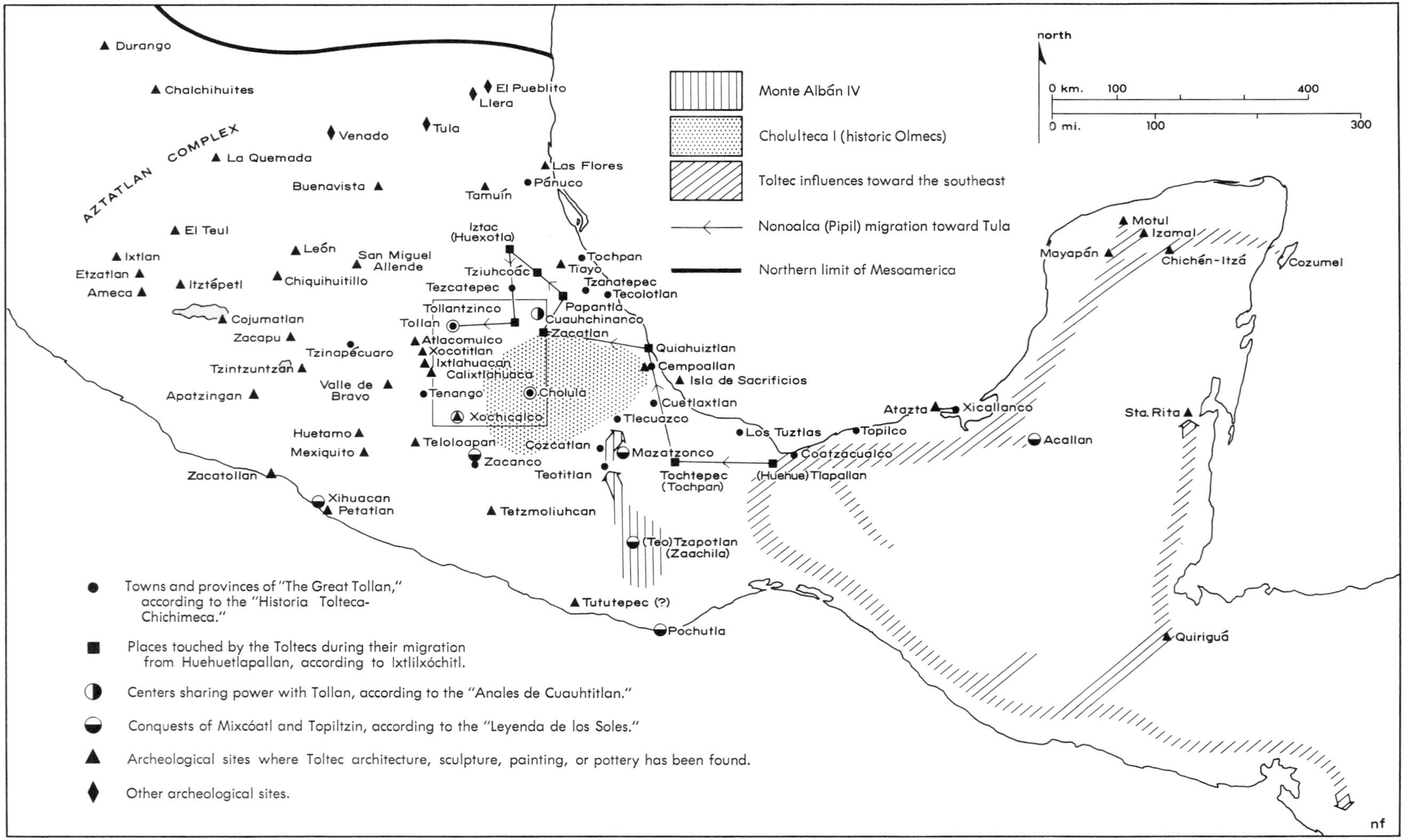

north

0 km. 100   100   300   400
0 mi.   100

Monte Albán IV

Cholulteca I (historic Olmecs)

Toltec influences toward the southeast

Nonoalca (Pipil) migration toward Tula

Northern limit of Mesoamerica

Durango ▲

Chalchihuites ▲

AZTATLAN COMPLEX

La Quemada ▲
Venado ◆
Buenavista ▲
El Pueblito ▲
Llera ◆
Las Flores ▲
Tula ◆
Tamuín ▲
Pánuco ●

El Teul ▲
León ▲
San Miguel Allende ▲
Chiquihuitillo ▲
Tula ◆
Tochpan ●
Tzapantepec ▲
Troya ▲
Tecolotlan ●

Itzíatlan ▲
Ameca ▲
Zacapu ▲
Tzintzuntzan ◇
Tzinapécuaro ▲
Valle de Bravo ▲
Iztac (Huexotla) ▲
Tziuhcóac ■
Papantla ●
Cuauhchinanco ●
Zacatlan ●
Quiahuiztlan ■
Cempoallan ■
Isla de Sacrificios ▲
Cuetlaxtlan ●

Cojumatlan ◇
Apatzingan ▲
Huetamo ▲
Mexiquito ▲
Tezcatepec ▲
Tollantzinco ●
Tollan ○
Atlacomulco ▲
Xocotitlan ▲
Ixtlahuaca ▲
Calixtlahuaca ▲
Tenango ●
Xochicalco ▲
Teloloapan ▲
Zacango ◑
Tlecuzco ●
Mazatzinco ■
Tochtepec (Tochpan) ◑
Los Tuztlas ●
Topilco ●
Coatzacualco ◑
(Huehue) Tlapallan ■

Xihuacan ○
Petatlan ▲
Zacatollan ▲
Tetzmoliuhcan ▲
Teotitlan ▲
Cozcatlan ●
(Teo) Tzapotlan (Zaachila) ○
Tututepec (?) ▲
Pochutla ○

Atzta ▲
Xicallanco ◑
Acallan ◑

Mayapán
Motul ▲
Izamal ▲
Chichén-Itzá ▲
Cozumel ◁

Sta. Rita ▲
Quiriguá ▲

Towns and provinces of "The Great Tollan," according to the "Historia Tolteca-Chichimeca." ●

Places touched by the Toltecs during their migration from Huehuetlapallan, according to Ixtlilxóchitl. ■

Centers sharing power with Tollan, according to the "Anales de Cuauhtitlan." ◑

Conquests of Mixcóatl and Topiltzin, according to the "Leyenda de los Soles." ○

Archeological sites where Toltec architecture, sculpture, painting, or pottery has been found. ◀

Other archeological sites. ◆

Map 7. Toltec migrations and the extent of the Toltec empire, A.D. 900–1200, based on historical

descendants of the ancient Náhuat population of Teotihuacan, although their culture had been transformed by Tajín and Central American contacts.

With the arrival of these elements there probably began the golden age of Tula, now governed by a ruler-priest as in the time of the Teotihuacan theocracy, and the monuments that we admire today were built. The Toltec empire grew in all directions; Mesoamerica touched its northernmost limit, never before reached, and so entered into direct contact with the cultures of the southwestern United States. (For the radiation of the Tula culture and the maximum expansion of Mesoamerica, see Maps 7 and 8.)

Later, however, the Tula empire disintegrated. Before the onslaught of barbarians, such as Xólotl's Chichimecs, the Mesoamerican frontier shrank southward to such an extent that the northern limit became the Sierra de Ajusco, between the Valleys of Mexico and Morelos. Mesoamerica then reached only somewhat north of Tepoztlan and Cuernavaca. Many years afterward, Tezozómoc of Azcapotzalco, and later the Mexicas, successfully attempted a sort of restoration of the old Toltec empire, and succeeded in reconquering lands for Mesoamerica that extended from very near San Juan del Río, Querétaro, to the Moctezuma River, a tributary of the Pánuco. But never again did Mesoamerica regain the northern limits reached under Toltec domination.

In the extreme northwest of this superarea, the region of southern Sonora and northern Sinaloa came initially within the cultural orbit of the southwestern United States; the Huatabampo complex found there by Ekholm (1942) is related to the southwestern cultures. Later, in the Toltec period, this northern region was conquered for Mesoamerica, when the Aztatlan complex flourished there. But at the conclusion of the period we get the impression that Guasave had been invaded by a people who made no pottery, or that it remained completely uninhabited. In Culiacan (Kelly 1945), by contrast, the pottery tradition continued to the days of the Spanish conquest, although to the south, in Chiametla (Kelly 1938), pottery was not made after the epigonal flowering of El Taste polychrome. Accordingly, it appears that this territory must have been subjugated by the warlike Indians of the western Sierra Madre in about A.D. 1350, with the result that communications between Acaponeta and Culiacan were cut and Culiacan was left completely isolated. In other words, more than a century and a half before the coming of Nuño de Guzmán's army, we find a situation very like the one in Sinaloa before Francisco de Ibarra reconquered the province of Chiametla from the barbarian Indians who had occupied it and cut off all communication between Culiacan and the rest of New Galicia.

In conclusion, it appears that in the Toltec empire cultural influences that probably came from the southwestern United States were combined with others such as the knowledge of metallurgy from Central America. The Tol-

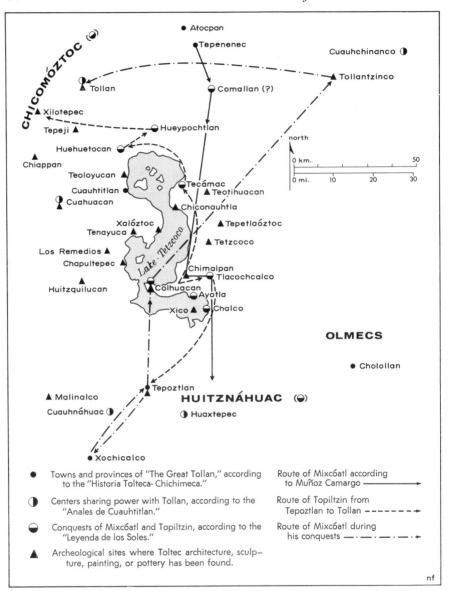

Map 8. The Toltec empire in the central valleys.

tec-Chichimecs, who are thought to have come from the northwest, and the Nonoalcas, who came from the southeast, were the two dominant groups in the Tula empire, and must have played an important role in the transmission of these influences. This militaristic state now became the foundation of a new order that involved an almost complete rupture with the Classic world, and for this reason the succeeding horizon has been called Postclassic.

I shall not deal here with this last phase of precolonial history, but I do

101. Carved stone reliefs in a ball court at El Tajín, Veracruz. Above: note the importance of the eagle and
the symbol for death. Below: a scene of human sacrifice. All three of the central personages are wearing what seem
to be stone *palmas* in their belts. Figures representing death look on from the left and above,
and a seated personage from the right.

want to emphasize that the destruction of the highest prehispanic cultures was not brought about by the Spaniards. What they encountered did not equal the splendor of earlier times. It is probable that those marvelous cultures had either destroyed themselves by social revolution, as Thompson and Olivé suggest in the case of the Maya, or perished in the turmoil, also indigenous, that was produced by the influx of disruptive peoples: the Otomí, the Olmecs, and the Toltec-Chichimecs. From then on, the glorious past remained absolutely destroyed, and once the Maya-Toltec renaissance was over, even the outstanding culture of Yucatán began to disintegrate. Only peoples who a few centuries before were numbered among the barbarians, such as the Tarascans and the Mexicas, remained proud and strong amid the ruins; and from the states they created, New Spain, from which Mexico comes, had to be forged.

Oaxaca in Ancient Mesoamerica

Part II is an effort to do for Oaxaca more or less what Part I does for Meso-america as a whole. It has been drastically simplified by the elimination of many technical terms and qualifying words or phrases. If this procedure makes it accessible to a larger number of readers, two aims will be fulfilled in com-pensation for the resulting loss of scientific precision of statement. First, it will save the time of members of the serious reading public, time too frequently wasted on objects unworthy of their attention. And second, wider interest in ancient Oaxaca will improve the prospects for needed research and the accom-panying technical publications, complete with all the howevers I have here surrendered.

Much of what follows is opinion, and in the absence of qualifiers and reser-vations it may seem arbitrary. But it is not simply my opinion in most cases, nor is it unfounded. Rather, what I have proposed here is a new synthesis of views currently held by those who specialize in the study of ancient Oaxaca.

Probably I have drawn most from the most experienced of all archeologists in this area—Alfonso Caso and Ignacio Bernal—but I also owe much to the published and unpublished work of others. During well over a decade I have been privileged to hear and participate in the discussions, formal and informal, in which professional opinion has been formed. Any attempt to provide a set of genteel footnotes for this assistance would be flummery. For what it is worth, I have appended a bibliographical note to this essay.

Certain other extremely important sources must be mentioned. During 1963 and 1964 I worked with the Oaxaca collection of Mexico's Museo Nacional de Antropología. This material had been put in order by Bernal in the 1940's, but when it was moved from San Angel to the old Museum much of his long labor was undone. In reordering this collection I have been, I think, the only person since Caso and Bernal to ponder, handle, and try to classify it all.

Since 1959 I have been connected in various capacities with the Frissell Museum of Zapotec Art in Mitla, which is not in fact limited either to art or to what may legitimately be called Zapotec. Here again, in the unending task of classifying Oaxaca materials, I have learned from the comments of Caso and Bernal as members of this museum's Board of Advisers.

The work of Richard S. MacNeish in the Valley of Tehuacan, on the northern borders of the archeological region of Oaxaca, has been of the utmost importance in the present context, and like many others I note gratefully his extraordinary generosity with time, effort, and his own unpublished data. Three former students of mine—Robert Chadwick, Kent Flannery, and James A. Neely—have worked for or with MacNeish, and have helped introduce me to the long series of crucial discoveries made during the years of the Tehuacan Archaeological-Botanical Project. I am particularly indebted to Flannery for the information in the Postscript on pp. 241–42, which was written in Mitla just before this volume went to press.

Douglas S. Byers of the R. S. Peabody Foundation, sponsors of the Tehuacan project, aided with further data. Dr. Frank H. Boos of Detroit has allowed me to see many of his unpublished photographs of the Oaxaca materials he located in collections all over the world, and his questions and comments have been very helpful in focusing my thinking.

In addition, Caso, Bernal, and MacNeish have read and criticized parts of this essay; so have Howard Leigh, Ross Parmenter, Ronald Spores, Peter Tschohl, and Charles Wicke. I have accepted most of their suggestions, but not all, and some of them disagree specifically with parts of what follows here. Part II is not then, I hope, a simple consensus—or worse, a lowest common denominator—of what my teachers and colleagues have written and said.

There are two sections in which I have most clearly ventured out beyond what my colleagues have been doing. On pp. 149–74 I have presented a psychological projection into the life of Monte Albán's great period simply because I think somebody among those few persons thoroughly steeped in such a culture ought to attempt this kind of sketch from time to time. On pp. 176–200 I have given some plain data (as I have generally avoided doing) because they were necessary to the argument presented in that section for a newly discovered major regional variant of Mesoamerican "Classic" or Early Urban culture.

Especially in the two sections just cited, then, but of course to some extent throughout, my own biases affect the selection and statement of what follows here. Every regional specialist has an obvious and inescapable tendency to consider his specialty important, and I cannot claim a miraculous immunity. Every region and period of ancient Mesoamerica produced a moving and characteristic art style, and each of these expresses best and appeals most to some particular temperament. Fortunately for me, it is the art of Teotihuacan that affects me most deeply and directly; thus I can admire the robust gran-

deur of Zapotec work or the refined preciosity of the last Mixtec products with nearly as much detachment as I have toward Maya or Aztec art. We all become fond of the familiar, because it offers us what is called ego reinforcement. A culture that has become familiar to an anthropologist through archeological or ethnographic work is as likely as anything else to provide such gratification, and consequently to threaten his objectivity in viewing the culture.

One who lives among the descendants of his archeological subjects has all kinds of feelings toward them, just as he must have toward other people he knows. Attitudes developed toward his contemporaries may be extended to the ancestral people and their archeological culture. I hope my awareness of this danger is a sufficient defense, for I have lived and worked for years among modern Zapotecs and Chochos. I do not know any Mixtecs.

In science, such personal factors are far from entirely negative. Morley and Thompson confessedly, and other Mayanists too, without a doubt, attribute as glorious a role to the ancient Mayas as they can within the limits of the known facts and scientific morality. Affected by the same subjective factors, and limited by the same facts and discipline, some of us are reacting, finding weak spots in their arguments, and gaining for other Mesoamerican peoples a share of the glory. If we overreach our data, we shall in our turn be exposed; and by this unending process our understanding of the Mayas and of the other Mesoamericans becomes gradually ampler and richer. Objectivity and discipline alone—without intuitive insight, esthetic sensibility, and imagination— are capable of producing neither scientific discovery nor achievements like Tajín and Tikal.

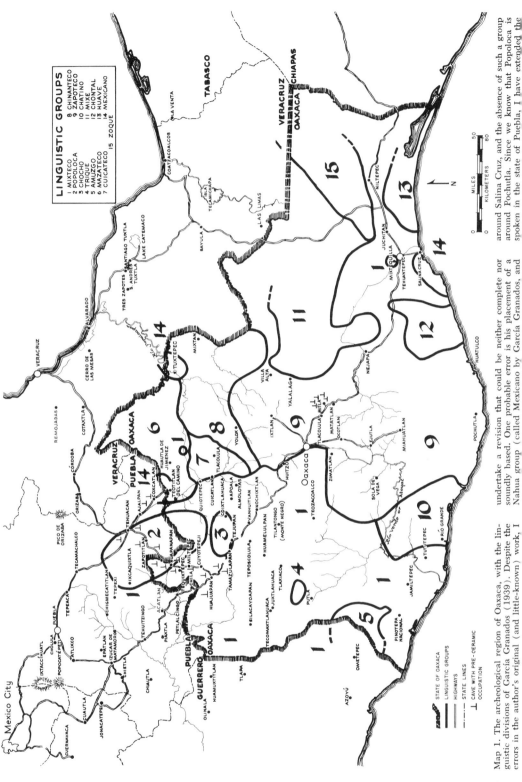

Map 1. The archeological region of Oaxaca, with the linguistic divisions of García Granados (1939). Despite the errors in the author's original (and little-known) work, I undertake a revision that could be neither complete nor soundly based. One probable error is his placement of a Nahua group (called Mexicano by García Granados, and around Salina Cruz, and the absence of such a group around Pochutla. Since we know that Popoloca is spoken in the state of Puebla, I have extended the

LINGUISTIC GROUPS

1 MIXTECO	8 CHINANTECO
2 POPOLOCA	9 ZAPOTECO
3 CHOCHO	10 CHATINO
4 TRIQUE	11 MIXE
5 AMUZGO	12 CHONTAL
6 MAZATECO	13 HUAVE
7 CUICATECO	14 MEXICANO
	15 ZOQUE

STATE OF OAXACA
LINGUISTIC GROUPS
HIGHWAYS
STATE LINES
CAVE WITH PRE-CERAMIC OCCUPATION

MILES
KILOMETERS

Oaxaca in Ancient Mesoamerica

JOHN PADDOCK

The boundaries of the modern state of Oaxaca correspond roughly to a region (Map 1) that may with some logic be regarded as a unit of Mesoamerican culture history. On the north, and apparently from the first habitation until modern times, this region includes the southern part of the state of Puebla; the easternmost fringe of the state of Guerrero is also included. The northeast corner of the state of Oaxaca falls into a physiographic and climatic province that belongs rather with Veracruz, but the people now living there are linguistically and otherwise linked with other Oaxaca peoples and distinct from those of Veracruz. At present, as at the time of the Spanish conquest, there is some slight extension of Oaxaca peoples into the territory of the state of Veracruz. There may have been a more important extension of Oaxaca peoples into that coastal region in earlier times.

Although some ancient travelers from Central Mexico, especially the Valley of Mexico, to Central America passed through Oaxaca, as the Inter-American Highway does today, an important alternative route lay east to Veracruz, south along the Gulf of Mexico to the Isthmus of Tehuantepec, and across the Isthmus to follow the Pacific lowlands to Guatemala. This route, too, is still in use, being the only railway link between Mexico City and the Guatemala border. Western and central Oaxaca may accordingly be seen as a region that could be bypassed if necessary in the comings and goings of people and ideas. Its isolation is much less assured than that of the Maya region, but in some periods it seems to have been singularly unmoved by events affecting the remainder of Mesoamerica. At other times its role has been very dynamic.

Much of the state is extremely broken, although it has few high mountain peaks. The cordilleras that mark the eastern and western edges of the north Mexican plateau come together in Oaxaca, and as a consequence most of the state consists of their apparently endless series of ridges, with a few rather high valleys here and there. Most of these valleys are small, but three of the largest of them come together at the modern city of Oaxaca to form a rich and centrally located area (called the Valley of Oaxaca) that has for a very long time been a natural capital. Along the Pacific coast there is a narrow strip of lowland, and at the Isthmus of Tehuantepec only a low continental divide separates this strip from the Atlantic lowlands. Oaxaca's Atlantic side includes only the foothills rising from these relatively broad Gulf of Mexico lowlands, except for one small corner of the state that extends into the coastal plain.

The range of climates in Oaxaca is enormous. Although most of the region is relatively arid, and most of it is also both hilly and at a fairly considerable elevation, there are true tropical forests as well as cool, damp mountain pine forests; there are low valleys where coffee and bananas thrive, and high ones where wheat is grown. In fact, almost every possible combination of altitudes from sea level to 10,000 feet, rainfalls from 2 to 100 effective inches per year, and lands from bare rock to deep alluvium may be found within the state.

In such a region man has had a great variety of environmental opportunities, and to whatever extent habitat may affect human development we should expect this variety to be benign. In Oaxaca the physical world man has needed at every stage of development has always been within a few days' walk.

EARLY MAN IN OAXACA

Up to now, mammoth bones found in Oaxaca have not been found together with points and knives such as those that served to establish the existence of early hunters—about 12000 to 8000 B.C.—in the Valley of Mexico. However, Coxcatlan Cave, six kilometers into Puebla from the Oaxaca state line, has yielded remains of early hunters of horse and antelope; and a similar finding in Oaxaca can probably be anticipated. The rich deposits of fossil bones just south of the city of Puebla are within an area that in some periods has been dominated by Oaxaca peoples, but it may be slightly too far north to be included with Oaxaca in these very early times.

The extinction of the large Pleistocene animals, mainly caused by decreasing rainfall and vegetation but no doubt completed by human hunters, forced the first Mexicans to increase greatly their exploitation of wild vegetable foods. It appears that these rude gatherers of seeds and fruits began practicing a simple and tentative plant domestication as early as 7000 B.C., working with members of the squash family. Long before 4000 B.C. along the present border of Oaxaca and Puebla, south of Tehuacan, the economic basis of Mesoamerican civilization had begun to take shape with the domestication of maize.

According to Richard S. MacNeish, whose research in Tamaulipas revealed very early plant domestication and whose later work in Chiapas confirmed it, the first cultivated maize should be found south of Tamaulipas and north of Chiapas. Some stone tools of the types used by early men in Tamaulipas and Chiapas occurred, he found, at a number of places in northern Oaxaca and southern Puebla, extending at least from Tamazulapan and Huajuapan, on the modern highway through Oaxaca, along the Huajuapan-Tehuacan road into Puebla. In this region he looked for the place having the least effective rainfall and therefore presumably the best preservation of ancient vegetable remains. With only slight rainfall and a very high rate of evaporation, the desert area from Tehuacan, Puebla, to Tecomavaca, Oaxaca, was his choice. The astonishing results of his excavations in this area include remains of the complete sequence of maize as it evolved from a wild plant to one so thoroughly domesticated that it could not survive without man's intervention.

Until very recently we were not able to speak of a human occupation of central Oaxaca until a much later time, when men were already on the verge of urbanism. Within the past decade, however, some stone implements from the central valleys in particular have been identified as belonging to an era when rudimentary cultivation was probably being practiced, but pottery still was not being made. This period seems to have been strikingly long in Mesoamerica, extending from about 7000 B.C. until well after 3000 B.C.

A complex of stone implement types found at several places in the area of Mitla, at the eastern extreme of the Valley of Oaxaca, is identified by MacNeish as being of a style that prevailed in the Valley of Tehuacan from about 4800 to 2500 B.C., or from approximately the first cultivation of maize until somewhat before the first crude pottery appeared there.

Several questions come to mind at once. Does this mean the Valley of Oaxaca was occupied during all the centuries from 4800 to 2500 B.C.? What is the relationship of its people to those of the Tehuacan Valley? Are there even earlier remains of human occupation in the Valley of Oaxaca? Are the makers of these stone implements the cultural ancestors of the later Valley of Oaxaca population? For the moment, unfortunately, we have no clear answers to these questions.

A potential source of confusion may be pointed out here. Right down to the Spanish conquest, a wide variety of stone tools continued in use throughout Mesoamerica; after about A.D. 1000 there were some metal tools in use, but stone tools remained plentiful. Moreover, although some chipped stone tools such as sacrificial knives for ritual use were made with great care and skill, others were made carelessly, especially after metals came into limited use. Even in very late sites, towns occupied at the time of the Conquest, certain crude chipped stone tools abound. Such tools have often been taken to indicate the habitation of a site by early man, and no doubt in some cases they do. But rude flint cores and flakes are thickly scattered about some late buildings in Oaxaca, and only the firm placement of hundreds of carefully

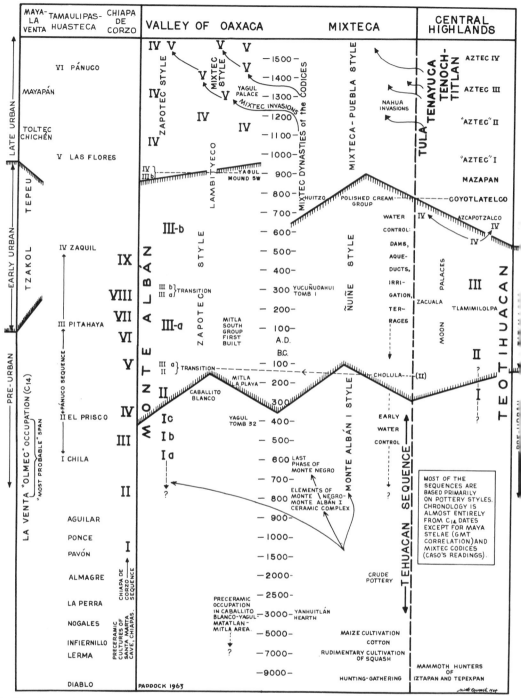

1. Chronological chart. With only minor or peripheral exceptions, this chart is based on dating criteria that are independent for each region: radiocarbon estimates, Maya stelae, and Mixtec codices. I think this is the first time such a chart has been published, for it has been the custom—inescapable until recently—to fill gaps in these charts by cross-dating from one region to another. That is, the presence of trade objects or the inference that some stylistic similarity proved contemporaneity was used to extrapolate a date from one column to another. The inevitable errors resulting have created false problems, which disappear when we make each column independent.

The exceptions to the independence of columns here are:

1. Note is taken of Caso's observation that certain traits of Teotihuacan II figurines appear in the distinctive urns of Transición II–III at Monte Albán.

2. The stylistic similarity of a few pieces from Yucuñudahui with others from Tombs 103 and 104 of Monte Albán is indicated as providing a plausible date for Transición IIIa–IIIb at Monte Albán.

3. Numerous similarities of Coyotlatelco pottery and certain late Mixtec products, as pointed out long ago by Noguera, are noted here without speculation about their place of origin.

4. What would otherwise be a blank space was filled by accepting Ekholm's 1944 sequence (Pánuco III through VI) even though it was based only on cross-relations. The beginning of this column, however, is covered by MacNeish's radiocarbon dates from Tamaulipas and his Pánuco excavations (1954, 1958).

5. Another empty space was filled by simply writing in, with some attention to Jiménez Moreno's interpretation of the Nahua chronicles, the series from Coyotlatelco through Aztec IV in the Valley of Mexico.

classified specimens in their various time levels will eventually make it possible to distinguish early ones from late ones.[1]

PRE-URBAN COMMUNITIES: MONTE ALBÁN I

Because much of Oaxaca is still practically untouched by archeology, we can offer only very tentative statements of what is likely to be found in the unexplored areas once exploration begins. Nevertheless, the number of satisfactorily fixed points is now large enough to give us the basis for at least a preliminary estimate of Oaxaca's role in a developing Mesoamerica (Figure 1).

MacNeish has established a sequence beginning well before 7000 B.C. and extending down to the Spanish conquest for the extreme north. Around the central Valley of Oaxaca there are, as mentioned, some stone implements apparently assignable to preceramic early agricultural semi-nomads. But the first period for which we have more or less adequate information is Monte Albán I. This period is so named because its remains directly overlie the bedrock at Monte Albán, the mountain that rises beside the modern city of Oaxaca.

There is grave doubt, as we shall see, that we should characterize this period at Monte Albán itself as pre-urban. However, remains of pottery made in the same style as that of Monte Albán I have been found at many other places throughout Oaxaca and in adjoining sections of Veracruz, Puebla, and Guerrero. A few bits of perhaps two or three of the dozens of pottery types used in Monte Albán I have turned up in MacNeish's Tehuacan excavations, in one instance in a layer dated as early as 800 B.C. (The first crude pottery in the same deposits seems to have been made somewhat before 2000 B.C.)

The Monte Albán I style is, then, very fragmentarily represented at a rather distant site as early as 800 B.C. The end of the period can be dated much more confidently as coming around 300 B.C. The pottery style of Monte Albán I—more precisely, the style destined to *become* that of Monte Albán I—must have been developing during the years 1500 to 1000 B.C. in various places, none of them larger or more advanced than what might properly be called a pre-urban agricultural village.

The entire Atlantic-slope boundary of Oaxaca borders the area of the well-known "Olmec" or La Venta culture, which reached its artistic peak at La Venta on the Gulf coast of the Isthmus of Tehuantepec. It is not strange, then, that certain strong resemblances should have been noted between parts of the "Olmec" and Monte Albán I cultures (Figures 2–7). We cannot yet say which one came first, or which one (if, indeed, either) played the dominant

---

[1] It follows that we should avoid using such terms as Stone Age or Neolithic in connection with Oaxaca peoples. Application of these terms to urban literate Mesoamericans is in fact quite meaningless, although very widespread. The original definitions, based on tool-making techniques and materials, are no longer used even in Old World archeology, for which they were developed. The rearguard action represented in the term Chalcolithic—used with considerable accuracy by Jiménez Moreno (p. 3)—is more a courteous bow to tradition than a meaningful classificatory device.

2. *Left:* the "Olmec" statue at Huamelulpan, Oaxaca.
Below: close-up of the same statue.

3. A brazier in Monte Albán I style,
apparently representing the young
god of fire. *Covarrubias collection,
Museo Nacional de Antropología (MNA).*

. An "Olmec" style figurine head from Chila, Puebla.
'rissell collection.

5. A water god effigy found at Monte Albán, with an early
form of the glyph C at the center of his headdress. *MNA.*

6. Three small lightning–rain (tiger–serpent) gods in Monte Albán I style. The largest is 14 cm. high.

7. Square pottery box with a lightning–rain god face (upper left) and three human faces. *MNA*.

role in their borrowing and lending. One major pyramidal construction series at La Venta has been dated by radiocarbon at about 800 to 400 B.C. Unhappily, the most characteristic and beautiful elements of "Olmec" culture remain unplaced with respect to these dated constructions.

Since the widely scattered finds of objects in Monte Albán I style consist chiefly of single ceramic specimens, we have no way of tracing the gradual development that must have taken place in the large area they come from. Our best information comes from Monte Negro, a mountaintop town in the Mixteca (the part of Oaxaca now occupied by the Mixtecs). This place was occupied for a relatively short time by people who used some pottery so much like that of Monte Albán I that it must have been made by the same potters; most of that found, however, is of local manufacture and quite poor compared with the Monte Albán product. Monte Negro is of great importance because it is more than a village (Figure 8). It has a clear system of streets and a number of public constructions; but for its rather small population and the lack of any surviving evidence of writing, it might be considered almost a small city. Its interest is increased by the fact that a radiocarbon date of about 650 B.C. has been determined from a sample of a wooden beam used *in the last days* of Monte Negro. The beam might well have been in use for several decades, and the cutting of the tree from which it came is what the radiocarbon process actually dates for us. Further, this date was determined at an early stage in the development of the carbon dating process, and doubt has been cast on it for that reason. Nevertheless, later applications of greatly improved procedures to related materials have tended to confirm it as at least approximately correct.

It is difficult to account for the apparent absence of humans in the lower parts of the Valley of Oaxaca during the several millennia of preceramic agricultural life. The soil is deep and rich, the rainfall sufficient for agriculture, the climate delightful. The surrounding mountains, where soil and climate are much less desirable, were inhabited. One ancient tradition—that a lake formerly occupied the bottom of the Valley—would explain it. Most experts insist that there is no evidence of a lake; but some point to several still existing swamps and ponds and a number of former shorelines, fan-shaped deposits, and other evidences of an ancient lake (Figure 9). If the lake really was there, and was drained when the present southern outlet was formed during a volcanic upheaval (earthquakes are frequent in Oaxaca), it would be easy to imagine why the early population left traces only on the slightly higher lands—such as the Mitla area—around the edge of the Valley, and why a culturally advanced population moved in suddenly and only relatively late to inhabit the fertile valley bottoms (Map 2).

In any case, sometime between 1000 and 500 B.C. a group appears to have taken possession of the Valley; and it began building in impressive scale on the top of Monte Albán. These people were using the pottery whose style was

8. Model showing the central section of Monte Negro at about 800 B.C.,
reconstructed under the direction of Jorge R. Acosta. *MNA.*

9. Three "fish plates" in the Frissell collection.
Not all such plates have pedestals, and they vary
greatly in size and in the degree of realism employed.

10. Grey ceramic bottle. *MNA.*

11. Olla of composite silhouette. *MNA.*

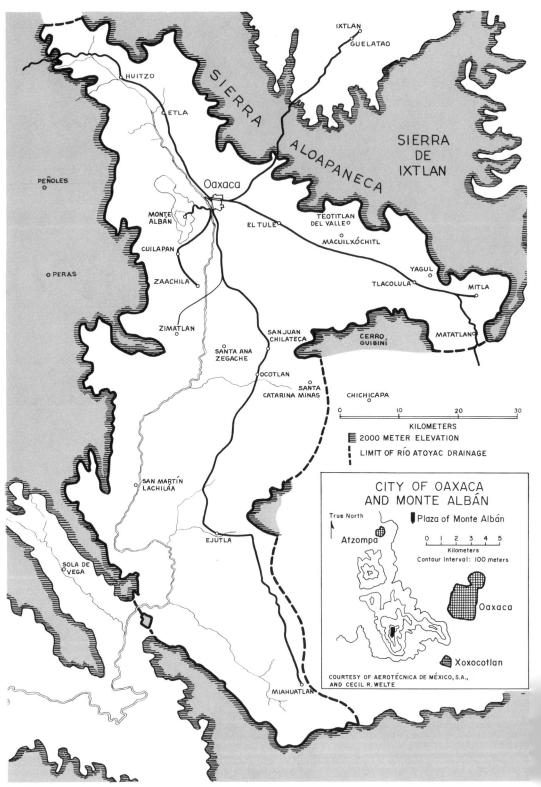

Map 2. The Valley of Oaxaca

12. Miniature olla in shape of gourd. *MNA.*

13. Vase with incised decoration typical of Monte Albán I. *MNA.*

already spread over much of Oaxaca (Figures 10–16). They buried their distinguished dead in tombs with offerings of pottery, and no doubt also of many perishable objects. Their pottery was technically excellent and made in lively forms (Figures 17–30, and below, pp. 245–55). The later overwhelmingly grand dimensions of the great plaza on top of Monte Albán may even have been outlined at this time, although we cannot be sure because the earliest buildings are covered by so many massive later constructions that very little is known of them. Whatever the buildings of Monte Albán I were like, the society responsible for them shows clearly all the usual archeological signs of class divisions; and, most important, before the period ended stone monuments were erected bearing calendrical inscriptions (Figures 31–47). In other words, both writing and a calendar implying some tradition of astronomical observation were in use.

We have described these first settlers on Monte Albán as pre-urban, but a good case can be made for granting them urban status. If future investigation should reveal that they were using writing early in the period, that the population was relatively large and dense, and that the later immense scale of the city was already projected by its earliest inhabitants, we may have to consider them urban. In this case we should also in all probability have to recognize that these Oaxacans were the first city dwellers in America.[2]

[2] The Valley of Mexico in these times had no semi-city more impressive than Cuicuilco, which though perhaps large in scale is rather rude in construction and lacks evidence of writing. The "Olmecs" of La Venta may or may not have had writing so soon; it is also not clear whether La Venta ever had the characteristics of a city. The lowland Mayas were still several centuries away from anything of this sort.

Text continued on p. 111

14. Grey ceramic bottle with incised decoration.
Frissell collection.

15. Grey plate without feet. *MNA.*

16. Miniature bowl with incised decoration. *MNA.*

17. Group of Monte Albán I pottery miniatures
most in animal forms. *MNA.*

19. Shoe-shaped effigy vessel. *Frissell Museum, courtesy Howard Leigh.*

8. Effigy olla with spout handle and ncised decoration. *Frissell collection.*

21. The Zegache vase: effigy of the god with the mask of a broad-billed bird. *MNA.*

0. Brazier in the form of a temple ith figures, apparently armed, and painted 'Olmec'' style face; the central figure is he young god with bird helmet; 'om Monte Albán. *MNA.*

22. Shoe-shaped vessel with duck head; from Monte Albán. *MNA.*

23. A figurine in the Frissell collection, Monte Albán I–II style.

24. A period I figurine from the Monte Albán excavations. *MNA.*

25. Figurine in Monte Albán I–II style.

26. Effigy vessel (with mouth mask of serpent?).

27. Effigy vessel in Monte Albán I style.

28. Reclining effigy; Monte Negro. *MNA.*

29. Animal effigy; Monte Albán. *MNA.*

30. Spout-handled olla with "swimmer" figure. *MNA.*

1. The Gallery of Danzantes at Monte Albán, extending from System M at left to the Danzantes Building at right.

32. Southeast corner of the Danzantes Building, showing how the line of Danzantes, forming the front of an older structure, continues into the body of the later one. Those visible at left of the modern doorway were partially uncovered by Dupaix at the beginning of the nineteenth century.

33. Danzantes uncovered by Dupaix.

34. *Above:* Danzantes inside the body of the later building. Those at left were uncovered by Sologuren and Belmar; t far right by Batres, all working around 1900. *Below left:* the Gallery of Danzantes, from the Danzantes Building ɔward System M. *Below right:* the Danzantes uncovered by Batres.

35. The Gallery of Danzantes, between System M at left and the Danzantes Building. Stelae 12 and 13, crossed by a diagonal shadow, are at the far left of the line. Reused later as construction material, many fragments of Danzantes have been found during exploration of other buildings; Caso examined 140 that had significant amounts of decipherable sculpture still visible on them, and there are many others. Monte Albán I offerings, burials, and pottery were found in a construction covering some of the Danzantes, thus placing them securely as not later than Monte Albán I.

. Danzantes of the Gallery. *Upper left:* Stelae 12 and 13.

36 (*cont'd*). Danzantes of the Gallery. Holmes (1897) showed the two Danzantes at left in the group at upper right as covered up to their necks by earth.

37. Fragment of a Danzante showing head and hand; Monte Albán.

38. Danzantes used as steps in the original building.

9. A Danzante reused as a building stone.

40. Fragment of a Danzante, probably of period I, used in construction of Mound J in period II.

1. A Monte Albán I style Danzante
uilt into Mound J of period II.

42. A Danzante in the style of Monte Albán I, used in the construction of Mound J.

43. A Danzante formerly on the South Platform at Monte Albán, now in the MNA.

44. The "Danzante del Museo," now in the MNA, but reported by Batres to have been found in front of Mound M

45. Danzante incorporated into a late rebuilding of the North Platform, Monte Albán.

46. Danzante reused in the North Platform.

47. A Danzante used as construction stor

THE BEGINNINGS OF EARLY URBANISM: MONTE ALBÁN II

In Monte Albán II, a short period beginning perhaps about 300 B.C. and ending before 100 B.C., we are confronted with the previous period's characteristics somewhat intensified, and with some new ones as well, including the paving of the great plaza of Monte Albán. Several large buildings of Monte Albán II are now known (Figures 48–52), and all evidence suggests that the life being led at this capital was of the kind we call urban and civilized.

The term Classic has long been used to refer to the period of the first urban, literate civilization of Mesoamerica. Unhappily, this term is now being used with three quite different meanings. For some it indicates a kind of culture resembling that of what Morley called the Old Empire in the Maya region, and the rather parallel developments of periods II and III at Teotihuacan and periods IIIa and IIIb at Monte Albán. When we knew less than we do now of Mesoamerican chronology, it was assumed that these more or less similar periods were all contemporaneous. Later some writers began using the term Classic to refer to the *time* of the Maya Classic: about A.D. 300 to

48. Wall of an ancient building—of Monte Albán I or II—recently exposed inside the body of Mound IV. From its base to the top, where the later floor of the temple atop Mound IV cut across it, the height is about 6 meters now; whether it was greater before construction of the later temple covering it cannot be determined.

900. It is now clear that the term in this sense has no particular meaning or utility outside the Maya region. To complete the confusion, some prominent Mesoamericanists prefer to conceive the Classic in a third and "classic" sense of the word: as referring to that which is most characteristic, essential, or typical. For them it is the time when the great regional divisions of Mesoamerica achieve their "classic" individual identities.

It would seem desirable to replace Classic with some term having a single meaning. Since the city appears to be essential to this kind of culture, the term Urban comes to mind. As measured by its effects on the further development of culture, on forms of human behavior, and on personal experience, the city quite possibly is man's most dynamic invention. We shall accordingly use the term Early Urban for the "first-generation" civilizations of Mesoamerica, those strongly theocratic systems that evolved not out of other urban civilizations but out of simpler forms (Figure 53). Their more militaristic successors of the last prehispanic centuries we shall call Late Urban. These are "second-generation" civilizations descended from the Early Urban theocracies.

The relationship of Monte Albán I and Monte Albán II is not so simple as might be assumed, for period I does not everywhere end with the beginning of II. Rather, II is a period identified by the appearance at Monte Albán of a number of traits limited largely to aristocratic and ceremonial circles (Figures 54–65), while on the level of the common people the ways of period I go on virtually undisturbed (Figures 66 and 67). At most sites where Monte Albán I culture is found, II does not appear at all. It is primarily because Monte Albán II objects are scarce that the period is considered to have been a short one. At many small places, since there is no evidence of II, period I seems to be succeeded directly by period III.

Just as there is some kind of affinity between Monte Albán I and the "Olmec" culture of La Venta, there are several resemblances suggesting links between Monte Albán II and what has long been identified as "the South." The recent excavations at Chiapa de Corzo, Chiapas, have somewhat clarified these resemblances, although the customary archeological assumption that similarity means contemporaneity may have to give way before contrary evidence from radiocarbon dates in this case.

Ever since Caso took note of the southern affinities he saw in Monte Albán II, the assumption has been that this change from the Gulf coast interests of Monte Albán I signified a breaking off of relationships with the Tenocelome or "Olmec" people or peoples. But a more recent opinion is that the suggestive stylistic succession of La Venta–Izapa–Highland Maya–Lowland Maya represents a historical sequence. Although we have little ceramic evidence to this effect, stone sculptures provide a spatially, chronologically, and stylistically persuasive indication of a major Mesoamerican dynamic movement. Whether this was a movement of people or only of an evolving art style, it seems at least possible that Izapa in Monte Albán's period II represented

Text continued on p. 119

49. The Plaza at Monte Albán, seen from the front of the South Platform. In left foreground, Mound J; background, the North Platform. At right, buildings forming the east side of the Plaza.

. View across the Plaza. Foreground: Mound J, left; Mound I, right. Background: Danzantes, left; System IV, right.

52. Mound J from the south, showing the passage through the pointed rear section of the building.

APPROXIMATE CULTURAL (NOT CHRONOLOGICAL) EQUIVALENTS

IN VARIOUS SCHEMES OF MESOAMERICAN DEVELOPMENT

Event markers (top of chart, left to right): SPANISH CONQUEST · FALL OF TULA · FOUNDING OF TULA · ABANDONMENT OF FIRST CITIES · BEGINNING OF PETÉN MAYA CLASSIC (MORLEY) · APPEARANCE OF REGIONAL CLASSIC ART STYLES · URBANISM AND WRITING · URBAN TRAITS BEGIN TO DEVELOP · FIRST POTTERY · FIRST PLANTING

VAILLANT AZTECS 1941	OTHERS	STEWARD-ARMILLAS 1948-49	BERNAL COMPENDIO 1950	CASO MIDDLE AMERICA 1952	WILLEY & PHILLIPS METHOD & THEORY 1955-58	PETERSON ANCIENT MEXICO 1956-59	JIMÉNEZ MORENO SYNTHESIS 1958	PIÑA CHÁN CULTURAL DEVELOPMENT 1952	PADDOCK OAXACA 1963
MIXTECA-PUEBLA PERIOD (1941) — AZTEC PERIOD	MILITARISTIC	INITIAL EMPIRE (MILITARISTIC)	FINAL HORIZON	HISTORICAL	POSTCLASSIC	HISTORIC	POSTCLASSIC — POST-TOLTEC	REGIONAL DEVELOPMENTAL HORIZON — MILITARISTIC PERIOD	LATE URBAN — NAHUA EXPANSION
CHICHIMEC PERIOD			TOLTEC PERIOD	TOLTEC			TOLTEC		RE-FORMULATION
	THEOCRATIC / WOLF 1959 / WAUCHOPE 1950		INTERREGNUM						
INDEPENDENT CIVILIZATIONS (1941) — LATE / EARLY	MAYA-TOLTEC NEW EMPIRE / MORLEY 1946 / MAYA OLD EMPIRE — CLASSIC	REGIONAL FLORESCENT (THEOCRATIC)	BAROQUE	CLASSIC	CLASSIC	CLASSIC — TERMINAL / BAROQUE / CLASSIC / TRANSITIONAL	CLASSIC — EPICLASSIC / FULL CLASSIC / EARLY CLASSIC	THEOCRATIC PERIOD	EARLY URBAN — DECADENT / BAROQUE / FORMAL / VANGUARD
	PROTO-CLASSIC		CLASSIC			PROTO-CLASSIC / PRE-CLASSIC	PRECLASSIC — (PROTO-CLASSIC) / UPPER		
MIDDLE CULTURES (1941)	URBAN FORMATIVE	(REGIONAL DEVELOPMENTAL)	DEVELOPMENTAL OR FORMATIVE	FORMATIVE	FORMATIVE		MIDDLE	FORMATIVE HORIZON — URBAN FORMATIVE PERIOD	PRE-URBAN — CULTIST
MIDDLE CULTURES (1937) — UPPER OR TICOMAN-CUICUILCO	VILLAGE FORMATIVE	FORMATIVE					LOWER	VILLAGE OR RURAL FORMATIVE PERIOD	POTTER
LOWER OR ZACATENCO COPILCO			ARCHAIC HORIZON	ARCHAIC	(PRE-FORMATIVE)				
EARLY CULTURES (1941)		INCIPIENT AGRICULTURAL OR "BASIC"	"THEORETICAL" HORIZON	PRIMITIVE	ARCHAIC	EARLY		PRIMITIVE HORIZON — INCIPIENT AGRICULTURAL PERIOD	PLANTER
		HUNTING AND GATHERING	HORIZON OF THE FIRST HUMANS	PREHISTORIC	LITHIC			PRE-AGRICULTURAL PERIOD	PRE-AGRICULTURAL — HUNTER

(Vaillant note at base of chart: DYNASTIC TOLTEC — TEOTIHUACAN OR CLASSICAL TOLTEC)

53. Chart of conceptual schemes of Mesoamerican development according to various authors. Included here are most of the more recent attempts to arrange Mesoamerican culture history in stages. It should be understood that the authors have not been consulted; this chart equates their concepts as I read them.

Vaillant altered slightly his idea of the Middle Cultures between 1937 and 1941, the latter date referring to the completion (not publication) of *The Aztecs of Mexico*. The ideas of Steward and Armillas are similar, and in some degree were a collaboration. There is room for doubt about whether Willey and Phillips intended to define Classic as here depicted or in closer correspondence with my own Early Urban. Their work was published in a journal in 1955, then revised for book publication in 1958. Peterson's manuscript (for *Ancient Mexico*) was finished in 1956, but publication was delayed and few changes were made before it appeared in 1959. The Jiménez Moreno "Synthesis" was written in 1958, but published late in 1959.

My own scheme is that used here, and has not been altered since 1963. Authors not included in this chart are those who have considerably chosen to stay close to one of the schemes presented here, thus avoiding further complication of an already difficult set of terms and definitions.

54. A Danzante in Mound J.

55. Tiger-man with glyphs, probably of period II, built into the South Platform.

56. A Danzante of Monte Albán II style, reused as construction stone.

58. From a rubbing of Danzante 41.

57. Danzante 41, period II style, in Mound J.

59. A period II Danzante used in the construction (period III) of the South Platform.

117

60. Large pottery box with glyph (of water?); Monte Albán. *MNA.*

61. The goddess 8 Z; Monte Albán. *MNA.*

62. Pottery jar with lid, a typical Monte Albán II form; from Monte Albán. *MNA.*

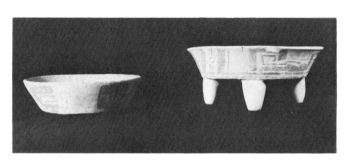

63. Bowls of a red-on-cream type diagnostic of Monte Albán II. Tetrapods (right) also are limited to this period. Shapes in this ware are numerous, but this is the most common. *Frissell collection.*

64. "Spider-foot" vessel; Monte Albán. *MNA.*

65. Sun god–macaw in his temple; an offering found deep down in the substructure of Mound B, Monte Albán. *MNA.*

66. Figurine of Monte Albán II; Monte Albán. *MNA.*

67. Miniature effigy vessels of Monte Albán I or II. *Frissell collection.*

simply a later stage of the same tradition that had drawn Monte Albán's attention to La Venta in period I.

Some time ago Caso suggested that the Monte Albán II style might possibly have been imposed in the Valley of Oaxaca by conquest (Figures 68–78). As possible evidence, he cited the upper-class and ritual character of Monte Albán II traits, their relatively sudden appearance in Oaxaca, and the presence of certain inscriptions in Monte Albán II style consisting of a place glyph with a human head upside down below it (Figure 79). As Caso pointed out, this might be a statement of the conquest of the place named. Leigh has offered another possible explanation of these inscriptions, suggesting that the heads are celestial deities passing under the earth (the mountain glyph) in order to resume their heavenly procession the following day. That Monte Albán II is a ruling-class phenomenon can hardly be disputed; but Leigh feels that it can be shown to have a plausible course of evolution out of period I, and even that a single masterful artist might have enough influence in favorable circumstances (as in Renaissance Europe) to account for the whole stylistic movement.

Monte Albán II has been conceived in the past as being in part a manifestation of the "Q Complex" postulated years ago by Lothrop and Vaillant. The pottery of Holmul I, deep in the Maya jungles, was another element; and the tentatively proposed Matzanel phase at the important Maya site of Uaxactún belongs in the same hypothetical grouping.

Whatever its origin, Monte Albán II brought some wonderful works of art into being, and in a style frequently quite different from that of period I, or in fact any period at Monte Albán or elsewhere. Some ordinary decorated dishes of this time are obviously similar to those of the Maya lowlands and Chiapas; but in no other region involved in the "Q Complex" was anything produced then fit to stand beside the jade bat god, the massive pottery head of Tomb 77, the standing pottery figures of Tomb 113, or the superb pottery "Scribe of Cuilapan" (Figures 80–88, 155).

Monte Albán II thus was by a wide margin the cultural capital of the "Q Complex" if that concept really refers to a meaningful social relationship; and the problem of what appears to be a discrepancy in the radiocarbon dates of Monte Albán II and the presumably contemporary phase—that is, the seemingly most similar one—at Chiapa de Corzo may profitably be seen from this viewpoint. For early Oaxaca we have the following series of radiocarbon dates:

Laboratory Number	Year Dated	Most Probable Date	Period	Place
C-424	1950	649 B.C.	Monte Albán I	Monte Negro
O-1210	1960	390 B.C.	Monte Albán Ic	Yagul
C-425	1950	275 B.C.	Monte Albán II	Monte Albán
O-1300	1961	240 B.C.	Monte Albán II	Caballito Blanco
C-426	1950	A.D. 300	Transición Monte Albán IIIa–IIIb	Yucuñudahui

These dates are all consistent with each other, and all fit easily into the long and detailed radiocarbon sequence established by MacNeish for the Tehuacan Valley. The 1950 dates were determined by the older solid carbon process. The 1960 and 1961 samples were gathered by different persons, using considerable care to avoid contamination, and are from sharply defined contexts. Some of the dates might indeed refer to pieces of charcoal that already were ancient at the time they were laid down where archeologists later found them; but the likelihood that all of them are uniformly in error in the same way, preserving their order in the previously established Monte Albán sequence but at some wrong age, is hardly very great. The Monte Negro and Yucuñudahui specimens are from beams; the Yagul one is from charcoal in a brazier, almost certainly not ancient when placed there. The Caballito Blanco specimen was in the wall of a building, and thus is more open to such suspicions; but the date on it suggests that it too actually corresponds in time to the Monte Albán II pottery fragments in the mound that overlay it. The form of the building also is known from only one other example—Mound J, of period II, at Monte Albán (Figure 89).

From Chiapa de Corzo we have a longer series of dates, and those referring to the periods said to resemble Monte Albán II most closely indicate that this development came in the first two centuries A.D. at this small place in Chiapas.

Text continued on p. 126

68. Tetrapod grey vase (made to be used with a lid?). *Frissell collection.*

69. Bowl with after-firing scratches outlining red-painted design; diagnostic in all respects of Monte Albán II. *MNA.*

70. Tetrapod bowl from Monte Albán. *MNA.*

71. Potstand (typical of Monte Albán II) holding a neckless olla or tecomate; Monte Albán. *MNA.*

72. Bowl with mammiform supports; Monte Albán. Both the shape and the "fresco"-painted decoration are typical of Monte Albán II. *MNA.*

73. Small painted brazier: the young god with bird helmet; Monte Albán. *MNA.*

74. Armadillo effigy with spout handle. *MNA.*

75. Urn in Monte Albán II style: the god with serpent mask. *Frissell collection.*

76. Bottle with effigy wearing serpent mask (eyes and hairdress look later than period II). *Frissell collection.*

77. Whistling vessel with monkey. When water was poured into the vessel, air was forced out through a whistle hidden in the monkey. *Frissell collection.*

78. The god with serpent mask; Tomb 77, Monte Albán. *MNA.*

79. Examples of the inscriptions on Mound J that Caso has tentatively identified as records of conquest. In each case there is a place (mountain) glyph, a two-stepped platform like a pyramid. Below it hangs a human head, adorned as if for war, and in one case (above, left) with the eyes shown closed. Calendrical glyphs—which could be names of personages or dates—accompany some of them.

81. The god 5 F; Monte Albán (slightly over life-size; head only).

80. Personage wearing headdress of the broad-billed bird, an important deity in Oaxaca; Tomb 77, Monte Albán. The face is life-size or slightly more.

82. God with mouth-mask of broad-billed bird; Temple of 7 Deer, Monte Albán. Over life-size. *MNA.*

83. Figure from Tomb 113, Monte Albán. Overall height less than that of Figure 80. *MNA.*

84. Large pottery brazier with headdress of tiger wearing broad-billed bird mask. *Frissell collection.*

85. Figure from Tomb 113, Monte Albán; about same size as Figure 83. *MNA.*

86. Figure from Tomb 113, Monte Albán. Slightly smaller than Figures 83 and 85. *MNA.*

87. Brazier very similar to fragmented polychrome examples found in Caballito Blanco excavations.

88. Giant polychromed figure of tiger; Monte Albán. *MNA.*

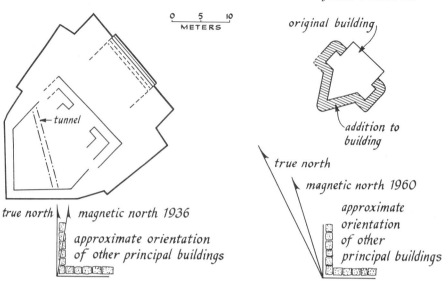

89. Mound J, Monte Albán (left), and Mound O, Caballito Blanco. Although their orientation with respect to other buildings at their sites is similar, their absolute orientation is not.

The apparent gap of several centuries may well be reduced by later refinement of both chronologies. It should be kept in mind too that cultural phenomena normally begin at one place and appear at others with some time lag; and that in remote places they often survive long after the great centers have moved on to other things. In view of the status of Monte Albán as a large urban center producing masterpieces of art, we may reasonably propose that this time gap results (if the judgment of similarities is correct) from the priority of Monte Albán.

An important site in the Mixtec region that might belong in this period is Huamelulpan, Caso and Gamio have found a number of stone sculptures there in a style suggestive of Monte Albán II, although the associated pottery—not at all strangely, in view of the Valley of Oaxaca sequences—seems more like that of Monte Albán I.

EARLY URBANISM BECOMES A TRADITION: MONTE ALBÁN IIIa

No cultural tradition would be recognizable unless it showed continuity, and none would be viable unless it could be adapted to changing conditions; but recognizable and viable traditions have been formed with strikingly different proportions of continuity and change. The Zapotec tradition that so distinctively crystallized around 100 B.C. at Monte Albán lies near one extreme, for it was still clearly recognizable over 1,500 years later on the irruption of the Spanish.

Change did occur, and present knowledge permits some division of this long tradition into periods. Future work will provide shorter subdivisions. Nevertheless, neither the abandonment of Monte Albán, nor the Mixtec conquest and occupation (some three centuries of it), nor, finally, the relatively trifling Aztec invasion caused any sharp break in Valley Zapotec ways. Except for the abandonment of Monte Albán and the later capture of a number of towns by the Mixtecs, change in the Valley of Oaxaca from the time of Christ until the Spanish conquest tended to be both very gradual and the work of the Valley's own Zapotec inhabitants.

The traits that distinguish period IIIa are first found in some tombs at Monte Albán and at Loma Larga, near Mitla, in offerings consisting in part of Monte Albán II materials; and there are also in these tombs a few ceramic figures, very rarely found elsewhere, which seem to have been produced only during a short period of transition from Monte Albán II to IIIa (Figures 90–98). In both these peculiar Transición urns and the ceramic and architectural complexes of Monte Albán IIIa there are hints of a new outside interest for the Valley of Oaxaca people.

Having maintained connections of some sort to the east in period I and to the south in period II, these Valley residents now looked to the north. Although few actually imported objects occur, many others of local manufacture begin to show a taste for the style of Teotihuacan in the Valley of Mexico (Figures 99–102). The headdresses and capes of the Transición figures, as well as a number of the Monte Albán IIIa vessel shapes, are strongly similar to those of Teotihuacan; yet in every instance the Oaxacans adopted these northern ideas only after coloring them strongly with their own traditions. Most of their pottery remained distinctively Oaxacan (Figures 103–11). There is no hint that Monte Albán was in some way dependent upon or subordinate to Teotihuacan (as so many other centers of the same time were); rather, one suspects that the Transición period at Monte Albán marks the moment when Teotihuacan's period II was beginning and Teotihuacan was for the first time a center of sufficient importance to attract the interest of the Valley of Oaxaca people. Recent considerable increases in our chronological knowledge suggest that a time around 100 B.C. is about right both for Transición in Monte Albán and for the beginning of period II in Teotihuacan.

The knowledge gained in the Monte Albán excavations makes it possible to divide the span of Zapotec culture from 100 B.C. to the Spanish conquest at several points. The resulting periods have been designated Transición, IIIa (ca. 100 B.C. to A.D. 300), IIIb (A.D. 300–900), and IV (A.D. 900–1521). Nevertheless, we ought to take note that periods III and IV of Monte Albán are in most senses a single tradition, interrupted only at Monte Albán, by its abandonment. The significance of this event is such, however, that we shall place IV with Late Urban developments. The relative simplicity of early IIIa gave way, with the enormous prosperity of IIIb, to elaboration, and finally in IV to an undeniable loss of quality. The outside interests that were so clearly perceptible in I, II, and IIIa were gradually assimilated, and in IIIb there was a completely integrated regional style. During period V there was a massive and largely successful invasion by the Mixtecs, bearing a sharply different culture; yet after three centuries of sharing the Valley of Oaxaca with these invaders, the Zapotecs were characterized by the Spanish chroniclers as very specifically different from the Mixtecs. The Aztec invasion, so greatly advertised by the Aztecs themselves, occurred near the end of this period; but it seems to have left no archeological trace whatsoever. (It may well have amounted to no more than the brief holding of a few strong points by small garrisons.)

No great skill is needed to find differences between objects of Monte Albán IIIa and those of late IV, over a thousand years later; but there seems to be no time of rapid stylistic change during all these centuries, and therefore our divisions are rather arbitrary. Period III is separated into phases IIIa and IIIb by the disappearance (through assimilation) of the last traces from periods I and II; the dividing "line" therefore is of necessity a twilight zone of considerable width—sometimes referred to as Transición IIIa–IIIb. The end of period IIIb is very clear at Monte Albán itself, for it marks the time when the metropolis was substantially (and perhaps rather rapidly) abandoned. Although burials continued to be made there, the temples were no longer maintained and no new ones were built. Offerings were continued, however, and when the temples began to crumble the offerings were placed in their rubble. No clear sign of this catastrophic event is to be found in the small cities throughout the Valley of Oaxaca; their culture of early period IV is entirely indistinguishable from that of late IIIb.

The most exhaustive analysis yet carried out is that of Caso and Bernal on the pottery urns that are the best-known product of the Monte Albán people. Those of periods I and II are much different in style from those of III and IV,[3] although the basic idea of a roughly cylindrical vessel with a figure on the front was there from the beginning, and some of the deities first represented in Monte Albán I and II were prominent (although in different style) also in III and IV (Figures 112–18). During period II the urns took on their definitive architecture, with the hollow vessel constituting the trunk and head of the seated figure. The IIIa urns were hand-modeled (Figures 119–35); those of IIIb were increasingly assembled from elements that had been stamped out in molds. During IIIb there was a strong tendency to elaboration, and the symbolic elements, grouped especially in the headdresses, came to dominate, with the human figure (or, it may be, the anthropomorphic god-figure) shown in decreasing detail and smaller proportion to the formal elements. Some simplification occurred in period IV, possibly because both workmanship and esthetic quality declined gradually throughout late IIIb and IV, to the point where the potters of period IV may not have been equal to the formidable task of constructing the large, complex, top-heavy urns of IIIb. The decadent trend is relieved here and there, naturally, by some excep-

---

[3] Because of this and other discontinuities, they do not extend their identification of the Monte Albán culture as Zapotec further back in time than IIIa.

Text continued on p. 140

. Transición urn, perhaps representing
e god Xipe; Monte Albán. *MNA.*

91. Urn of Transición II–III; the god with serpent mask.
Frissell collection.

. Transición urn; glyph C and serpent mask in headdress.
issell collection.

93. Transición urn with serpent mask and a glyph C
with rare single stream of water in the headdress.

95. Urn of Transición. *Frissell collection.*

96. Fragment of nearly life-size figure; Mound X, Monte Albán. *MNA.*

94. Urn of the god 5 F; from the Loma Larga tomb, Mitla. *MNA.*

97. Transición urn with serpent mask and glyph C in headdress.

98. Vessel of rather Teotihuacanoid form, with effigy in Monte Albán IIIa style and wearing a bat headdress; Monte Albán. *MNA.*

99. Teotihuacan vessels and influences at Monte Albán during Transición II–III. *MNA.*

00. Reclining dog. *MNA.*

101. Vessel showing several similarities
to Teotihuacan style; Monte Albán. *MNA.*

2. Teotihuacanoid vessels of Monte Albán IIIa. *MNA.*

103. Vases of 1 Tiger (left) and 2 J (right). Vessels with the glyphs of these two deities are more commonly found joined. *Frissell collection.*

104. A bowl with panel of carved serpentine-cloud designs that is diagnostic of Monte Albán IIIa; from Monte Albán. *MNA.*

105. The carved decoration of Monte Albán IIIa. *MNA.*

106. Small bird-masked figure of the goddess 1 F; Monte Albán. *MNA.*

107. Monkey effigy with carved panel. *MNA.*

108. Two spout-handled effigy-vessels with carved panels.
Frissell collection.

9. Gigantic pottery head of tiger. *MNA.*

Large pottery year sign; Cerro de Atzompa, Monte Albán. *MNA.*

Bowl with fixed cups inside. *Frissell collection.*

112. The water god in Monte Albán I.
Covarrubias collection, MNA.

113. The water god of period II,
Monte Albán. *MNA.*

114. The water god in Transición II–III.
Covarrubias collection, MNA.

115. The water god of Monte Albán IIIa
(shown as head only). *MNA.*

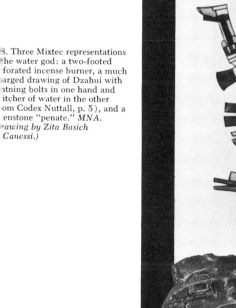

, Cocijo in his most common form:
water god of Monte Albán IIIb. *MNA.*

117. The water god of Monte Albán IV. This badly made and poorly
preserved example was found at Monte Albán; because of the difficulty
of distinguishing IIIb from IV, no handsomer specimen could be
shown with confidence that it really is of period IV. *MNA.*

3. Three Mixtec representations
he water god: a two-footed
forated incense burner, a much
arged drawing of Dzahui with
ntning bolts in one hand and
itcher of water in the other
om Codex Nuttall, p. 5), and a
enstone "penate." *MNA.*
*awing by Zita Basich
Canessi.)*

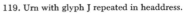

119. Urn with glyph J repeated in headdress.

120. Urn with glyph F
in headdress.

121. Plain urn, female figure of Transición
or early IIIa. *Frissell collection.*

123. Small IIIa urn
with rare serpent-
water or reptile's-eye
glyph in headdress.

122. The god with two vessels on his back. *MNA.*

An *acompañante* from Monte Albán.
A.

125. Small IIIa urns in the Frissell collection, strikingly different in construction from most urns; but note similarity in body treatment to Figure 98 (p. 130).

The goddess with Yalálag headdress, wearing *chquémitl* and skirt of types still in use. *MNA.*

127. Large figure of the god with serpent mask. *MNA.*

128. Personage holding a monkey under his arm. *Frissell collection.*

129. The goddess 11 Death. *MNA.*

130. The Idol of Yogana.
Frissell collection.

131. God with serpent mask. Like many figures of saints, he has virtually no body; the hands alone suggest it. Note that he also has only three toes on each foot. *Frissell collection.*

133. God with Cocijo in his headdress. *Frissell collection.*

. God with headdress of broad-billed bird.
A.

134. Acrobat juggling a stone with his feet. The incomplete lady behind or above him is unidentified. Detail from the late Mixtec Codex Vindobonensis, p. 44.

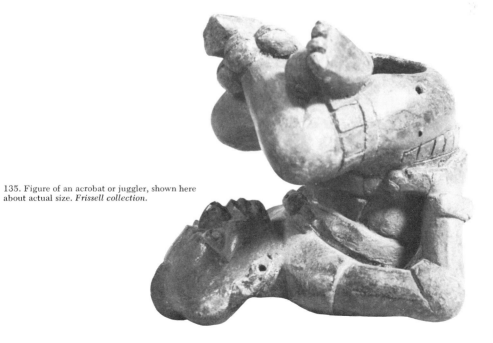

135. Figure of an acrobat or juggler, shown here about actual size. *Frissell collection.*

tional artist's masterful work. In IIIa and early IIIb the material was usually
a hard-baked, lightweight, rather fine-grained light grey clay. In period IV
it usually was rather poorly baked, gritty, heavy, blackish red-brown. Even
more impressive than this technological degeneration is the gradual loss of
definition and sureness from the often brilliantly sharp modeling of the individually carved faces on the urns of IIIa to the blurring and heavy uniformity
of mold-made faces in later times.

Since most IIIa buildings are thoroughly buried under larger IIIb constructions at Monte Albán, and since period IV does not exist there in architecture, the development of architecture remains much less precisely defined
than that of pottery sculpture. In general the tendencies are parallel to those
revealed in the urns. The few known buildings of periods I and II include
some of imposing size. Their lower walls are nearly vertical, and often made
of large blocks of stone. Beginning in IIIa, the lower walls often were bat-
tered, the simple vertical rise of earlier times now broken up into the widespread Mesoamerican *talud y tablero* or slope and panel, with a framed decorative panel projecting slightly above the top of the sloping wall. One structure of enormous mass that apparently is attributable to IIIa is the South
Platform at Monte Albán. Its lowest wall is high and vertical, and incorpo-
rates a number of stelae. The architecture of IIIb was similar to that of IIIa,
and what little is known of period IV architecture from the exploration of
Valley sites suggests that there was no marked change from IIIb, but only a
general slackening of standards.

Funerary architecture offers another sequence. The tombs of Monte Albán
I were little more than stone or adobe boxes. The tombs of period II had
peaked roofs and side niches; the niches remained characteristic of Monte
Albán tombs up to the Spanish conquest. During IIIa there was an increase
in overall size; the niches of some tombs are so large that the cruciform tomb
is only a step away. The grandest of the Monte Albán tombs in the architectural sense were built at the end of IIIa and the beginning of IIIb; some
of these have sculptured decoration on the façades as well as mural paintings
inside. Those of late IIIb and IV were smaller again, and less elaborate in
construction. Through all these changes, elaborate tombs remained far more
numerous in Oaxaca than in other regions of Mesoamerica.

In some respects the writing system and the closely associated calendar
seem to show an extreme of conservatism. Some of the day signs and certain
other traits dating from period I underwent only relatively minor modifications through the entire course of Valley history down to the Spanish conquest (Figures 136 and 137). Several other glyphs that are first known from
Monte Albán II, though some may be earlier, also lasted until the Conquest.
In fact, the calendar-writing complex apparently achieved full development
in period II except for a few details. Aside from a handful of examples painted
on walls, Zapotec writing is known only from carvings on stone and pottery;
there were paintings on skin or cloth as well, but no surviving examples are

known. (Leigh's article on one Zapotec glyph, pp. 256–69 below, provides a detailed sequence.)

All the sequences so far mentioned belong to the world of the public or to that of the wealthy. We turn next to a more humble object, the common serving dish. In period II this was a rather thick but neatly finished and thoroughly baked grey bowl, with a flat bottom and nearly vertical sides. It was commonly about one-third as high as it was wide. (This form may have begun, in fact, in period I;[4] but other bowl forms are better known from that period.) With only slight alterations, the everyday serving bowl of Monte Albán II remained in use until the Spanish conquest. In IIIa its nearly vertical sides were made to slope outward somewhat, so that it acquired the form of a truncated cone; but it still was made of light grey clay, well formed and well baked. In IIIb it tended to be slightly larger, and darker in color; at times the inside bottom was decorated with carelessly made undulating lines, not incised but smoothed with a polishing stone. The material became slowly grainier, as in the urns. The evenly if not highly polished interior of IIIa tended to be less well done in IIIb; the exterior was not well smoothed in IIIb, and careless application of the polishing stone to this unprepared surface produced irregular streaks. In late IIIb and IV the bowl tended to become smaller again, but it retained the truncated cone shape, perhaps now less clearly defined. The exterior finish was still poorer, showing now the strong irregularity of clay squeezed roughly into shape with the fingers and never effectively smoothed at all. The interior too at times was only carelessly smoothed, and rarely polished. Nevertheless, we must note that through all this sequence of change, the grey-to-black color—obtained only through much care in achieving a reducing atmosphere in the firing—was preferred.

We have not yet defined period IIIa except by contrasting its stonework and pottery with those of earlier and later periods. However, there is something we can say about it in its own right. In earlier treatments, this period has been characterized as the beginning of the Mesoamerican "Classic" in its Monte Albán aspect; and in one sense of the word it is indeed the beginning of classic (true, pure, typical) Zapotec style. Although Teotihuacan style is plainly present in some objects of IIIa, much of the culture was by this time fully central Oaxacan. Period IIIa may be regarded from another viewpoint as the final phase of a centuries-long process of assimilation during which outside ideas were reworked and ultimately (at a point that defines the end of IIIa) absorbed. As a phase of the familiar stylistic cycle of archaic, classic, and baroque, IIIa is early classic; I and II still have some echoes of peasant art from simpler times, and may therefore be called archaic in this sense, while IIIb is baroque and IV in many ways may be called decadent.

[4] MacNeish found well-made stone bowls of the same form beginning from 4000 to 5000 B.C. at Tehuacan, and remaining in use until well after the form had appeared in pottery during the second millennium B.C.

As an early classic phase of artistic development, IIIa may be characterized in another way. It has been pointed out frequently that the pottery dishes and figurines made by the agricultural villagers of Mesoamerica before the rise of cities have a very attractive quality of freedom, in contrast to the formality of later urban products. One might say that there is a playful feeling in the early work—playful in the sense that as in play, one is not oppressed by the irrevocability of real life. One can experiment; one's mistakes can be forgotten or corrected. In Early Urban work, by contrast, one gets the impression that it matters very much to do things properly; thus the formal quality. (Monte Albán II seems to represent a time of transition in which old-style playful figurines were still made, but new-style formal urns were gaining ground.) In all such observations as these we must keep in mind that the village artisan of early times, no matter how informally and playfully free, could not expect to invent very much in one lifetime: he was working within the limitations of available materials, of known techniques, and of a heritage of ideas. The urban artisan of later times, for all that he worked within much more specifically defined limitations, remained an individual and in some cases an artist; and such a man can always find some detail not fixed by tradition in which to apply his own peculiar vision.

The question of militarism in the Mesoamerican "Classic" is still far from any final resolution, but for Monte Albán the data may be somewhat clearer than for the other major centers of its time, at Teotihuacan and in the Maya lowlands. At Teotihuacan there is little evidence of any military activity at all. In the Maya lowlands the paintings and sculptures that show fighting and captives are of the *late* Maya "Classic," after Teotihuacan had been abandoned. As noted above, some inscriptions of Monte Albán II may record conquests. The famous stelae of the South Platform, surely of period III and perhaps of IIIa, include figures of bound captives and of a conqueror thrusting his lance into the hill glyph representing some still unidentified town (Figures 143–49). Some warrior figures in pottery, too, are known from period III (Figure 150). However, before we characterize Early Urban times at Monte Albán as militaristic, we ought to note that whereas the city enjoyed the military advantages of any hilltop, there is no hint of fortification. Further, there are no signs that it was ever fought over or prepared for fighting. Since fortifications are obvious at some later Valley sites, and armed warrior figurines are very common at these later towns, the contrast with Monte Albán may be meaningful.

Bernal's data on the number of populated places in two of the three arms of the Valley of Oaxaca suggest an explanation here. Although he warns that his survey of archeological sites was not of a kind which could produce definitive conclusions, it is suggestive that he found surface fragments of IIIa pottery at only 50 or 60 sites; IIIb–IV fragments (combined because of the difficulty of distinguishing between them) were identified at over 200 sites in the

Text continued on p. 149

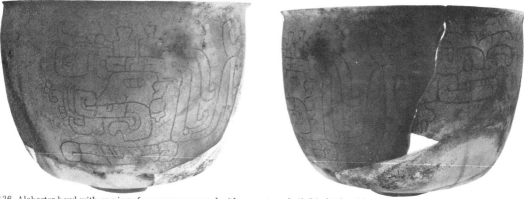

136. Alabaster bowl with carving of a personage or god with serpent mask (left); his headdress terminates in a serpent's head (right). *Frissell collection.*

137. The Lápida de Bazán, a thick onyx slab found in Mound X at Monte Albán. *MNA.*

140. The Xipe of Tomb 103, Monte Albán. *MNA.* In his left hand he appears to hold a trophy head; he wears a belt of seashells cut so that they tinkle. (Compare Figure 175, p. 168.)

9. Large pottery cylinder covered with ⁄phs, found at Cerro de Atzompa, ⁊nte Albán. *MNA.*

1. The god 1 Tiger; from Suchilquitongo, Huitzo. ⁊A.

142. *Acompañante* with glyph C in his headdress; from Macuilxóchitl.

143. Front and side of Stela 2, Monte Albán. The figure on the front of the stela stands on a place (mountain) glyph; his arms, terminating in tiger claws, are bound behind him, and he wears a complete tiger skin and mask. On the back of the stone the sculptor began the same carving upside down, but abandoned it. *MNA*.

144. Stela 6, Monte Albán; behind it, the front of System M. The scene shows a man standing on a place glyph, his arms bound behind him.

145. Stela 9, Monte Albán, at the foot of the grand stairway of the North Platform. Apparently late in style, it is crowded with carvings on all sides. In the background, System IV.

146. Stela 3, South Platform, Monte Albán; another bound captive on a place glyph.

147. Stela 8, South Platform, Monte Albán. Still another bound figure standing on a place glyph; this one, like some of the others, is uttering something, as indicated by the speech glyph issuing from his mouth.

147

148. Stela 10 of Monte Albán. *MNA*.

149. Stela 4 of Monte Albán. A man named 8 Deer (glyph below his right arm) stands on a place glyph, thrusting a lance into it with his left hand. *MNA*.

150. Standing figure, apparently a warrior. This piece was stolen from the Museo Frissell on December 24, 1959.

same area. We may conjecture from these figures that the new urban social system of IIIa was extremely productive, and that the Valley of Oaxaca was prospering. City life and the high level of organization in associated rural areas had made possible a new kind of exploitation of the environment,[5] yet at this time the population was still rather small with respect to the land area. As time went on, however, the abundant food supply allowed a steady population increase, and before the end of IIIa all the best land in the Valley had been occupied. The often bitter quarrels over boundaries that plague Oaxaca to this day very probably date back to early Monte Albán IIIb, when the Valley for the first time was filled with human inhabitants to the limit of its sustaining capacity.

BAROQUE EARLY URBANISM: MONTE ALBÁN IIIb

Period IIIb is the best known archeologically of all the Monte Albán periods. Among other things, it is the time when Monte Albán's population reached its peak and when nearly all the now visible buildings there were constructed. Finally, it is the most dramatic period of the city's history, since the great flowering of Monte Albán IIIb—and its parallels in Teotihuacan III and Maya Tepeu—came just before the great collapse of Early Urbanism in Mesoamerica. One of the most interesting questions about IIIb is why the immense social, economic, and physical structures of Monte Albán suffered so striking a failure after well over a millennium of growth.

Abandonment of the great "Classic" capitals of Mesoamerica is much discussed as a major mystery, but this is looking at it wrong end to; the mystery is how they were able to go on so long and accomplish so much with so little sign of trouble. These were, we have said, "first-generation" urban centers—the first cities in their part of the world, and derived from simpler forms of society. They began with a system capable of highly effective exploitation of their environment, but with a relatively small population. So long as the growing population could find new land on which to increase production, all was well. Surpluses went into the building of more and more overpoweringly majestic monuments. Offerings in gratitude to the gods were splendid, and the priests who enjoyed a monopoly of specialized knowledge, including technical as well as religious procedures, lived sumptuously (Figure 151).

The Valley of Oaxaca has obvious mountain boundaries; but any region has equally effective functional limits. So long as any needed increase in the food supply could be produced by bringing new lands within the region under cultivation, the Early Urban system worked smoothly. Once the land was all cul-

---

[5] Except for the astronomical calendars, stone carving, pottery, and the control of water resources, Mesoamerican civilization was rather notable for its low technological level. Thus large, beautiful, elaborately decorated buildings were often structurally poor; the principle of the wheel was known, but the only wheeled vehicles were toys; the true arch was not developed. Even when metallurgy tardily arrived, few metal tools were made. Therefore the demographic expansion is attributed to social, not technological, innovations.

151. Offering found in the patio of the house built over Tomb 103, Monte Albán. The scene represented is a funeral. The dead man, symbolized by a head carved from stone on a small stone pyramid, is surrounded by an orchestra, the seated figure of the old god of fire (or a priest representing him), and five priests standing in full ceremonial costume. The figures of the five priests are unusual in that the elaborate headdresses are removable; otherwise they are one-piece pottery figures. Placeable in Transición IIIa–IIIb or the beginning of period IIIb, the house of Tomb 103 probably was built at the peak of Monte Albán's prosperity and before the decline of craftsmanship had had much effect.

tivated, some increase was still possible from more intensive cultivation. Having reached the limit of this technique, the Valley people may have tried to extend the economic boundaries of their region and to draw upon surrounding lands to help in the ever more costly maintenance and constant enlargement of Monte Albán. Perhaps the warriors on Monte Albán stelae of period III are men who set out to bring new areas under the city's dominion, and the captives are the leaders of towns they conquered.

The conquest of neighboring regions might have produced some momentary relief from economic pressures, although Bernal's survey indicates that the striking uniformity of ceramic remains throughout the Valley extends only to the geographical limits of the Valley itself. In any event, there was probably never any real integration of outside communities into the Valley's way of life. Valley lands, under more and more intensive exploitation, were depleted (as pioneers of new social forms the Early Urban people could not know the hazards in them). Hillsides, cleared of their forest cover and planted, soon eroded away, except in areas where terracing was customary. As the supply of wood for construction and fuel was cut back, the daily trip to the sources became longer. Yet new buildings in the religious centers kept going up, each grander than the one before; in order to cover the last version, a new pyramid always had to be larger. Increasing difficulties seem to have been met with intensified appeals to the gods. This meant more spending for offerings and buildings, compounding the problem.

The immense prestige conferred by a millennium of success was no doubt sufficient to tide Monte Albán's ruler-priests over the first few crises. (With the economy pushed to an extreme, any complication such as a dry year provoked a crisis.) But repeated exposure of the priests as unable, after all, to bring the rains or solve other problems finally rendered the public less eager to expend its scant worldly goods on tribute to the gods. Perhaps the people were literally not able to keep up with the priesthood's demands on their time and resources. Under such conditions, any real difficulty whatever can be enough to set off a long series of catastrophic breakdowns. Institutions that have seemed unassailable are then revealed as having already been long poised on the edge of disaster.

Monte Albán in period IIIb was a nearly incredible enterprise. It occupied not only the top of a large mountain, but the tops and sides of a whole range of high hills adjoining, a total of some fifteen square miles of urban construction (Figures 152–54). Human labor may be characterized as cheap under some circumstances, but a man's time is never cheap in a pre-industrial economy, where what he eats has to be produced by hand labor. Except for the possibility of catching more or less rainwater during four or five months of the year, the population of Monte Albán had to drink water carried up the mountain—as much as 1,500 feet—in jars. This alone would be costly; but the quantities of water required in building construction make the location of a large city on this high ridge even more astonishing. In addition, the maintenance of a major religious capital such as Monte Albán would necessarily require the services of thousands of specialists: priests, artists, architects, the apprentices of all these, and many kinds of workmen, including servants for the dignitaries and their families.

In purely economic terms, in fact, the whole accomplishment seems fantastic. But if we attempt to comprehend it in those terms alone we are neglecting the crucial factors. For over a century we have been living in a world where technology has been the great hope, solving one problem after another. Perhaps we may be forgiven if we have come to demand material-mechanical explanations for everything, overlooking the possibility that they may often be insufficient.

With a technology in which the wheel was not used for transport, there were no draft animals, and no metals were used, how could Monte Albán be built at all? Was there some totalitarian system for mobilizing the entire population to labor on those gigantic temples? To carry the water? To work for weeks grinding a jade pebble (Figures 155–64) by invisible degrees into a work of art? To bring offerings over the mountains, on foot, from the two oceans? Was it a slave state that collapsed when the victims revolted?

To ask these questions only in economic, technological, and political terms will produce only some of the needed answers. Questions about religion and art must be included, and they may in this case be the most basic ones. At the end there was no vengeful destruction of Monte Albán; the temples came down, but they fell stone by stone over the silent years for lack of repairs. Reverent offerings were still made there secretly in Spanish colonial times. Even now one may see, almost any day, large pilgrimages in Mexico. It is common for tens of thousands of men, women, and children to walk 50 or more miles to a shrine. They are not slaves; they would revolt if *denied* the right to make their pilgrimage. If they were asked, they would gladly bring a jar of water, or a log, or a stone; or they would give a few days' labor.

Every known human culture is overelaborated in some direction or other. Sometimes this tendency only goes beyond the positively economic; at other times it reaches extremes that are strongly anti-economic, even threatening the very existence of the society. But men seem to need to show their mastery of their environment, to reassure themselves that while the forces of nature may be unpredictable and menacing, culture itself is not limited to what it *must* be; man creates it and he can extend it beyond necessity if he wants.

Ancient Mesoamerican culture was strikingly impractical on two counts: its indifference to (or contempt for) technology, and its extraordinary devotion to esthetic principles. (Since the extreme development of religion was a central integrating factor in the society, we shall not treat it as impractical.) The nearly unbelievable phenomenon of Monte Albán IIIb cannot be understood except in terms of these noneconomic attitudes.

Men capable of manipulating a calendar based on astronomical events were obviously able to perceive that building a metropolis on a mountain range was a costly business. But the view is magnificent.

The works of Zapotec culture remain always sober and formal, but always robust and often marvelously well made; the greatest of them all is the capital city. For all the magical beauty of Teotihuacan's city plan and integration into its landscape, the Zapotec architects of the same period matched—or perhaps anticipated—the accomplishment in their own way. They left for us at Monte Albán a city of unrivaled majesty in a setting that would have overwhelmed lesser men before they began (Figures 165–73).

The men and women who toiled up that long hill with some offering for the gods—food for their priests, wood or water for their temples—may have felt in their tired bodies that a valley location would be more "practical." But these people were participating in the life of a metropolis; they could see that they were making it possible. They could stand dazzled before those mighty temples, stroll half an hour to circle the immense open plaza, watch the stunning pageantry of the ceremonies, stare as fascinated as we at the valley spread mile after mile below. They knew that no other such center existed for hundreds of miles—and even then their city had only rivals, not superiors. They were proud, and they were reassured at this enormous work of art as evidence that man too has power.

Monte Albán was a place electric with the presence of the gods (Figures 174–88). These gods were the very forces of nature with which peasants are so respectfully intimate. Lightning-rain was represented by a tiger-serpent. The mysterious powers of more realistic animals—serpent, vampire bat, opossum, mountain lion, owl—were called upon to bridge the conceptual gap and make possible objective representations (as animals) of the abstract forces of the universe. The ultimate drama of human sacrifice does seem to have been carried out at Monte Albán, although rarely; sacrifice did not become a common affair and a rationalized form of punitive execution as it later did among the haunted Aztecs.

Every temple stood over half a dozen temples of centuries before. Buried in the great temples were ancient high priests of legendary powers, now semideified; centuries of accumulated wealth in offerings, centuries of mana in ceremonies, centuries of power and success, lay deep inside that masonry. But with their own humble hands, or those of their remembered ancestors, the common people had made the buildings.

No whip-cracking slave driver was needed. The satisfaction of helping to create something simultaneously imposing, reassuring, and beautiful is enough to mobilize endless amounts of human effort. Mexico's shrines of today are in most cases far less beautiful, and the worshipers' participation (with money) is far less satisfyingly direct; but they still come by the thousands, voluntarily.

In the dynamic art of Monte Albán IIIa we see a new major tradition being

Text continued on p. 174

152. Air view of the Valley of Oaxaca: Monte Albán, center foreground; city of Oaxaca, left foreground. Taken from above Huitzo, looking southeast, July 1964.

153. Air view, Plaza of Monte Albán, south to north, August 1963.
The Valley of Etla is in the background.

154. The Plaza of Monte Albán, seen by air from north to south.
Taken just before sunset, January 1958.

156. A jade figure of Monte Albán II; from Monte Albán. *MNA.*

155. The bat god of Monte Albán II. It is made of 25 pieces of jade shaped to fit together, with shell for eyes and teeth; the pendants, curiously, are of a common greenish stone. Found at the Adoratorio near Mound H, Monte Albán. *MNA.*

157. Greenstone figurines of period IIIa, from Monte Albán, showing similarities to Teotihuacan and Guerrero work. *MNA.*

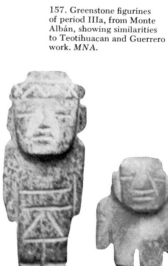

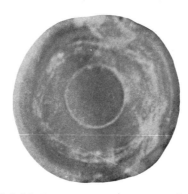

158. Objects of *tecalli*, a white to greenish stone often wrongly called alabaster or onyx. From Monte Albán; early IIIb. *MNA*.

159. A Maya jade found by Batres in 1902. Along with others, it was in a late Maya pottery vessel, apparently placed under a cement floor, in Mound B, Monte Albán. *MNA*.

160. Jades of Monte Albán IIIb. *MNA*.

161. A IIIb jade. *MNA*.

162. Three greenstone plaques
of Monte Albán IIIb–IV.
MNA.

163. Greenstone figures of Monte Albán IIIb–IV. *MNA.*

64. Greenstone figures of Monte Albán IV, showing little if any difference from Mixtec work of the same times. *MNA*.

165. View from north to south across the Plaza, Monte Albán; afternoon. Taken from the mound on the north side of the Patio Hundido, or Sunken Plaza, within the North Platform. (See Figure 166, No. 15.)

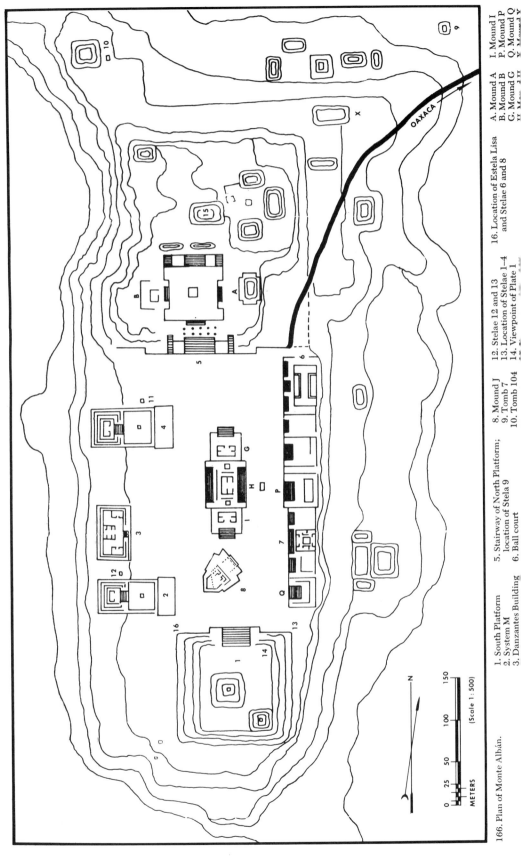

166. Plan of Monte Albán.

1. South Platform	5. Stairway of North Platform;	8. Mound J	12. Stelae 12 and 13	16. Location of Estela Lisa
2. System M	location of Stela 9	9. Tomb 7	13. Location of Stelae 1–4	and Stelae 6 and 8
3. Danzantes Building	6. Ball court	10. Tomb 104	14. Viewpoint of Plate 1	

A. Mound A   I. Mound I
B. Mound B   P. Mound P
G. Mound G   Q. Mound Q

162

57. The central buildings seen from the east side of the Plaza. The sunken Adoratorio in the foreground is where the bat god (Figure 155) was discovered. In the background are the Danzantes Building and System IV.

. Interior patio of System M.

170. An interior patio on the North Platform, north of Mound A.

171. The face of the North Platform.

173. The southwest corner of the Plaza, as seen from the South Platform: System M, the Danzantes Gallery, and the Danzantes Building.

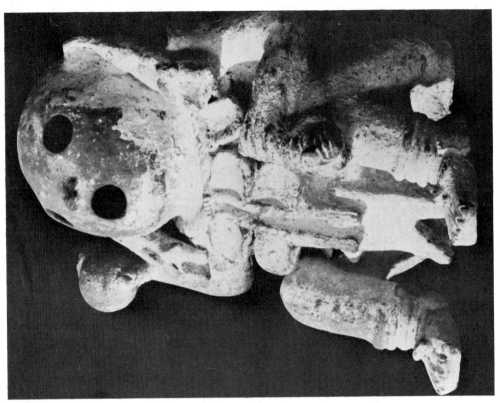

175. The Xipe of Tomb 58, Monte Albán: end of IIIb. MNA. (See Figure 140, p. 145.)

177. The god of the glyph L; a rare example of an "urn" in stone. *MNA*.

176. A typical Cocijo of period IIIb; compare Figure 116.

178. A female *acompañante* with glyph C
in her headdress. *MNA.*

179. The god 2 Tiger. *MNA.*

180. Vase with glyph of 13 Monkey. *MNA.*

181. Xipe carrying olla; Tomb 51, Monte Albán. *M*

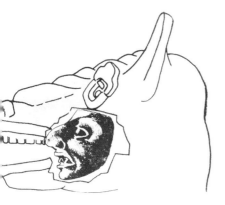

182. Man wearing an animal (*coatimundi?*) disguise. *MNA*. The man's face is visible inside the open mouth of the animal. (*Drawing after Abel Mendoza in Caso and Bernal 1952.*)

182. Pottery figure of an old man, probably a sacrificer. (The lower left figure is rotated.)

186. The bat god. *MNA.*

A very simple Cocijo of period IIIb.
ell collection.

187. The tiger god. *MNA.*

Some IIIb urns. Left to right: an unidentified old man; the god 5 Turquoise;
ompañante with glyph C in headdress. *MNA.*

created—not out of nothing, but out of inherited and imported themes. Human genetics, we may safely assume, operated then as it does today. If generation after generation of genuinely talented artists were available and were given the aristocrat's right to work in the cultural capital, we may be sure that the society was one in which the upper class drew constantly on the lower for fresh talent. In numbers and in abilities, aristocracies do not reproduce themselves. If the ruling class remains creative, it necessarily does so by means of effective recruiting from below.

In spite of all its power and prosperity, period IIIb shows a very slow but inexorable falling off in the quality of its art. This is a matter not of the evolution from classic to baroque, but of a decline in the quality of the baroque. We may conclude that the ruling class was becoming more and more exclusive, less and less open to talent of all kinds from below.

The same increasing rigidity of the ruling class was one of the causes of the final collapse. Less and less inventive, it was more and more fanatically devoted to tradition. The old ways were effective in the old days, and any troubles being suffered today must be caused by a departure from those sacred ways. These feelings ran deep and lasted long. In the seventeenth century, almost 150 years after the Spanish conquest, Balsalobre complained bitterly of widespread idolatry in the Valley of Oaxaca, and was able to collect readily identifiable descriptions of some deities whose cult we know goes back at least to Monte Albán IIIa.

Perhaps the very effectiveness of the psychological mobilization of the public, so identified with the temples and their rituals, reinforced the inflexibility of the priesthood, the stubborn reliance on unchanging ways in the face of inescapably changing conditions, that we have seen as leading to the ultimate breakdown.

The end of Early Urbanism in Monte Albán before A.D. 1000 was similar in some ways to the end of Early Urbanism around A.D. 650 in the Valley of Mexico, and after A.D. 900 in the Maya lowlands. One significant difference was that in the adjoining Mixtec region, the new era was already several centuries old at the time the old era ended at Monte Albán. Late Urban Mesoamerica was in existence at least in some small Mixtec city-states by about A.D. 700. The background to this important development must be sought in a period for which until very recent times we have had next to no information about the Mixteca.

THE MIXTECA IN EARLY URBAN TIMES

The Mixtec region is one of the best known in all Mesoamerica during very early and very late times, but some of the intervening periods are still almost completely blank archeologically. The work of MacNeish has given us a new and strikingly detailed picture of life in the Tehuacan Valley and some adjoining parts of the Mixteca during the long preceramic period. The Monte Negro explorations, plus scattered finds in Monte Albán I style at other places, had already made possible a tentative general characterization of life there during approximately the last millennium before Christ. In addition, Wicke (1965) has now concluded that the western part of the Mixteca is a likely place of origin for a single culture from which both Jiménez Moreno's Tenocelome (the former La Venta "Olmec") and Monte Albán I–Monte Negro are descended. The ceramics of MacNeish's Santa María phase of the Tehuacan Valley (900–200 B.C.) resemble those of Monte Albán I; and by the end of this phase the larger villages had ceremonial structures. At this time the Tehuacan Valley may have been peripheral to Monte Albán, which by then had astronomy, writing, and large stone buildings.

After Monte Albán I–Santa María times, the Mixteca enters upon its most mysterious period. Since in both earlier and later times its people were quick to adopt—when they did not introduce—major Mesoamerican innovations, we may propose that their culture was affected by Monte Albán II on one side and Teotihuacan I on the other, even though these centers did not then have the widespread influence they later enjoyed. The beginnings of Early Urbanism in the Mixteca may be inferred also from their reflection in the Tehuacan Valley, where the Palo Blanco phase (200 B.C.–A.D. 700) corresponds closely to Early Urbanism as defined here. MacNeish considers this phase, characterized by villages surrounding hilltop ceremonial centers with many public buildings, a provincial extension of Monte Albán III.

During the following Venta Salada phase (A.D. 700–1540), MacNeish believes the Tehuacan Valley was more or less completely incorporated into the Mixteca (by cultural leadership, conquest, and perhaps colonization). But Venta Salada is Late Urban, and what I should like to suggest here is that the Tehuacan Valley may in fact have been peripheral to some center or centers in the Mixteca as well as to Monte Albán during the preceding (the Early Urban and even the late Pre-urban) horizons. Another possibility is that the Mixteca may have been a mediating region between Monte Albán and the Tehuacan Valley. We do know that the part of the Mixteca closest to the Valley of Oaxaca was a cultural satellite of Monte Albán, and the northern part may have been similarly subordinate to Cholula-Teotihuacan. Except perhaps for the Monte Albán III conquest stelae, there is no evidence that the subordination was in any sense military. The relationship may well have been simply a reflection of the artistic, religious, and commercial leadership of the great cities.

In the area close to the Valley of Oaxaca, the site of Yucuñudahui has produced one of the few bits of true archeological illumination for Early Urban times in the Mixteca. A tomb there has been dated by radiocarbon at A.D. 298. Caso, in his report on the excavations (1938), notes that "the shape of the tomb, the glyphs on the stones that decorated it, and the pottery found inside it all are different from anything known before now, although they also show relations with the cultures of Monte Albán and Teotihuacan" (Figure 189). At this point, then, even the part of the Mixteca closest to Monte Albán was diverging from the ways of the metropolis, and developing its own style. Several pottery vessels from the Yucuñudahui tomb are closely related to Monte Albán forms current during the time of transition between periods IIIa and IIIb at the metropolis. Other vessels from the tomb are foreign to Monte Albán. Caso mentions three small jars with spout handles which have their rims turned completely outward and down; the edges are cut in the shape of battlements, or in a repeating step design (Figures 190–93). "Seler considered this type to be derived from Teotihuacan," Caso goes on, "but to judge from the places it is found, in the south of the state of Puebla and the north of Oaxaca, it might better be considered a Mixtec influence on southern Puebla and Teotihuacan pottery." This observation must be considered together with the comments of Jiménez Moreno in this volume (pp. 43–47 and 61–64) and with those that follow here.

Only a short time ago it would have been quite impossible to go beyond what Jiménez Moreno says about some as yet unnamed regional style or culture that may have existed in the Mixtec region before the Late Urban Mixteca-Puebla culture. No one would propose seriously that the region had been abandoned during these centuries. However, all of us have tended to assume without giving the matter much thought that it was a cultural backwater, where life was a mixture of provincial Teotihuacan ways and equally provincial Monte Albán ways. And so in part it was; but a significant third component may be seen in at least one part of the Mixteca. This third component is not Mixteca-Puebla, but earlier; not provincial Monte Albán or Teotihuacan, though often mixed with one or both. There seems to exist a pre-Mixteca-Puebla *style*, then, in the Mixteca-Puebla *region*.

The evidence of such a style—not to call it a culture just yet—is found in the Mixteca Baja, a relatively low trough of the upper Balsas River basin lying between the Cholula highland and that of the Mixteca Alta, the Coixtlahuaca-Tilantongo area. Jiménez Moreno has prophetically mentioned the Mixteca Baja and its towns of Acatlan, Puebla, and Huajuapan, Oaxaca. It is precisely in and near these places that the "new" style is found. Taking the Mixtec name for this region from the Alvarado dictionary of 1593, we may call it the Ñuiñe style. (Ñuiñe means literally Hot Land.)

Probably the best known by far of the region's distinctive traits falls in the time period of the Ñuiñe style: Thin Orange pottery,[6] which Carmen Cook has shown to have been made, perhaps exclusively, at Ixcaquixtla, a southern

---

[6] Thin Orange should not be confused with Fine Orange, which was produced and very widely traded around A.D. 1000. Export Thin Orange is very thin and hard, having a rather coarse temper. Fine Orange is so called because it has either a very fine temper or none at all. Several varieties were produced, all coming from the Gulf lowlands. In shapes and decoration it has nothing in common with Thin Orange (Smith 1958).

189. Cup with human figure; Tomb 1, Yucuñudahui. *MNA.*

. Ollita with false spout handle; nb 1, Yucuñudahui. *MNA.*

191. Ñuiñe ollita. *MNA.*

. Ñuiñe ollita; provenience unknown. ssell collection.

193. Ñuiñe ollita with false spout handle; from Huajuapan. *Frissell collection.*

194. Pottery duck from the Mixteca, probably of Monte Albán II or IIIa times. Both the material and the workmanship are strongly suggestive of Teotihuacan. *Frissell collection.*

Puebla village in the Ñuiñe region. MacNeish estimates that the large-scale export of Thin Orange occurred between A.D. 200 and 500. Thin Orange itself has such an immense distribution that it would do little to help define the homeland of a style; but in most of the Ñuiñe region many local imitations of it, all failing to achieve the quality of the original, were made (Figures 195–98 and Plate 4). Acatlan, also in southern Puebla, is the important modern pottery center where a ware very similar to ancient Thin Orange is produced today; and Acatlan is the center too of a unique ancient trait of Ñuiñe style, the *cabecitas colosales.*

Miguel Covarrubias referred a number of times, although apparently only in conversation with friends, to what he called the *cabecitas colosales* (colossal headlets), which interested him because of their conceptual similarity to the true *cabezas colosales* of his beloved La Venta "Olmecs." Both the huge ancient stone heads and the small later pottery ones are complete sculptures, having no bodies nor even necks; they are also naturalistic and usually almost spherical. In the storerooms of the Museo Nacional in Mexico City there are a number of *cabecitas colosales,* all recorded as having come from Acatlan; and the same provenience has been given for other examples I have located of these rather uncommon objects (Figures 199–207). They definitely do not belong to the Teotihuacan culture, or to that of Monte Albán, or to the Mixteca-Puebla culture of the "Postclassic" as defined by Vaillant. Their nearest stylistic relatives may be certain strongly naturalistic pottery sculptures of central Veracruz.

Along with a number of pottery vessels of imitation Thin Orange form and paste and a small spout-handled jar (Figure 193) of the kind Caso found at

195. Vessels of "domestic" Thin Orange from Huajuapan. *Frissell collection.*

196. A Teotihuacan-Guerrero-style figurine made of a stone resembling that ground up for temper in variants of Thin Orange.

197. Solid pottery head (fragment), made of extremely coarse-grained Thin Orange paste; from Huajuapan. *Frissell collection, courtesy of Manuel Mejía G.*

198. Beads(?) from Tequixtepec. The stone seems to be the same kind ground for use as temper some kinds of Thin Orange pottery. *Frissell collection.*

200. Another *cabecita colosal* in the Frissell collection. This one shows evidence of tooth filing.

199. A *cabecita colosal* in the Frissell collection. These are not fragments, but are complete as heads alone.

201. A *cabecita colosal* in the collection of Howard Leigh, Mitla.

202. A variant of the *cabecita colosal*. Frissell collection.

203. *Cabecitas colosales* in the storerooms of the MNA.

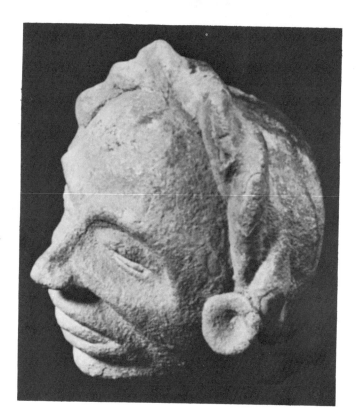

204. Like all the other known examples, this *cabecita colosal* is said to come from the region of Acatlan, Puebla; even those reported from Guerrero come from an area close to Acatlan. *Frissell collection.*

205. Another view of the head shown in Figure 204.

206. A similar head. *Howard Leigh collection.*

207. *Cabecitas colosales* exhibited in the MNA.

Yucuñudahui, I once bought in Huajuapan a slab of plain, dark grey, onyx-like stone, polished on one side, which was said to have formed a part of the lining of a small tomb in which the pottery was found. This trait may be of little importance, and so far as I know it extends from Huajuapan into the Mixteca Alta rather than over the Mixteca Baja or Ñuiñe. In excavations at nearby Tamazulapan (in the Mixteca Alta), Bernal and his students found two fragments of this same polished stone.

But any complex of traits at a given time and place is made up of this kind of intersection of numerous more or less continuously varying characteristics. Extending in the opposite direction from Huajuapan is an unusual way of making floors. At first glance, these floors look like abnormally thick examples of the common "stucco" or lime cement floor of Mesoamerica. At southern Puebla sites, and at a site I know near Huajuapan where imitation Thin Orange is abundant and Mixteca-Puebla pottery seemingly absent, these very thick floors are strikingly distinctive. They are made of ground *tepetate*, a calcareous hardpan that is common in the Mixteca Alta as well as in the Ñuiñe. (In the Mixteca Alta *tepetate* is often cut into blocks and used in construction; it is soft when fresh but hardens on exposure to air.)

Many important carved stones, of a style clearly earlier than the Mixteca-Puebla, occur in the Ñuiñe. Only some forty of these stones have so far been discovered, but they are sufficient to establish the existence in the Ñuiñe of a significant regional division of Early Urban Mesoamerica. Some of these stones were originally thought of as manifestations of either Teotihuacan or Monte Albán culture. Recent discoveries make it clear that they are neither. The beautiful long stone (Figure 208), apparently a lintel, that was recently removed from Huajuapan to a place of honor in the Museo Nacional, was presented in a drawing by Caso (1937) as illustrating Teotihuacan calendar glyphs. In 1956 he published another drawing of it, and one of the Miltepec stone (Figure 210), noting that these and other carved stones in the Mixteca are somewhat different from those of Monte Albán but that they use the bar to represent 5, unlike the later Mixtec codices (Caso, 1956a). As typical Ñuiñe artworks, the Huajuapan and Miltepec stones have debts to both Teotihuacan and Monte Albán, but they fall clearly and completely within the style of neither metropolis. (See also Figure 233.)

In spite of the large-scale excavations at Teotihuacan under Mexican government auspices during the early 1960's, no stone stelae such as those of the Gulf coast, Monte Albán, or the Maya region have been found there. Isolated glyphs occur at Teotihuacan on pottery and on painted walls, but Caso had to go as far afield as Huajuapan to find a true calendric inscription on stone in what he then quite naturally considered to be Teotihuacan style. In view of Caso's unsurpassed knowledge of Mesoamerican writing, his comment in 1963 upon first seeing photographs of the Ñuiñe stelae is of considerable interest. After pointing out several traits they share with the Monte Albán stelae, a glyph in La Venta style, and some Teotihuacan stylistic traits, he concluded, "This is a new glyphic system."

At several villages to the northeast of Huajuapan, along the road to Tehuacan, handsome examples of Ñuiñe stone carving are to be found (Figures 209–12). The largest number are at Tequixtepec, and one of these alone (Figure 213)[7] is almost enough to make one suspect that an Early Urban regional style of importance might be found here. According to those (Carmen Cook, Don Leonard, Fredrick Peterson, and MacNeish) who have visited the archeological site from which the stones were brought down to the modern town of Tequixtepec (Figures 214–25), the ancient settlement had a number of buildings made of well-cut stone. Late Teotihuacan figurines (periods III and IV) have been found on the surface of the site, and are said by Peterson to be true Teotihuacan examples rather than simply figurines having a resemblance to those of Teotihuacan.

However, it was a ceramic rather than a stone sculpture that finally forced us to confront the problem of whether there does really exist in the Ñuiñe a major "Classic" regional style. Starting in 1955, I had paid regular visits to an archeological site near Huajuapan whose inhabitants, while plowing land or building houses, occasionally came upon burials having interesting offerings. In the course of a dozen or so visits, I bought many whole or fragmentary pottery objects, most of them in the common shapes of Thin Orange but coarser in quality than the "export" Thin Orange found at Teotihuacan. Although the paste composition of these objects is similar to that of the Ixcaquixtla product, their color is distinctive; the orange is often more or less clouded with grey, and in some cases wholly greyed. That this darkening was at times the result of a controlled reduction is revealed in the fact that the glossy black of the vessel in Figure 193 was produced with the same apparently local paste. Besides the specimens I acquired by purchase at Huajuapan, I picked up many sherds on the surface of the site that have the same characteristics.

In April 1962, on a routine visit to the site, I was offered for sale a most extraordinary vessel, which we may perhaps call an urn (Figure 226). Since its combination of traits was completely without precedent, my first reaction—like that of many who have seen it since—was that it must be a fake. Close inspection revealed that it was not. It is made of the same near-Thin Orange that I have acquired over the years at the same site. Caso and Bernal, who inspected it in Mitla the following day, agreed on its startling unfamiliarity of style and its authentic age. They estimate, on the basis of its resemblance to known styles, that it is of late "Classic" origin.

The Huajuapan urn in some ways resembles the elaborate *braseros* or incense burners of late Teotihuacan: it is made of stamped-out flat ceramic

---

[7] A photograph of this stone has been published by Carmen Cook (1960: 360) as an illustration to an article on another topic.

Text continued on p. 193

208. The lintel of Huajuapan (now in the MNA) as it was displayed in Huajuapan's civic center.

209. One of the Huajuapan carvings, now in the MNA. *Drawing by Carolyn B. Harris, after a sketch by Alfonso Caso.*

210. A Ñuiñe stone now built into the rectory at Miltepec. Only the 5-bars, a pan-Mesoamerican trait, and the trilobed ornament at the left are shared with Monte Albán carvings.

211. Fragment of a Ñuiñe stone; Huapanapan.

212. A carved Ñuiñe stone preserved in the municipal building at Huajuapan. The circular element is one of the distinctive Ñuiñe traits; Mesoamerican glyphic cartouches are usually rectangular, frequently rounded at the corners.

213. Two views of the Ñuiñe stone first
published by Carmen Cook. *Left:* as it stands
in the public square of Tequixtepec.
Below: in its original position. It may represent
a conquest scene: a personage whose name
is expressed in the circular cartouche and the
numeral 11 below it is shown striking a human figure
with a club held in the hand emerging from the
right side of the cartouche. The falling personage
lies across a place-mountain glyph exactly like
those used on the Monte Albán stelae.

214. Stone in a Tequixtepec home. Feather-crested tiger on place glyph, left, utters twice the name of 1 Flint, or perhaps declares war in words as cutting as flint knives.

215. Stone in the plaza, Tequixtepec; note two flint(?) signs, lower left; Olmecoid glyph, lower right; complete divided glyph C, with teeth, center.

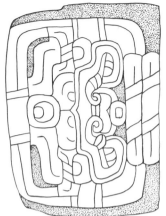

216. Stone in the Tequixtepec plaza. Because of the complexity of its inscription and the erosion of the already shallow carving, interpretation is very difficult. The drawing, by Charles Wicke, will be of assistance. The numeral at the bottom, in which the two 5-bars are plain, might represent 11 if the circular element above belongs with the bars. The large symmetrical element above the numeral somehow suggests an earth monster.

218. A Tequixtepec plaza stone. Resting on the two 5-bars at bottom are what might be the bases of a sun-ray, part of the late Mixtec year glyph, as well as a possible numeral 1. The central cartouche may contain (sideways) a temple or house; at top is a representation of flowing water.

217. Another stone in the Tequixtepec public square. The top third appears to be occupied by a group combining the bowknot known from Teotihuacan and Monte Albán with, perhaps, a local form of year glyph. The center third is 5 Flower. The bottom third is a place glyph shown as a pyramid with stairs in the middle.

189

219. Two views of a Tequixtepec stone that has two carved and two plain sides, as if it had been carved this way to be used in a corner. *Left*: on this side a rabbit(?) is shown in the upper right corner. *Right*: the adjoining side; 3 Monkey is identifiable here.

220. Another Tequixtepec stone with two adjoining carved faces.
Above: One face shows the two flint(?) glyphs so frequent here, and a hand
extending from the cartouche holds a decorated object that doubles
over and hangs. *Right:* Glyph C with teeth, a 5-bar,
and a serpent(?) appear on the other face.

221. A Tequixtepec stone, now in a house in Tehuacan,
with a hand extending from the cartouche and holding
a hanging decorative object;
compare Figures 220 (left) and 233.

222. Stone built into a house wall, Tequixtepec.

223. Another stone incorporated into a Tequixtepec house.

224. Stone effigies in Tequixtepec: those at upper left
and lower right seem to be
complete, the one at lower
left a fragment; the effigy
at upper right is a vessel.

225. Tequixtepec pottery objects: a potstand of polished grey ware, a head of coarse Thin Orange–like paste,
and a polished cream bowl with red-painted rim and interior incising. *Frissell collection.*

pieces of symbolic forms, assembled on a tubular framework (Figure 227) and including a representation of a human.[8] Moreover, unlike the Teotihuacan *braseros,* but like the Monte Albán "funerary urns," the Huajuapan urn has a large vessel on the back. (Those of Monte Albán are always found empty; the Huajuapan urn was full of fine ash.) All these resemblances, however, are purely general and do not extend to the specific elements of which the urn is made up.

Unlike the Teotihuacan *braseros,* which bear only human faces, the Huajuapan urn has a partial representation of the body as well. The Teotihuacan *brasero* masks, which are often of extraordinary beauty in the austere Teotihuacan style, seem all to be representations of young (or at least unwrinkled) persons. By contrast, the Huajuapan urn shows us a strikingly wrinkled personage, apparently male (Figure 229).

This old man wears a headdress of great complexity (Figure 228). The semicircular element at the rear no doubt is the feather crest so common throughout Mesoamerica. The tiger apparently forms a part of the headdress, the forward part of his body projecting out over the man's head. The tiger as represented here would not be wholly out of place at Monte Albán, although such tiger figures are very common in the Mixteca also. Necklaces of shells are worn by both the tiger and the man, and a double string of them also encircles the man's head. Feathers are more familiar for this headband, but these seem much more likely to be shells.

The old man's right arm (along with the right side of the glyphic element below it) is missing; the break seems to be ancient. In his hands he is holding a cartouche that has the day sign Dog (Caso's interpretation) inside, and the numeral 9 below. Approximately where the old man's feet and lower legs would be if they were shown, a glyphic element having the form of a vessel in cross section rises far enough to enclose the 5-bar. This "vessel" seems to be made of a pottery version of what might well be the common Mixtec codex representation of water, especially in the form of a river; and its intact left side terminates in a leaf. Both the leaf and the water signs occur at Monte Albán in connection with the Zapotec glyph C, as Leigh explains below (pp. 257–61). The four elements, two on each side, that enclose the old man are identical except that the color of the pottery varies from orange to dark grey. They look very much like representations of flowing water, each having also a leaf.

[8] The use of stamped-out elements in assembling elaborate symbolic sculptures in pottery is common to Teotihuacan III–IV and Monte Albán IIIb, which is the major reason for assigning the Huajuapan urn to the late phases of Early Urban times. A large stela found in Río Grande, on the Pacific coast of Oaxaca, also has a human figure, which is apparently being embraced from above and behind by a tiger (Figure 230). The Río Grande stela cannot as yet be confidently assigned to any known Mesoamerican culture, although there is some agreement that it has a relatively late (Xochicalco) glyph (Caso 1963a).

The "vessel" form of Zapotec glyph C seems to be repeated, upside down, in the complex figure that projects from the base of the urn. The numeral 7 is clear here, but interpretation of the remainder is very difficult. Caso suggested that the element above the numeral 7, in which a folded strip of cloth or paper seems to rise from and return into a cartouche form, might be a year sign; that is, he felt that this doubled-over strip might be a regional variant of the interlacing trapezoidal forms involved in the Teotihuacan and late Mixtec year signs. The same combination of the "vessel" form with parallel strips projecting from it and terminating in circles (jades?) may be seen, inverted (that is, right side up), on an unusual pottery vessel in the British Museum for which no provenience is known (Figure 231).

Faint traces of a watery black painted decoration appear in vertical lines on the rectangular base of the Huajuapan urn. There are traces also of a white coating on the glyph 9 Dog. Careful cleaning might reveal more evidence of painted decoration, but since it would also remove some of the evidences of authenticity that the piece probably still needs, it has not been attempted.

The dental mutilation so plainly shown by the old man seems to be of type B-4 in the Romero classification; its appearance suggests that it may be combined with type A-4. Type A-4 is known most commonly from the Maya region, although examples from Tlatilco and Xochicalco are listed by Romero as well. Type B-4 has been found at Monte Albán in a late "Classic" context that accords with the chronological placement suggested by the use of molds in making the Huajuapan urn. The combination of A-4 and B-4 has been found, it appears, only in the Maya region if at all. However, it is not entirely clear that such a combination is represented on the urn.

A pottery sculpture of an old man having some rather striking similarities of detail has been illustrated by Caso and Bernal in *Urnas de Oaxaca*, Figure 329. This piece, which is in the Museo Nacional of Mexico, is recorded as having come from Huapanapan—a town on the Huajuapan-Tehuacan road. The Oaxaca collections of the Museo Nacional yield only a few other pieces from the same region; nearly all of them are foreign to any previously defined Mesoamerican style (for example, see Figures 232, 234, and 235).

But was there, in this now very dry and impoverished region, a social apparatus capable of producing a Mesoamerican "Classic" regional style worthy of the name? We have long thought of the Mixteca as lacking truly urban architecture. Yet we now know many sites in the Mixteca where very large or very numerous constructions exist, notably Cuthá, Diquiyú, Quiotepec, Calipa, Venta Salada, Silacayoapan, Cerro Jazmín, and Cholula. Not all these are within the Ñuiñe, but most or all of them flourished in the time of the Ñuiñe style. Many other examples await discovery, and among places where there are strong indications of important settlements in the Ñuiñe region and period, we may mention Tequixtepec, Huajuapan, Acatlan, and possibly Silacayoapan. Finally, there are many known sites where architecture of relatively moderate scale exists. Both before and after the Ñuiñe style, the Mixteca emphatically was important.

Irrigation works have been found at over 150 sites in the Tehuacan Valley by MacNeish, Peterson, and Neely. Some of these are dated as "Classic"—that is, they are contemporary with the Ñuiñe style and in the immediately adjoining region. MacNeish says that there unquestionably did exist in the Ñuiñe a population and a social apparatus sufficient to account for the regional style. It may be observed here that irrigation probably gave the region a vastly different aspect in ancient times.

On the opposite side of the Ñuiñe, in the Mixteca Alta, contemporary phenomena again suggest that there is nothing incredible in the regional development we are examining. Yatachío, a relatively small and poor site near Tamazulapan, shows few or no traces of Teotihuacan connections,[9] with much stronger indications of Monte Albán influence and with abundant local or regional material not ascribable to contact with either metropolis. The important Tomb 1 of Yucuñudahui, mentioned previously, is known best for its half dozen pottery vessels in the general style of Monte Albán; but most of the vessels from this tomb are of a local or regional style that cannot be easily related to Monte Albán. Many of these "independent" pottery pieces of Yucuñudahui are strongly similar to the pottery of Huajuapan, San Juan Viejo (Diquiyú), and southernmost Puebla.

As Jiménez Moreno has pointed out, the Ñuiñe is a natural low-altitude corridor between the "Olmec" regions of the Atlantic side (La Venta) and the Pacific (Guerrero), adjoining the important southern Morelos-Itzocan "Olmec" area as well. No law of nature would prevent such a region from falling into relative eclipse for a few centuries, or returning to prominence later on. The Ñuiñe seems to have been eclipsed by Teotihuacan-Cholula on one side, and Monte Albán on the other, during the earlier phases of Early Urban times. Its return to importance, which was accompanied by the production of the Ñuiñe style, seems to be an event of late Teotihuacan times, perhaps extending into the years just after the abandonment of Teotihuacan.

There are several lines of evidence suggesting that a part of the population of Teotihuacan may have been made up of Mixtecs or their relatives, perhaps Chocho-Popolocas or Mazatecs. After they abandoned Teotihuacan in the

---

[9] What we interpreted as Teotihuacan connections (for example, Thin Orange pottery) in 1952 may now be considered Ñuiñe connections instead, at least in regions much closer to the Ñuiñe than to Teotihuacan. One wonders also about the objects discovered by Noguera in 1936 in a large, well-stocked tomb at Tehuacan, which were attributed at that time to Monte Albán and Teotihuacan. Although MacNeish suspects that at least architecturally and ceramically the Tehuacan Valley has long been distinguishable from the Mixteca, it might be illuminating to examine the Tehuacan offerings again in the light of recently increased knowledge. Perhaps, for example, some vessels with a Monte Albán-like appearance could be shown through laboratory analysis to have been made in the Mixteca and the Tehuacan Valley itself.

Text continued on p. 200

226. The Huajuapan urn. *Frissell collection.*

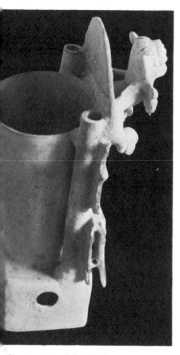

Construction of the Huajuapan urn.

228. Headdress of Huajuapan urn figure.

The face of the old man on the Huajuapan urn.

230. Stela of Río Grande, Oaxaca. *MNA.*

231. *Above:* pottery vessel of unknown provenience. *Below:* a detail. *British Museum.*

232. Two figurines from Huapanapan. *MNA.*

233. Bancroft's copy of the Dupaix drawing of a Ñuiñ stone in Huajuapan. Dupa drawing shows clearly a h extending from the cartou the running water glyph is like that of Figure 218. Present whereabouts unkr

198

34. The god with mouth-mask of a
serpent; a small vessel having the form
of a Valley of Oaxaca urn, but made
of coarse Thin Orange–like paste
with micaceous temper and coming from
Acatlan, Puebla. The crossed bands
on the forehead appear on some Monte
Albán II urns. A third projecting
decoration at the top center of the
headdress is missing.

35. A small Ñuiñe triple effigy vessel of coarse micaceous Thin Orange–like paste. Each of the grotesque faces has
a headdress made of the glyph C, complete with teeth below and flowing water above (see Leigh paper below, Figures 26, 54).
Grissell collection, courtesy of José Luis Franco.

seventh century A.D., these people might well have resettled with others who spoke their own language—in Cholula, the Ñuiñe, and the Mixteca Alta. They would obviously bring with them metropolitan ways and objects, including the Teotihuacan III and IV figurines Peterson reported finding at Tequixtepec.

Such speculations are perhaps idle until we know more, and yet they have a kind of inevitability. The existence of a style such as the Ñuiñe is almost demanded by what we know. The Mixteca-Puebla style, which in a sense spread throughout Mesoamerica in Late Urban times, must have an origin; yet we have had no inkling of how it developed, or from what materials. We know when: between the fall of Teotihuacan and the rise of Tula, or in Ñuiñe times. We know where: very probably in the Mixtec region, and preferably on the Cholula side of that region. The Ñuiñe is the indicated place. As a post-Teotihuacan repository of Teotihuacan skills, it would have had the materials.

LATE URBANISM: THE MIXTEC CITY-STATES

In order to discuss the events of Late Urban times in the region now called the Mixteca, we need a new name for the group of peoples that includes the Mixtecs proper and their neighboring linguistic and cultural relatives such as the Chocho-Popolocas, Mazatecs, Chinantecs, Cuicatecs, Ichcatecs, Amusgos, and Triques; but that excludes the also neighboring and fairly closely related Zapotecs and the remoter although still related Pame-Otomí and Mangue-Chiapanec peoples. I propose to call this group the Tetlamixteca.[10] Although the geographic and general cultural nearness of the Tetlamixteca conforms only imperfectly to the pattern of linguistic relationships among them, that is a normal consequence of their recent changes of homes and of dominance.

Especially with respect to certain of the Mixtec city-states, we know much more about the Late Urban period in the Mixteca than we do about previous periods. Our knowledge is due largely to the existence of several Mixtec historical manuscripts, which Caso has read and shown to be accurate (Figures 236–40 and Plates 5–12). We also have references to the places and peoples concerned in the chronicles and archives of the sixteenth century. In a purely archeological sense, we have only scattered data on the Tetlamixteca in Late Urban times.

Jiménez Moreno has begun the discussion of our topic in Part I when he speaks of the abandonment of Teotihuacan and the scattering of its inhabitants, probably including some Tetlamixteca (whom he identifies tentatively as Mazatecs and Chocho-Popolocas). Although he traces in detail his hypothesis of the Nahuat-Pipil migrations to the Gulf coast and on to Central America, he provides only a few sentences, dense with provocative leads, on the Tetlamixteca refugees of Teotihuacan and their probable flight to the Mix-

10 "Tetla-" is a Nahuatl prefix indicating nearness. The only alternative, "para-Mixtec," seems to me even less attractive.

teca to join their relatives there. In Part III below there are relatively detailed considerations from several viewpoints of some consequences in the Valley of Oaxaca of these events in the Mixteca.

Why is it proposed here that Late Urbanism begins in the Mixtec region, and not—for instance—in the Valley of Mexico with the abandonment of Teotihuacan? Primarily because all available evidence points strongly to a loss of cultural leadership in the Valley of Mexico, beginning with the dispersal of the Teotihuacanos and ending only with the Spanish conquest. Although the Valley of Mexico did indeed return to *political* leadership during Late Urban times and especially with the Aztecs, this should not be confused with overall cultural leadership.

Late Urbanism as here conceived involves more than a transfer of political power from the theocracies of the Early Urban to the military of the Late; it involves also a reformulation of Mesoamerican culture. To judge from the extreme, almost incredible poverty of the architectural remains left over the ruins of late Teotihuacan by the people (presumably Toltecs) who also left Coyotlatelco and Mazapan pottery there, these rude folk were no cultural innovators. During that same period in the Mixteca and Cholula, then a Tetlamixteca city, the central artistic ideas of Mixteca-Puebla culture were appearing. By the time the Toltecs had learned enough to build Tula, they had made historically recorded (and archeologically confirmed) alliances with the anciently rooted, sophisticated Tetlamixteca.

The construction of Indian America's most massive building, the great pyramid of Cholula, seems to have been carried out precisely during the time when Cholula was a Tetlamixteca metropolis. This same period is that of the appearance at Cholula of the finest polychrome pottery. The art style that spread to the farthest corners of Mesoamerica—Tamuín, in the Huasteca; Guasave, in Sinaloa; Santa Rita, in British Honduras—in the Late Urban period emphatically is a Mixteca-Puebla phenomenon, as Vaillant and Caso proposed, and not a Toltec one. Right up to the Conquest the Tetlamixteca remained leaders in a cultural sense, and the Valley of Mexico Nahuas, for all their military-political dominance, remained willing followers.

Other Mesoamericans may have been militarists as early as the Mixtecs; the Huastecs, for instance, are a possibility. But the combination of militarism with leadership in the Mixteca-Puebla cultural style seems to be attributable first to the Mixtecs. We may appeal here to the histories kept by the Mixtecs themselves.

The codices studied by Caso refer to many towns, far from completely identified as yet, throughout the Tetlamixteca region. The ruling dynasties of the sixteenth century were recorded in Spanish archives as Mixtec speakers, and these dynasties are traceable in the codices for several centuries before the Conquest; in at least one case the First Dynasty (meaning the first Mixtec dynasty) was founded before A.D. 700. No doubt there are many references to the non-Mixtec peoples of the Tetlamixteca group in these codices, but at present we do not know how to identify them. Many towns that appear in the codices in various relationships to the principal ruling dynasties are also still to be identified. Those whose name glyphs are already known are clustered in the Mixteca Alta, not very far from the Valley of Oaxaca. The prehispanic codices thus have contributed rather little to our knowledge of the Ñuiñe up to now, although future investigations may alter this state of affairs. Certainly early postconquest documents abound with data—still very little studied—on the Ñuiñe in Late Urban times.

The famous Mixtec conqueror 8 Deer "Tiger Claw," who ruled from Tilantongo, may be seen as an early example of Late Urban militarism. Born in A.D. 1011, he died sacrificed in 1063 (Caso suggests that he may have been sacrificed at Cuilapan in the Valley of Oaxaca). For some years it has been clear that 8 Deer "Tiger Claw" brought all or nearly all of the Mixteca Alta under one rule. The many small city-states involved were linked by a combination of conquest, alliance, and strategic marriage. Now we know in addition that 8 Deer's dominion extended to the Pacific, where he governed the Coast Mixtec province of Tututepec. The inevitable and important questions aroused by this discovery (which we owe to Mary Elizabeth Smith) are whether 8 Deer's dominions also extended over the Ñuiñe and perhaps even on to Cholula and the Tehuacan Valley; and whether he began the Tetlamixteca invasions of the Valley of Oaxaca.[11]

In Caso's expositions of the historical content of Codices Bodley and Selden II, as well as in a number of shorter works, he has provided us with a detailed picture of the political system of the Mixteca Alta in Late Urban times. Religion, mythology, kinship, marriage, military force, alliance, economic power, and no doubt other factors as well all were integrated into a constantly shifting political system, a system that at any given moment encompassed many, though probably never all, of the small dominions of the Tetlamixteca region.

Ethnic relationships in the region probably were more complex in preconquest times than today. Within the larger Tetlamixteca group Mixtec speakers today are an overwhelming majority, but in Early Urban times the Mixtecs

---

11 Of interest here is the relation, if any, of 8 Deer "Tiger Claw" to the handsome Stela 4 of Monte Albán (Figure 149, p. 148), which shows a man named 8 Deer standing on a place glyph and thrusting a lance into it as if in sign of conquest. There are several grounds for doubting that Stela 4 shows a conquest by 8 Deer "Tiger Claw." First, since there are only 260 possible calendric names, approximately one of every 260 persons born in Oaxaca necessarily was named 8 Deer. There was a Mixtec ruler, in fact, at Yanhuitlan in the early fifteenth century who was named 8 Deer "Fire Serpent"; and there may well have existed also a Zapotec 8 Deer who is shown on Stela 4. Second, there is no sign of the surname "Tiger Claw" on the stela, although the personage shown on it wears a tiger's head as the centerpiece of his necklace. Finally, it is probable on stylistic grounds that the stela antedates the birth of 8 Deer "Tiger Claw," perhaps by as much as several centuries. See Caso and Smith (in press) and Smith (1963: 276–88).

Text continued on p. 209

Woman spinning; Codex Vindobonensis, p. 9.

237. Ritual bath using typical Mixtec pitcher;
Codex Vindobonensis, p. 12.

. Use of fire drill; Codex Vindobonensis, p. 12.

239. Priest offering decapitated bird;
Codex Vindobonensis, p. 18.

. Procession: man playing shell bugle, man carrying torch, woman carrying incense burner;
lex Vindobonensis, p. 18.

241. Mixtec *penates* (greenstone figurines). Some represent the rain–lightning god Dzahui, but many are small images of a dead man bundled up for burial, seated in Mixtec fashion; these were buried with the dead. *MNA.*

242. Large *penate* in form of rain god. *MNA.*

243. Small *penate* from Tehuantepec.

244. Black bowl of a typical Mixtec shape. *MNA.*

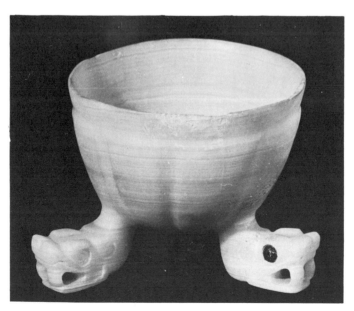

245. Stone bowl with serpent in Mixtec style. *MNA.*

. Stone plaque illustrating Mixtec technique
sing only tubular drill and straight saw. *MNA.*

247. The Lápida de Tlaxiaco: the moon, with rabbit
(not man) seen on its face. *MNA.*

. The Lápida de Tilantongo: the lord 5 Death. *MNA.*

249. Decorated miniature vessel of unknown use.

250. Life and death? From Soyaltepec. *MNA.*

251. Ladle of a kind very common in the Mixteca.

252. Man with spearthrower and shield; a whistling vessel. Graphite decoration on polished orange-red, a common Mixtec ware of Monte Albán V. *MNA.*

253. Woman wearing *quechquémitl*, pain white and polychromed after firing.

254. Polychrome pitcher decorated with shells and butterflies with tiger heads.

255. Kneeling man; Tomb 13, Yagul. Orange-red polished slip over cream paste, graphite decoration. *Museo Regional, Oaxaca.*

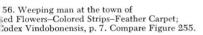

256. Weeping man at the town of Red Flowers–Colored Strips–Feather Carpet; Codex Vindobonensis, p. 7. Compare Figure 255.

257. Miniature polychrome animal effigies. *Frissell collection.*

259. Typical pear-shaped olla of Huitzo Polished Cream.

258. Effigy vessel with a Mixtec-style mouth, made of Plumbate, a ware exported from Guatemala to all parts of Mesoamerica around A.D. 1000. *Frissell collection.*

260. Bowl of Huitzo Polished Cream; the painted decoration is red-brown. Graphite paint and incision also appear at times on this pottery.

261. Huitzo Polished Cream o

262. Huitzo Polished Crea
bowls. Except at Huitzo,
this pottery is extremely
rare in the Valley of
Oaxaca, and seems to com
from the adjoining area
(Sosola?) of the Mixteca.

208

263. Polychrome animal (deer?) head. *MNA.*

may have been only one among several more or less equal ethnic groups. The great mass of Mixtecs at that time probably lived well north of Oaxaca—Early Urban Cholula would be the probable capital. In the Tetlamixteca region of Oaxaca the Mixtecs did not dominate either numerically or otherwise.

When the Otomí and Nahua groups of north central Mesoamerica began to press successfully southward at the end of the Early Urban period, one consequence was similar pressure from the Mixtecs in the Tetlamixteca region of Oaxaca, and ultimately in the Valley of Oaxaca as well. In some cases there was a Mixtec ethnic invasion, resulting in the foundation of new towns or the displacement of non-Mixtecs from old towns; in other cases non-Mixtec towns were brought under the domination of a Mixtec ruling caste, installed either locally or elsewhere (see below, pp. 314–35 and 367–85). By the device of political marriage, daughters of non-Mixtec local ruling families were taken into this Mixtec conquering caste, where they learned the Mixtec language and produced Mixtec-speaking children. Although their sons might enjoy relatively strong claims to power, these ladies themselves often lived more or less as hostages.

Seen as it is today, the Tetlamixteca region is emphatically not one over which we can readily imagine these petty dynasties scheming, fighting, and marrying for centuries; but we must remember that it was referred to as a rich area by those who saw it soon after the Spanish conquest (see pp. 369–70 below). The wealth of its ruling classes is relatively well known from the codices, from the sixteenth-century chronicles and the Aztec tribute rolls, and from such finds as Tomb 7 of Monte Albán and Tombs 1 and 2 of Zaachila (see pp. 336–44 below). The way of life typical of the ordinary citizen of these times remains almost completely unknown. The site that provides most of our archeological data is Yagul, but its situation in the traditionally Zapotec Valley of Oaxaca is rather special, and only the study of comparable sites in the Tetlamixteca zone will enable us to distinguish late Tetlamixteca culture with confidence from late Zapotec culture.

LATE URBANISM IN THE ZAPOTEC WORLD: MONTE ALBÁN IV

We should be cautious in speaking of Late Urbanism among the Zapotecs— at least those of the Valley of Oaxaca—because their Early Urban ways tended to persist, at the expense of Late Urban alternatives, right down to the Spanish conquest. This persistence, whatever its cause, accounts for the sharp contrast of their culture with that of the neighboring and distantly related Tetlamixteca peoples. As we have seen, the Tetlamixteca were probably the first Late Urban people in Mesoamerica; their culture had been Late Urban for centuries by the time they invaded the Valley of Oaxaca. Nahua peoples such as the Toltec-Chichimecs or Aztecs, having arrived on the scene late, never had an Early Urban phase at all. It would almost seem that the Oaxaca peoples, old in the ways of Mesoamerican civilization, had to decline to Late Urbanism, while the latecomers of Nahua speech had to rise to it.

From the abandonment of Monte Albán as a functioning city during the tenth century until the Spanish conquest, the culture of the Valley Zapotecs is called Monte Albán IV; but it was in fact an unbroken continuation of IIIb in most ways, including the slow decline that had set in long before (Figures 264–70). No metropolis replaced Monte Albán; there was, then, no Zapotec metropolis at all after Monte Albán IIIb, and the Zapotec situation came to resemble more the Mixtec one, with many small cities subjected only to rather ephemeral unification. The only known effort to establish a new Zapotec state was the legendary, and still archeologically unproven, political centralization upon Zaachila. And at the time of this movement, there was a certain disunity even in the Valley of Oaxaca; for despite Zaachila's political ambitions, religious power was concentrated at Mitla, and the Zapotec government in exile at Tehuantepec (at the high tide of Tetlamixteca invasion) concerned itself more with Mitla than with Zaachila.[12]

Monte Albán IIIb–IV apparently had very little direct contact with the rest of Mesoamerica until the Tetlamixteca, including the Mixtecs proper, and later the Aztecs, irrupted upon the scene. Before these invasions there seems to have been some military activity in Zapotec territory, but perhaps only of a local or small-scale nature. If the inscriptions of Monte Albán II may not refer to conflicts at all, the stelae of period III unquestionably do. At the time of the early Spanish chroniclers, the Valley Zapotecs were re-

---

[12] A recent linguistic study adds a point of interest here. The dialect of Zapotec spoken in the Isthmus of Tehuantepec has now reached a degree of differentiation suggesting a minimum separation of five centuries from the other speakers of the language, and the Valley dialect to which the Isthmus one shows the closest relationship is that of Mitla.

corded as having been long in conflict with the Mixes, and the Isthmus Zapotecs with the Mixes, Zoques, and Huaves, who had once dominated in Tehuantepec. The time dimension in these chronicles is highly unreliable, however, and we cannot be sure whether these Zapotec invasions of the Mixe region and the Isthmus antedate the Tetlamixteca invasions of the Valley of Oaxaca. The linguistic study discussed in note 12 suggests that they do not, for a similar study gave a similar date for the separation of Cuilapan Mixtecs in the Valley of Oaxaca from the main body of Mixtec speakers.

Whether or not military activities had something to do with the abandonment of Monte Albán in some indirect way—for as we have seen, there is no evidence of fighting there—the fact and the approximate time of its becoming a ghost city are well established. At this time there probably was a sudden strong increase in the population of the small Valley cities, but they have as yet been little studied from this point of view.

Mitla, as Bernal shows, was not then as we see it now, centered upon a group of splendid palaces north of the river. Its center was instead south of the river, marked by groups not of palaces but of temple-crowned pyramids. Both the pyramids of period IV and the palaces of V are represented on the top of a heavily fortified hill outside the city. Wherever there is a gap in the cliffs that protect most of its perimeter, the hilltop is closed off by massive stone walls (Figure 271); the only remaining entrance is a long passage between two of the walls. Mitla itself is exposed, built on a gentle slope. That such a fortress should become a part of the community and should bear remains only of the late periods—as it seems to do—is more than suggestive of the rise of militarism.

Separated from the fortress of Mitla by a large, barren hill and a mile or two of open fields is another hill of extraordinarily similar form, that of Yagul. The Yagul hill is larger than the hill of the Mitla fortress, and the small city is compactly placed on its lower slopes, just below the fortress itself (Figures 272–74). The hilltop fortress is nearly identical with that of Mitla, and the identity of parts of the Yagul and Mitla palaces is almost complete (see pp. 351–59).

As early as Monte Albán II, on ceramic evidence, the Yagul-Mitla area had a certain identity of its own that distinguished it from Monte Albán and the rest of the Valley. The concentration of religious power at Mitla in the political heyday of Zaachila may therefore have been a reflection of an already ancient tendency. Tlacolula, as the locale of one of Mexico's largest Indian markets, and Mitla, as a Zapotec traditional holy place, are as important today among the Indian population of the Valley as the more central Oaxaca and Zaachila.

Just as the present-day towns of Tlacolula, Mitla, and Matatlan form a compact and intimately related group at the eastern terminus of the Tlacolula Valley, the ancient sites of Yagul, Caballito Blanco, Lambityeco, Loma

Larga, Mitla, and Matatlan ought to be regarded as possibly having been interrelated in ancient times. Unlike Monte Albán, the area has clear remains of very ancient preceramic occupation. In Monte Albán I at least Yagul and Mitla were inhabited, although they were very small places compared to Monte Albán. Monte Albán II is represented, but it may be that Transición II–III is more important in the Mitla area. At this time Matatlan, Caballito Blanco, Loma Larga, and perhaps Mitla and Yagul apparently experienced a local boom, with abundant production of quite special ceramics of a sort very rare at Monte Albán. The rich tomb found by Martín Bazán at Loma Larga made it the type site for Transición II–III. At Caballito Blanco Mound O, a simplified miniature of Monte Albán Mound J—the Observatory —was built, collapsed, and was rebuilt with enlargements.

At Yagul there is little indication of activity during these times, and it may be that the community for some reason transferred its center to Caballito Blanco, several hundred yards away. Similarly, the occupation of Caballito Blanco appears to have ended, at least as regards construction of public buildings, at the beginning of Monte Albán III; and it seems possible that the community simply moved on to nearby Lambityeco, which shows no evidence of occupation before Monte Albán III.

Of Lambityeco's two or three dozen mounds (they cannot be counted exactly because some of them lie in Tlacolula and have been damaged or even leveled), the only one that has been excavated archeologically lies at the outer edge of the group. It may well therefore represent a construction carried out at the peak of the community's population. Its period seems to be IIIb and early IV, with only doubtful indications of IIIa and a striking absence of V. Some fragments of pottery found at its base have been identified by Robert E. Smith as Balancán Fine Orange, a Toltec-period product of the Gulf coast lowlands.

At just about the time of the abandonment of Lambityeco, around the end of IIIb and the beginning of IV, there was a great building boom at Yagul (Figure 275). Coinciding as it seems to with the beginning of building at the Mitla fortress, this suggests a general movement to fortified and naturally defensible sites, a local reflection of a change occurring throughout Mesoamerica.

The Fine Orange imports of Lambityeco and other specimens excavated at Yagul combine with the local production of imitations to tell us of an awakening interest in other regions. In most respects, Caso and Bernal have found in Valley pottery development no clear reflection of the abandonment of Monte Albán or the occupation, apparently not much later, of fortified hilltop sites. Thus the evolution of many ceramic forms arrives finally at a period designated simply as IIIb–IV. However, a few forms are known to occur in IV only. One of these is the bat-claw vase (Figure 276), a small conical tumbler with claws obviously very distinct from the tiger-claw representations on earlier forms. The nearly life-size pottery figure of Xipe found by Linné in an early Toltec deposit over the ruins of Teotihuacan years ago is holding exactly such a bat-claw vase in one hand.

Inscriptions on stone seem to show a new development in period IV: the simpler inscriptions of period III, made with combinations of symbols and figures that are very large relative to the stone surfaces on which they are carved, give way in period IV to the use of smaller stones covered with much more finely carved scenes including considerably more detail (Figures 283–85). Although this description might seem to suggest a Mixtec influence, the elements themselves are clearly distinct from those found in Mixtec inscriptions. (A very few carved stones are known that may represent a Zapotec-Mixtec cultural mixture, but neither their provenience nor their time can be placed with any exactness.) The Zapotec stones carved in period IV seem designed to be viewed from much nearer than those of period III. Since no city of period IV was comparable in size to Monte Albán, which probably set the style in period III, this change may simply reflect the move to much smaller ceremonial precincts.

What little architecture tentatively assignable to period IV has been uncovered in the Valley has been the source of very slight illumination. As Bernal found at San Luis Beltrán, and as I found at Lambityeco, there is not much that could not be characterized as typical also of late Monte Albán. The buildings at San Luis Beltrán are less well constructed than those of Monte Albán, but San Luis is a small place and this difference would be expected even if there were no chronological difference. At Lambityeco some simple grecas have been added to a building that otherwise offers nothing new; but even the grecas had appeared very tentatively, in a primitive form, at Monte Albán. At Tlanechico and Cuilapan Bernal found nothing useful for period IV. Zaachila, which may eventually be the richest site for the period, has been equally frustrating. When in 1962 (after previous groups had been forced to flee for their lives in 1947 and 1953) a crew led by Roberto Gallegos and protected by soldiers did finally carry out some small-scale excavations there, the result was a rich and illuminating find—of period V (see pp. 314–35 below). Yagul, where there was surely an important occupation during IIIb and IV, is so completely covered with period V structures that it has been almost impossible to explore earlier remains there.

Mitla should be another rich source of data on period IV, but Caso's work (with Borbolla) in 1935 showed that the palace groups north of the river were begun in period V, that is, after the Tetlamixteca invasions. My own 1963 work in the Adobe Group indicated that it, too, was built in period V in an area previously unoccupied.[13]

---

[13] Whether these northern groups were built by the Tetlamixteca invaders, by the Zapotecs after a reconquest of Mitla, or by both peoples in some kind of forced or voluntary coexistence is not clear. Bernal's work in the present volume (pp. 346–51) is a step toward the clarification of ethnic relationships in this troubled period. Bittler's work at the Mitla fortress will add further data (Paddock 1965).

Text continued on p. 225

264. Urns all made from the same mold; Monte Albán IIIb–IV. *Frissell collection.*

265. *Hachas.* Although more common in Tehuantepec, examples have been found in Mitla and in the Monte Albán excavations. *Frissell collection.*

266. The goddess 2 J. *Frissell collection.*

267. Figurine of the goddess 13 Serpent.

268. The god of the glyph L. *Frissell collection.*

69. A stamped-out female figurine of IIIb–IV.

270. Whistle-figurine of IIIb–IV.

271. An exterior wall of the Mitla Fortress, showing how construction was combined with natural features.

272. Air view from the south of the Mitla Fortress.

273. Yagul in profile, seen from the east (near the Mitla Fortress).

274. Yagul from the air, from southwest to northeast; July 1964.

275. Tomb 28, Yagul. The carved stone door, pulled aside, forms the left side of the picture; across the top, in darkness, is the carved stone lintel of the doorway from the walled but unroofe exterior antechamber into the interior antechamber, whose floor is littered with stones left by ancient looters. The illuminated doorway, with its own carved lintel, leads into the main chamber of the tomb— which had been emptied long before the Spanish conquest.

276. One of the few forms peculiar to Monte Albán IV is the bat-claw vessel (left), accompanied here by a rare variant effigy.

277. Mold-made figurine of period IV.

278. Another diagnostic trait of period IV is the jar with a lid made to be tied on. *MNA*.

279. So badly made that he is almost unrecognizable is this warrior figurine, mold-made, painted white, then probably decorated in colors.

280. A very late, painted urn, judged to be of period IV. *Frissell collection.*

281. A typical figurine head of Monte Albán IV style from the Valley of Oaxaca; these are abundant at both Lambityeco and Yagul.

282. Warrior(?) with flint knife and shield. *Frissell collection.*

283. A period IV stone in a house at Matatlan. Glyph C, center top; man and woman (probably being married) in middle. Incomplete figures at bottom suggest the stone is incomplete.

284. Lápida 2 of the MNA, left, has a glyph C at top and two apparent marriage scenes in the panels below. The incomplete Lápida 3, below, is virtually the same except for identities of the personages involved and, no doubt, date and place.

285. Period IV stone from Cuilapan, exhibited in the Museo Regional de Oaxaca. Although it obviously contains an abundance of detail, probably historical in large part, no one is able to read it as Caso has read the Mixtec codices. For a contemporary Mixtec stone carving, see Figure 248.

86. A building complex at Guiengola that is much like Systems M and IV of Monte Albán.
At this mountain site in Tehuantepec, the short-lived Zapotec-Mixtec alliance
inflicted a costly defeat on the Aztecs in the late fifteenth century.

287. One of the Guiengola pyramids, with much of its original plaster covering still in place.

288. A building complex at Guiengola, showing how small terraces at various places on the mountain were adapted to construction.

289. A "false mosaic" greca stone at Guiengola. This kind of carving, in place of the usual Mitla mosaic, was used on Tomb 30 at Yagul (see Wicke article below) and for lintels and other elements where mosaic construction was impossible for technical reasons at both Mitla and Yagul.

In spite of all the difficulties, we have some fairly solid starting points from which to begin constructing a picture of life in period IV. First of all, we may clear away an obvious doubt that is certain to arise. Since there was a massive Tetlamixteca invasion of the Valley, and most of the towns in the Etla and Tlacolula Valleys were subjugated if not populated by the invaders, how do we know Monte Albán IV culture was not simply cut off and replaced by the Monte Albán V culture of the Tetlamixteca? The answer is conclusive: Fray Juan de Córdova was able not only to write a detailed grammar and vocabulary of the Valley Zapotec language after the Spanish conquest, but to include in his works a kind of encyclopedia of Zapotec culture. Still later writers, down to Balsalobre in the seventeenth century, corroborate him. The 1580 *Relaciones*, like Burgoa in 1670, provide details on the existence of two different cultures among the Indians of the Valley at the time of the Conquest and later, and give these cultures the names Mixtec and Zapotec (see p. 378).[14] It is true that the Zapotec people and culture may have been temporarily forced into exile in the Isthmus of Tehuantepec (Figures 286–89), but the ability of the Indians to maintain their own ways under Spanish pressure makes it clear that the Zapotecs were entirely capable of keeping their traditions alive in spite of Mixtec military successes and occupations.

[14] The richness of documentary sources for the study of late Zapotec culture is still, sadly, known only in a general way. Córdova and Burgoa were republished by Mexican scholars during the 1930's and 1940's, but their potentialities remain only that. The national and local archives are even less known.

THE MINORITY PEOPLES

What about the less numerous peoples of Oaxaca? Is it possible that they too possessed cultures and histories of importance? The fact that we have here grouped most of them with the Mixtecs under the name Tetlamixteca should not mislead us; some of them surely did play distinguishable roles in Meso-american development, and at certain times their importance may have been greater than their numbers would suggest.[15]

For postconquest times, geographic and linguistic provinces within the Mixteca are well defined. Preconquest divisions are less clear, although arche-ology has already provided some tentative outlines. In some cases the con-gruence of archeological and linguistic divisions permits hypothetical iden-tification of one of the minority peoples with one of the provinces.

Recent studies indicate that the minority peoples became linguistically sep-arate at times ranging from early agricultural Potter days to Late Urban days; thus some did not yet exist as separate groups until very late in Oaxaca his-tory. Instead, some centuries ago there was a smaller number of groups speak-ing a smaller number of languages ancestral to the more numerous ones of recent times.

Linguists who disagree about both methods and results in other instances agree that at the time of the first domestication of plants in America, what later became central Mesoamerica was probably inhabited by a people speak-ing a single language, ancestral to the present-day Otomangue or Macro-Mixtecan group of languages. Dialects within this ancestral language gradu-ally became separate languages, ancestral in turn to several modern groups, including three which are probably recognizable if we call them Otomían, Zapotecan, and Mixtecan. Each of these three modern groups achieved its present divisions by means of a series of splits which began about 4,000 years ago and has not yet ended.

The Otomían branch is now and may always have been located north of the Oaxaca archeological region, and therefore it does not greatly concern us. The Zapotecan branch for some reason is accorded only two component names, although some specialists say there are seven different languages in it (six are called Zapotec, and one Chatino). The Mixtecan branch is roughly coterminous with the Tetlamixteca group defined earlier. The minority peoples of this group are the Amusgos, Chinantecs, Chocho-Popolocas, Cui-catecs, Ichcatecs, Mazatecs, and Triques. In and close to the Isthmus of Te-huantepec live several other minority peoples. The Mixes, Zoques, and Hua-ves seem to constitute a distant branch of the Maya language group; and the Oaxaca Chontals are related to the North Mexican Yuman group.

Recent census figures explain why we call these people minorities, but this

---

[15] Jiménez Moreno in Part I has suggested, for example, that the Mazatecs and the Popo-locas were important at Teotihuacan.

modern situation is not necessarily of very long standing. Consider the Aztecs, for example, who came into the Valley of Mexico in small bands probably numbering less than a thousand persons in all. By the time of the Conquest, perhaps 300 years later, there were several hundred thousand of them. Conceivably the Mixtecs, or for that matter the Zapotecs, benefited in the same way from a few centuries of prosperity. Adversity can effect an equivalent decline (see pp. 234–36 below).

Exploitation of documentary materials on the minority peoples is beginning; witness Cline's paper in Part III. Identification of these peoples as they appear in the Mixtec codices will make new resources available, and important linguistic studies are already under way. Historically oriented ethnography will also help, although most of what has been done so far is the work of a single dedicated man, Robert Weitlaner.

Archeology will ultimately have to provide the bulk of the data. Cline, Delgado, and Weitlaner have made tentative beginnings in the Chinantla. There are obvious connections with the neighboring La Venta "Olmec" region in early times. In late times the Chinantla became a province, although a strongly distinct one, of the Mixteca. The eggshell-like polychrome pottery of the Chinantla, though it appears in Mixtec shapes, is far more fragile than the thin, strong polychrome of the Mixtecs; and the Chinantecs' fugitive paints, emphasizing yellow and blue, are sharply different from the Mixtecs' more durable paint and overwhelming emphasis on maroon, orange, grey, white, and black. Gold found in late Chinantec tombs—one late enough to have also some Spanish glass beads—is not distinguishable from Mixtec work. The Yolox tombs, described by Delgado as Zapotec, are decorated with painted greca motifs like those of the Mixtec codices and those found on the tombs and palaces of Mitla and Yagul. Also found in the Chinantla are grey pottery offerings very much like those of Monte Albán V found in the Mitla area.

Although Seler marked a number of apparently Mixtec pottery objects from his turn-of-the-century trips as coming from Cuicatlan, the Cuicatec capital, we should remember that they had been brought to Cuicatlan to be sold, and perhaps brought from a considerable distance. Weitlaner has reported some apparently Cuicatec archeological finds (Figure 290), but they are not readily distinguishable from Mixtec ones. The suggestive geographical position of the Cuicatecs with respect to the Valley of Oaxaca is discussed later in this volume (pp. 376–77).

About the Triques there is little to be said. Some remains of large ancient centers are close to their present location; conceivably these may once have been Trique towns of importance. This, however, is a still uninvestigated possibility and no more.

Our first glimpses of the archeology of the Tehuantepec area have been sufficient to assure us that it is fully as complex as should be expected in an isthmus where for millennia all sorts of Indians arrived, came into contact, and either settled or moved on. Besides the predictable late Zapotec and Mixtec remains, the Isthmus is already known to hold traces of occupation with strong Gulf coast and perhaps Mayoid traits, as well as Pre-urban remains of considerable variety and predominantly lowland characteristics.

The Tehuacan Valley, where MacNeish has given us a solid and detailed sequence of thousands of years, has surely been populated by some of the Oaxaca minority groups in times past. Mazatecs and Popolocas live in and near it now, although since about A.D. 1500 Nahua speakers have been invading it, and Mixtec rulers seem to have enjoyed dominion before that time (Figures 291–93). Unfortunately for our purposes here, MacNeish's history only sets the stage; it remains to establish the identity of the actors.[16]

The Amusgos have been proposed, on purely linguistic evidence, as the founders of Monte Albán—that is, the people of Monte Albán I. This hypothesis cannot be proved, of course; but it at least presents no serious conflict with known archeological data. More information on the Amusgos may come in time from Brockington's studies of Pacific coast sites.

One of the few places in the Tetlamixteca region where even small-scale excavations have been carried out is the area of Tamazulapan and Coixtlahuaca. The relatively large, well-watered valley of Tamazulapan-Teotongo-Tejupan, a rich agricultural area, is populated by Chochos and a few Mixtecs. The nearby tiny, dry, almost hopelessly eroded valley of Coixtlahuaca is at the opposite edge of the Chocho enclave; there was formerly a Mixtec population in the city, and a surrounding country population of Chochos. But the archeological site of Coixtlahuaca is a rich one. The Spanish confirmed the sixteenth-century importance of this capital by building an enormous and beautiful church there (Figures 294–96); the Aztec tribute rolls also record it as an important center. Archeological work at Tamazulapan, by contrast, has disclosed an interesting but relatively poor ancient settlement, and the town's early Spanish church is small (Figure 297).

What accounts for these findings? How could the Mixtec rulers of Coixtlahuaca maintain a great center in a small and relatively unproductive valley, while in the large and fertile adjoining valley of Tamazulapan the Chochos were content with an overgrown village? It would appear almost certain that the Tamazulapan valley and its Chocho inhabitants were politically subordinate to the Mixtec rulers in Coixtlahuaca, and subject to taxation and the like in their masters' interests. (Coixtlahuaca may have lived in part from its role as a trading center too; but we know from a number of documents that it was a major center of political power.) According to the Mixtec histories, as we have seen, this sort of arrangement was the norm in the Mixteca from A.D. 700 until the Spanish conquest. The Tamazulapan and Coixtlahuaca excavations appear to bear out the histories on this important point.

---

[16] A beginning in this direction will be offered in the final publications of the Tehuacan project.

. Sacrificial knife found in a cave in the Cuicatec region by Robert Weitlaner and the late William R. Holland.
of three, it was used by present-day Cuicatecs to sacrifice animals in curing ceremonies. *MNA.*

Xantiles from the region of Teotitlan del Camino. They are hollow, made to be set over braziers
hat smoke will come out their mouths. Very similar figures, much larger, were made in neighboring
acruz, also in late times. No convincing etymology is known for the name given these figures. *MNA.*

292. *Xantil* in the form
of a rain god.

293. *Xantil* said to be from the Mixteca Alta,
where they have not been reported previously.

294. Ruins of the open chapel adjoining the Coixtlahuaca Dominican church-monastery.

295. Lateral façade of the Coixtlahuaca church.

8. The center of Coixtlahuaca as seen from across the narrow valley.
The enormous sixteenth-century church-monastery dominates the town.

9. The church of Tamazulapan in 1952. A mismatched high tower has since been added on the left.

THE CLOUD PEOPLE

Intricately cross-cutting the already bewildering variety of geography and climate in Oaxaca are peoples speaking—depending on where we place the line between dialects and languages—from one to two dozen different mutually unintelligible languages, each of which appears in a number of local dialects. The major waves of ancient Mesoamerican culture change, from plant domestication through irrigation and urbanism to empire building, reached some places as irresistible floods and others as minor ripples. Meanwhile, each local environment and subculture favored some physiques and temperaments and combined with other factors to produce peoples who differ physically and whose cultural differences may extend to their basic views of man and life and the universe.

The preceding pages have described, rather summarily, various aspects of the human diversity that ancient Oaxaca compresses perhaps as much as any region of the world. There are several approaches by which we can abstract some order from these riches. Oaxaca was first populated not by a mass immigration but by a few tiny bands of physically and culturally homogeneous men; it was affected, even if not uniformly, by cultural currents that spread throughout Mesoamerica; its development in some respects parallels that of all regions populated by men; and its location with respect to the rest of Mesoamerica is stable.

Although the northern and southern boundaries of Mesoamerica shifted through time, an immensely important characteristic of ancient Oaxaca was its always central location with respect to the other major divisions of Mesoamerica. At a number of critical points in Mesoamerican development, one or another region seems to have been the first to make some innovation that then diffused to and affected the rest. In several important instances this region was Oaxaca itself. In nearly all the others, a neighboring region was the source, assuring early access to the innovation. Even when the late Zapotec world effectively closed itself off from outside influence, as seems to have happened in Monte Albán IIIb–IV, the adjoining Tetlamixteca area was a center of major innovations.[17]

It is MacNeish's revelation of the process by which the Indians first domesticated plants—above all maize—that places Oaxaca for the first time in the center of Mesoamerican events. Mesoamerica itself, in fact, begins acquiring its identity with precisely this achievement, and it takes place not in a neighboring area but in the archeological region of Oaxaca itself.[18]

---

[17] There is no need to review here the participation of Oaxaca in Mesoamerican history; the developmental concepts defined in these pages are intended to be equally applicable throughout Mesoamerica. Extension of such concepts to all early civilizations requires only the sacrifice of detail.

[18] As MacNeish emphasizes, there is no particular reason to suppose that plant domestication occurred first in the Tehuacan Valley sites where he discovered traces of it. His estimate of the area in which plant domestication first occurred in America is all or nearly all within the archeological region of Oaxaca as defined in this volume.

Irrigation too is first known in Mesoamerica as found in the Tehuacan Valley; but so much remains to be learned of it that our next milestone perhaps should rather be the "Olmec" culture, which we may conceive as the innovative center of Mesoamerican development during one period. But the "Olmec" or Tenocelome culture as seen at La Venta is a phenomenon already ripe, sophisticated, brilliant. Where are its origins? Covarrubias proposed years ago that they would be found in Guerrero, and we cannot dismiss his proposal, the more so since his ideas on the time and dynamic importance of La Venta, long regarded as fanciful, were fully borne out in the end by radiocarbon dating. Charles Wicke, after exhaustive study of the development of Tenocelome style, thinks the gigantic "Olmec" sculpture of Huamelulpan (Figure 2), in the Mixteca Alta of Oaxaca, is one of the earliest major Tenocelome works. A common origin for the Monte Albán I culture and that of La Venta would explain their similarities and differences without resort to the troublesome device of "influences" from one on the other. There are three possibilities, then, for the origin of Tenocelome culture: (1) the area of western Oaxaca and eastern Guerrero, that is, within the archeological region of Oaxaca itself; (2) farther west in Guerrero, a region bordering on ancient Oaxaca; (3) in the Gulf lowlands, another region bordering on ancient Oaxaca.

Our next milestone is urbanism. As we have seen, Monte Albán has some claim to being regarded as the first Mesoamerican community to achieve urban status. Recent findings tend more and more to suggest that Monte Albán (closely followed by Teotihuacan) was for a time the dynamic center of Mesoamerica in this respect. We do not know when Monte Albán first reached the status of metropolis—that is, a large city dominating a considerable area that includes other cities. Quite possibly Teotihuacan was the first Mesoamerican metropolis; but even so Monte Albán would be not later than second, and the area of Teotihuacan's dominance of course adjoins the Ñuiñe of northern Oaxaca.

After the fall of Teotihuacan in approximately A.D. 650, Mesoamerica seems for a time to have had no single leading innovative center. Teotihuacan's great influence was not inherited by the groups who camped on its ruins and built crooked mud walls over its magnificently frescoed plaster ones. What innovative and influential force the era offered appears in capitals of neighboring regions: El Tajín of northern and central Veracruz, Cholula in the Tetlamixteca area, and Xochicalco in Morelos. Neither Tajín nor Xochicalco survived into fully Late Urban times as a significant center.[19]

On the map Tajín, Cholula, and Xochicalco appear to form a kind of axis; and it is the Tetlamixteca city of Cholula that is central. There is at least one material indication that these capitals of adjacent regions were indeed in con-

[19] Both show unmistakable signs of incipient Late Urbanism, for example the sacrificial scenes in the Tajín friezes (see Part I above, Figure 101) and the militarist aspect of Xochicalco's city plan. Nevertheless, they seem to me to be more like final flowerings of Early Urbanism than vanguards of Late Urbanism.

tact with each other, even if none of them can be singled out as clearly dominant. Although it had been known at least since Monte Albán II (on pottery),
the step-fret or greca or xikalkoliwki and its variants became very conspicuous. At Xochicalco and Tajín grecas were used prominently as architectural
decoration, covering an entire building at the latter site; at Cholula they may
or may not have been used on the buildings, but they nearly replaced other
motifs in the decoration of dishes. Again as architectural adornment, they appeared in the Valley of Oaxaca (at Lambityeco; the Mitla palaces are later)
and around Uxmal in the Maya area.[20]

Tajín, for all its greatness at its peak (and its tastes affected faraway regions), survived into Late Urban times only briefly and feebly; its successor
capital, Cempoala, far from serving as a center of cultural innovation, drifted
toward an acceptance of Tetlamixteca ways. Xochicalco also survived into
the early years of Late Urbanism, but was then abandoned. Uxmal and other
Yucatán centers experienced a revival as the relatively passive partners in an
acculturation of Maya Early Urbanism with Central Highland—usually considered Toltec—Late Urbanism. But Toltec Late Urbanism, like that of the
Aztecs, was heavily indebted to the Tetlamixteca peoples.

Of all the regions that had post-Teotihuacan flowerings of Early Urbanism
with traces of Late Urbanism, then, only the Tetlamixteca appears to have
been in the initial stages of something new and dynamic; the others were at
the end of something old and exhausted. Mixtec dynamism in the several centuries preceding the Spanish conquest has been so well set forth by Covarrubias that we need not dwell on it here.

We have attributed to "the archeological region of Oaxaca" and to its ancient peoples and cultures a vital role at several crucial moments of Mesoamerican culture history. This claim raises at least two serious questions. Is
there, in a social and cultural sense, such a unit as the archeological region
of Oaxaca? If there is such a unit, is the role we assign to it within its possibilities?

Let us start with the second question. Although according to contemporary
government planners, as well as many other observers, Oaxaca today is one of
the poorest, least developed regions in Mexico, it was not always thus. Recent
studies by Cook, Borah, and Simpson have placed the Indian population of
Central Mexico—roughly Mesoamerica west of the Isthmus of Tehuantepec—

---

[20] This was the time when lowland Maya culture achieved its greatest brilliance and area of
dominion. Although occasional examples of Maya art are found in contexts as early as that
of Teotihuacan, the dazzling achievements of the Early Urban Mayas seem in general to
have been very remote and exotic for their contemporaries west of Tehuantepec. The art
of Xochicalco, flourishing during the late Maya heyday, does undeniably show several Maya
traits; yet even there the presence of four or five Maya technicians and artists would account
for everything. Late "Classic" Maya culture shows, like Tajín and Xochicalco, some Late
Urban characteristics, but it too failed to survive the period of change.

at from 20 to 28 million at the time of the Conquest. According to numerous independent indications, the Conquest population of Oaxaca was larger than that of the present day. It would appear from the findings of MacNeish, Woodbury, and Neely that this larger population may have depended for its subsistence on enormous networks of dams, aqueducts, and terraced irrigated fields, so arrayed as to make the utmost of the water supply in a way not approached by most modern inhabitants of the region (there are a few small areas of intensive modern irrigation). Ancient irrigation works have been found not only in the fertile bottom land of the Tehuacan Valley, but in surrounding areas as well, areas that are now virtually uninhabited desert.

These water control systems were well developed in Early Urban times in the Tehuacan Valley, and already existed several centuries before Christ. There is no reason to think that comparable exploration of other areas will fail to discover such irrigation systems elsewhere. It is scarcely conceivable that so vital a technique could have been kept secret, above all when we know of fairly considerable and frequent migrations, as well as constant trade, between regions. Assuming, then, that irrigation systems and techniques were at one time widespread, and that they had been in use for some 2,000 years before the Spanish arrived, how could they have simply dropped from sight in so large a part of Mexico?

This question too is answered by the demographic histories of Cook, Simpson, and Borah. According to their heavily documented estimates, the Indian population of Central Mexico dropped from over 20 million in 1519 to under 17 million in 1532, about 6 million by 1550, under 2 million by 1580, and about 1 million around 1600. This nearly complete destruction of the Mexican Indians was largely the consequence of the introduction from Europe of a series of diseases to which they had no resistance.

Abundant Spanish colonial records tell of the repeated epidemics and their catastrophic effects. One result of the decrease in population was the consolidation of towns, since many of them were reduced to populations so small as to be impractical administrative and economic units. When towns were consolidated, the new settlements naturally were located on the choicest lands. As the population was withdrawn from the lands where irrigation was relatively difficult or intricate, the only surviving persons who knew the local systems and their peculiarities were moved to new locations where they were neither eager nor able to pass their knowledge on to their children. In this way the knowledge of how to operate specific systems was lost; and in time, since the population was more and more concentrated on choice lands where efficient water and land conservation was unnecessary, the general principles were forgotten too. Finally even the memory of such a technology was lost. Spanish and Arabic techniques, meanwhile, were introduced in those places where intensive cultivation still went on.

After about 1650, when a very slow recovery of population began, there was a corresponding movement back into the usable but less choice lands. Except in a few areas (including especially some parts of the Mixteca Alta) where ancient terraces have continued in use and some new ones seem to have been built from time to time, exploitation of the land by the new post-1650 settlers has been of the kind that results in disastrous erosion.

The present-day aspect of much of the Mixteca is utterly desolate; over large areas all soil has been washed away and sterile bedrock is exposed. Misled by present appearances, many writers (including Jiménez Moreno in the present volume) have concluded that the region was poor agriculturally in prehispanic times also, and have accordingly questioned its demographic and cultural possibilities. The firsthand testimony cited on pages 369–70 below bears conclusive witness to the contrary.

Ancient Oaxaca did, then, have the population and other resources needed to make it repeatedly a leader among the Mesoamerican regions. It remains to consider to what extent we can justify treatment of this very diverse region as a unit.

Bernal, in his monumental bibliography of Mesoamerica, defined the archeological region of Oaxaca as extending into the states of Guerrero and Puebla, and set its limits at a linguistic boundary: the division between the modern speakers of Mixtec and Popoloca and their non-Oaxacan neighbors (Nahuas in most cases). The present-day situation is virtually the same as that of the sixteenth century, and he has thus defined the archeological region as it was in late prehispanic times. Since there is no sharp geographical division corresponding to this linguistic one on either the west or the north, it probably shifted more or less constantly during the preceding millennia. Nevertheless, the presence of the Ñuiñe style during Early Urban times in both Puebla and neighboring Oaxaca suggests that a similar cultural (and perhaps ethnic) boundary existed then. Again, the Monte Albán I style of late Pre-urban centuries appears to have occupied an area corresponding roughly with that of Bernal's Late Urban archeological region. As for the north and west, then, there are good grounds for proposing that Oaxaca was repeatedly, if not continuously, a region distinguishable from its neighbors.[21] On the east the natural boundaries, by contrast, are abrupt and are defined in terms sharply affecting human occupancy. With apparently only brief exceptions, the Gulf coast lowlands and the Isthmus of Tehuantepec have constituted cultural as well as geographic frontiers.

Ancient Oaxaca has thus been a genuine cultural unit, distinguishable from neighboring regions on all sides. Its boundaries have been breached from time to time by both inward and outward migrations, invasions, and cultural diffusions; but in general its identity has been clear.

The kind of identity that holds deepest interest for the actors of history

---

[21] Settlements of Oaxaca peoples in the Valley of Mexico might have taken the form of extensions of its boundaries at some times and of something more like colonization at others.

themselves, and for the spectators as non-scientific fellow human beings, clearly is that of ethnic groups.[22] For Oaxaca ethnic identity has been important both in distinguishing Oaxacans from outsiders and in dividing Oaxacans among themselves.

Except for the Chontales and the Zoque-Mixe-Huave group, which are all small populations and all located in the extreme southeast, ancient Oaxaca is an ethnic-linguistic unit. It began in simple and complete unity, that of a single people having a single language and culture.[23] For some thousands of years there was a trend toward differentiation; two great trunks were slowly formed from the original unit, and each of the trunks, without having lost all of its resemblances to the other, then underwent internal differentiation into a number of branches. An integrative countertrend that began at least 700 years ago has slowly gathered force, without replacing the process of divergence, until it has become almost wholly dominant in recent years and promises soon to wipe out the remaining differences within Oaxaca.

The two main trunks of Oaxaca linguistics are of course the Zapotec and the Mixtec. Recent estimates by Swadesh and his co-workers suggest that the single people who gave origin to both trunks became separated perhaps somewhat after 2000 B.C. Further separations within each trunk have taken place occasionally until very recent times, so that each now includes half a dozen or more distinct languages. However, only two names (Chatino and Zapotec) have been assigned to all those of the Zapotec trunk, while each modern language of the Mixtec trunk has a different name.

It is important to understand that even after the Zapotec and Mixtec trunks separated, many centuries were required for them to develop truly distinct cultures, languages, and identities. Thus up through the time of Monte Albán I, or until shortly before the time of Christ, archeological remains throughout Oaxaca and the related parts of Puebla and Guerrero suggest much more cultural similarity than difference. Still later, well into the first millennium A.D., Ñuiñe style clearly overlapped that of Monte Albán III in some areas even though considerable distance intervened (and linguistic evidence indicates that the Tetlamixteca and Zapotec peoples were already long established in their present locations).

[22] Since we cannot often be entirely certain about it, identification of the peoples who make archeological events has been deplored as poor science. Further, ethnicity is an elusive concept; ethnic identity may be based upon any of a number of criteria, or a combination of them. But ethnic identity remains a significant social reality. Here we shall rely primarily on language, to date the best understood criterion for Oaxaca.

[23] On linguistic evidence, Harvey (1962) proposes northeast Oaxaca as "the most probable center of dispersal of the Otomangue languages." Matching the linguistic data with MacNeish's archeological evidence for this region, its social organization, and the appearance, one by one, of domesticated plants, Harvey concludes, "It appears beyond all reasonable doubt that the Tehuacan sequence pertains from at least the El Riego phase [MacNeish 1964a, 1964c] terminating 7,000 years ago to an emergent Otomangue linguistic stock."

A sharp although not total differentiation was finally achieved with the development of Late Urbanism in the Mixteca, contemporary with late Monte Albán IIIb in the Valley of Oaxaca. Then, not more than five centuries later, the Mixtec invasions of the Valley brought about an intimacy of coexistence that prohibited any long maintenance of cultural or biological "purity." As always, persons interested in promoting ethnic friction for their own ends continued to emphasize the differences; quotations down to the mid-twentieth century could be added to those cited below (p. 378) from 1580. But the tide of history has been running the other way.

At the time of the Mixtec invasions differentiation had reached its maximum, yet even then the rival peoples had something in common. For example, whereas the shape of a plain Mixtec (Monte Albán V) dish is sharply different from that of its Zapotec (Monte Albán IV) contemporary, their grey color, a result of their both being made in reducing kilns, sets them apart from comparable vessels of adjoining regions. The contrasting traditions of Monte Albán IV and V maintained their identities until the Spanish conquest and after, as we have seen; but their contact also appears to have produced the beginnings of still a third one. Although examples are rare, at both Monte Albán and Yagul there are tombs whose offerings include objects of both Mixtec and Zapotec styles. A few objects hint at a fusion of the two traditions, and Bernal (pp. 346–51 below) suggests the possibility that even such a masterwork of ancient America as the Mitla palaces might be the product of this fusion.

The ethnic mixing of Mixtecs and Zapotecs probably was almost wholly limited to the ruling class and its political marriages before the Spanish conquest. Since then it has still been greatly impeded in many places by hostility between the two groups. Nevertheless, as early as 1670 Burgoa (who presumably was himself performing the ceremonies) testified that Zapotecs and Mixtecs often intermarried in Zegache. In present-day Mitla, intermarriage of the town Zapotecs with Mixtecs from the outlying settlements is common, and marriages with the Mixes from the adjoining mountains are not really rare.[24]

Although the Nahuatl-speaking Aztec and Tlaxcalan guides of the early Spanish explorers innocently contributed a confusion here,[25] the clear fact is that what is taking place is not a new integration, but a reunion. A particularly dramatic proof is that even today, nearly 4,000 years after their separation, the Zapotec and Mixtec peoples still call themselves by the same name and still say it in a very similar way. Most peoples around the world have self-names that translate as something like The Men, or The People. The Mixtecs call themselves Ñusabi, or Cloud People, which in Nahuatl is Mishtékatl. The Zapotecs call themselves (depending on dialect differences) something like Ben'Zaa, which likewise means Cloud People; the particle sa or zaa refers to

[24] It would be interesting to have a study of the marriage records of Zaachila, which is bitterly split into Zapotec and Mixtec moieties.
[25] As they did also by saying that Teotihuacan was the ancient Toltec capital.

cloud in both cases. Perhaps just to provide a different name for a people they regarded as different, the Aztecs made a phonetic rather than a semantic translation of Ben'Zaa, into Tsapotékatl or Zapote People. There is no evidence that the Zapotecs ever called themselves such a name (although they use it today when speaking Spanish); the Zapotec word for zapote is entirely different. Although the languages naturally have a significant proportion of other similarities surviving from their common origin, the psychological role of the self-name gives it special importance.

Origin myths might reasonably be expected to provide another link, but those of both peoples are utterly unsatisfactory for this use. According to their genealogical codices, the Mixtecs are descended from a divine pair who were born from a tree (or from the earth in some versions) less than 1,500 years ago. The Zapotec origin myths as written down shortly after the Spanish conquest take them back to the famous Chicomostoc or Seven Caves, which is the legendary place of origin of the late Nahua invaders of the Valley of Mexico and is mentioned also by northern Mixtecs in early postconquest documents. Since Chicomostoc is little or no earlier than the Mixtec divine pair, and Zapotec linguistic identity is, obviously, as old as the Mixtec, there is a discrepancy of some 2,000 years between the Mixtec and Zapotec origin myths and the linguistic evidence. But the Zapotec myths are the same ones that fail to mention Monte Albán as having a place in Zapotec history (see p. 367).

As for clouds, they too seem to have been left out, one suspects with as little reason as Monte Albán. The valleys of Oaxaca, Tehuacan, Cholula, and Mexico are semi-deserts where rain is life. The Cloud People already bore that name before irrigation was developed to mitigate slightly their dependence on rain, and there are good indications that they already lived about where they do now.[26]

In those remote times, the small groups who spread out to settle the complicated emptiness of Oaxaca were parting from each other to begin their millennia of slow divergence countered only by occasional, difficult contacts. As techniques improved and population grew, contacts became easier and more frequent, and finally inescapable and hostile. Integration then was attempted several times by means of conquest. The Zapotecs of the Monte Albán III stelae, the Mixtecs of period V, the Aztecs, and the Spanish all tried and failed to reunite the Cloud People. The struggling national governments of 1810 to 1910 likewise made little impression on Indian Oaxaca; but modern medicine, communications, and education are erasing in a few decades the ethnic identities that survived centuries of empire builders. A new sense of national identity as Mexicans is emerging, but age-old loyalties persist. The present-day state of Oaxaca rather closely corresponds to the lands of the Cloud People, and within the nation it has a character distinctively its own.

[26] As well as in the Valley of Mexico and other areas later taken over by the Nahua invaders.

BIBLIOGRAPHICAL NOTE

General surveys of Oaxaca archeology at any length have been so rare that I believe the present essay is only the third of its kind. Caso's *Culturas mixteca y zapoteca* was prepared in the late 1930's, published in revised and enlarged form in Mexico in 1939, and reissued, in English, as Nos. 21 and 22 of the *Boletín de Estudios Oaxaqueños.* In 1961 Bernal prepared a long article for the *Handbook of Middle American Indians.* Although the volume of the *Handbook* which includes Bernal's article is not yet available, I have had access to the manuscript.

As I pointed out in my notes for the English version of Caso's *Culturas*, in 1940 Oaxaca archeology was interpreted (often even by Caso himself) as reflecting local variants of cultural phenomena originating elsewhere. Since then, the work of Caso and others has forced us little by little to see Oaxaca as a major innovating center.

Bernal's *Handbook* article differs from the present survey in several ways. First, it omits aspects of ancient Oaxaca covered by other authors in the same volume of the *Handbook.* Second, I have tried to avoid duplicating Bernal's data as much as possible. And finally, Bernal is almost aggressively Monte-Albán-centered with regard to internal Oaxaca affairs, but is not notably Oaxaca-centered with regard to Mesoamerican development in general, whereas I have given somewhat opposed views on these and other issues. The Bernal article therefore will be essential reading for any serious student of ancient Oaxaca.

Three short essays by Eduardo Noguera, published in *Esta Semana* between 1935 and 1946, appear together with many other useful notes in *México prehispánico* (1946). Bernal's *Compendio de arte mesoamericano* (1950) provided brief coverage of Oaxaca. A major event in the history of Oaxaca archeology was the publication in 1957 of *Indian Art of Mexico and Central America,* in which Miguel Covarrubias gave two full chapters to ancient Oaxaca. In spite of an alarmingly freewheeling approach that frightens off most archeologists, Covarrubias combined an immense fund of knowledge with an artist's insight, making up in creativeness what he lacked in discipline. Unhappily, the captions are often in error, since the author did not live to correct them.

Bernal wrote an *Official Guide* to Monte Albán and Mitla in 1957, and in 1958 gave two talks on Oaxaca archeology that later appeared as Nos. 1 and 7 of the *Boletín de Estudios Oaxaqueños.* (This series includes several short articles treating aspects of ancient Oaxaca, but no other general ones except Caso's in Nos. 21 and 22.) During 1958 Jiménez Moreno wrote the "Synthesis" that appears here in English as Part I. The VII Mesa Redonda of the Sociedad Mexicana de Antropología was held in Oaxaca in 1957, and the large collection of papers submitted to it was published in 1960 as Volume XVI of the *Revista Mexicana de Estudios Antropológicos.*

Two works of basic importance appeared in 1962 in honor of the XXXV International Congress of Americanists for which the papers of Part III (below) were written. These are the *Vocabulario en lengua mixteca* (1593) by Alvarado, reissued in facsimile with three preliminary studies by Jiménez Moreno; and Bernal's heroic *Bibliografía de arqueología y etnografía de Mesoamérica y el Norte de México,* which includes a virtually total bibliography of ancient Oaxaca up to 1960 and provides the definition of the archeological region of Oaxaca used in the preceding pages.

Some works of less than pan-Oaxacan scope are *La Mixteca: su cultura e historia prehispánicas,* by Barbro Dahlgren (1954), a compilation from published chronicles; "The Genealogy of Tlazultepec," an article by Ronald Spores (1964), which provides in a few paragraphs a solid characterization of late preconquest Mixtec culture; and Linné's *Zapotecan Antiquities* (1938).

Postscript 1970

Several book-length reports will be written about the work done in Oaxaca archeology from the beginning of 1966 to the end of 1969, but that work is still continuing on all fronts. Meanwhile, preliminary accounts may be found in the sources mentioned on p. ix, where the names of those responsible are also cited. Here there is space for no more than the briefest outline of what has been learned.

By around 7000 B.C., humans were leaving implements and caches of wild foods in small dry caves near Mitla. Most of their tools were nearly identical to those reported for the Tehuacan Valley people by MacNeish, and development appears closely parallel until after 2000 B.C. However, the Valley of Oaxaca is much more hospitable to man. Before 1000 B.C. there were many large villages along its rivers, which then carried greater volumes of water than at any later time. All Mesoamerica, including the Valley of Oaxaca, was "Olmec" in culture at 1000 B.C. The Valley people supplied craft objects to the Tenocelome, or inhabitants of the Gulf Coast "Olmec" climax area, but we do not know whether they were the same people, kinfolk, or unrelated.

From about 900 to 600 B.C. the superb ceramic complex of Monte Albán I may be seen evolving in the large river-bottom villages (if the legendary lake did occupy the Valley, its floor had many aquatic human inhabitants). However, we still know of no antecedents for the writing system used in early Monte Albán, where major construction seems to have begun about 600 B.C. Vague hints of "Olmec" style in the Monte Albán Danzante carvings are now understandable not as reflections of a foreign style but as the vestiges of a local style of several centuries before.

Early Monte Albán times at Macuilxochitl, an important town on the Valley floor, are vividly if incompletely illuminated by the Dainzú discovery, where elaborately protected players are shown in a strenuous ball game unlike those previously known. They are incised in outline like the Danzantes, but resemble only one or two of them (Figures 57 and 58, p. 117).

After the period of the Dainzú carvings (probably in Transición II–III), some Valley of Oaxaca people lived at Teotihuacan and used Oaxaca-style domestic pottery; they also imported from Oaxaca some fine effigy urns of Transición style. An embassy? Traders? Pilgrims? We can only guess.

Like its beginnings, the end of Monte Albán as a functioning center is better dated now. A number of tightly clustered radiocarbon dates from Lambityeco and Mitla place early Monte Albán IV—at or shortly after the abandonment of Monte Albán—around A.D. 700. A startlingly early date of A.D. 835 for Monte Albán V remains from Mitla is more credible in the light of these period IV dates. They are confirmed by the occurrence of a brief and early period IV, followed by a rapidly dominant V, at Miahuatlan.

In the Mixteca Alta, scattered finds show habitation in preceramic times. Later remains parallel those of the Valley from about 900 to 200 B.C. Peak prosperity at Teotihuacan and Monte Albán may have accompanied a depressed period in the Mixteca Alta, which then flourished and became important after they had declined.

The Mixteca Baja has provided further examples of the traits cited (pp. 174–200) as possible elements of a Ñuiñe style, but whether all these traits do in fact form a single complex remains to be seen. Some late Mixtec or Mixteca-Puebla traits have now been traced to the Ñuiñe period and region.

The narrow Pacific coastal plain, whose exploration has only begun, shows a rich and varied culture history and an unexpected individuality. Remote as it was from the Mesoamerican mainstream at some times, at others it was powerfully affected by such great events as the collapse of Classic Maya civilization.

PART III

Papers on Ancient Oaxaca

It was with Part III that Ancient Oaxaca *began: a small book of conference papers with a brief introduction. (The conference was a symposium on ancient Oaxaca during the XXXV International Congress of Americanists in Mexico City, in August 1962.) That introduction grew, to the surprise of the author and the consternation of the publisher, into Part II—which itself proved to need introducing by the present Part I.*

Part III is a group of studies taking up a handful of the numberless specific questions into which Oaxaca culture history must be divided for detailed analysis. It is not a random handful. Some more and some less, some by design and some not, all of them bear not only upon ancient Oaxaca, but at least briefly or indirectly upon the "Mixtec problem." One group of them is designed specifically to provide definitive answers to certain questions about the Mixtecs and their close cultural relatives (the group of peoples we called the Tetlamixteca in Part II), and the role they played in the Valley of Oaxaca.

As recently as 1960, when Ignacio Bernal asserted in a Paris congress that the Mixtecs had settled in parts of the Valley, it was suggested in reply that the presence of Mixtec styles in Zapotec-speaking areas was caused by the Zapotecs' having taken over typical Mixtec styles in the centuries immediately preceding the conquest. The last four of the eight papers to follow—those by Caso, Wicke, Bernal, and Paddock—ought to make unlikely any further dispute over whether in fact there were Mixtec invasions of the Valley.

The other four papers were variously motivated. Neither Chadwick nor Leigh, obviously, thought of his paper as an approach to the "Mixtec problem." Chadwick, nevertheless, with due reservations, brings the Mixtecs into Monte Albán I. When Leigh finished his analysis of the Zapotec glyph C, he had no way of knowing that I would soon be finding it in the Mixteca Baja and presenting the concept of Ñuiñe style; his paper antedates Part II by at least two years. A form of glyph C which he predicted ought to exist did in-

deed turn up—on a Ñuiñe stone. The glyph occurs also on several Ñuiñe ce-
ramic effigies, and Leigh's analysis of its evolution suggests that they are
contemporary (if similarity is assumed to mean contemporaneity) with Monte
Albán IIIb.

Cline's Mazatecs are a component of the Tetlamixteca group, and accord-
ing to Jiménez Moreno may have played an important part in Teotihuacan.
Along with many other groups they are candidates for a role in Bernal's hy-
pothetical separate invasions of the Valley of Oaxaca by Eastern and Western
Mixtec groups of slightly different culture.

Robertson and Caso disagree about the source of the Borgia Group of
codices, although both would probably allow a Tetlamixteca attribution for
these important manuscripts. Caso has preferred to place the group as "Po-
blano-Tlaxcalteca," while Robertson, within his careful definition of Mixtec,
insists on a Mixtec origin.

Six of the eight papers have appeared in the Actas *of the 1962 Congress*
(published in 1964). The Chadwick and Leigh papers, although prepared for
the Congress, were not presented then because the authors did not attend;
they are published here for the first time. The Caso, Bernal, and Paddock
papers were presented originally in Spanish and appear here in English ver-
sions by Paddock. A ninth paper read at the Congress, by Roberto Gallegos,
was omitted both from the Actas *and from this volume in deference to the*
author's wishes.

Duplication of illustrations already published in the Actas *has been avoided*
where possible, and many new drawings and photographs have been ob-
tained for the present version. The papers by Cline, Wicke, Bernal, and Pad-
dock have been slightly revised and amplified for this volume. Many of the
essential illustrations for Caso's article appear here through the kindness of
Jorge Gurría Lacroix, Executive Secretary of the Mexican Instituto Nacional
de Antropología e Historia. For other important aid with illustrations in Part
III we are indebted to Ross Parmenter.

The Tombs of Monte Albán I Style at Yagul

ROBERT CHADWICK

The only tombs of Monte Albán I style so far discovered at the site of Yagul in the Valley of Oaxaca were excavated by Bente Bittman Simons, David Sanchez, and me, between January and March of 1960, in an exploration sponsored by Mexico City College (since March 1963 called the University of the Americas) and approved by the Mexican Instituto Nacional de Antropología e Historia. The discovery was mentioned in *American Antiquity* in the following note: "On the hill above the site [Yagul], where the fortress is located, a complex of burial compartments formed by little rows of adobe bricks yielded some important burials with associated Monte Albán [period I style] ceramics, including two outstanding, esthetically superior pieces: a face-effigy cylindrical brazier with strongly Olmecoid features, wearing a glyph-bearing helmet, and a tripod vessel with face-effigy supports. Sherd finds corroborated the clear presence of Monte Albán I at Yagul, which completes the continuity of occupation at this key Oaxaca site from Preclassic times to around the time of the Conquest (Monte Albán I–V)."[1]

Apart from this one brief mention, no account of the Monte Albán I style tombs at Yagul has been published. Any searching interpretation would thus be premature, and for the most part I shall restrict my report to description. However, some suggestions about the early population of ancient Oaxaca will be offered; for although the difficulties of relating ethnic groups to artifacts are formidable, this should not rule out the attempt.

Anne Middendorf Sosnkowski has described the Monte Albán I tombs found at the type site as follows: "The six tombs of period I, with the exception of Tomb 94, which undoubtedly was constructed at the end of the epoch, are very simple. Lacking doors and niches and having flat roofs, they resemble boxes. Two of these tombs, one of which is made completely of adobe, were

[1] Notes to the papers in Part III will be found at the end of each paper.

used for the burial of children. In this period the practice was made of digging a tomb beneath a building already constructed. All of the tombs with one ... exception have dirt floors."[2] In one of the children's tombs, clay toys were found that bore a marked resemblance to the Danzante figures. Middendorf Sosnkowski notes, too, that Tomb 107 was located beneath six stucco floors, and was constructed under a building, presumably a temple, one of whose foundation walls served as a side of the tomb.[3]

Ignacio Marquina describes the oldest tombs of Monte Albán as having rectangular floor plans and vertical walls, generally of small dimensions, and roofed with flat slabs of stone.[4] Miguel Covarrubias has called Monte Albán I tombs "rectangular cysts covered with stone slabs."[5] It has also been stated that Monte Albán I tombs were *fosas* (graves) not exceeding 0.50 meters in height, with flat roofs and no doors.[6] A tomb found at Monte Negro in the Mixteca Norte and containing an offering of Monte Albán I style was of the same form as those of Monte Albán.[7]

At Yagul, all four of the tombs belonging to period I (numbers 31, 32, 33, and 34) agree structurally (apart from some minor variations) with those excavated at Monte Albán. The all-important difference between the Yagul period I tombs (Figure 1) and those at the type site is, of course, that the

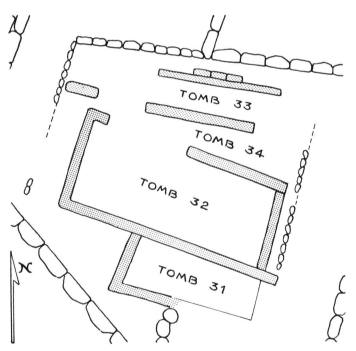

1. Tombs of Monte Albán I style, Terrace F, Yagul. *Drawing by José Luis Franco.*

Yagul tombs were made of adobe, not stone. Adobe construction is rare at Monte Albán,[8] and adobe tombs are apparently rare in Mesoamerica as a whole. Pedro Armillas says he knows of no other adobe tombs in Mesoamerica, and Melvin Fowler believes that none exist east of the Mississippi River in the United States.[9]

The recent discovery of an adobe tomb in Chiapas, therefore, deserves mention. The tomb, at the site of Chiapa de Corzo, "measured about 2.93 meters east-west by 1.40 meters north-south. Its walls were made of large unfired adobe bricks and reached a height of 1.05 meters. For its floor, the soil had been pounded and coated with a grey clay. Large irregular sandstone slabs once formed the roof, but had soon collapsed inward against the walls, where they providentially smashed or covered up many of the objects in the offering, thus saving them from subsequent molestation by the grave robbers. The male occupant apparently had been fully extended on his back, his head to the east, but the skeleton was badly disturbed and scattered by post-interment events."[10] Agrinier suggests a date in the first century A.D. for this tomb, in which two carved human bones were found that showed traces of early Monte Albán style together with Olmec-influenced Protoclassic Izapa style. Dixon had earlier proposed a date of about A.D. 300, some five or six hundred years later than the date of the Yagul tombs.[11]

A cruciform subterranean structure of adobe was found at Yagul in 1956, but it was too small to have been a tomb, even by the standards of Monte Albán I, and was thought to be some kind of cache.[12] It had been completely emptied, apparently in ancient times, but a placement in Monte Albán I is a definite possibility. The fact that it was roofed with beams of stone strongly resembling the columnar basalt used in constructions at La Venta would support such a dating.[13]

In addition to dating based on the structural similarities between the Yagul examples and other Monte Albán I tombs (similarities that will be discussed later), the Yagul group has been dated to Monte Albán I times by the radiocarbon method. An Olmecoid *brasero* of the young god of fire (Figure 2) was recovered from one of the tombs, and a charcoal sample taken from it. The Exploration Department and Geochemical Laboratory of Humble Oil and Refining Company, Houston, Texas, reported that the most probable date for this sample was 390 B.C., with an estimated laboratory counting error of ± 275 years at the one sigma level.[14]

The objects from the Yagul tombs were identified by Bernal as belonging stylistically to phase C of Monte Albán I.[15] This identification is consistent with the early radiocarbon date of about 650 B.C. reported from a sample of a beam taken at Monte Negro, the Monte Albán I style site in the Mixteca Norte;[16] with the report of the Humble Oil laboratories that the most probable date on a sample from a Monte Albán II site very near Yagul (Caballito

2. The young god of fire; Tomb 33, Yagul.

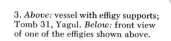

3. *Above:* vessel with effigy supports; Tomb 31, Yagul. *Below:* front view of one of the effigies shown above.

4. Part of the offering found in Tomb 31, Yagul.

Blanco) was 240 B.C., with an estimated counting error of ± 150 years at the one sigma level;[17] and with the previous date of 275 B.C. for a period II sample from Monte Albán itself.[18]

The Yagul *brasero*, which is thought to be the finest of its kind yet discovered, is an example of a class of objects that Covarrubias regards as typical of the Monte Albán I culture.[19] Caso, in commenting on the distribution of *braseros* of this type, says that they are found from southern Puebla to Guatemala.[20]

A second important artifact of period I, a tripod vessel with face-effigy supports, was recovered from Tomb 31 at Yagul (Figure 3). According to Caso and Bernal this piece is unique in Oaxaca archeology.[21] Although many otherwise similar vessels are known from Monte Albán and the surrounding region, none had ever been found before with human heads as legs. It must be noted, however, that a similar object was found by Lothrop in a tomb at Zacualpa, Guatemala, and has been described as a flat-base bowl standing on three cylindrical legs, the legs being partly concealed by features of human faces. Wauchope illustrates and discusses other Zacualpa pots with effigy-head legs, including one human effigy; and he had previously made a study of effigy-head supports. Practically all examples, he says, are late.[22]

Similar vessels from the Postclassic are frequently found in the Tehuantepec area, and Gann and Thompson have pointed out that "three-legged pots, with a face moulded at the extremity of each hollow leg," are common in the Archaic (Preclassic) culture of the Valley of Mexico.[23] According to John Paddock, this type of vessel is also common in Postclassic Cholula.[24]

As we have said, the four Yagul period I tombs are, with minor variations, structurally similar to those found at Monte Albán. Tomb 31 perhaps follows the Monte Albán specifications more exactly than the other three. This tomb, which contained the tripod vessel described above, was rectangular, constructed on an east-west axis, and approximately 0.50 meters high. It was 0.64 meters wide and 1.80 meters long, and its walls were formed by five courses of adobe bricks, which were covered with cream-grey stucco both inside and outside the burial chamber. Each brick measured approximately 0.10 by 0.215 by 0.165 meters. The bricks were obviously not fired. According to Eduardo Noguera, the firing of bricks did not begin until Classic times.[25] No roof was found *in situ*, but judging by the number of adobe bricks recovered inside the tomb, it is probable that the roof was made of them and had collapsed. Since no worked stone was recovered, the roof may have been supported by wooden beams, although no evidence was found to support this idea. The Monte Albán I style tomb of Monte Negro had wooden beams.[26]

The skeleton uncovered in Tomb 31 was lying on a packed earth floor and had been much disturbed; it could be ascertained, however, that the occipital portion of the skull faced west—an orientation characteristic of 80 per cent of Monte Albán I burials.[27] Most of the funerary offerings of 14 pottery vessels (Figures 3–5) were placed around the feet of the extended skeleton,

5. Offering of Tomb 32, Yagul. The vessel at upper right is very similar to one found in Tomb 31 and not shown in Figure 4.

6. Incised decoration on pottery fragments found in and around Tombs 31–34, Yagul.

though it was not possible to determine what the original posture of the pots had been. There were no signs of cremation in this primary burial, although there was an ash deposit throughout the tomb. The person buried in Tomb 31 had a height of approximately 1.40 meters (4 feet 5 inches).

Tomb 32 shared its southern wall with Tomb 31, but was different in several respects. It was somewhat longer and wider, and contained two burials. Only the lower burial had funerary offerings and it is conceivable that the upper one had been an "offering" or companion for the lower one. No floor was found below the lower skeleton, but traces of a stucco floor were discovered at approximately the level of the upper burial. There were no remains of a roof *in situ*, but a large number of fallen adobe bricks were recovered from the tomb. Both skeletons were extended, with skulls to the west.

Tomb 34 shared its southern wall with Tomb 32, and is important because it was the only one found with part of a roof in position. The roof, probably flat, was composed of several adobe slabs that rested on the north and south walls of the tomb. The chamber yielded no funerary offerings, but was completely filled with ashes and charcoal, from which a large number of diagnostic Monte Albán I sherds were recovered. No skeletal remains were found, with the exception of two small pieces of charred bone, and it is not certain whether these bone fragments were human or not.

It is interesting to note that although there is no evidence for the practice of cremation at Monte Albán, several burials that Richard S. MacNeish, Melvin Fowler, and I recently excavated at Coxcatlan Cave on the Puebla-Oaxaca border gave evidence of cremation or "ritual burning" as well as the practice of cannibalism. The age of the Coxcatlan Cave burials has been placed by carbon 14 as approximately 8,000 years.[28] The Coxcatlan Cave burials suggest an elaborate ritualism, for the two adult burials were oriented east-west and contained offerings of at least seven baskets. Although we cannot consider the type of burial at Coxcatlan a direct antecedent of that at Yagul, it is nonetheless interesting that burial ritual was already quite complex in the Oaxaca region by about 6000 B.C. It is possible, therefore, that Tomb 34 at Yagul does represent an example of cremation; and Melvin Fowler has offered the suggestion that perhaps the body or bodies were burned elsewhere, and that the tomb served only as a repository for the ashes.[29]

The Olmecoid *brasero* mentioned earlier was recovered from Tomb 33, which shared its southern wall with Tomb 34. Both tombs had approximately the same dimensions: 0.39 meters high, 0.415 meters wide, 1.50 meters long. Only the north and south walls of these tombs were found. Thus whereas Tombs 31 and 32 were rectangular burial chambers with four distinct walls, Tombs 33 and 34 had only two walls each, Tomb 34 having also part of a roof *in situ*. In Tomb 33 the skeleton was extended, with the skull to the west.

The adobe tombs at Yagul speak quite clearly of a complex ceremonialism for burials in the period called Monte Albán I. As Bernal has said, "At this

7. Incised decoration on objects from Tombs 31 and 32, Yagul.

8. Grey tripod bowl found in area of Tombs 31–34, Yagul.

9. Spiral-incised pedestal bowl, Tomb 31, Yagul.

11. Bowl fragment decorated with wet-leaf impression; Patio F (area of Tombs 31–34), Yagul.

10. Incised black pedestal bowl found at Tamazulapan (Mixteca Alta), Oaxaca, in 1952. *MNA*.

time we are certainly not dealing with what could be called a primitive culture (even though it is the first culture found in the Valley). It is, on the contrary, well advanced. The simple fact of knowing definitely that by this time these people could write and had a calendrical system which could be inscribed on stone shows how far they were from primitive. Naturally all the usual complex that goes with this type of advance, with writing and a calendrical system, was present already; that is, we have the whole of the ceremonial pattern such as is found in most of Mesoamerica. By this we understand naturally the type of culture which is organized around, or rather led by, a small group of people, this small group of people being priests. Therefore, the whole of the culture, or at least the high culture, is organized and centered around the people who lead it—the priests, who are interested essentially in religion and in the ceremonies that accompany religious practices. This ceremonialism seems to be the most typical of all traits of really ancient Mexican culture. It is already the most characteristic trait of Monte Albán I."[30]

With regard to the ethnic composition of the Oaxaca metropolis, Caso and Bernal have expressed the opinion that the ancestors of the present-day Zapotecs probably were the people of Monte Albán III.[31] A suggestion about the people who might have been the carriers of the traits of high culture in Monte Albán I might be of interest here. (Let me repeat that I am fully aware of the dangers involved in attempting to correlate artifacts with linguistic and ethnic groups, but the goal of archeology, after all, is the study of people; the study of artifacts is a means to that end.) I have suggested elsewhere that the Tenocelome, as Jiménez Moreno calls the people of La Venta (this volume, p. 7), may have been the ancestors of the people who later possessed the culture that we call Mixtec.[32] Jiménez Moreno believes that the place of origin of the Mixtecs was in Mixtan, a locality on the Oaxaca-Veracruz border near Playa Vicente—that is, in Olman, the rubber country.[33] Covarrubias, too, has given his opinion that the Mixtecs and related peoples originated the "Olmec" art style of La Venta.[34] Thus the people who were later known as Mixtec might have participated also in the culture of Monte Albán I.

This hypothesis is not new, or altogether without support. Jiménez Moreno has written that there are indications that "the two centers [La Venta and Monte Albán] were just then the most highly evolved of all; and probably for this reason they acted more or less in unison as the guiding forces of the cultural development, a sort of La Venta–Monte Albán civilizing axis" (this volume, p. 17). And Bernal has said that "certainly the Monte Albán culture . . . is affiliated with, or we might say a local development of, a larger culture which we usually call Olmec."[35] (It should be noted, however, that Bernal does not agree that there is significant positive evidence that the Mixtecs played a part in the culture of Monte Albán I.)[36]

Caso has also suggested that early Mixtecs might have been connected with the culture of Monte Albán I.[37] And Alberto Escalona Ramos makes this statement: "I suggest the possibility that the Mixtecs, inhabitants of phase I of Monte Albán, displaced by the Zapotecs of phase II, moved northward, some arriving in Xochicalco, where they initiated phase II. Contact with Monte Albán persisted throughout Xochicalco phase II."[38]

Finally, it is interesting to note that Caso has asked the following question, which to my mind lends support to the kind of hypothesis I am offering here: "Does Monte Albán I represent an ancient occupation of Mixtecs or their 'Olmec' ancestors? We cannot as yet answer this question, but the discovery of Tomb 111 (of the first period) suggests that this may be the case."[39]

NOTES

1. H. B. Nicholson, "News and Notes," *American Antiquity,* XXVI (1960), 143.

2. Anne Middendorf Sosnkowski, "An Area Study of the Distribution of Tombs in Meso-america" (unpublished Master's thesis, Department of Anthropology, Mexico City College, 1957), p. 11.

3. *Ibid.*

4. "Son de planta rectangular y muros verticales, en general de pequeñas dimensiones techadas con losas planas." Ignacio Marquina, *Arquitectura prehispánica,* Memorias del Instituto Nacional de Antropología e Historia, S.E.P., No. 1 (México, 1951), p. 337. Plate 94 shows plans of typical Monte Albán I tombs.

5. Miguel Covarrubias, *Indian Art of Mexico and Central America* (New York, 1957), p. 154.

6. Laurette Séjourné, "El simbolismo de los rituales funerarios en Monte Albán," *Revista Mexicana de Estudios Antropológicos,* XVI (1960), 79.

7. Alfonso Caso, "The Mixtec and Zapotec Cultures: The Mixtecs," *Boletín de Estudios Oaxaqueños,* No. 22 (1962), p. 26. See also Caso, "Resumen del informe de las exploraciones en Oaxaca, durante la 7ª y la 8ª temporadas 1937–1938 y 1938–1939," *Actas,* XXVII Congreso Internacional de Americanistas, II (México, 1942), 163.

8. Jorge Acosta, "Informe de la XVI temporada de exploraciones arqueológicas en la zona de Monte Albán, Oaxaca" (unpublished report, Archivos Técnicos, INAH, 1947), p. 12.

9. Personal communications to the author, 1962.

10. Pierre Agrinier, *The Carved Human Femurs from Tomb 1, Chiapa de Corzo, Chiapas, Mexico,* Papers of the New World Archaeological Foundation, No. 6 (Orinda, California, 1960), p. 1.

11. Keith Dixon, "Two Masterpieces of Middle American Bone Sculpture," *American Antiquity,* XXIV (1958), 57–61.

12. John Paddock, "The 1956 Season at Yagul," *Mesoamerican Notes,* No. 5 (1957), pp. 24–25.

13. Philip Drucker *et al., Excavations at La Venta, Tabasco,* Bulletin 170 of the Smithsonian Institution, Bureau of American Ethnology (Washington, D.C., 1959), Plate 21.

14. *Mexico City Collegian,* October 27, 1960, p. 1. For a discussion of the radiocarbon date, see "Yagul Brasero C-14 Date" (anonymous), *Katunob,* Vol. II (1961), No. 2, pp. 7–8, and Paddock's reply, "Yagul Brasero C-14 Date (cont'd)," *Katunob,* Vol. II (1961), No. 4, pp. 7–13.

15. Personal communication from Ignacio Bernal to John Paddock, 1960.

16. Willard F. Libby, *Radiocarbon Dating* (Chicago, 1952), p. 92.

17. *Mexico City Collegian,* July 13, 1961, p. 1.

18. Libby, p. 92.

19. Covarrubias, p. 145.

20. "Los incensarios de este tipo se encuentran desde el sur de Puebla hasta Guatemala."

Alfonso Caso, *Exploraciones en Oaxaca, quinta y sexta temporadas, 1936–1937* (Tacubaya, 1938), p. 23. For a description of other examples of *braseros*, see Alfonso Caso and Ignacio Bernal, *Urnas de Oaxaca*, Memorias del Instituto Nacional de Antropología e Historia, No. 2 (México, 1952), p. 326.

21. Alfonso Caso and Ignacio Bernal, personal communication to John Paddock, 1960.

22. Samuel K. Lothrop, *Zacualpa: A Study of Ancient Quiche Artifacts* (Washington, D.C., 1936), p. 18; Robert Wauchope, *Excavations at Zacualpa, Guatemala* (New Orleans, 1948), pp. 137–39.

23. Thomas Gann and J. Eric S. Thompson, *The History of the Maya* (New York, 1931), p. 6.

24. John Paddock, personal communication to the author, 1960.

25. Eduardo Noguera, personal communication to the author, 1962.

26. Caso, "The Mixtec and Zapotec Cultures: The Mixtecs," p. 26.

27. Séjourné, p. 79. According to Séjourné, the majority of the tombs of Monte Albán I style were oriented east-west; most of the burials had their skulls pointing west.

28. Richard S. MacNeish, *Second Annual Report of the Tehuacan Archaeological-Botanical Project* (Andover, Mass., 1962), pp. 8–9.

29. Melvin Fowler, personal communication to the author, 1962.

30. Ignacio Bernal, "Monte Albán and the Zapotecs," *Boletín de Estudios Oaxaqueños*, No. 1 (1958), pp. 2–3.

31. Caso and Bernal, *Urnas de Oaxaca*, pp. 370–72.

32. Robert E. L. Chadwick, "The Olmeca-Xicallanca of Teotihuacan: A Preliminary Study" (unpublished Master's thesis, Department of Anthropology, Mexico City College, 1962), p. 60. See also Chadwick, "The Ethnohistory of Postclassic Tehuacan" (Andover, Mass., in press); ——, unpublished dissertation, University of Alberta, Calgary, Canada (in preparation); and "Exploración y reconstrucción de la plaza de la Pirámide del Sol, Teotihuacán, México, 1963–1964" (unpublished report, Archivos Técnicos, INAH, 1964), pp. 50–63.

33. Wigberto Jiménez Moreno, "El enigma de los Olmecas," *Cuadernos Americanos*, V (1942), 124.

34. Covarrubias, p. 77.

35. Bernal, "Monte Albán and the Zapotecs," p. 3.

36. Bernal, personal communication to the author, 1962.

37. Caso, "Resumen," p. 183. Also see Caso, "The Mixtec and Zapotec Cultures: The Mixtecs," p. 8.

38. "Sugerimos la posibilidad de que los mixtecos, pobladores de la fase I de Monte Albán, desplazados por los zapotecas de la fase II, se desplazaron hacia el norte llegando algunos hasta Xochicalco, y dando lugar a la fase II. El contacto con Monte Albán persistió durante la fase II de esta ciudad." Alberto Escalona Ramos, "Xochicalco en la cronología de la América Media," *Revista Mexicana de Estudios Antropológicos*, XIII (1952–53), 354.

39. "¿Monte Albán I representa una antigua ocupación de los mixtecos o de sus antepasados 'olmecas'? No podemos resolver todavía esta cuestión, pero el hallazgo de la tumba 111 (de la primera época) lo sugiere." Caso, "Resumen," p. 183.

The Evolution of the Zapotec Glyph C

HOWARD LEIGH

Drawings by Rubén Méndez

One of the first signs by which people learn to identify Zapotec art is that known as the glyph C, so named by Alfonso Caso more than thirty years ago in his original study of Zapotec hieroglyphics.[1] It is almost like a trademark, both because it occurs so much among the Zapotecs and because it seems to have been used only by them.[2] At the time Caso named it, the glyph was believed to represent a stylized jaguar, and this conception of it has been generally accepted by later writers.[3] In the present study, however, nothing has been found to indicate that the jaguar was involved in any way.

The glyph had been developing for many centuries before its commonly recognized form was achieved in the period known as Monte Albán IIIb. After that period, which ended with the abandonment of Monte Albán, the glyph went into decline. It suffered many changes before its final extinction, which probably occurred some centuries before the Spanish conquest. Countless examples are known for period IIIb, and some forty of them are shown here. They come from ceramics, inscription stones, and paintings known to be of that period (Figures 41, 43–82).

The glyph C is an extremely complicated affair, and to understand it in isolation would be quite impossible. For this reason I have introduced a considerable number of drawings that are not of the glyph itself but seem in some way related to it or help to explain certain of its elements. Some of the relationships shown here have long been recognized,[4] whereas others seem to have become apparent only as a result of this study.

To arrange the drawings in exact chronological order is a difficult task, especially within a given epoch, since the simplest forms are not by any means always the oldest. The glyphs of Monte Albán IV are for the most part simpler than those of earlier periods, but they can also be very complicated (Figures 85, 86). It must be understood, therefore, that the arrangement is only roughly chronological.

The most impressive part of studying glyph C during two millennia is the sense of continuity one receives. There is always a reaching back and bringing forward of an element that has gone out of use, often centuries before. When at the beginning of this century Goudy and Kennerley wanted to design new type, they went back to French sixteenth-century type and to the capitals on Trajan's Column, bringing forward styles of letters long out of use. A similar operation seems to have taken place in the long history of the glyph C. Presumably the Zapotec priests could do this because they had manuscript books kept from very early times, and because they had before them ancient inscriptions on stone.

No attempt has been made to study the geographical distribution of the glyph C. Such a study could be made from the materials in the Museo Frissell de Arte Zapoteca at Mitla, and those in the Museo Regional of Oaxaca; the Frissell collection comes from some 180 localities. But even these materials would hardly give a complete picture. That the glyph has been found throughout most of the vast Zapotec region is fairly certain. This seems to confirm Burgoa's claim that there was a certain uniformity of culture, and perhaps ecclesiastical jurisdiction, throughout that large area.[5]

Anybody familiar with the glyph C in the period of its greatest frequency, Monte Albán IIIb, would have little reason to suspect that it was related to the glyph of periods I and II. But if one examines its forms in periods IIIa and Transición II–IIIa, a continuity with the early forms is at once apparent, as Caso and Bernal have pointed out.[6] Having gone backward to the earliest manifestation of the glyph, let us now reverse the process and follow its long career from the beginning.

The earliest and simplest form of the glyph C is that of a vase seen in cross section and having a horizontal band. This band is often decorated with the undulations that represent water (Figures 3–6), and with the water zigzag (Figure 7). If anyone needs convincing that a vase is indeed represented, the forms in Figures 1, 2, 4, and 12 prove the point beyond question. Glyphs 4, 10, 11, and 12 occur with numbers in bars and dots, and doubtless represent the calendrical day-sign Water (Nahuatl, *Atl*; Zapotec, *Nisa*).

But there is more to it than this. The vase was an important element in the complicated symbolism of astro-calendrical religions; much of that symbolism is found on the stones and pottery of Monte Albán I and later periods, and most strikingly in the mosaic designs on the palaces of Mitla. Phyllis Ackerman has written an excellent summary of this ancient symbolism,[7] and although her study was not of Mesoamerica, such ideas are as likely to turn up in the New World as not. It is possible to cite in the art of Monte Albán such symbols as the twin brothers, the S glyph (clouds), the felines of the Milky Way, the mountain glyph (earth), the inverted mountain glyph (sky), the Greek key, the Greek cross (cardinal points), the Malta cross (260 days) as in the Codex Fejérváry-Mayer,[9] half of the gamma cross (the rotation of

constellations around the Pole Star), the net of the sky god, the *Tomoye* (the Japanese name for a three-lobed form found also at Teotihuacan),[10] the fish, the stick through a circle (Polaris), the tree, etc. None of these symbols has to do with the glyph C, but because of their presence we may feel fairly certain of the symbols that do concern it.

In tracing the development of glyph C, we find that in the periods Monte Albán I, II, and Transición II–III we are dealing with the symbol of the flowing vase, and from Monte Albán IIIa onward with a "powerful, inedible animal."[11] The animal in this case is the alligator (Nahuatl, *Cipactli*; Zapotec, *Chila*), day sign for the first day of the Mesoamerican calendar and sometimes spoken of as the Earth Monster or the Sky Monster. It would be difficult to overestimate the importance of this symbol in the art of the Zapotec and Maya civilizations.

First let us consider the symbol of the flowing vase. A god stands or sits, holding in both hands a vase out of which flow two streams in opposite directions. Equally common is a representation of a god holding a vase without any flowing streams. Another representation is of a god with a stream of the Milky Way flowing from his mouth (Figure 8). He is shown as being at the center of the Milky Way, and the mouth of the vase forms its hiatus, from which the streams flow in opposite directions; for, as Ackerman says, "while the hiatus in the Milky Way is not in its center as we see it, iconography stylizes by regularizing the natural fact."[12] The symbolism is, of course, air and moisture, i.e. creative force.

The glyph shown in Figure 1 is taken from Danzante 55 of Monte Albán I. Exactly above this glyph on the stela are the heads of two felines, "powerful, inedible animals," "the felines of the Milky Way."[13] On the abdomen of the Danzante figure is the head of a god from whose mouth flows a stream that turns upward. From the circle (the mouth of the vase), in the position of the sex, flows another stream, which joins the first and turns downward, the two forming the serpent's forked tongue. (Again, the serpent often represents clouds: air and moisture or wind and rain, the creative force. See Figure 8.) The flowing streams are shown also on a pottery vase of Monte Albán I (Figure 9).

In case it is not immediately apparent, the glyphs of Figures 1 and 4 are the same as those of Figures 2, 3, 5, and 6, the former two figures being a sectional view of a pot with a horizontal band, and in the one instance (Figure 4) with the water undulation motif. In Figure 7 a leaf element has been added. This leaf is to recur with frequency on the glyph C over a very long period of time.

Only three examples from Monte Albán II are shown here (Figures 10, 11, 12). Figure 10 has two bars below it. Although the water undulation is missing, the day sign Water was doubtless understood.

In the transitional period between Monte Albán II and III, the early form of the glyph with its water undulation is set into a squared U-form with curling

14

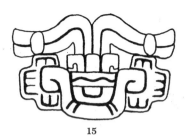

15

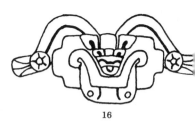

16

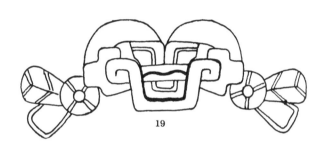

17

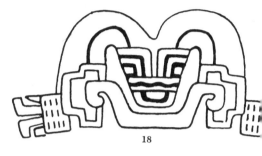

18

19

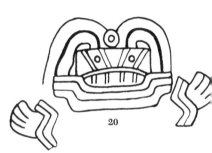

20

21

22

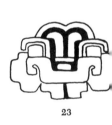

23

24

25

ends (Figures 13, 14), and double streams are added to the vase, flowing out
in opposite directions (Figures 15–19). In Figure 17 three leaves have been
inserted above the vase. A small Transición pottery urn in my collection has
a leaf on the right side of the headdress, and a rain god on the left. Figure 20
was drawn from a small Transición urn, but may be regarded as a "sport,"
having no followers. Then there is a beautiful Transición urn in the Frissell
collection, which shows in the headdress of the figure the upper jaw of an
alligator (Cipactli-Chila), with a leaf on either side (Figure 21 and Figure
92, this volume, p. 129).

Immediately afterward, in Monte Albán IIIa, teeth appear on the under-
side of the squared U-form (Figures 22–26).[14] Teeth had not been present on
the glyph in the Transición period, but the alligator, Cipactli-Chila, was there.
During period IIIa the glyph shows a tendency to represent this important
calendrical sign as first in the list of days. The Zapotec name was written by
Fray Juan de Córdova as both Chilla and Chila. The first spelling is more frequent in Córdova's works, but the second is probably more correct, since
the Spanish double-l sound seems to be foreign to Zapotec phonetics.[15]
The glyph in Figure 26, taken from a fragment, is an exact duplicate of one
on a head from the district of Miahuatlan in the Frissell collection, a head
that is clearly in the style of period IIIa. Two other heads in the Leigh collection show fragments of the same glyph, again in the style of IIIa. There
exist a number of urns (including one in the Frissell collection) that show a
Transición-style glyph C with what seem to be two fragmentary Cipactli
heads facing in opposite directions. At my request, Frank H. Boos has kindly
searched through his vast corpus of photographs of Zapotec art, and has provided me with a photograph of a fine fragment in the American Museum of
Natural History, New York (Figure 27), which shows exactly what I had
hoped to see. I had long felt sure that these twin Cipactli were intimately connected with the glyph C.

There now appears a glyph that cannot be called glyph C, but is used like
it on inscription stones, urns, and braziers (Figures 28, 32, 33). For identification purposes I have had drawn a Cipactli glyph from the Ídolo de Yogana
(Frissell collection) with its mirror image (Figures 30, 31). It forms exactly
the glyph seen in Figures 28, 32, and 33. Figure 28 has leaves, as did Figure
21; it was drawn from a large jaguar urn in the Leigh collection, where it
forms the central element in an elaborate headdress. Figure 35 shows it in
perspective. Figures 36–39, which show how various elements fall into place,
help us to understand the real glyph C as it appears in Figures 40, 41, 43, and
44. Figure 42, from Stela 4 of Monte Albán, is introduced here as an example
of a more realistic representation of the alligator. It is seen from the front
and lacks the lower jaw; in other words, it is the same as glyph C in period
IIIb.

Mathematical signs in the form of bars, dots, and scrolls have been added

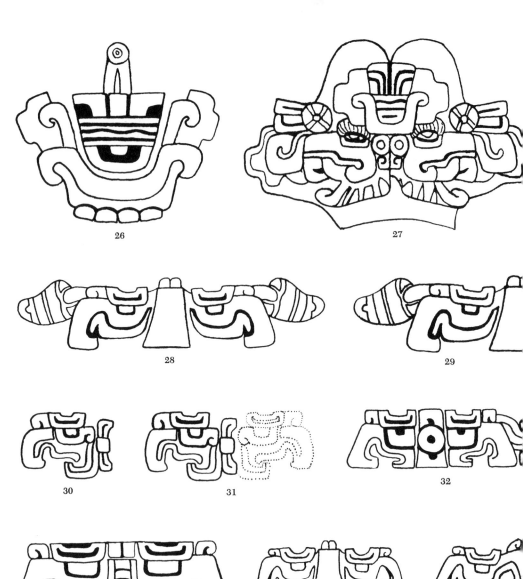

26

27

28

29

30

31

32

33

34

35

36

37

38

39

40

41

42

to the glyph as it appears in Figures 43, 44, and 48. Figure 49, from the top of a stone in the American Museum of Natural History, has elements of the glyph C, but appears to be entirely mathematical.

The glyphs from the Lápida de Bazán and Tomb 105 of Monte Albán show the appendages that Caso has called "eyes of the sky" (i.e. stars).[16] They look like eyes, and Chila-Cipactli is, after all, sometimes referred to as the Sky Monster.

Except for the Lápida de Bazán and Stelae 12 and 15, the inscription stones of Monte Albán do not show the glyph C, so far as I know. The many stones that do show it do not come from Monte Albán itself. Perhaps stelae were not much in vogue in period IIIb, and the great site was heading for abandonment at the end of that period. The infrequency of the glyph is striking, to say the least.

The glyphs in Figures 41 and 43–49 are from wall paintings and inscription stones. Those in Figures 50–82 are from pottery objects. In Figures 41–54 the flowing streams are absent; in 55–81 they are present.

Figure 50 was drawn from a small *Cocijo* (rain god) urn in the Leigh collection. The glyph has as its central ornament a sign for 260; on the back of the urn are two numerical bars that are not shown in the drawing. Caso has described all the many cross glyphs as symbols of turquoise, which is an aquatic symbol. I believe that any of the cross glyphs can represent the day sign Rain (Nahuatl, *Quiáhuitl*), and that they can also be given a numerical interpretation.

From period II on, the glyph C sometimes occurs with numbers as if it were a day sign. There is no doubt that in periods II and Transición it represents the day sign Water (Atl, Nisa), and in II and IV the alligator, Cipactli-Chila. Of course there is another glyph, a water undulation within a cartouche, representing Atl-Nisa from period II on.

Everybody concerned with the archeology of Oaxaca knows how difficult it is to identify artifacts of period IV, that long period between the abandonment of Monte Albán and the Spanish conquest. That the glyph C survived into the period is certain, but it is equally certain that it was on its way to extinction at this time. Some ten weeks of excavation at Lambityeco, a site occupied only during period IV and perhaps a part of IIIb, produced only a single example of the glyph; even that was a fragment broken from a small vase of a style characteristic of IIIb. It was striking to see a whole row of figurines in which not one had a glyph C in the headdress.

To illustrate the glyph C in period IV, I have chosen to start with the examples on the beautiful Stela of Cuilapan in the Oaxaca Museum. The glyph shown in Figure 83 occurs in the lowest of the stone's three sections, directly above a Mountain glyph that is flanked by Cipactli glyphs facing in opposite directions. This arrangement seems to me to represent the three periods of 260 years that constituted period III. The first is represented by the Mountain

Text continued on p. 268

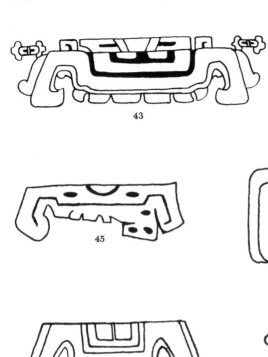

43

44

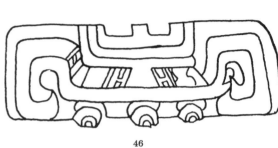

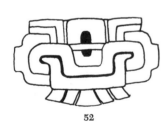

45

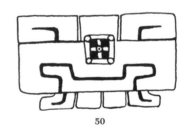

46

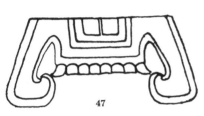

47

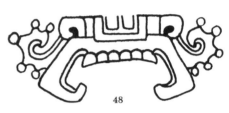

48

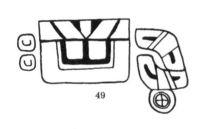

49

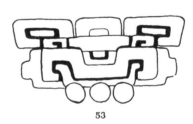

50

51

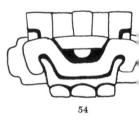

52

53

54

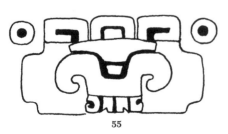

55

56

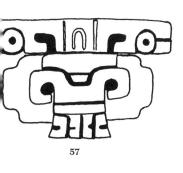

57

58

59

60

61

62

63

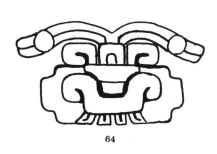

64

65

66

67

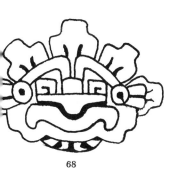

68

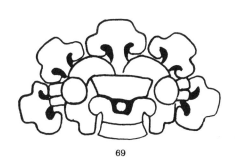

69

70

71

72

73

74

75

76

77

78

79

80

81

82

83

84

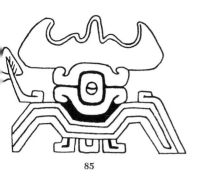

85

86

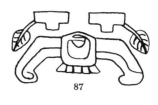

87

88

89

90

91

92

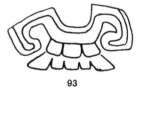

93

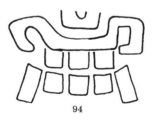

94

95

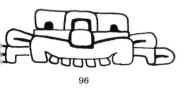

96

97

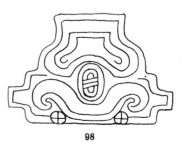

98

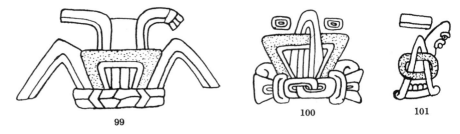

99   100   101

glyph, the second by the Cipactlis, the third by the Cipactli front view, or glyph C.

If this is correct, period IIIa lasted 520 years, and IIIb 260 years, the time of the classic glyph C. It was a period of luxuriance, but also of decline. Figures 85 and 99 are taken from the same Cuilapan stone, where they form the headdress of four personages (each is shown twice) engaged in carrying out a religious ceremony. Figure 85 bears a leaf, which was usually absent in IIIb. An exception is a large urn in the Leigh collection that shows three leaves behind the glyph. Leaves are present also in Figures 87, 88, and 89. In Figure 88 it will be noticed that the person or god inserted in the glyph wears another glyph C as a headdress. I have included here a drawing of a Maya jade figurine showing a Cipactli with leaf (Figure 91). In Figure 99 an element from the year sign (shaded), with streams flowing out from it, has been brought into the glyph. A handsome year sign on a carved tile from Zaachila has a leaf inserted. Caso long ago suspected a relationship between the year sign and the glyph Cipactli.[17] There seem to be elements in Figure 99 that are similar to the year sign on the Stela di Roma (Figure 100). If any sign was more durable than the glyph C, it was the year glyph (Figure 101), and we await with interest Caso's promised study of it.

NOTES

1. Alfonso Caso, *Las estelas zapotecas,* Monografías del Museo Nacional de Arqueología, Historia y Etnografía (México, 1928), *passim.*

2. Since this was written, the Ñuiñe material described in Part II of this volume has come to light. On the Ñuiñe stelae, as well as at Xochicalco and in Veracruz, the wide U-shaped element of the glyph C is frequent.—Editor.

3. Sigvald Linné, *Zapotecan Antiquities and the Paulson Collection in the Ethnographical Museum of Sweden* (Stockholm, 1938), p. 140.

4. Alfonso Caso and Ignacio Bernal, *Urnas de Oaxaca,* Memorias del Instituto Nacional de Antropología e Historia, No. 2 (México, 1952), p. 29.

5. Fray Francisco de Burgoa, *Geográfica descripción,* Publicaciones del Archivo General de la Nación (México, 1934), II, 121.

6. Caso and Bernal, Figures 27, 28, etc.

7. Phyllis Ackerman, "Ancient Religions," in Virgilius Ferm, ed., *The Dawn of Religions* (New York, 1950), *passim.*

8. Alfonso Caso, "Relaciones entre el Viejo y el Nuevo Mundo. Una observación metodo-

lógica," *Cuadernos Americanos*, CXXV (1962), 160–75. In English: "Relations between the Old and New Worlds: A Note on Methodology," *Actas y Memorias del XXXV Congreso Internacional de Americanistas* (México, 1962), I, 55–71.

9. *Codex Fejérváry-Mayer*, in Edward King, Lord Kingsborough, *Antiquities of Mexico* (London, 1831–48), Vol. III.

10. John O'Neill, *The Night of the Gods: An Inquiry into Cosmic and Cosmogonic Mythology and Symbolism* (London, 1893–97), p. 635.

11. Ackerman, p. 5.

12. *Ibid.*, p. 13.

13. *Ibid.*, p. 5.

14. In some cases these teeth seem clearly to have been filed; probably the most obvious examples here illustrated are Figures 23, 51, 55, 56, 57, 79, and 82. The chronological and geographical distribution of these mutilations has been studied by Javier Romero in his book *Mutilaciones dentarias prehispánicas de México y América en general* (México, 1958).

15. Fray Juan de Córdova, *Arte en lengua zapoteca* [1578] (Morelia, Michoacan, 1886), p. 6. See also Córdova, *Vocabulario en lengua çapoteca* [1578]. Edición facsimilar, S.E.P. (México, 1942).

16. Alfonso Caso, *Exploraciones en Oaxaca. Quinta y sexta temporadas 1936-1937* (México, 1938), p. 88.

17. Caso, *Las estelas zapotecas*, p. 47.

The illustrations for this paper have been taken from the following sources. Figs. 2, 15, 18, 21, 24–26, 30, 31, 33, 40, 43, 51, 53, 54, 56, 58, 67–73, 81, 84, 86, 95, and 97 from the Frissell Collection, Mitla. Figs. 9, 13, 17, 19, 28, 29, 34, 50, 55, 57, 63, 66, 75, 76, 78, 80, 82, 90, and 98 from the Leigh Collection, Mitla. Figs. 3, 5, 6, 14, 16, 22, 23, 59, 60, 62, 64, 65, 74, 77, 79, 96, from Caso and Bernal, *Urnas de Oaxaca*. Figs. 10 and 11 are from inscriptions on bedrock at Caballito Blanco, Oaxaca. Figs. 83, 85, and 99 from pieces in the Museo Regional, Oaxaca. Figs. 61, 92, and 94 from Seler, *Gesammelte Abhandlungen*, II, 338, 355, and 361 (figs. 61, 86a, 86b, 102, and 103). Figs. 27 and 49 from fragments in the American Museum of Natural History, New York.

The following illustrations were taken from Monte Albán materials: figs. 1 and 8, Danzante 55; fig. 4, Stela 12; fig. 12, urn from Temple of 7 Deer (in Museo Nacional de Antropología, México); fig. 32, Stela 1; fig. 41, Tomb 104; fig. 42, Stela 4; fig. 44, Lápida de Bazán (in MNA); fig. 45, Stela 15; fig. 46, Tomb 105.

Drawings of figs. 47, 48, 52, 87–89, 93, and 94 are after Caso, *Las estelas zapotecas*. Fig. 47 is Lápida 13 ("de Manuel Martínez Gracida," present location unknown); fig. 48, Lápida 1, MNA; fig. 52, Lápida 6, Museo Regional, Oaxaca; fig. 87, Lápida 2, MNA; fig. 88, Lápida 3, MNA; fig. 89, Lápida 14, in Matatlan; fig. 93, Lápida 4, MNA; fig. 91 from a jade figurine in the collection of Fred Olsen; Fig. 100 is from the Stela di Roma, Museo Pigorini, Rome, No. 57085 (published in Caso 1956). Fig. 101 is from a stone in the monastery wall at Cuilapan, Oaxaca (shown on p. 374, this volume). The present location of the urn from which fig. 20 was taken is unknown.

Some of the drawings in this article are of pieces illustrated in Part II of this volume:

Leigh fig.	Part II fig.	Leigh fig.	Part II fig.	Leigh fig.	Part II fig.
4	36a	30	130	89	283
1, 8	36d	44	137	87, 88	284
12	82	41	138	83	285
21	92	42	149		

Examples of the glyph C illustrated in Part II but not referred to in this article are figs. 5, 93, 97, 112, 114–17, 142, 176–78, 182a (smaller figure at left), 185, 188 (figure at right), 215, 220, 223, 235, and 268.

Colonial Mazatec Lienzos and Communities

HOWARD F. CLINE

The Mazatec Indians occupy parts of the former Districts of Teotitlan, Cuicatlan, and Tuxtepec in the Mexican state of Oaxaca, a relatively small area in the state as a whole (Map 1). Their principal Indian neighbors are the Cuicatec, the Popoloca, and the Chinantec (Map 2). The Mazatec are not well represented in historical and anthropological literature, and most published material on them (chiefly a growing body of data on linguistics) is recent.[1] Modern ethnological reports, archeological accounts, and historical documents are relatively sketchy and sparse.[2] In these there are occasional minor references to lienzos and native "pinturas," but to date no systematic discussion of these Mazatec pictorial documents has appeared in print. What follows here is an attempt to summarize what we now know about them. We shall deal first with materials that were hitherto incorrectly attributed to the Mazatec area, and then with various post-Conquest pictorial documents that are unquestionably Mazatec.

LIENZOS INCORRECTLY ATTRIBUTED TO THE MAZATEC AREA

In the rather large, if scattered, body of descriptive writings about Mesoamerican pictorial documents, the 1905 article by Walter Lehmann stands out as a major pioneering contribution.[3] Unfortunately, that great Americanist incorrectly ascribed to Mazatec hands one item in the group of pictorial documents he discussed. Those who have uncritically followed Lehmann in describing and classifying such documents have, by repetition, perpetuated his initial error.[4]

Lehmann listed only one lienzo under the general rubric "Les Peintures mazatèques": Lienzo Seler I ("Lienzo de Santa María Ichcatlá"), then in the hands of its owner, Eduard Seler.[5] The original document is not now available for study; but the Lehmann description of it leaves little doubt that rather than being Mazatec, it belongs to a group of pictorial and lienzo items

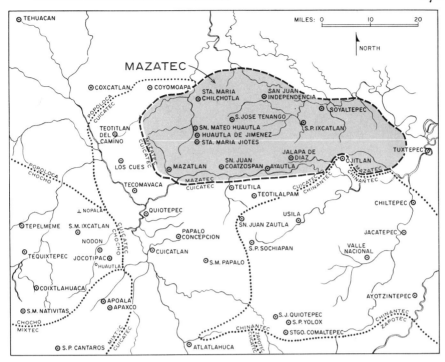

Map 1. The Mazatec area and neighboring communities.

related to the Mixteco-Chocho area, whose main center is around Coixtla-huaca, Oaxaca. Santa María Ixcatlan is part of that complex (Map 1).

There is a San Pedro Ixcatlan in the Mazatec region, but no Santa María Ixcatlan. In any case, the content and toponyms of Seler I show that it is not Mazatec. The lienzo includes, for instance, the place name "Nopala," a non-surviving community that appears on other prose and pictorial documents from Santa María Ixcatlan, notably the 1579 *Relación* of the town.[6] As late as 1939, San Antonio Nopala was remembered as one of the ancient Chocho pueblos connected with Santa María Ixcatlan.[7] Seler obtained the document from Manuel Martínez Gracida, a well-known antiquarian of Oaxaca, who in addition provided him with a companion document known as Seler II, an unpublished lienzo unquestionably connected with Coixtlahuaca and the surrounding area.[8] Martínez Gracida, also known as the compiler of that massive work *Cuadros sinópticos* (1883) (a description of all the places in Oaxaca), placed Santa María Ixcatlan in the Mazatec parish of Huautla, al-though the detailed description provided him by a local official clearly linked it with Coixtlahuaca.[9] Seemingly Martínez Gracida's error was accepted by Seler, then by Lehmann, and later by all those who have followed them. Sub-sidiary lines of testimony, not presented here, combine to indicate that Seler I is not Mazatec; it is clearly Chocho-Mixteco. The decisive datum is Leh-mann's: his 1905 statement that Seler I comes from Santa María Ixcatlan.

There is one other pictorial document incorrectly listed as Mazatec. In a

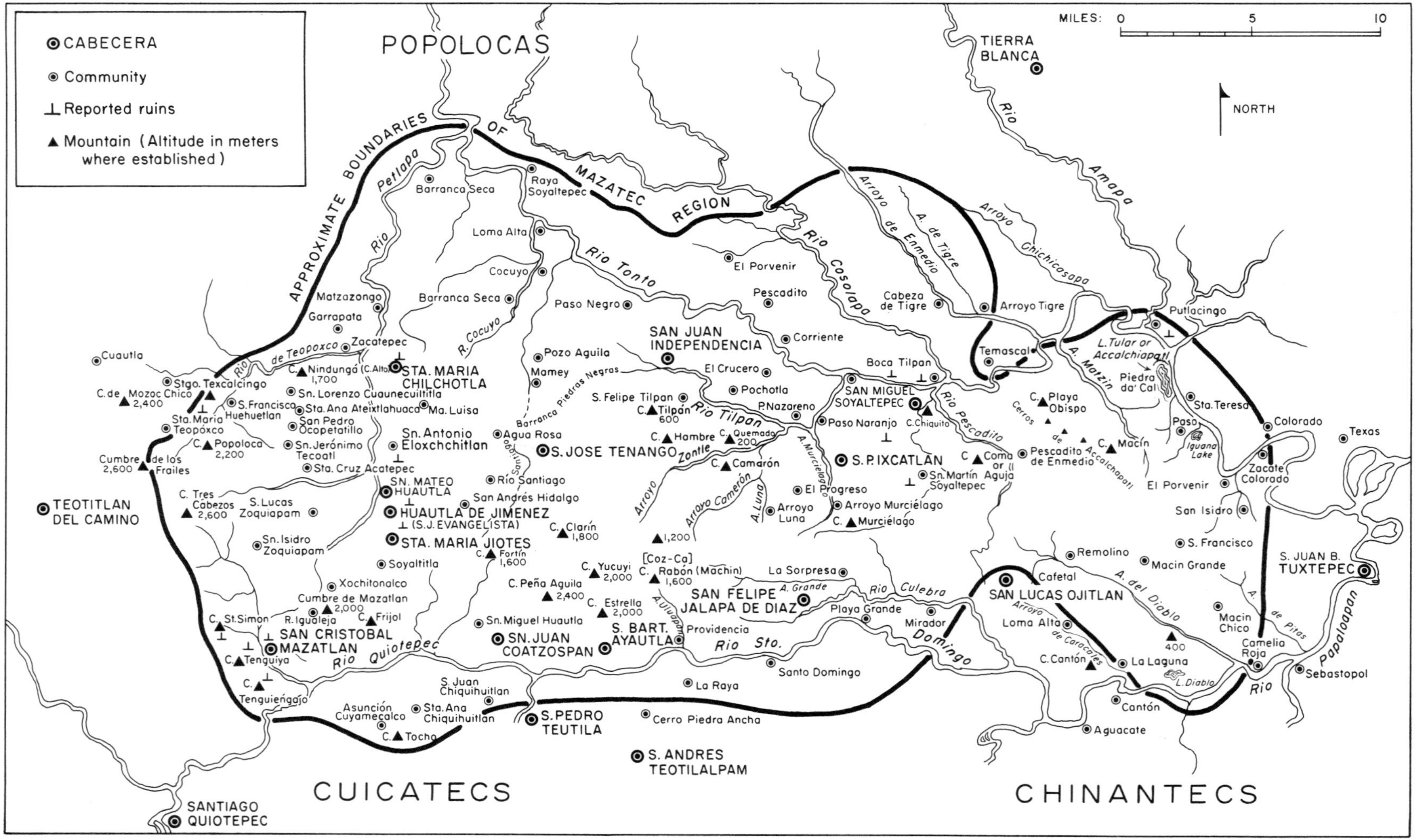

Map 2. The Mazatec area.

very superficial classification of Mexican historical codices made by J. S. Harry Hirtzel in 1928, Codex Fernández Leal appears as the sole entry for post-Conquest Mazatec items.[10] In the sources utilized by Hirtzel, notably Peñafiel (1895), there is nothing to relate this document with Mazatec areas.

There has been some doubt among modern students about where Codex Fernández Leal fits in, since there is little detailed study on which to rely. It has customarily been known as "Cuicatec" because its nineteenth-century owner claimed to be a descendant of the rulers of Quiotepec, who were allied with those of Cuicatlan.[11] Only Hirtzel (who never really justified his classification) placed it among Mazatec pieces. There is no evidence at present to substantiate this claim.

THE COLONIAL MAZATEC LIENZOS AND COMMUNITIES

So far as we know, no *original* Mazatec lienzos exist today in any public collection or even in private hands. The originals all seem lost. None of the documents described below appears to have been cited or known in 1905 by Lehmann, although Frederick Starr had published one by 1902. The usual published secondary sources dealing with the description and classification of Mesoamerican pictorial documents also omit them. Because of this obscurity and neglect, I shall summarize what I have learned about them.

So far only three of these lienzos have been discovered. All are post-Conquest, and each is known only in an imperfect copy. The three are the Lienzo de San Pedro Ixcatlan–San Miguel Soyaltepec, alias Lienzo de Tuxtepec; the Lienzo de Santa María Chilchotla; and the Mapa de San Juan Evangelista Huautla de Jiménez. The first two are unpublished. Starr reproduced his poor photograph of the Huautla document in a limited edition, copies of which are now rarities.[12]

In trying to interpret pictorial documents of this kind, we are always faced with the problem of identifying and locating colonial places on them, and establishing their relationship to modern communities. There are, however, certain materials that help us in such an undertaking, and I shall try to provide them for the three lienzos in question. First a word about these aids.

Among the most important text sources on the historical geography of the area is the *Suma de visitas.* According to Borah and Cook, data for this area were compiled for the *Suma* between about 1544 and 1548. To supplement this information we have the *Libro de tasaciones,* with entries as late as 1565.[13] I have used these sources as a basis for Maps 3 and 4. Of nearly equal importance in locating colonial places is the 1581 *Relación geográfica* for Teotitlan del Camino, both map and text having been published.[14] I have used this source in Map 5.

To return to the lienzos themselves, the only known extant copy of the Lienzo de San Pedro Ixcatlan–San Miguel Soyaltepec is deposited in the Peabody Museum Library, Harvard University.[15] There it is labeled "Lienzo de

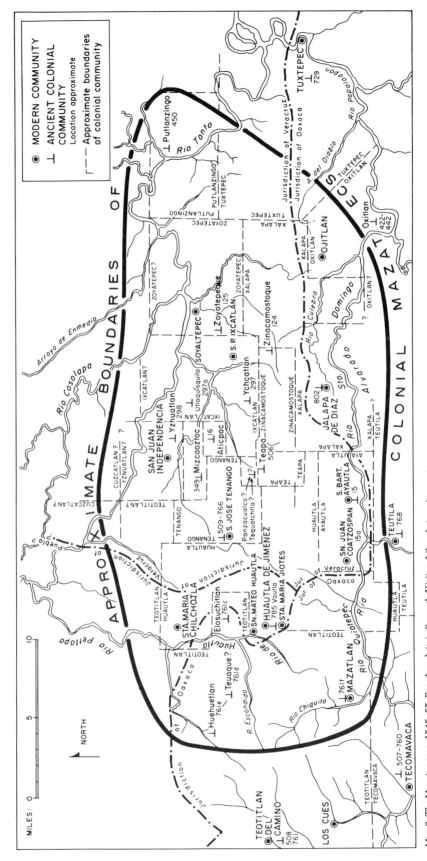

Map 3. The Mazatec area, 1545–65. Based on data in *Suma de Visitas, Libro de tasaciones*, etc.
Numbers refer to descriptions in *Papeles de Nueva España* (*PNE*), Volume I.

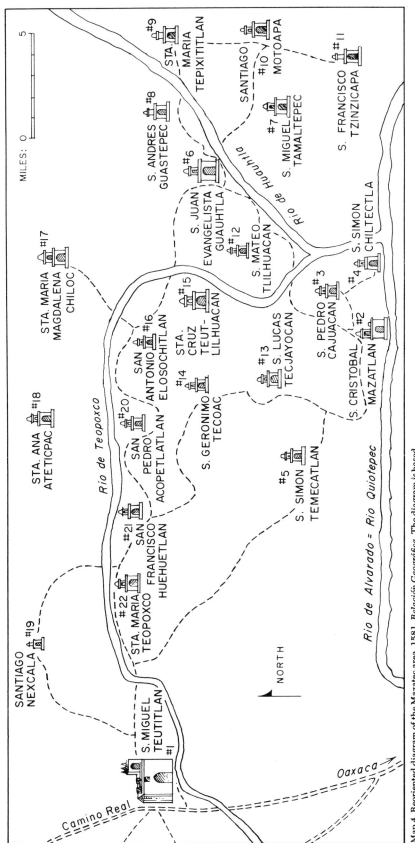

Map 4. Reoriented diagram of the Mazatec area, 1581. *Relación Geográfica.* The diagram is based on "Traza del Partido de Teutitlan del Camino, Oaxaca," in *PNE,* IV, 213. Numbers correspond to numbers on Map 5.

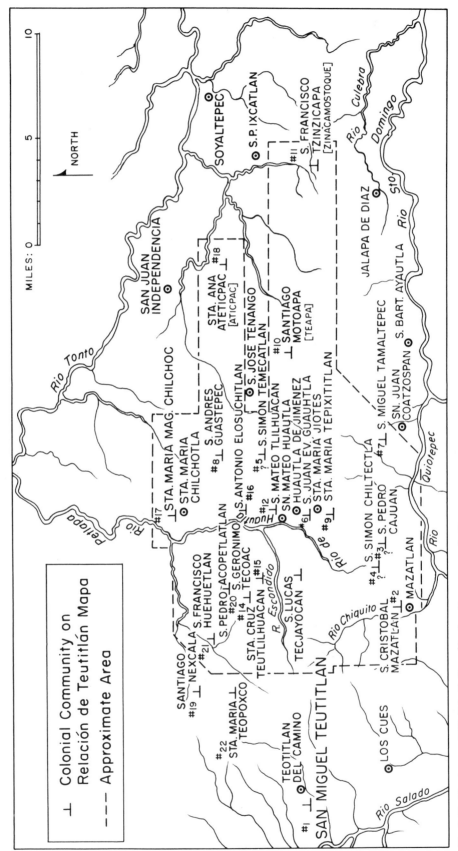

Map 5. The Mazatec area, 1581. *Relación Geográfica.* Locations are approximate.
Numbers correspond to numbers on Map 4.

Tuxtepec," but here we have preferred to name it for the two places that are most important in it.[16] The lienzo is drawn on what appears to be linen paper, which is pasted on another sheet of linen paper. The Peabody copy is 49 x 59 inches (150 cm. side x 125 cm. high). In addition to native glosses, it has several modern penciled notes in English, some apparently by Alfred M. Tozzer, some by other hands. Tozzer's note reads "Rio Tonto & Rio Papaloa- pam. A historical scene of Spaniards and Indians, containing a gloss which is not Nahuatl, and place names around the periphery." The Peabody copy seems to have been drawn or traced in pencil, and then covered with grey watercolor, on which black ink or watercolor appears. The copy thus has no colors, but the unidentified penciled notes in English refer to colors that presumably appeared on the original or the local copy from which the Pea- body copy was taken.[17]

The Peabody version either is, or is related to, a copy of the lienzo made in 1912 by someone in an expedition from the newly formed Escuela Interna- cional de Arqueología y Etnología Americana. At this time Franz Boas was the School's Director, and he was followed in the post by Alfred M. Tozzer.[18] In 1912 Boas and William H. Mechling, who joined the school as a Fellow of the Hispanic Society of America, found the lienzo in the possession of Ma- riano Espinosa of Tuxtepec, Oaxaca, who permitted them to have it copied. A supplement to the School's 1912 Annual Report indicates that a students' copy of the lienzo was on display, and also could suggest that perhaps the original document remained in Indian hands.[19] Of the several mentioned copies—Espinosa's, Boas-Mechling's, and the students'—it is now uncertain which is the Peabody document.

Figure 1 is a photocopy of the Peabody copy.[20] Figure 2 is a diagram of the lienzo. The central feature is a baptismal scene below an unglossed com- munity, with two colonial Spaniards on the left and another on the extreme right, a friar and Indians in the center; a confused and corrupt Nahuatl gloss accompanies the scene.[21] A single place name, "Metza apatl," appears as a boundary marker, near the center. Near it is another large, unglossed com- munity. Various watercourses are shown, and around the edges are place signs and personages, many of which are also accompanied by glosses, and in some instances numbers. Detailed analysis reveals that the one unglossed community is San Pedro Ixcatlan, and the other San Miguel Soyaltepec. Most of the other places are also identifiable. Map 6 locates the communities de- picted on this lienzo; it is based in part on data supplied by Espinosa, the former owner of the document.

The date "1521" in the gloss does not refer to the date of production of the document, but to a historical event of that year, the putative first contact with Spaniards. If the encomenderos pictured on the lienzo are to be identified with the de Nava family of Oaxaca (to which several published colonial sources refer as sixteenth-century holders of San Pedro Ixcatlan), the earliest

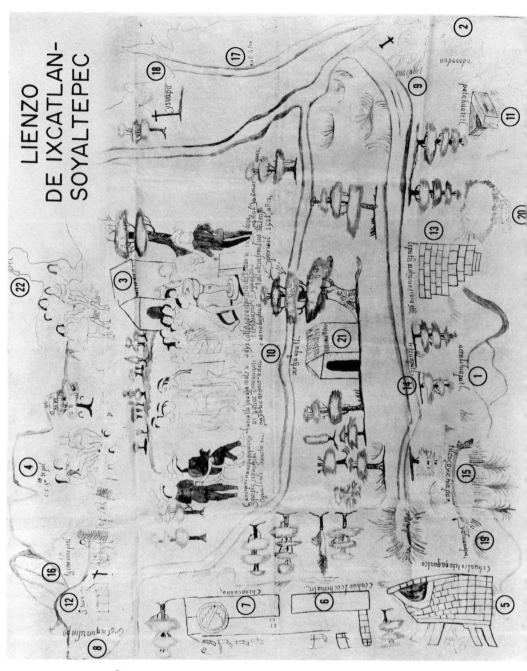

1. Photostat of the Lienzo de
Ixcatlan-Soyaltepec. *Peabody
Museum, Cambridge, Mass.*
Numbers correspond
to numbers in Figure 2.

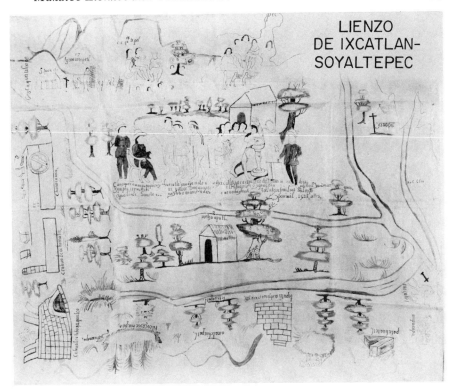

2. Diagram of the Lienzo de Ixcatlan-Soyaltepec. Place names are as given on the lienzo. Espinosa place names, if different, follow in parentheses. 1 Accalchiapatl. 2 Anpanapa (Ampanapa). 3 — (Ayizcatl). 4 Cacahuatepetl. 5 Cehualco-Tetzotacoalco. 6 Cenhualco-Chimaliz. 7 Chinacaostoc (Chinacasto). 8 Coscaquauhliapa (R. Coz-ca). 9 Mazatitl. 10 Metza apatl (Matza apatl). 11 Patahuatetl. 12 S. Juan. 13a Tepatli. 13b Acotzinco (Acotzingo, Acotxinco, Acoltzinco). 14 Tetza apatl (Plan de Atilpatl). 15 Tilcocoyochiapac. 16 Tzinacatepetl (Tzinacantepetl). 17 Xalilalco. 18 Ysuapa (Isuapa). 19 Yzhuanapa. 20 [Ocelotl]. 21 Zoyatepec. 22 [Tzinacatepetl] II [Atzcatepetl [see 16], Txinantepetl [Señorío de Tuxtepec]). 23 — (Pochtlancingo [Señorío de Tuxtepec]).

date at which the lienzo could have been composed is about 1550. It could be later, but probably not much beyond 1600. The central gloss, around the baptismal scene, is confused. The Appendix to this paper, which relies heavily on Espinosa's work, discusses it in more detail.[22] The content of the document seems to be historical-cartographical, and is possibly connected with litigation over tribute payments, native land boundaries between the two major communities, or succession in their cacique lines.

The Lienzo de Santa María Chilchotla is apparently of the same nature. In 1937, in connection with ethnographic and linguistic investigations of the Chinantla and surrounding regions, Bernard Bevan visited the western Mazatec area, and in 1938 he returned there for a short field season shared by Dr. and Mrs. Jean B. Johnson and Louise Lacaud.[23] Although the details are now somewhat hazy, Bevan writes that in 1937 he saw and was allowed to take black and white snapshots of a copy of the lienzo, then in the possession of "an

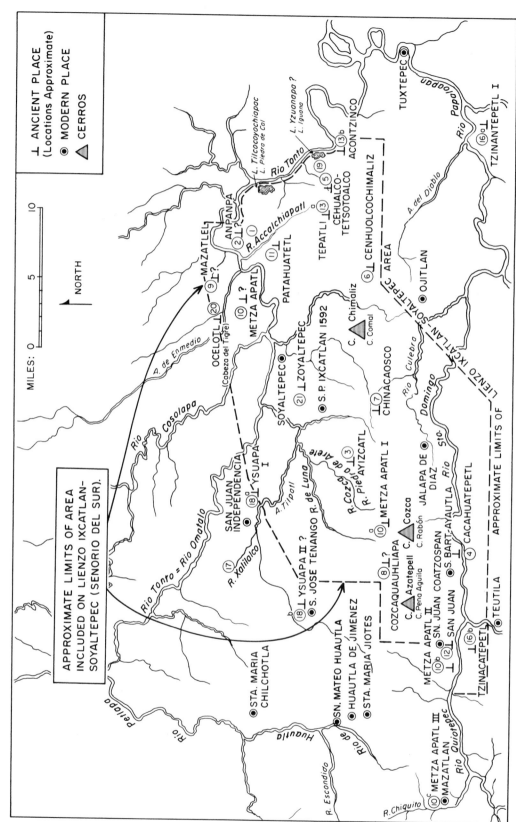

Map 6. The area represented in the Lienzo de Ixcatlan–Soyaltepec.
Numbers correspond to numbers in Figure 2.

otherwise undistinguished Mazatec Indian who held the now meaningless hereditary title of *cacique*."[24]

The positive copies of the three 1937 Bevan small photos are now in the files of Johnson's widow, Irmgard Weitlaner Johnson (Coyoacan, D.F.); the original negatives are apparently lost. I have reproduced one of these photos in Figure 3, and my reconstruction in Figures 4 and 5 is based on tracings from enlarged re-photographs of the three small Bevan snapshots. The original document is apparently lost. Its history and pedigree are unknown. For study and comment we have only the present unsatisfactory reconstruction, which may derive from a wholly unknown earlier item.

One can read on the reconstruction, in nineteenth-century handwritten block letters, the following legend: "Copia de un lienzo tejido a mano cuyos trazos y carácteres apenas son perceptibles; no tiene firma y se presume data del año de 1751." To the left of this is a small note in cursive modern hand, with an almost illegible signature: "Sta. María Chilchotla, octubre 20 de 1924, J. Hernández [?]." At the edge of each of two stylized churches, one with a baptism scene, are two other main glosses. One says "La yglecia vieja. Aquí bautismo Sr. Dr. Marge yglecia del sapo años 1751." The other reads "La yglesia del partido de Sta. María del Chilchotlan, año de 1758, a mes enero 22."

The photographs and the reconstruction based on them do not enable us to state with any certainty the dimensions or material of this copy. The lienzo appears to be painted, perhaps in colors, on woven cotton cloth. It would also seem to be between 7 and 8 feet long, and about 4 feet wide. The photographs leave out one small section at the upper left-hand margin. It still is not clear whether this document is a nineteenth-century copy of a presumed 1751 copy, or whether this is a 1924 copy of that nineteenth-century copy.

We are by no means certain what purpose the document was meant to serve. The contents seem to be historical-cartographical. Around the edges as well as on the central portions are various watercourses, boundary markers, and landmarks, some with glosses. At the lower right is a row of nine stylized figures, apparently caciques, with the blurred notation "desde 1710."[25] A line of footprints around the edges suggests that the main purpose of the document was to delineate the town's eighteenth-century boundaries. Figures 4 and 5 diagram some of these data. Map 7 has been compiled from various sources to indicate the area covered by the lienzo.

For a suggestion of the possible provenience and history of the document, let us examine for a moment the "hereditary cacique" who showed the lienzo to Bevan. Wilhelm Bauer (1908) provides a few data on this cacicazgo or lordship. He notes that the last Mazatec "king" was one Manuel Vicente, who was said to have died in 1869 at the age of 103. His status as cacique was apparently recognized by the Mexican government until 1857, when hereditary titles of this nature were abolished; in fact, the native leadership persisted informally for many years. On Manuel Vicente's death the cacicazgo fell to

3. Lienzo de Chilchotla. *Bevan photo.*

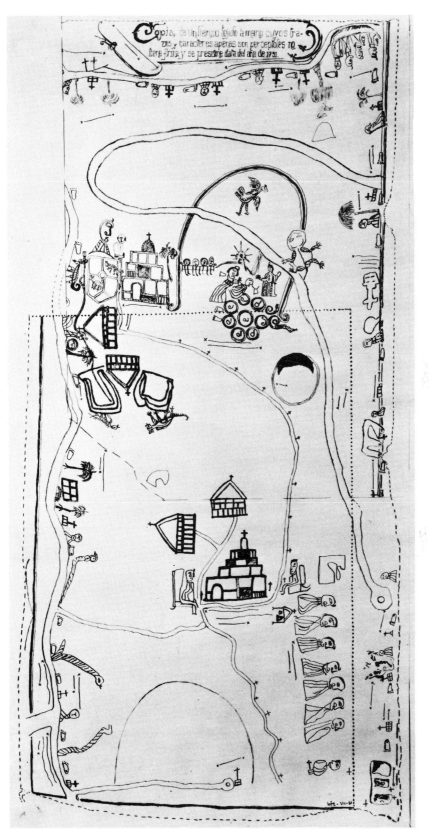

4. Reconstruction of the Lienzo de Chilchotla.

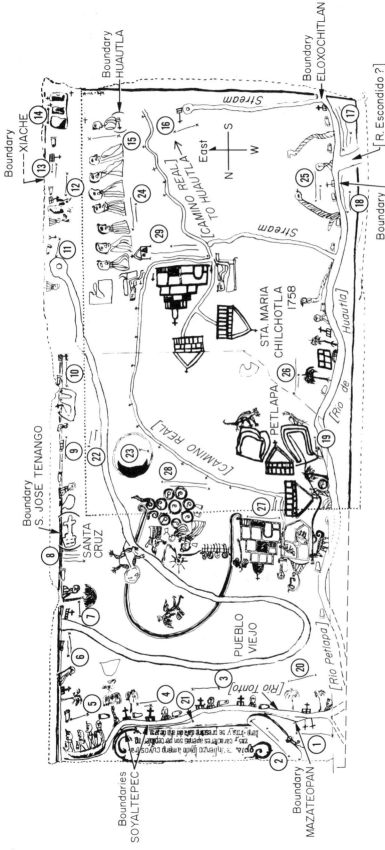

5. Diagram of the Lienzo de Chilchotla. 1 Otro lado de Mazateopan. 2 Sta. Ma. Chilchotla. Octubre 20 de 1924. J. Hernandez. 3 Lace daza Ollaliecu. 4 -ieonapse-- Alta. 5 Palo Palma. 6 A Rio Suquipa la Raya S [oyaltepec?]. 7 Palo Flore. 8 Iqual piedra de la Sta. Cruz Raya la Nopale Sn. José Tenango. 9 Aqui pudere Piedra de Cal. 10 Medio temas aqui. 11 [illegible word]. --tla--tepec. 12 [illegible]. 13 [alz?]xiache Raya. 14 [illegible]. 15 Palo de Raya de Huautla. 16 Agua [illegible]. 17 Otro lado Raya de pueblo San Antonio Elosuchitlan. 18 Otro lado Raya de S. Fran. Huehuetlan. 19 Petlapa. 20 La Raya Chicotlan. 21 Otro lado pasa llano de la gente de Suyatepequiz. 22 Piedra Colorado. 23 Leña. 24 Linea el cacique viene de año 1710. 25 Aqui la Raya de los Cascaveles. 26 Aqui se llama llano (?) de Suyatepequi. 27 Y la Iglecia vieja. 28 Aqui vautismo Sr. Dn. Marge Yglesia del Sapo de años 1751. 29 Y la Iglesia del Partido de Snta. Maria de Chilchotla. Años de 1758 a mes enero 22.

284

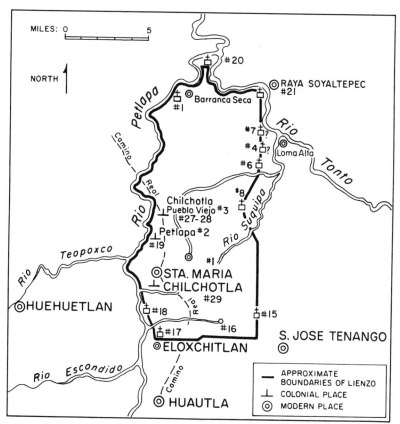

Map 7. The area represented in the Lienzo de Chilchotla. Numbers correspond to numbers in Figure 5.

an unnamed Mazatec whom Bauer calls "the last cacique, ruler [Beherrscher] of Chilchotla"; this man was assassinated in the 1880's by discontented followers.

His widow, interviewed in 1903 by Bauer near Chilchotla on the Finca Sta. Helena, apparently provided Bauer with data on the caciques of this area. He says that they were always selected by one or more related towns, for a life term; that they received voluntary tributes in the form of maize, beans, sugarcane, coffee, or clothing; and that a strong personality seems to have been the chief quality that won a man election. The duties of a cacique combined those of judge and religious leader, since he was in charge of all cult practices. Upon election, each cacique chose a "holy animal" to represent him, and this animal was given a place of honor in the village church of Chilchotla; the animals included snakes, tigers, eagles, alligators, and black dogs, these last being considered especially important.[26]

Apparently Huautla and Chilchotla were related towns under the same general cacique. The Mapa de Huautla (with which we shall deal next) has a picture of a cave showing remains of the "kings." Caves of this kind are described by the local compilers of data on Chilchotla for the *Cuadros sinópticos* (1883) as the cemeteries of "kings and nobles of the Mazatec nation," from which the compilers extracted skeletal materials and pottery from a central crypt.[27]

Finally, we come to the Mapa de San Juan Evangelista Huautla de Jiménez. In 1900, on one of his pioneering journeys through Mexico, Frederick Starr visited a small portion of the Mazatec region and spent a short time in Huautla. While he was there, he was shown Mazatec documents, including the Mapa de Huautla, of which he made a photographic copy.

In both his *Notes on the Ethnography of the Indians of Southern Mexico* (1902) and *In Indian Mexico* (1908), as well as in unpublished journals deposited in the Ayer Collection (Newberry Library, Chicago), Starr mentions the original document. It was kept, apparently, in the *palacio municipal*, together with a quarto volume of land documents bound in parchment, dated 1763. It is possible that in 1902 Starr issued a single-sheet publication of his photograph of the Mapa, for in his famous *Notes* he mentions his intention of publishing it, and in the later *In Indian Mexico* he mentions the publication as a fact.[28] Figure 6 is a photograph of the published Mapa de Huautla, from the copy of this rare item preserved in the New York Public Library.[29] Unfortunately, there seems to be a portion omitted on each side margin; at the left, the town of Huautla seems bisected, and at the right, the photograph reveals only the first part of a place name (Figure 7).

The original Mapa, whose present whereabouts are unknown, was said by Starr to be "painted on a strip of coarse cotton, probably native-woven, in red, black, yellow, and brown, and measures about 7 feet by 3 feet 10 inches." He notes mountains, valleys, streams, caves, trees, houses, churches, and villages, together with "various astonishing birds and animals," on this detailed landscape. He referred to it as "a quaint piece of painting" and "a curious geographical chart."

Starr's informants thought that the Mapa was about the same age as the dated documents of Huautla's title, 1763. This comports well enough with data provided in *Cuadros sinópticos*. The compilers tell us that the church in Huautla was constructed in 1766. The history they provide is taken from Torquemada and other printed sources.[30] None of the other churches shown on the Mapa is dated in this source.

From the Starr photograph it would seem that this document sets forth the eighteenth-century boundaries of Huautla, which is shown (unglossed) at the center of the extreme left margin. The various neighboring communities, linked by labeled roads, are shown as groups of buildings. These places are shown in Map 8. Near the upper center of the Mapa is depicted a cave with skulls, and on or above the mountains at the top are various birds. Of the

6. Mapa de Huautla. *After Starr, ca. 1903.*

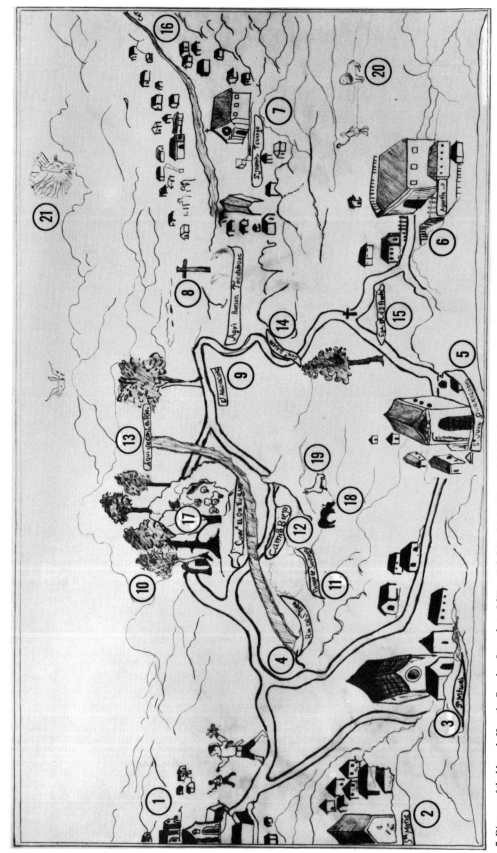

7. Diagram of the *Mapa de Huautla. Based on Starr photo.* 1 [Huautla]. 2 Sta. Maria [Jiotes]. 3 S. Miguel [Huautla]. 4 Rio de Santiago. 5 S. Juan Quaxospam. 6 Ayautla. 7 S. Joseph Tenango. 8 Aqui llaman Tecolotepec. 9 El Aguacate. 10 Cueva el Oxtiupam. 11 Parage de Santiago. 12 Camino Biejo. 13 Aqui se cons. el Rio. 14 Cam. de Abajo. 15 Eya. de las 3 Pinoles. 16 Cat--- [name incomplete]. 17 [skulls]. 18 [deer]. 19 [bull?].

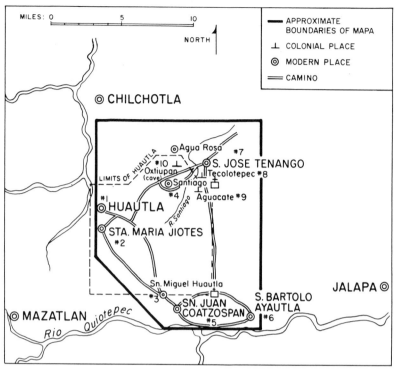

MILES: 0 — 5 — 10

NORTH

— APPROXIMATE BOUNDARIES OF MAPA
⊥ COLONIAL PLACE
◎ MODERN PLACE
═ CAMINO

◎ CHILCHOTLA

◎ Agua Rosa #7
#10 ⊥ ◎S. JOSE TENANGO
LIMITS OF HUAUTLA Oxtiupan (cave) ‖Tecolotepec #8
◎Santiago
#1 #4 ⊥ Aguacate #9
◎HUAUTLA
◎ STA. MARIA JIOTES #2

Sn. Miguel Huautla
#3 S. BARTOLO JALAPA ◎
SN. JUAN AYAUTLA
COATZOSPAN ◎ #6
◎ MAZATLAN Quiotepec #5
Rio Quiotepec

Map 8. The area represented in the Mapa de Huautla. Numbers correspond to numbers in Figure 7.

rivers, only the Río Santiago is labeled. At the center left margin is San José Tenango; two crosses show the eastern limits of Huautla.

Before discussing the data we have gathered, let us summarize them. From published sixteenth-century documents a fair number of colonial Mazatec communities can be located, many of which appear also on copies of the three lienzos. In addition, the lienzos add some local detail. The key to Map 9 lists these colonial Mazatec places, generally attempting to correlate modern communities with ancient ones; Map 9 locates them, so far as our present knowledge will allow.

COMMENTS ON MAZATEC COLONIAL ETHNOHISTORY

It is premature to attempt to outline the ethnohistory of the Mazatec in late pre-Conquest or early colonial times; the documentation is inadequate. However, attempts in this direction have been made. Most recent (1955) is a synthesis by Alfonso Villa Rojas.[31] It draws heavily on Espinosa (1910) and on an unpublished study by Gonzalo Aguirre Beltrán entitled "Los pobladores del Papaloapan."[32] Relying on these sources, Villa Rojas attempted to map the communities, but neither he, nor apparently Aguirre Beltrán, utilized the lienzos here discussed. When Espinosa made errors or unsupported generalizations, these are uncritically repeated by Villa Rojas. But he does add some

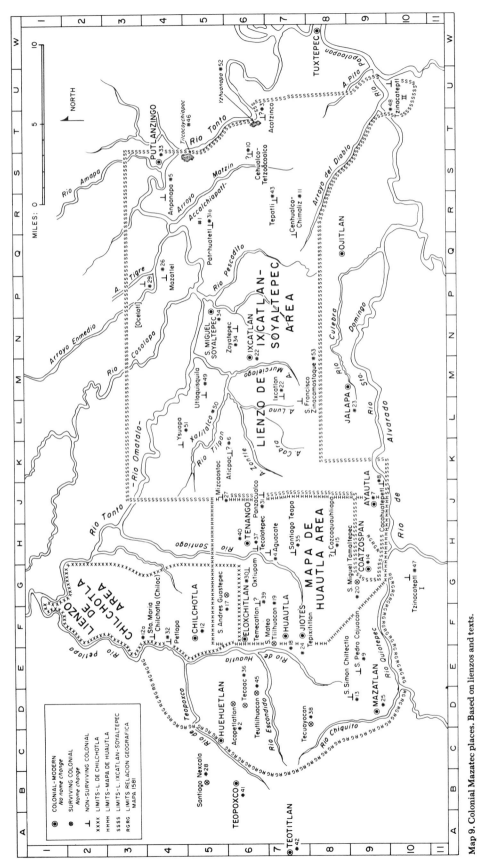

Map 9. Colonial Mazatec places. Based on lienzos and texts.

290

No. in Map 9	Place or Community (with variants and probable modern location)	Coordinates in Map 9
1	Accalchiapatl (mod. Arroyo Matzin)	R-S/4-7
2	Acopetlatlan, S. Pedro (mod. Ocopetatla)	D/6
3	Acotzinco	T/7
4	Aguacate	H/6
5	Anpanapa (var. Ampanapa)	R/4
6	Aticpac, Sta. Ana (var. Ateticpac)	K/6
	Atzcatepetl, see 48	
7	Ayautla, S. Bartolomé (mod. Ayautla)	J/7
	Ayizcatl, see 22	
8	Cacahuatepetl	K/9
9	Cajuacan, S. Pedro (mod. S. Pedro)	E/7
10	Cenhualco Tetzoacoalco	T/6
11	Cenhualco Chimaliz	R/7
12	Chilchotla, Sta. María (vars. Chiloc, Pueblo Viejo; mod. Chilchotla)	F/5
13	Chiltectla, S. Simón (mod. Coyotepec)	D/9
	Chinacaostoc, Chinacasto, see 53	
14	Coatzospan, S. Juan (var. Quaxospan; mod. Coatzospan)	G/9
15	Cozcaquauhliapa	H/8
16	Eloxchitlan, S. Antonio (var. Elosuchitlan; mod. Eloxochitlan)	F/6
17	Guastepec, S. Andrés (mod. S. Andrés Hidalgo)	G/6
18	Huautla, S. Juan Ev. (vars. Vautla, Guauhtla; mod. Huautla de Jiménez)	F/7
19	Huautla, S. Mateo (var. Tlilhuacan; mod. S. Mateo Huautla)	F/7
20	Huautla, S. Miguel (var. Tamaltepec; mod. S. Miguel Huautla)	G/9
21	Huehuetlan, S. Francisco (mod. Huehuetlan)	C/5
	Isuapa, see 51	
22	Ixcatlan, S. Pedro (vars. Ychcatlan, Ayizcatl; mod. Ixcatlan)	M/7
23	Jalapa, S. Felipe (var. Xalapa; mod. Jalapa de Diaz)	M/8
24	Jiotes, Sta. María (var. Tepixititlan; mod. Jiotes)	F/7
25	Mazatlan, S. Cristóbal (vars. Matza apatl, Metza apatl; mod. Mazatlan)	D/9
26	Mazatetl	P/4
27	Mixcaostoc	J/5
28	Nexcala, Santiago (mod. Texcalcingo)	B/5
29	Ocelotl (mod. Arroyo Tigre)	P/4
30	Oxtiupam (Cave)	G/6
31	Panzacualco	J/6
	Parage Santiago, see 35	
31a	Pata huatetl	R/5
32	Petlapa	F/4
33	Putlanzingo (var. Pochtlancingo; mod. Putlalcingo)	S/4
	Quaxospan, see 14	
	Tamaltepec, S. Miguel, see 20	
34	Soyaltepec, S. Miguel (var. Zoyatepec; mod. Soyaltepec)	N/6
35	Teapa, Santiago (var. Parage Santiago; mod. Santiago Viejo)	H/7
36	Teocoac, S. Gerónimo (mod. Tecoatl)	D/6
37	Tecolotepec	H/7
38	Tecuayocan, S. Lucas (mod. S. Lucas Zoquiapan)	D/8
39	Temecatlan, S. Simón	G/6
40	Tenango, S. José	H/6
41	Teopoxco, Sta. María	B/6
42	Teotitlan, S. Miguel (var. Teutitlan; mod. Teotitlan)	A/7
43	Tepatli	R/7
	Tepixititlan, see 24	
44	Tetza apatl	Unlocated
	Teutitlan, see 42	
45	Teutlilhuacan, Sta. Cruz (mod. Sta. Cruz Acatepec)	D/6
46	Tilcocoyochiapac	S/4
47	Tzinacatepetl I (var. Tzinancatepetl)	G/10
48	Tzinacatepetl II (mod. Sebastopol)	U/10
	Tzinzicapa, see 53	
49	Utlaquisquila	M/5
	Vautla, see 18	
	Xalapa, see 23	
50	Xalilalco (mod. R. Tilpan)	K-M/5
	Ychcatlan, see 22	
51	Ysuapa (var. Yzhuatlan; mod. S. J. Independencia)	K/4
52	Yzhuanapa	T/6
53	Zinacamostoque, S. Francisco (vars. Tzinzicapa, Chinacaostoc, Chinacasto)	M/7
	Zoyatepec, see 34	

useful data from other sources, and his short, pioneering synthesis, though historiographically unsatisfactory, provides a valuable starting point for further investigations.

The most important source, though also inadequate, is Mariano Espinosa's *Apuntes históricos* (1910), on which all must rely to some degree.[33] We have seen that he owned a version of the Lienzo de Ixcatlan–Soyaltepec, and his text indicates that he had seen or used the Lienzo de Chilchotla, or a document very like it. His work is particularly valuable because he obtained information from Indians of his day about the places and events depicted, thus preserving in print traditional data that do not appear on the documents themselves. With these aids he sketched the history of the Mazatec. Basing himself on a misreading of the date on the Lienzo de Chilchotla, he posits a history beginning in 1190, and the subsequent splitting of the Mazatec realm into two Señoríos, North (Huautla-Chilchotla-Mazatlan) and South (Ixcatlan-Soyaltepec). His data on the Señorío del Norte are sketchy and ambiguous. From the almost exact correlations of the place names and other data on the Lienzo de Ixcatlan–Soyaltepec and in Espinosa's text, it is self-evident that the pictorial document was his major source. He omits a few minor places shown, and adds one or two others, with valuable information on their location, presumably from his Indian informants. Many of his assertions about the history of given communities, however, are drawn from secondary sources, often unidentifiable. The various statements about "invasions," for instance, seem to stem from Clavijero and other common treatments of pre-Conquest history. Therefore, though it is still the chief document for work on Mazatec ethnohistory, Espinosa's *Apuntes* must be used with extreme caution by those seeking real historical data.

Thus we still lack a reliable historical treatment of the Mazatec. Some puzzling features in the small extant literature are yet to be resolved, such as the identification of the mysterious "Guatinicanames" recently discussed by Robert J. Weitlaner.[34] At the same time, however, we have at our disposal sources not hitherto utilized, among which are the three lienzos here examined.

SUMMARY

To conclude, let me list the main points of our discussion:

1. Neither Seler I nor Codex Fernández Leal is Mazatec. Earlier literature classifying them as Mazatec is incorrect.

2. At present there are only three available Mazatec colonial lienzos: Ixcatlan-Soyaltepec; Chilchotla; Mapa de Huautla.

3. None of these exists in the original; all are more or less defective copies. So far only the Mapa de Huautla has been published, in a limited, rare edition.

4. Using data from these lienzos and other colonial sources, we are able to reconstruct the locations of about 50 colonial Mazatec places (Map 9).

5. In 1910, Mariano Espinosa utilized materials from the Lienzo de Ixca-tlan-Soyaltepec (which he once owned in copy), and from a document that may have been the Lienzo de Chilchotla, for his historical sketch of the ancient Mazatecs. His assertions, resting in part on a misreading of dates and on very subjective views, must be further verified before they can be accepted professionally. Those using Espinosa have followed him too uncritically.

6. Most of the investigation of the ancient and modern Mazatec areas remains to be done. It is an interesting, important, and neglected region that warrants further consideration.

APPENDIX

Lienzo de Ixcatlan-Soyaltepec. Notes on the Central Gloss.

The central scene on the lienzo is a baptismal episode, and on either side of it are figures in Spanish dress. Accompanying it is a four-line gloss in rather corrupt Nahuatl, possibly compounded by copyist's errors or omissions. Read from left to right, the gloss appears as follows, according to my transcription (hyphens denote illegible or missing letters):

[Line 1]: CANCIQUECNANEQUEOQUIZEY -HUECATLAYOU MOTE N--- UAYXCATLAY OCACIPACTLI D JUAN DE -ENDOÇA

[Line 2]: YQUIPIA CEPUATTCHI --UI YQUAC OMOQUAOTE ---- T- TLAHUANOCO YQUA ACOHU -PANOL JUAN MARQUES

[Line 3]: OQUALHUIC SANCTO ----NAYHUAN COMENDERO ---O DE NABA YHUAN TOTLATZIN FRAI LUIS BALEOJO

[Line 4]: 1521 AÑOS

In a private communication (March 14, 1961), Miguel León-Portilla was kind enough to provide me with a reconstruction of this material, together with a literal translation. The translation, if the gloss is read as a four-line composition, gives a confused statement, as follows: SOLO CUANDO VINIERON A ENCONTRAR DE LEJOS CUANDO ERA DE NOCHE SE LLAMABA CON ROSTRO OSCURO LAGARTO SEÑOR D. JUAN DE MENDOZA TENÍA VEINTE Y [MÁS DE CINCO] AÑOS FUERON BAUTIZADOS SE LES MOJÓ SUS CABEZAS ESPAÑOL JUAN MARQUÉS VINO SANTO [----] A Y ENCOMENDERO [----] O DE NAVA Y NUESTRA REVERENCIA FRAY LUIS BALEOJO. EN EL AÑO 1521.

Restudy and analysis led me to the conclusion that, rather than a single gloss, the materials in fact formed four subglosses, each connected with the picture or group of pictures beneath which it is found. When broken into these elements, the statements would be as follows:

[Gloss 1]: SOLO CUANDO VINIERON DE LEJOS A ENCONTRAR TENÍAN VEINTE Y [MÁS DE CINCO] AÑOS CUANDO ERAN BAUTIZADOS SANTA IGLESIA

[Gloss 2]: CUANDO ERA DE NOCHE SE LLAMABA EL CON ROSTRO OSCURO LAGARTO, SEÑOR D. JUAN DE MENDOZA SE FUÉ BAUTIZADO. SE LE MOJÓ SU CABEZA NUESTRA REVERENCIA FRAY LUIS VALEOJO

[Gloss 3]: ESPAÑOL JUAN MARQUÉS EN EL AÑO 1521

[Gloss 4]: ENCOMENDERO ----O DE NAVA

Glosses 3 and 4 deal with Spaniards historically known and identifiable. Juan Marqués was one of Cortés's captains, who campaigned in the Tuxtepec area in

1521. Probably he was the first Spaniard seen by Mazatecs. A companion in arms (and also one of Cortés's group) was Juan López de Ximena, to whom Cortés granted Ixcatlan, to be held in encomienda, at an early date. The sixteenth-century chronicler Andrés de Tapia lists him as having died in about 1540; his sons held the encomienda, inheriting it through the widow of Juan López de Ximena, Francisca de Nava, whose name they apparently chose to bear. A report of about 1548 states that three sons held the place. We do know from the *Libro de tasaciones* that in 1565 the encomendero of Ixcatlan was Pedro de Nava (second holder), and that his son, Diego de Nava (third holder), was in possession as late as ca. 1603. Unfortunately, Gloss 4 is mutilated, so that it is not clear whether the text refers to Pedro or to Diego; in the first case the dates would be ca. 1546–70, and in the second ca. 1570–1603.

The two portions of the material around the baptismal font seem open to the following interpretations. Gloss 1 suggests that when the group of Indian *principales* (local leaders) was baptized by an itinerant priest, all the *principales* were at least 25 years old. Espinosa and others record activities of missionaries in this and adjoining areas, but in insufficient detail to permit definitive dating.

Gloss 2 seems to refer to the figure with his face obscured in the baptismal font. It seems to say that before becoming a Christian, i.e., in time of night or darkness, his native name was Lagarto, that he took the Christian name of Juan de Mendoza, and that Fray Luis de Valeojo performed the ceremony, wetting his head.

So far, we have been unable to identify the friar Luis de Valeojo with any certainty. Espinosa provides contradictory data; in one instance he names him as an Augustinian chaplain of Cortés, and in another as the famous Franciscan Luis de Fuensalida, basing his assertions on a passage in Chimalpahin that I have been unable to find. In a private communication (July 9, 1962), the Franciscan historian Lino Gómez Canedo stated that it was highly unlikely that Fuensalida worked in the Chinantla, or that he can be identified with the Fray Luis de Valeojo who appears on this lienzo. So the friar remains unidentified.

From these data we can arrive at certain conclusions. Depending on the identification of the encomendero, the document cannot antedate 1546, possibly 1570. The date 1521 refers to a historical event, the appearance of Juan Marqués, who is shown. At the time the missionaries came, the Indian *principal* was Lagarto, who took the name Juan de Mendoza, a common name among Oaxaca *principales* in that area. We do know, from the *Libro de tasaciones*, that in 1546 the Indian rulers were D. Juan [de Mendoza?] and D. Manuel, who made up a *tasación*, or tribute schedule, after informing viceregal authorities that no such stipulation had been in effect when Juan López de Ximena was encomendero. This use of Christian names in 1546 suggests that the baptisms had taken place before that time, a fact that does not in itself affect the dating of the document. In short, the central gloss or gloss complex is historical.

The several place names, in some cases combined with numbers, suggest that the data around the edges of the central gloss are geographical-cartographical. They probably refer to a text document now unknown. Some of the places were earlier communities that contemporary documentation does not record; but for some of them Mariano Espinosa had obtained data from Mazatecs before 1910. In my opinion, the "árbol genealógico" for this area about which Espinosa vaguely speaks is the group of figures at the top and central portion of the lienzo, under the incomplete place name " ——pec." The Peabody copy does not carry the data near these figures that perhaps appeared on the original or the copy used by Espinosa.

NOTES

1. Most of the earlier literature to his day is cited by Daniel G. Brinton, "On the Mazatec Language of Mexico and Its Affinities," *Proceedings of the American Philosophical Society*, XXX (1892), 31–39, reprinted in his *Studies in South American Native Languages from MSS. and Rare Printed Sources* (Philadelphia, 1892), Appendix II, pp. 11–20. See also Manuel Orozco y Berra, *Geografía de las lenguas y carta etnográfica de México* (México, 1864), pp. 46, 188; and Francisco Belmar, *Ligero estudio sobre la lengua Mazateca* (Oaxaca, 1892).

More recent contributions include Irmgard Weitlaner Johnson and Jean Bassett Johnson, "Un cuento mazateco-popoloca," *Revista Mexicana de Estudios Antropológicos*, III (1939), 217–26; George M. and Florence Cowan, "Mazateco: Locational Morphemes," *Aboriginal Linguistics* (Cuernavaca), I (1947), 3–9; Kenneth L. and Eunice V. Pike, "Immediate Constituents of Mazatec Syllables," *International Journal of American Linguistics*, XIII (1947), 78–91; George M. Cowan, "Mazateco Whistle Speech," *Language*, XXIV (1948), 280–86; Eunice V. Pike, "Phonetic Rank and Subordination in Consonant Patterning and Historical Changes," *Miscellanea Phonetica*, II (1954), 25–41; her "Tonally Differentiated Allomorphs in Soyaltepec Mazatec," *International Journal of American Linguistics*, XXII (1956), 57–71; and her *Vocabulario mazateco* (México, 1957); Sarah C. Gudschinsky, "Native Reactions to Tone and Words in Mazatec," *Word*, XIV (1958), 338–45; and her "Mazatec Kernel Construction and Transformations," and "Discourse Analysis of a Mazatec Text," *International Journal of American Linguistics*, XXV (1959), 81–89, 139–46; María Teresa Fernández de Miranda, "Toponimia popoloca," in *A William Cameron Townsend*... (México, 1961), 431–47.

2. Wilhelm Bauer, "Heidentum und Aberglaube unter den Maçateca-Indianern," *Zeitschrift für Ethnologie*, XL, Part VI (1908), 857–65; Jean Bassett Johnson, "Some Notes on the Mazatec," *Revista Mexicana de Estudios Antropológicos*, III (1939), 142–56; George M. Cowan, "El motivo 'mariposa' en la cultura mazateca contemporánea," *Yan* 2 (1953), 92–94; Demetrio Mejía, "Informe que el suscrito presenta... relativo a la exploración de las ruinas del Cerro de Tenguiengajo, en la municipalidad de San Cristóbal Mazatlán...," Museo Nacional, *Anales*, IV (Part 2, 1888), 17–23; Nicolás León, "Informe sobre las ruinas del cerro de Moctezuma y la gruta de Eloxochitlán, 1906," *Boletín de Instrucción Pública* (México), VI (1906), 645–50; and his "Entre los indios mazatecas: Exploración de los monumentos arqueológicos del Cerro de Motecuhzoma y de la gruta de Nindondahe en San Antonio Eloxochitlán (Estado de Oaxaca). Álbum fotografico" (n. p., 1906). It contains 31 photos and a map of the Distrito de Teotitlan.

3. Walter Lehmann, "Les Peintures Mixtéco-Zapotèques et quelques documents apparentés," *Journal de la Société des Américanistes de Paris*, n.s., II (1905), 241–80.

4. José Alcina Franch, *Fuentes indígenas de Méjico: Ensayo de sistematización bibliográfica* (Madrid, 1956), p. 84, reprinted from *Revista de Indias*, XV: 421–521; Manuel Carrera Stampa, "Fuentes para el estudio de la historia indígena," in *Esplendor del México Antiguo* (México, 1959), II, 1194.

5. Lehmann, "Peintures," p. 278. "The provenience of this document is probably within the region of the Mazatecs and Chinantecs."

6. For the sixteenth-century area, see the *Relación geográfica* and mapas described in Carlos E. Castañeda and Jack Autrey Dabbs, *Guide to the Latin American Manuscripts in the University of Texas Library* (Cambridge, Mass., 1939), Item 955. The maps appear as Figures 2a and 2b in Donald Robertson, "The Relaciones Geográficas of Mexico," XXXIII Congreso Internacional de Americanistas (San José, 1958), *Actas*, 3 vols. (San José, 1959), II, 541. Francisco González de Cossío, *El libro de las tasaciones de pueblos de la Nueva España: siglo XVI* (México, 1952), pp. 599–601, reproduces tribute documents for Ixcatlan and Nopala (1543–62).

7. Sherburne F. Cook, *Santa María Ixcatlán: Habitat, Population, Subsistence*. Ibero-Americana: 41 (Berkeley, Calif., 1958), pp. 12–13, 20. Robert J. Weitlaner has obtained a ms. map labeled "Santa María Ixcatlan, Plano topográfico, 1870," which is apparently based

on earlier native sources; the location of Nopala is that given in 1580 and in 1939 by Cook's informants.

8. Bio-bibliography of Manuel Martínez Gracida appears in *Diccionario Porrúa: Historia, Biografía y Geografía de México* (México, 1965), p. 961. *Lienzo Seler II* is discussed briefly in Lehmann, "Peintures," pp. 278–79. In 1960 this document was still preserved in the Museum für Völkerkunde in Berlin; a black and white copy made by or for Lehmann is in the Lehmann Collection, Ibero-Amerikanische Bibliothek (Berlin).

9. J. Aguilar, "Jefatura política del distrito de Teotitlán del Camino," in Manuel Martínez Gracida, *Colección de cuadros sinópticos . . . 1883* (Santa María Ixcatlan, p. 564) (Oaxaca, 1883), pp. 543–65.

10. J. S. Harry Hirtzel, "Notes sur le classement des manuscrits anciens du Mexique," Société des Américanistes de Belgique, *Bulletin*, I (1928), 66–70.

11. The original of this codex is now in the Bancroft Library, University of California. The basic general description is given in Antonio Peñafiel, *Códice Fernández Leal* (México, 1895), with the plates out of their true order. John B. Tompkins, "Codex Fernández Leal," *Pacific Art Review*, II (1942), 39–59, reproduces photos. Minor commentary appears in Robert Barlow's review of Tompkins, *Tlalocan*, I (1944), 383–84, and in César Lizardi Ramos, "Paradero del Códice Fernández Leal," *Boletín Bibliográfico de Antropología Americana*, XVII, Part I (1955), pp. 234–35.

12. Only one copy, that of the New York Public Library, is listed in the Union Catalog of the Library of Congress.

13. *Suma de visitas de pueblos por órden alfabético: Manuscrito 2800 de la Biblioteca Nacional de Madrid. Anónimo de la mitad del siglo xvi*. Francisco del Paso y Trancoso, ed., *Papeles de Nueva España*, 7 Vols. (Madrid, 1905–6), Vol. I. Woodrow Borah and S. F. Cook, *The Population of Central Mexico in 1548. An Analysis of the* Suma de visitas de pueblos. Ibero-Americana: 43 (Berkeley, Calif., 1960), p. 36. See No. 6 above for *Libro de tasaciones*.

14. Francisco de Castañeda, "Descripcion del pueblo y corregimiento de Teutitlan . . . 15 setiembre 1581," in Paso y Troncoso, *Papeles de Nueva España*, IV, 213–31; Mapa on p. 213.

15. I am indebted to Ross Parmenter of New York City for drawing this document to my attention. Franz Boas presented this copy to the Peabody Museum in 1916. J. O. Brew, Director, and Margaret Currier, Librarian, Peabody Museum, kindly arranged to have large photostatic copies made for me for detailed study.

16. I am grateful to John B. Glass of Harvard University for providing detailed descriptions of this lienzo and for a number of bibliographical notices from his files.

17. Data supplied by Glass. He reports, for instance, that adjacent to the unglossed ocelot is the word "yellow," in English.

18. A sketch of this interesting international school, which closed in 1920, appears in Juan Comas, "Bosquejo histórico de la antropología en México," *Revista Mexicana de Estudios Antropológicos*, XI (1950), 103–5. The present writer has been unable to find the administrative files of the School; the Hispanic Society has informed me that no reports made by Mechling can be located. The School's Directors were Seler (1910–11), Boas (1911–12), Tozzer, Engerrand, and Gamio.

19. Franz Boas, "Informe del Presidente de la Junta Directiva. Escuela Internacional . . . Año escolar de 1911 a 1912" (México, 1913), p. 5, and "Anexo [sic] al informe . . . 1911–1912" (México, 1913), p. xix, which states that the students' copy of the lienzo was on display. It adds an ambiguous reference, "Los indios mazatecos, quienes viven al oeste de Tuxtepec, tienen un lienzo antiguo, en el cual los límites y los pueblos antiguos de su territorio se indiquen." This could apply to any of the three documents reviewed here. Data supplied by Glass.

20. The author's thanks go to J. O. Brew, Director of the Peabody Museum, for authorizing the photographing of the lienzo and the publication of the photo, and to John Glass for supervising the photography.

21. I am grateful to Miguel León-Portilla for helping to reconstruct the gloss and pro-

viding a literal translation. An extended note on the central gloss appears here as the Appendix.

22. Mariano Espinosa, *Apuntes históricos de las tribus chinantecas, matzatecas y popolucas* (México [1910]), pp. 49–68. The same work, *Reedición con notas y apéndices preparada por Howard F. Cline*, Papeles de la Chinantla, 3, Museo Nacional, Serie científica, 7 (México, 1961), pp. 93–107.

23. Jean Bassett Johnson, "Some Notes on the Mazatec," p. 142.

24. Bernard Bevan to Howard Cline, 1961; ms. is in the administrative files of the Hispanic Foundation.

25. Presumably the nine kings on the "pintura" of the Señorío del Norte mentioned by Espinosa, *Apuntes históricos* (1961 ed.), p. 96. He apparently read the date 1710 as 1190, a year to which he assigns an invasion of Mazatec territories and a new dynasty.

26. Bauer, "Heidentum und Aberglaube," pp. 859–60.

27. J. Aguilar, "Jefatura política de Teotitlán del Camino," *Cuadros sinópticos*, pp. 560–61.

28. Frederick Starr, *Notes upon the Ethnography of Southern Mexico. Part I* (author's ed., Davenport, Iowa, 1900), reprinted from Davenport Academy of Natural Sciences, *Proceedings* (June 1900), pp. 74–79. Frederick Starr, *In Indian Mexico: A Narrative of Travel and Labor* (Chicago, 1908), pp. 228–38, esp. p. 236; on p. ix Starr lists as a published document "The Mapa of Huauhtla. Reproduction. Single sheet, mounted." Unfortunately Starr's diary for the period covering his trip to Huautla (Diary No. 31) is missing from the nearly complete holdings of the Ayer Collection of the Newberry Library. He does record in No. 31 (December 1900), p. 27, a visit to President Porfirio Díaz, to whom he presented a photo of the Mapa de Huautla, along with other gifts.

29. Starr, "Mexican Literary Curiosities" (Chicago [1903–4]), No. 4, The Mapa de Huautla. This is listed as a halftone, 16 x 27.5 cm. I am indebted to Robert Kingery, Chief of the Reference Department, New York Public Library, for arranging to have this item photographed for me.

30. Aguilar, "Jefatura política," pp. 558–59.

31. Alfonso Villa Rojas, *Los mazatecos y el problema indígena de la Cuenca del Papaloapan*, Instituto Nacional Indigenista, *Memorias*, VII (México, 1955), 59–74.

32. Gonzalo Aguirre Beltrán, "Pobladores del Papaloapan" (ms., n.d.), cited by Villa Rojas, *Los mazatecos*.

33. See n. 22 above. Brief notes on Espinosa appear in Howard F. Cline, "The Chinantla of Northeastern Oaxaca, Mexico: Bio-Bibliographical Notes on Modern Investigation," in *Estudios antropológicos publicados en homenaje al doctor Manuel Gamio* (México, 1956), pp. 637–38; in his "Problems of Mexican Ethnohistory: The Ancient Chinantla," *Hispanic American Historical Review*, XXXVII (August 1957), 284–86; and in his "Mapas and Lienzos of the Colonial Chinantec Indians, Oaxaca, Mexico," in *A William Townsend*, pp. 50–60.

34. Robert J. Weitlaner, "The Guatinicaname," in *A William Townsend*, pp. 199–205.

The Mixtec Religious Manuscripts

DONALD ROBERTSON

A group of six prehispanic Mexican manuscripts of religious or ritual content, recorded only with native "glyphs" or signs, has come down to us with no specific indication of its provenience. It is known as the Borgia Group, being named after the main manuscript of the six, the Codex Borgia. The other five are the Codices Laud, Fejérváry-Mayer, Cospi, and Vaticanus B, and Mexican Manuscript No. 20 of the Bibliothèque Nationale in Paris.[1] It is generally agreed that the group comes from what Vaillant called the Mixteca-Puebla culture. Opinions differ, however, when it comes to trying to establish more precise geographic origins, the regions of Puebla-Tlaxcala, coastal Veracruz, and Cholula all having been suggested. The linguistic affiliations proposed are equally diverse.[2] In an earlier study I have indicated disagreement with all of these non-Mixtec attributions for the group.[3]

Eduard Seler, with his monumental facsimiles and commentaries, set the direction taken by later studies of these manuscripts, and most scholars, including Walter Lehmann, Cottie Burland, and Karl Anton Nowotny, have followed his lead in concentrating on the content (i.e., iconography) of the works.[4] Certain passages or chapters of the texts lend themselves to detailed explanation. First and foremost is the Tonalámatl or Book of Days (the graphic presentation of the 260-day native ritual calendar), a feature that appears in more than one version. Sixteenth-century colonial written sources from the Nahuatl-speaking areas of the Valley of Mexico give such detailed descriptions and complete information for interpreting the 260-day calendar (or Tonalpohualli) that the area of doubt about this phase of native religion is quite small. One can assume that only minor differences separated the Nahua Tonalámatl known through the early colonial sources from the phase of the calendar represented by these manuscripts.

Other chapters and large and important sections of the Borgia Group have been interpreted by using a deductive approach based almost solely upon analysis of the native signs or "glyphs." Written confirmation, whether in the form of accompanying written glosses (of which there are virtually none) or in the form of extensive written commentaries from anywhere in Mexico drawn up during the colonial period, is scanty for the material contained in these chapters and sections.

As for solving the problem of a place of origin for the ritual manuscripts, the iconographic studies of Seler and his followers have been unable to match the success achieved by Alfonso Caso in his iconographic studies of the history manuscripts.[5] It seems likely that approaches *supplementing* iconography will be needed to break the riddle. One of these ancillary approaches is the formal study of graphic style.

In the study of European art the iconographic approach has demonstrated definite limitations, especially as a means of defining styles or schools of art. The study of iconography alone is rarely able to establish a provenience that is otherwise unknown, particularly in a situation in which the artists of several closely related schools are working within a common religious system. Throughout Christian Europe, for instance, a young girl wearing a blue robe and carrying a small male child represents the Virgin Mary. Other criteria, most of them essentially formal, must be sought to distinguish between paintings of the Virgin by Sienese and Florentine contemporaries. Iconography is better adapted to comparing the art of places with different theologies (or different interpretations of a common theology) than to studying the art of two nearby places that have the same religious traditions. As Lionello Venturi phrased it, "the iconographical method is an obstacle in the understanding of art, because the types and compositions of mythological and sacred scenes may remain almost the same throughout the most profound differences in artistic civilisations and individual imaginations. Since to create in art does not mean to invent, the repetition of motives popularly accepted is clearly distinct from the personal contribution of the artist and the taste of an epoch or school."[6]

The formal analysis of Mexican preconquest manuscript painting, which I am proposing as a supplement to the iconographic study of the manuscripts, is ultimately based upon the work of Giovanni Morelli. Morelli first presented and applied his approach in the late nineteenth century to the problems of attribution in Italian painting. Writing under the pseudonym Ivan Lermolieff, he proposed that instead of the relatively subjective criteria current in his day, more objective standards for determining the styles of individual painters could be established.[7] He said in effect that the careful study and comparison of how ears, nostrils, fingernails, and other iconographically unimportant parts of the human body were painted would show us the "handwriting," as it were, of individual artists, and that this handwriting, often

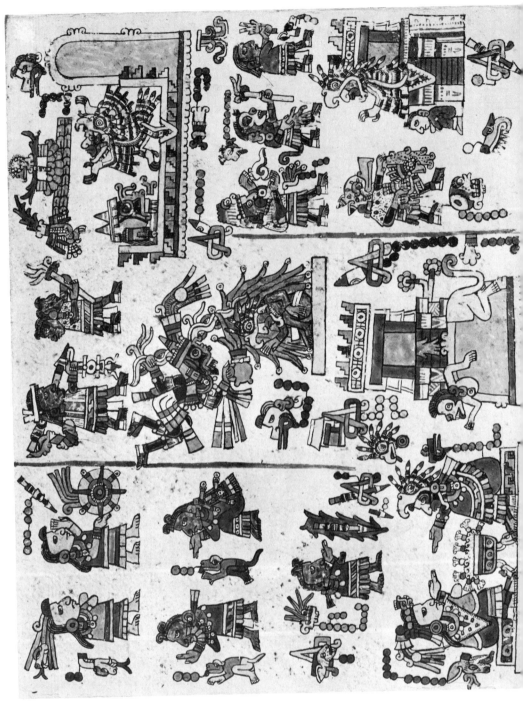

1. Codex Nuttall, p. 5 (obverse).
Mme. Nuttall's pagination
is used throughout.

demonstrated only in minor details, was a significant way of identifying the styles of particular artists (and thus by extension particular schools).[8]

The application of Morelli's method to Mexican colonial easel painting has already been tried with success by Abelardo Carrillo y Gariel.[9] The method can also be applied to the prehispanic Mexican ritual manuscripts and Mixtec history manuscripts. A workable approach would be to investigate the problems of format, the representation of space, the treatment of line and color, and finally, the particular method of presenting the forms used in the manuscripts—human, animal, botanical, and geographical. In this preliminary study we shall have to limit ourselves to discussing the qualities of line and color and the forms and parts of the human body.

An examination of this kind is quite distinct from an iconographic investigation, whose aim is to interpret the *meaning* that forms convey through gesture, color, and linear patterning. A formal analysis is not concerned with the content of forms but with how they are presented to the viewer. With respect to the religious manuscripts, such an analysis has two advantages: it removes the forms from a subjective framework of interpretation when meaning is unknown, and it is an equally important device to remove them from association with possibly irrelevant factors when a known religious meaning exists, allowing them to be studied *in vitro*, as it were. Religious content can be misleading for studies intended to establish provenience, since it is often part of a much wider configuration in time and space than the pattern of distribution of a single regional artistic style.

The native-style manuscripts of the Borgia Group are so markedly different from the three extant prehispanic Maya manuscripts that a Maya provenience has never been proposed for them; the Maya manuscripts can thus be dismissed from our discussion. The only other significant number of manuscripts believed to be prehispanic is the group known as the history manuscripts —Codices Vienna (Vindobonensis), Nuttall, Selden, Bodley, and others. These have been established as dealing with Mixtec history, and can therefore be safely assumed to come from the Mixtec area of Mexico. Since their prehispanic date is now generally accepted, they provide us with a useful standard of comparison for the Borgia Group.

According to the definition used in this paper, the style of the history manuscripts is the prehispanic Mixtec style. Thus when a similar style governs relief sculpture—whether in cast gold or carved bone—it, too, can be included under the rubric "Mixtec style." Similarly, when the *tipo-códice* pottery shares these traits, it is in Mixtec style no matter where it is encountered archeologically (Plates 18–20, 26, and 29). This definition is limited to a series of traits that can be analyzed from the point of view of form; it does not include iconographic, linguistic, or geographical qualifications of the terms "Mixtec" or "Mixtec style."

The historical codices Vienna and Nuttall are screenfolds, and are both painted on animal skins. They are similar in content in that they deal with the prehispanic history of the Mixtec area.[10] They are also similar in the organization of the page. The persons, historical events, and signs for personal and geographical names and dates are drawn within a series of red guide lines. In both manuscripts the forms exist in a two-dimensional space that has a direction, which, like the movement of lines in a European book, is determined by the direction of reading.

The graphic styles of Codices Nuttall (Figures 1–3, Plates 10–12; also pp. 316–18, 342, this volume) and Vienna (Figures 4–5, Plate 5; also p. 203, this volume) are remarkably alike. Complex and rich linear patterns qualify the use of color on figures. Lines are precise and sure, but they have a fluidity that indicates they are hand-drawn rather than traced, laboriously copied from a model, or done with the somewhat mechanical precision of a ruler. Eyes follow two main patterns: one consists of two concentric circles; in the other, the upper lid is drawn as a straight horizontal line, and the lower lid has a half-pear-shaped profile with its larger end toward the nose. Noses are large and fleshy and make an obtuse angle with the forehead. Hands have a wide variety of gesture. The fist tends to be curvilinear, the nails angular. In Codex Vienna hands sometimes have a graceful curvilinear shape. In some instances the feet of standing figures establish a ground line with precision; in others no such single precise ground line is established, the two feet of a single figure being inconsistently placed in space. The feet of men seated on thrones dangle in space, rest securely on an imagined ground line, or even extend below the line of the base of the throne. Seated women are shown both in a proper seated position and in the "Aztec woman's pose" with legs tucked under the rump, a position that is still to be seen in parts of Mexico (Plate 5). Standing figures show the proportions of the human body most clearly—tall torsos, large heads, and short, stocky legs.[11]

The Mixtec history style as seen in its finest recognized exemplars, the Codices Nuttall and Vienna, is one of considerable sophistication and even elegance. Nuttall and Vienna, however, represent only one phase of the style, for when we compare them with other manuscripts—Selden (Plate 6) and Bodley (Plate 7), for instance—we see significant differences.[12]

Codices Selden and Bodley differ from Nuttall and Vienna in their use of a markedly heavier line, not only comparatively, but in relation to the size of the forms it bounds. It is less consistently used as a frame for areas of color; colors may merely be juxtaposed and not separated by a framing line. Colors are more crudely and less evenly applied, and have a smaller range. Eyes are considerably larger in proportion to the size of the face as a whole. Noses, as in Nuttall and Vienna, are large and fleshy, but have an angular base and descend from a much lower brow. Hands have angular fingers and do not give so convincing a demonstration of the ability to hold objects. Seated fig-

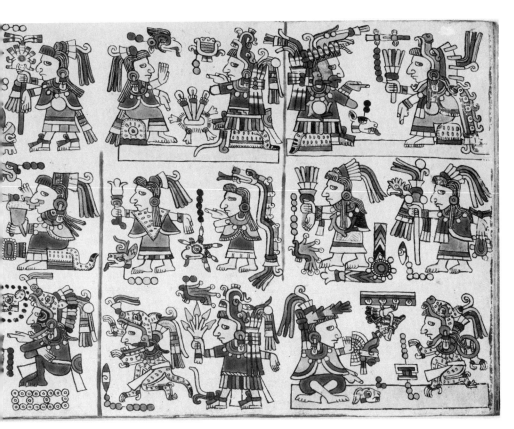

Codex Nuttall, p. 32 (obverse).

Codex Nuttall, p. 61 (reverse).

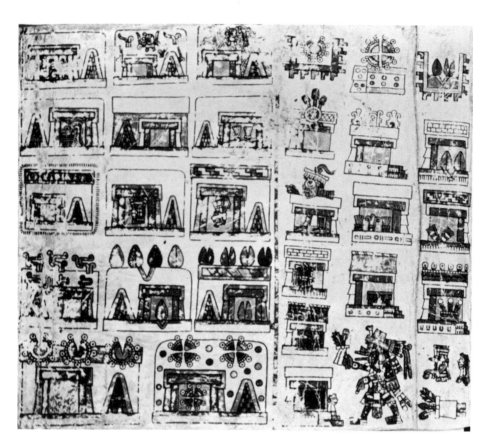

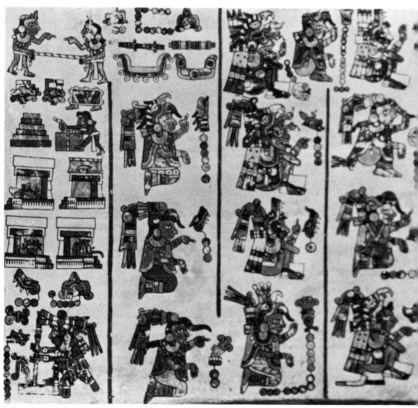

4. Codex Vienna (Vindobonensis) obverse. *Above*, p. 31; *below*, p. 32.

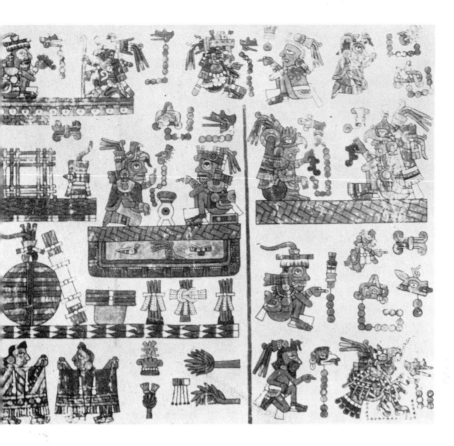

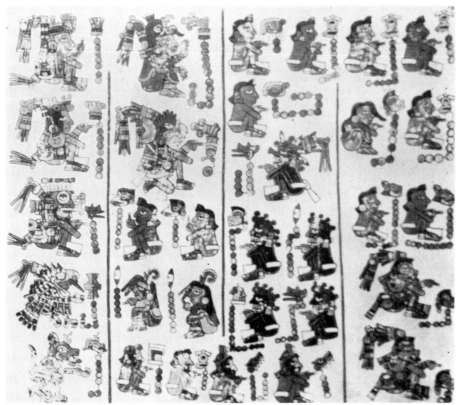

Codex Vienna obverse. *Above*, p. 35; *below*, p. 36.

ures of men in Codex Bodley are seldom shown with dangling feet, although this does occur in Codex Selden. Among well over 200 examples of seated women in Bodley, none is shown in the "Aztec woman's pose."[13] Standing figures establish a ground line, especially when on a mat. Feet vary: sometimes only the big toe is shown, sometimes all the toes. Sandals are rarer, and when drawn they are colored brown rather than left white as in the Nuttall and Vienna conventions.

Selden and Bodley, undoubtedly Mixtec in terms of their content, were thus not made by the same artist, nor does either of them come from the same school as Nuttall and Vienna, if we define school as a single city or artistic center or a limited period of time.

The ritual manuscripts have clear differences among them, but this does not mean that we need postulate a division of the group into subgroups. The unit of Mixtec history manuscripts, which is generally accepted despite differences in graphic style, prepares us for a wide degree of tolerance in considering examples of another such unit or single group.

Codices Borgia, Laud, and Fejérváry-Mayer have the following characteristics in common: all are screenfolds, are painted on animal skins, deal with ritual or religious subject matter, are commonly considered prehispanic, and have approximately square pages. However, Codex Borgia, the main example (Figure 6), is larger than Codices Laud and Fejérváry-Mayer, and is drawn with a precise and sure line of great strength.[14] This line may overlay areas of color, thereby enriching them. Eyes are like those in the Nuttall-Vienna manuscripts. The noses, however, are larger, and the bridge of the nose is stressed. There is an angular junction of the nose and the high, sloping forehead. Hands, which are drawn with great care, often have long, elegant fingers spread out in fan fashion. Fists are curvilinear and graceful. Nails are sometimes rounded, and sometimes angular as in Codex Nuttall. In some cases seated figures have floating feet; in others they establish a ground line. Seated women are rarely shown in full front view (a pose rare in Codex Nuttall); they are sometimes in the "Aztec woman's pose," and usually appear on thrones or animal-skin pillows. Standing figures rest upon a ground line when shown standing on a mat or path, and usually imply a consistent ground line in other cases. Feet consistently have dangling toes; if sandaled, the toes overlap the sole of the sandal, and if bare, the feet follow the same pattern as though to imply the missing sandal sole. The sandals themselves are drawn with linear patterns reminiscent of Codex Nuttall.

The complex and rich patterns of lines of Codex Borgia are found again in Codices Laud (Plate 8) and Fejérváry-Mayer (Plate 9), but beside them are figures of an almost puritanical frugality. Human figures are sometimes reduced to the simplest of patterns. Lines have such geometric precision that it

Codex Borgia, p. 65.

Codex Vaticanus B, p. 53.

seems almost as if a ruler and compass had been used, and this mechanical quality sets them apart from all the other manuscripts discussed so far. Eyes follow the patterns we have already established for Codices Nuttall and Vienna; noses, too, follow patterns by now familiar except that they have a more precise geometric base. Seated men seem to float when on thrones, although sometimes they establish a ground line. Seated women use the "Aztec woman's pose," and in some cases are shown full front. Standing and kneeling figures imply a ground line. Hands are carefully drawn, and feet are sometimes shown in an unusual plan view in Codex Laud. (The same view of the feet may be seen in the Zaachila tomb sculptures, shown in Plates 13–17.)

In terms of the style of the figures, the differences separating Borgia from Laud and Fejérváry-Mayer are less pronounced than those that separate Nuttall-Vienna from Selden-Bodley. Since the four history manuscripts are accepted as being Mixtec despite their divergences of style, we can assume that the three ritual manuscripts also have a single artistic origin—either a single school in the narrow sense, or at least two or more very closely related schools in an extended sense.

From an iconographic point of view, there is greater consistency among the history manuscripts than among the ritual manuscripts. This is because the histories often show the same persons acting out the same historical activities at the same moments in time at the same places. The differences among the ritual manuscripts must be considered, for they have been divided in the past into several distinct groups on the basis of iconographic studies of content. It is probable that the seemingly different natures of the manuscripts in the Borgia Group are so perceived more because of their obvious diversity of content (iconography) than because of any formal diversity (style). The members of the Borgia Group may not represent different styles in the larger sense of language or geographic distance so much as different phases of a single, rich religious tradition. They record different parts of the same religious complex—either a single style in the large sense, or closely related substyles in a more restricted sense. Future iconographic investigations following this direction may very well enrich our knowledge of the content of the manuscripts and the complexity of the religion of the Mixteca-Puebla culture as a whole.

The ritual and history manuscripts, as exemplified respectively in the Codex Borgia and the Codex Vienna, present us with remarkable similarities of style. The complexity of linear patterns qualifying areas of color and the precision of line (not the traced line of Laud nor the ponderous line of Bodley) link the two manuscripts, as do the patterns of the human eye, the nose, the relation of the nose to the forehead, and the elegance of the human hand, with its ability to grasp and to hold. In both manuscripts, within the same limits, seated figures, male and female, run variations upon these themes, and standing figures establish the same canon of proportions for the human body. This similarity persists in the conventions governing the human foot, in which toes often overlap sandal soles, and bare feet may follow the same pattern.

The main differences are those that derive from diversity of content. The history manuscripts, which deal with the unique facts of history, demand a different organization of the material and the individual pages from that required by the ritual manuscripts, which deal with the recurring cycles of religion and ritual.[15] I suggest that this gross difference has hitherto clouded our view, and that a close comparison of details will show the similarity to be fundamental, the difference superficial. I also suggest that Codex Borgia is so closely related to Codices Vienna and Nuttall that an attribution of Mixtec style is fully justified. The factors linking Borgia to Fejérváry-Mayer and Laud are clear enough to justify our saying that if Borgia is Mixtec, the other two ritual manuscripts must be Mixtec as well.

Codex Vaticanus B (Figure 7) is another important religious manuscript, and as such deserves comparison with Codex Borgia.[16] The two codices have been linked, almost without a dissenting voice, as an inseparable pair, and hence make interesting objects of study from the point of view of their respective graphic styles. The pairing of these manuscripts has been predicated in the past less upon their formal characteristics than upon their similarity of content. This similarity is especially evident when they are compared in detail.[17] Both manuscripts are painted on animal skins, both are approximately square, and both are generally accepted as preconquest. However, there are also striking differences: figures in the Vaticanus manuscript are large, coarse, and ill-adjusted to the red lines that define the space surrounding them—so much so that feet or the attributes of figures often overlap the red frame lines, and the figures seem compressed into a space too small for them. The Borgia figures are drawn so that there is a nice adjustment of the figure to the surrounding space; frames are not overrun, and maintain their integrity and perform their essential function of establishing a carefully designed ambient area for the figures. Vaticanus is essentially less elegant than Borgia, being executed by a hurried or even careless hand. Line is heavier and less sure in defining forms. Color overlays linear patterns and lacks the clarity of Borgia. It is often used without a frame line, and it is sometimes applied in rough taches that become almost splotches. Hands are drawn crudely, with little or no reference to anatomical limitations. Arms and hands seem to be thrown out into space, and legs and feet establish a ground line in only the most rudimentary sense; in most cases feet dangle like those of a puppet.

The differences separating Borgia from Vaticanus B show that the prehispanic ritual manuscripts, like the history manuscripts, include works of divergent styles. These differences rule out the possibility of either a single school or an extremely widespread single style. It seems, then, that we should postulate a Mixtec style for Codices Borgia, Laud, and Fejérváry-Mayer as companions to the history manuscripts. But the range of style difference separating Vaticanus B from Borgia is such that copying or possibly a distinct provenience for Vaticanus B, perhaps even a non-Mixtec provenience, is quite tenable as an attribution.

Finally, let me add that we should not hesitate to link the ritual manuscripts that use a dot-and-bar number system with those that do not when formal characteristics point to such an association. The stelae of Xochicalco give ample evidence that the dot-and-bar number system was used on the northwest side of the Mixtec area; both Monte Albán and the Maya area used it on the east, and it occurs in the Gulf coast region to the northeast as well. Within the heart of the Mixtec region it is found at Yucuñudahui. In other words, it is not a criterion by which Mixtec work can be distinguished from non-Mixtec.

It is possible that we shall ultimately be able to establish an almost measurable system of criteria for identifying styles from specific regions or even specific cities. Caso, along with Ross Parmenter and Mary Elizabeth Smith, is pursuing the study of the Mixtec history manuscripts and lienzos and the persons and places they depict. Their studies in the future may be of the utmost importance for locating the places of origin of the manuscripts. Perhaps we shall then be able to apply this system of criteria to other kinds of paintings, especially to that of the *tipo-códice* ceramics and even in some of its phases to relief sculpture in bone, stone, and cast gold.

NOTES

I wish to thank the American Council of Learned Societies for a Grant-in-Aid, which supported the research used in this paper. John B. Glass, Consultant on Mexican Pictorial Manuscripts, Hispanic Foundation, Library of Congress, has been helpful in bibliographic matters.

1. *Il manoscritto messicano Borgiano del Museo etnografico della S. Congregazione di Propaganda Fide; riprodotto in fotocromografia a spese di S.E. il Duca di Loubat a cura della Biblioteca Vaticana* (Rome, 1898); *Codex Borgia: Eine altmexikanische Bilderschrift der Bibliothek der Congregatio de Propaganda Fide Herausgegeben auf Kosten Seiner Excellenz des Herzogs von Loubat, erläutert von Dr. Eduard Seler* (3 Vols. in 1; Berlin, 1904–9); and Eduard Seler, *Comentarios al Códice Borgia,* trans. Mariana Frenk (México and Buenos Aires, 1963), 2 Vols. and Atlas (color reproduction with Seler's explanatory drawings opposite each page). Carlos Martínez Marín, *Códice Laud, introducción, selección y notas,* INAH Investigaciones 5 (México, 1961). *Codex Fejérváry-Mayer: An Old Mexican Picture Manuscript in the Liverpool Free Public Museum, 12014/M, Published at the Expense of His Excellency the Duke of Loubat, Elucidated by Dr. Eduard Seler* (A. H. Keane, trans.; Berlin and London, 1901–2). *Descripción del Códice Cospiano manuscrito pictórico de los antiguos Náuas que se conserva en la Biblioteca de la Universidad de Bolonia reproducido en fotocromografía a expensas de S.E. el Duque de Loubat* (Rome, 1898). *Il manoscritto messicano Vaticano 3773; riprodotto in fotocromografia a spese di S.E. il Duca di Loubat a cura della Biblioteca Vaticana* (Rome, 1896) and *Codex Vaticanus No. 3773 (Codex Vaticanus B): An Old Mexican Pictorial Manuscript in the Vatican Library Published at the Expense of His Excellency the Duke of Loubat, Elucidated by Dr. Eduard Seler* (A. H. Keane, trans.; Berlin and London, 1902–3). "Le Culte rendu au

soleil (Tonatiuh)" in Eugène Boban, *Documents pour servir à l'histoire du Mexique* (Paris, 1891), I, 329–48; Atlas, Plate 20.

2. See, for example, Alfonso Caso, "Las ruinas de Tizatlán, Tlaxcala," *Revista Mexicana de Estudios Históricos*, I (1927), 139–72; José Luis Franco C., "La escritura y los códices," *Esplendor del México antiguo* (México, 1959), I, 361–78; Walter Lehmann, "Les Peintures Mixtéco-Zapotèques et quelques documents apparentés," *Journal de la Société des Américanistes de Paris*, n.s. II (1905), 241–80; Henry B. Nicholson, "The Mixteca-Puebla Concept in Mesoamerican Archeology: A Re-Examination," *Selected Papers of the Fifth International Congress of Anthropological and Ethnological Sciences, Philadelphia, September 1–9, 1956: Men and Cultures* (Philadelphia, 1960), pp. 612–17; Fredrick A. Peterson, *Ancient Mexico* (New York, 1959); *Codex Borgia* (Seler commentary); George Clapp Vaillant, *Aztecs of Mexico: Origin, Rise, and Fall of the Aztec Nation* (Garden City, N.Y., 1947).

3. Donald Robertson, "The Style of the Borgia Group of Mexican Pre-Conquest Manuscripts," in *Studies in Western Art: Acts of the Twentieth International Congress of the History of Art*, ed. Millard Meiss *et al.*, Vol. III: *Latin American Art and the Baroque Period in Europe* (Princeton, N.J., 1963), pp. 148–64, Plates XLIX–LII.

4. For Seler's editions of the manuscripts, see n. 1 above. The other main studies are Lehmann, "Peintures"; Cottie A. Burland, "Some Descriptive Notes on Ms. Laud Misc. 678, a Pre-Columbian Mexican Document in the Bodleian Library of the University of Oxford," in XXVIII Congrès International des Américanistes, *Actes de la Session de Paris, 24–30 août, 1947* (Paris, 1948), pp. 371–76; and Karl Anton Nowotny, *Tlacuilolli: Die mexikanischen Bilderhandschriften, Stil und Inhalt, mit einem Katalog der Codex-Borgia-Gruppe*, Monumenta Americana 3 (Berlin, 1961).

5. Alfonso Caso, "El Mapa de Teozacoalco," *Cuadernos Americanos*, Vol. XLVII, No. 5 (Sobretiro al XXIX Congreso Internacional de Américanistas; New York and México, 1949), pp. 3–40; his *Explicación del reverso del Codex Vindobonensis*, Memoria de El Colegio Nacional 5, No. 5 (México, 1951); and his *Interpretation of the Codex Bodley 2858*, boxed with facsimile in color (México, 1960). The history manuscripts are discussed in detail later in this paper.

6. Lionello Venturi, *History of Art Criticism* (New York, 1936), p. 228.

7. Ivan Lermolieff [pseud. of Giovanni Morelli], *Kunstkritische Studien über italienische Malerei*, 2 Vols. (Leipzig, 1890–93).

8. Venturi, p. 238, both notes by implication the limitations of Morelli's method and points out its value: "That which he brought to the art of connoisseurship was . . . a rigorous attention to details."

9. Abelardo Carrillo y Gariel, *Técnica de la pintura de Nueva España* (México, 1946).

10. *Codex Vindobonensis Mexic. 1, Faksimileausgabe der mexikanischen Bilderhandschrift der Nationalbibliothek in Wien*, Walter Lehmann and Ottokar Smital, eds. (Vienna, 1929). A more recent edition is *Codex Vindobonensis Mexicanus 1 (Österreichische Nationalbibliothek Wien)*, ed. Otto Adelhofer, Codices Selecti 5 (Graz, 1963); see also Caso, *Explicación*, n. 5 above. *Codex Nuttall: Facsimile of an Ancient Mexican Codex Belonging to Lord Zouche of Harynworth, England, with an Introduction by Zelia Nuttall* (Cambridge, Mass., 1902).

11. Within a single manuscript more than one style can exist, as Caso has pointed out: "The obverse [of Codex Vienna], which is the principal part of this manuscript, is by another hand, much more skillful and careful than that which painted the reverse." (*Explicación*, p. 9.) The differences are mainly in the line, which is more calligraphic and fluid on the reverse side, and which varies less in width and is firmer and thicker on the obverse. Heads are larger and dominate the figure more completely on the reverse. We need not concur with Caso's qualitative judgment while agreeing that the manuscript is the work of two hands. However, the similarities of obverse and reverse are such that for the purposes of the following discussion the differences can be ignored. For details from the obverse of Codex Vienna, see Plate 5 and Figures 234–38 in Part II above, p. 203.

12. Codex Selden was unpublished except for the lithographed edition of Edward King,

Lord Kingsborough, *Antiquities of Mexico* (London, 1831–48), Vol. I, No. 5. In 1964 the Sociedad Mexicana de Antropología brought out a facsimile edition of the Selden with Caso's commentary. Codex Bodley has recently been published in a full-color facsimile in Mexico; see n. 5 above.

13. See p. 14 of Caso's commentary to the edition of Codex Bodley, n. 5 above.

14. Codex Borgia was published in facsimile by the Duc de Loubat. Seler made an exhaustive commentary, which includes the Borgia Group as a whole; see n. 1 above. For Codices Laud and Fejérváry-Mayer, also see n. 1.

15. I pointed this out in "The Style of the Borgia Group." (See n. 3 above.) One consequence of the differences between historical and ritual content is that the Mixtec sign for year, the interlocking A-O, is common in the histories, where specific years are constantly referred to, but extremely rare in the religious manuscripts, where events are in a cyclical setting. (But see pp. 51, 52, and 71 of Codex Borgia for the use of this sign.)

16. See reproduction and Seler commentary cited in n. 1 above.

17. Nowotny, *Tlacuilolli*, has convenient tables of concordance for the content. See also Seler's commentary on Codex Borgia.

Plate 1. The plaza of Monte Albán, seen from the southeast corner. The Observatory, Mound J, is in the foreground.

Plate 2. Effigy-vessel of Monte Albán I style. Surface color, polish, and incisions with red paint rubbed into them are all typical of the period. *Frissell collection.*

Plate 3. Tripod bowl of typical Monte Albán I shape, color, and incised decoration; it was later covered with "fresco" painted decoration in the style of Monte Albán II. *Frissell collection, courtesy of Manuel Mejía G.*

Plate 4. Objects made of coarse Thin Orange-like paste for local distribution. All but one (head, upper left, from Tequixtepec, Oaxaca) are from Chila, Puebla. *Frissell collection.*

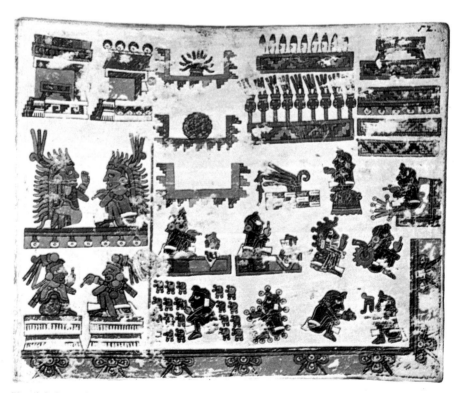

Plate 5. Codex Vindobonensis, p. 52. From the edition published in 1963 by Akademische Druck- u. Verlagsanstalt, Graz, Austria.

Plate 6. Codex Selden 3135 (A.2), p. 13. *From the original in the Bodleian Library, Oxford.*

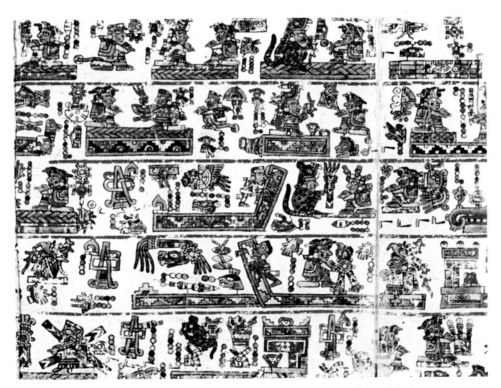

Plate 7. Codex Bodley 2858, parts of pp. 15 and 16. *From the original in the Bodleian Library, Oxford.*

Plate 8. Codex Laud, pp. 34 and 33 (l. to r.), Paso y Troncoso pagination, or pp. 37 and 38 (l. to r.), Kingsborough pagination. *From the original in the Bodleian Library, Oxford.*

Plate 9. Codex Fejérváry-Mayer, p. 24, Seler pagination. *From the original in the Liverpool Free Public Museum.*

Plate 10. ♂6 Water "Colored Strips," Codex Nuttall, detail of p. 35. *From the original in the British Museum.*

Plate 11. ♂1 Grass, Codex Nuttall, detail of p. 34. *From the original in the British Museum.*

Plate 12. ♂3 Vulture (above), and glyph of Culhuacan-Cuilapan (below); Codex Nuttall, detail of p. 61. *From the original in the British Museum.*

Plate 13. ♂9 Flower, sculpture in Tomb 1, Zaachila. *Drawing by Abel Mendoza.*

Plate 14. ♂5 Flower, sculpture in Tomb 1, Zaachila. *Drawing by Abel Mendoza.*

ate 15. Interior (rear of main chamber), Tomb 1, Zaachila.

ate 16. Plaster sculpture near front, east wall of the main amber, Tomb 1, Zaachila.

Plate 17. Sculpture opposite that shown in Plate 16; perhaps the Lord of the Land of the Dead.

Plate 18.

Plate 19.

Plates 18, 19, 20. Different views of a tiny Mixtec polychrome cup with a hummingbird on the rim (shown in Plate 20 at about actual size), from Tomb 1, Zaachila.

Plate 20.

late 21. Polychrome tripod vessel, Zaachila.

Plate 22. Polychrome pitcher, Zaachila.

late 23. Polychrome brazier with deer feet and perforated handles, Zaachila.

Plate 24. Life-size polychrome head of a man, Zaachila.

Plate 25. Animal-head pitcher with tubular spout, Zaachila.

Plate 26. Polychrome tripod (deer-foot) bowl, Zaachila.

Plate 27. Polychrome ring-base bowl, Zaachila.

Plate 28. Polychrome bird's head, Zaachila.

Plate 29. Polychrome ring-base bowl, Zaachila.

Plate 30. Three polychrome vessels from Tomb 30, Yagul.
Restoration drawing by Abel Mendoza.

Plate 31. Yagul polychrome tripod vessel with emblems probably representing Mixcóatl. *Drawing by Abel Mendoza.*

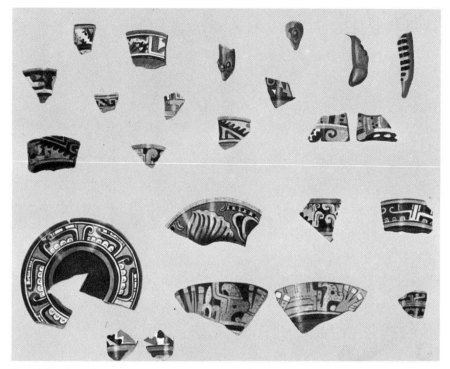

Plate 32. Yagul polychrome fragments. *Drawing by Abel Mendoza.*

Plate 33. Offering found in the Palace, Yagul: polychrome
fragments and a greenstone necklace with penate.
Drawing by Hipólito Sánchez Vera.

Plate 34. Yagul polychrome fragments. *Drawing by Abel Mendoza.*

Plate 35. Yagul polychrome fragments. *Drawing by Abel Mendoza.*

36. Yagul polychrome tripod vessel. *Restoration drawing bel Mendoza.*

Plate 37. Yagul polychrome tripod vessel. *Restoration drawing by Abel Mendoza.*

Plate 38. Yagul polychrome tripod vessel. *Restoration drawing by Abel Mendoza.*

Plate 39. Yagul polychrome tripod vessel. *Restoration drawing by Abel Mendoza.*

Plate 40. Unrolled collar of tripod shown in Plate 39. *Drawing by Abel Mendoza.*

The Lords of Yanhuitlan

ALFONSO CASO

In the National Archives of Mexico there is a group of unnumbered files, dated 1580, which contains some very important information about the rulers of Yanhuitlan.[1] We learn from these documents that Don Gabriel de Guzmán, who was *cacique* or lord of Yanhuitlan in 1580 and died in 1591, was a son of Don Diego Nuqh and Doña María Coquahu, also lords of Yanhuitlan. Nuqh means Six Movement or Six Earthquake in Mixtec, and Coquahu means Two House. This Diego Nuqh probably is the Diego Hoyd (*sic*) who was governor of Cuilapan in 1560.[2]

The documents say also that Doña María Coquahu, ♀ Two House, was a daughter of the lords Namahu and Cavaco. Na mahu means Eight Death, and Ca uaco is One Flower (*v*, of course, is often used for *u* in old Spanish spelling). Now a certain Lord ♂ Eight Death and his wife Lady ♀ One Flower appear in the Codex Bodley (19–III); we can find their surnames there as well, along with the name of the place they ruled. His full name is ♂ Eight Death "Tiger-Fire Serpent," and hers is ♀ One Flower "Tiger Quechquémitl." The place they rule is represented by a symbol made up of Feather Carpet–Jawbone–Arrow Beak (Figure 1).[3]

♂ Eight Death "Tiger-Fire Serpent" was a son of the third king of the Fourth Dynasty of Tilantongo, a man named Xico or ♂ Ten Rain "Tláloc-Sun" (Figure 2);[4] he was also a brother of ♂ Yacqua or ♂ Four Deer, who was the ruler of Tilantongo at the Spanish conquest and who died without having been baptized.[5] In fact, the last personages mentioned on the obverse of the Codex Bodley are ♂ Eight Death (Na mahu) and his brother ♂ Four Deer (Yac qua). We know that Na mahu was still alive in 1533.[6]

Now Doña María Coquahu, who inherited the right to rule Yanhuitlan, as we have seen was a daughter of the lords of the place called Feather Carpet–Jawbone–Arrow Beak; therefore that must be the glyph for Yanhuitlan.

1. Codex Bodley 19–III. Na mahu and Ca uaco at Feather Carpet–Arrow Beak.
All drawings by Abel Mendoza.

2. Codex Bodley 20–II. Xico or ♂ 10 Rain of Tilantongo.

3. Codex Bodley 11–IV. ♂ 5 Eagle and ♀ 9 Serpent at Feather Carpet–Arrow Beak (parents of ♀ 11 Serpent "Flower," wife of ♂ 8 Deer "Tiger Claw" of Tilantongo).

4. Codex Bodley 15–III.

5. Codex Bodley 24–V.

7. Codex Bodley 24–III. ♂ 6 Water and ♀ 1 Reed at Feather Carpet–Cacaxtli.

6. Lienzo de Teozacoalco.

We learn further that a brother of Doña María, Don Domingo de Guzmán or ♂ Seven Monkey "Tiger-Torch,"[7] became regent of Yanhuitlan because his nephew was a minor; he defended the principality against the Spaniard Gonzalo de las Casas and died in September 1558. His sister Doña María Coquahu, ♀ Two House, married the prince Don Diego Nuqh, ♂ Six Movement, who is mentioned in these documents as ruler of the towns of Tamasola and Chachoapan.

Thus the transmission of the lordship of Yanhuitlan, first to a lady married to a prince of Tilantongo, and from this pair to their daughter (who married the lord of Tamasola and Chachoapan), had taken place through the female line. The line of succession went on as follows: the eldest son, Don Matías de Velasco, inherited the lordships of Tamasola and Chachoapan, the towns from which his father came; and the second son, Don Gabriel de Guzmán, who was now of age, began to govern in Yanhuitlan (his uncle, the regent Don Domingo, died in 1558), thus inheriting the lordship there. This was, the document says, the order always followed in such matters: the eldest son inherited the lordship of the father, and the second son that of the mother.

We have some knowledge of still other caciques of Yanhuitlan: Don Francisco de Guzmán, son of Don Gabriel, who governed until 1629; Don Baltazar de Velasco y Guzmán, his nephew, who succeeded him in 1629; and all those who appear in the chart on pp. 332–33, which carries the succession down to the middle of the nineteenth century.

If the place indicated in Codex Bodley by Feather Carpet–Arrow Beak is Yanhuitlan, we can carry the genealogy back to 1061, since Bodley 11–IV (Figure 3) shows as rulers there a Lord ♂ Five Eagle and Lady ♀ Nine Serpent, parents of ♀ Eleven Serpent "Red Flower" or "Tiger Flower," one of the wives of the conqueror ♂ Eight Deer "Tiger Claw." Between this mention of the parents-in-law of ♂ Eight Deer "Tiger Claw" in 1061 and the next reference to the place in connection with ♂ Eight Death "Tiger-Fire Serpent," who died in 1536 and must have been born around 1490, there is a gap of more than four centuries during which I can find no other mention of it in the codices. It seems likely therefore that Yanhuitlan must have another glyphic place name besides the one of Feather Carpet–Arrow Beak.

In other places the feather-mantle sign appears in combination with other symbols, just as the arrow-beak glyph is sometimes combined with a wall rather than a feather carpet. We must keep in mind that Mixtec place names vary greatly. For example, Teozacoalco is represented at times by a wall that is being bent by a little man, and at other times by a flower (Figures 4, 5, 6).

Another example that is worth noting in connection with the genealogies of Yanhuitlan and Cuilapan is this: in Bodley 24-III (Figure 7) there is shown a Lord ♂ Six Water "Colored Strips" who marries the Lady ♀ One Reed "Sun Jewel," and the place they rule is represented by a feather carpet and a *cacaxtli* (a frame for carrying loads on one's back). Now in Codex Nuttall 35 (Figure

8. Codex Nuttall, p. 33. Pages 33—35 of Codex Nuttall record the genealogy of certain rulers at a place called Red Culhuacan—Flames—Huauhtli. Probably this refers to Yanhuitlan and its connection with Cuilapan. The rulers are identified by a distinctive headdress, which is known only among the rulers of this town and refers to the god Xipe Totec. Among these lords we see ♂ 2 Dog "Flint Braid" (upper right corner, p. 34), who also founded the Third Dynasty of Teozacoalco. On p. 35 (lower left corner), as the last ruler of the Xipe dynasty, ♂ 6 Water "Colored Strips" is shown. He was born about 1315 and is the last lord of this genealogy to be recorded in the Nuttall.

Probably a lord of this family is the personage buried in Tomb 1 of Zaachila, for the sculptured personages of the tomb wear the same Xipe headdress as the lords shown on pp. 33—35 and on p. 61 of Codex Nuttall, p. 303 above.

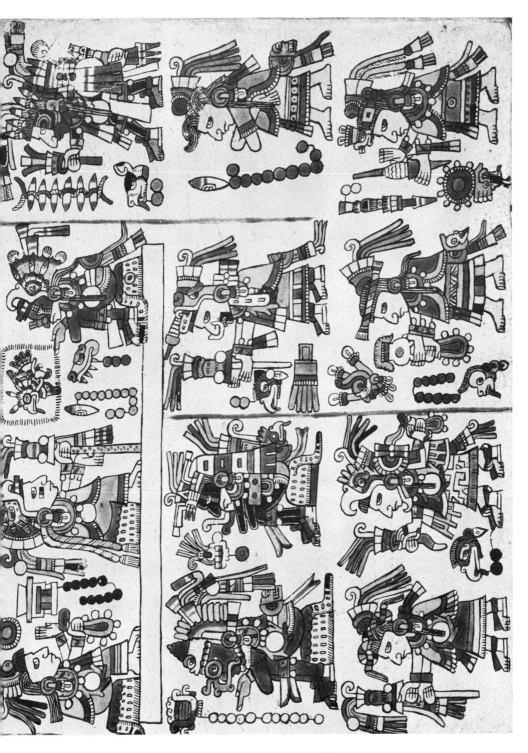

9. Codex Nuttall, p. 34.
♂ 2 Dog "Flint Braid" is
the figure in the upper
right corner; ♂ 1 Grass is
the second figure from
the left, center row.
See also Plate 11.

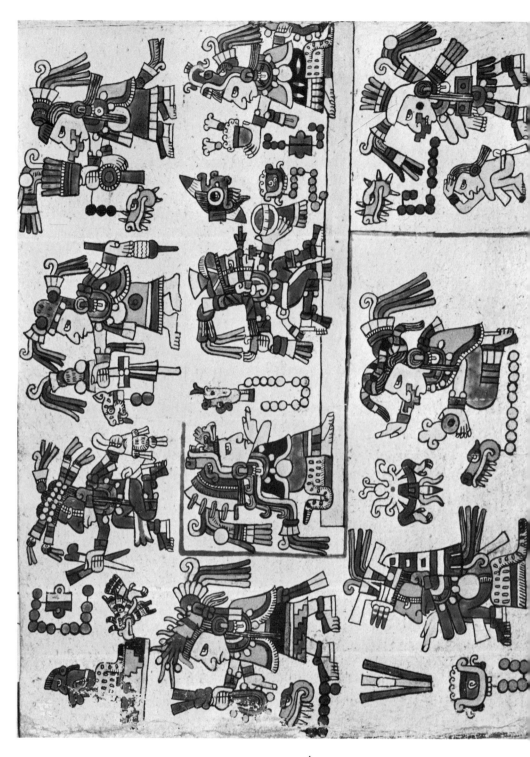

10. Codex Nuttall, p. 35. ♂ 6 Water "Colored Strips" is the first figure on the left, bottom row. See also Plate 10.

10) there is a Lord ♂ Six Water "Colored Strips" (Plate 10) who is the last in a genealogy that begins in Nuttall 33 (Figure 8) at a place with a rather complicated glyph. This glyph consists of a twisted hill that shoots flames and has five caves in it, a tree, and a river or lake in which there is a quetzal. We may call it Culhuacan–Tree–Quetzal River (center bottom).

This ♂ Six Water "Colored Strips" is a son of ♂ Eleven Water "Tláloc-Flint" and ♀ Thirteen Serpent "Feather Serpent"; one of his sisters, according to Nuttall 35, is ♀ Three Alligator "Turquoise Fan." Bodley 17-IV (Figure 11) shows the same ♂ Eleven Water "Tláloc-Flint" as married to ♀ Thirteen Serpent "Feather Serpent" and ruling at Feather Carpet–Cacaxtli. Their daughter ♀ Three Alligator "Turquoise Fan" appears as wife of ♂ Two Water "Fire Serpent," last king of the Third Dynasty of Tilantongo and Teozacoalco. Therefore, Culhuacan–Tree–Quetzal River and Feather Carpet–Cacaxtli must be the same place. In Selden II, 13-IV, we find this confirmed, for ♂ Six Water "Colored Strips" appears there as ruler of Feathers-Cacaxtli (Figure 12, Plate 6). We find the glyph also in Bodley 22-II (Figure 13), where there is a ruler ♂ Eight Deer "Fire Serpent" who is at once nephew and son-in-law to ♂ Six Water "Colored Strips," since he is a son of ♂ Thirteen Eagle, brother of that man's wife (Bodley 24-III; 24, 23-III), and married to a daughter whose name we do not know. Thus ♂ Eight Deer "Fire Serpent" begins a new dynasty in Feathers-Cacaxtli or Culhuacan–Tree–Quetzal River.

Can we link Feather Carpet–Cacaxtli to Feather Carpet–Arrow Beak, which we have identified as Yanhuitlan? It seems that we can. On page 33 of Codex Nuttall we see the place we have called Culhuacan–Tree–Quetzal River, and above it a temple of the god Xipe, here called by his calendar name of ♂ Seven Rain. The dynasty begins on the day 1 Flint in the year 1 Flint. The founding king of this new dynasty is ♂ Nine Serpent "Xipe" (Figure 8, upper left), whose wife (to his right) is ♀ Eleven Rabbit "Venus Quechquémitl-Xipe," who may be his sister; the second king is ♂ Five Flower "Xipe," who appears married to ♀ Four Rabbit "Quetzal" (lower left). Both these kings and the first of the queens are wearing a highly distinctive headdress that elsewhere in the codices is worn only by people from the same town; for instance ♂ Six Water "Colored Strips," whom we have already mentioned, has one. These lords with their peculiar headdress may be seen in Figures 8–10 and 14, and in Plates 9–14.

In Tomb 1 of Zaachila (Figures 15–34 and Plates 13–29), recently discovered by Roberto Gallegos, there appear two personages named ♂ Nine Flower and ♂ Five Flower who wear exactly the same headdress as the Nuttall rulers (Plates 13–14, Figures 21–22).[8] Although we cannot be sure that ♂ Nine Flower of Zaachila is the same person as the ♂ Nine Serpent of Nuttall, we can be confident that ♂ Five Flower is the same one mentioned in Nuttall 33, and that he is the great-grandfather of ♂ Six Water "Colored Strips."

Though there is a great variety of male headdresses in the codices, this

Text continued on p. 329

11. Codex Bodley 17–IV. ♂ 11 Water and ♀ 13 Serpent, parents of ♀ 3 Alligator and ♂ 2 Water and lords of Feather Carpet–Cacaxtli.

12. Codex Selden II, 13–IV. ♂ 6 Water at Feathers–Cacaxtli.

13. Codex Bodley 22–II. ♂ 8 Deer "Fire Serpent" at Feather Carpet–Cacaxtli.

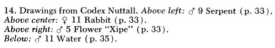

14. Drawings from Codex Nuttall. *Above left:* ♂ 9 Serpent (p. 33). *Above center:* ♀ 11 Rabbit (p. 33). *Above right:* ♂ 5 Flower "Xipe" (p. 33). *Below:* ♂ 11 Water (p. 35).

Patio with tombs, Zaachila, from the top of the "Castillo" or highest mound.

Exterior antechamber, façade, and door of Tomb 1, Zaachila.

19. Interior antechamber and main chamber, Tomb 1, Zaachila.

20. Painted plaster sculpture on rear wall of Tomb 1, Zaachila. See also Plate 15.

21. ♂ 9 Flower, Tomb 1, Zaachila. See also Plate 13.

22. ♂ 5 Flower, Tomb 1, Zaachila. See also Plate 14.

23. Plaster sculpture of owl,
interior antechamber,
Tomb 1, Zaachila.

24. Sculpture on wall opposite that shown in Figure 23.

25. A niche as found, Zaachila.

26. Tripod vessel with death figure; from Tomb 2, Zaachila.

27. Polychrome tiger-claw vessel, Zaachila.

28. Tiger-claw vessel, Zaachila.

29. Carved and (at far right) incised bones,
Zaachila. Large bones of deer, jaguars, and humans
were worked into these and other forms by the Mixtecs,
who at times—as in some of the Monte Albán Tomb 7
examples—inlaid turquoise to emphasize the designs.
The glyphic content of the carvings is usually ritual,
referring to deities and the religious calendar; but some
examples seem to record historical events and their dates.

30. Jade handle, Tomb 2, Zaachila.

31. Gold lip plug with pendant, Zaachila.

32. Gold ring with eagle holding pendant;
from Tomb 1, Zaachila.

33. Gold disks, Zaachila.

34. Gold pendant, Tomb 2, Zaachila.

distinctive one, connected with the god Xipe, is found only on the persons mentioned here and on another king of the same place, ♂ Three Vulture "Xipe" (Nuttall 61; Plate 12 and p. 303 above).

We know that the Mixtecs of Cuilapan who lived in Zaachila had come from Yanhuitlan or from a town called Almoloyas, west of the Santo Domingo River, where the local Mixtecs had made themselves vassals of Yanhuitlan in order to obtain protection against their Cuicatec neighbors.[9] Further, in the *Relación* of Cuilapan we are told that a lord of Almoloyas married a daughter of the ruler of Zaachila (Teozapotlan), and that the Zapotec king gave him Cuilapan as a dowry.[10] (However, the *Relación* of Teozapotlan says that before 1280 the Zapotec king of that place married a Mixtec lady.) Since then the Mixtecs had established themselves in Cuilapan, although not in large numbers.[11] Later, shortly before the Spanish conquest, a lord of Yanhuitlan and the lord of Zaachila married two sisters; the lord of Yanhuitlan was given Cuilapan on this occasion. The Mixtecs then arrived in such numbers that they took control of Zaachila, and had "within the capital a kind of castle"; they also surrounded Zaachila with newly founded Mixtec towns.[12]

In view of these facts it is not strange that Mixtec tombs should be found in the mound or "castle" at Zaachila, nor that ♂ Five Flower should be shown in Tomb 1 adorned in exactly the same manner as in Codex Nuttall 33; the personages buried in this tomb at Zaachila thus may be seen to be related to those mentioned on pages 33 to 35 of Nuttall.

We know that these people came from a place called Culhuacan–Tree–Quetzal River, which is the same as the place referred to as Feathers-Cacaxtli. We have seen, too, that the rulers who are shown at Feathers–Arrow Beak are the same ones who, according to the National Archives documents, were ruling at Yanhuitlan in 1533, and whose descendants we can follow until well into the nineteenth century. Therefore there must be a relationship between Feather Carpet–Arrow Beak (Yanhuitlan) and Feather Carpet–Cacaxtli (Cuilapan).

Special attention should be given to the fact that in the Bodley 14-IV, V (Figure 35), ♂ Eight Deer "Tiger Claw" is apparently sacrificed at a place called Hill with Arm, Wall, and Cacaxtli–Feather Carpet–Maguey (century plants) and Other Plants. Is this the same place as Feather Carpet–Cacaxtli? If so, ♂ Eight Deer would have been sacrificed in Cuilapan.

If we look at the genealogies on pp. 331–33, three facts become apparent. (1) Two personages from Arrow Beak or Yanhuitlan, ♂ Five Eagle and ♀ Nine Serpent, are the parents of the fourth wife of ♂ Eight Deer "Tiger Claw." The marriage occurs probably in 5 Flint, i.e. 1056. (2) Culhuacan–Tree–Quetzal River, where the local deity is ♂ Seven Rain "Xipe" and which is the place ruled by the ♂ Five Flower "Xipe" who is portrayed in Tomb 1 of Zaachila and on page 33 of Codex Nuttall, is the same place as Feathers-Cacaxtli. The lords of Feathers-Cacaxtli, ♂ Six Water "Colored Strips" and his wife ♀ One Reed "Sun Jewel," were the parents of the woman who married ♂ Eight Deer

35. Codex Bodley 14–IV, V. The
sacrifice of ♂ 8 Deer "Tiger Claw"
at Hill–Arm–Feather Carpet–
Cacaxtli.

"Fire Serpent," who may be the personage buried in Tomb 1 of Zaachila. (3)
Since we know that the rulers of Cuilapan came from Yanhuitlan, possibly the
genealogies of Culhuacan–Tree–Quetzal River–Feathers-Cacaxtli, which may
be Cuilapan, and of Arrow Beak–Feathers, which is Yanhuitlan, are connected. However, the earliest mention I have found in the archives of a Cuilapan cacique is of Don Ángel Villafañe y Alvarado, who died before 1620 and
probably came to the rulership of Cuilapan through his wife, whose name we
do not know. His son, Baltazar de Velasco y Guzmán, was cacique of Yanhuitlan and Teposcolula; another son, Ángel de Guzmán, was cacique of Cuilapan and Tututepec. It was a son of Baltazar, however, Francisco Pimentel
Guzmán y Alvarado, who inherited the *cacicazgo* of Cuilapan, for Ángel's
son, Jacinto, died without heirs.

   ♂ Eight Deer "Fire Serpent," the last personage who appears in Codex
Bodley, must have been born in about 1400, since his nephew is born in 1435.
The first mention of a colonial cacique is of a man probably born in about
1580. Thus we have a gap of roughly 180 years, or six or seven caciques, for
whom we have no data, unless, as in the case of Yanhuitlan, Cuilapan may be
represented in more than one way.

   In a file classified under the title "Lands" in the National Archives, we
find that a woman named Juana de Lara was cacique of Cuilapan and
died in 1717; she was a daughter of Jerónimo de Lara y Guzmán (born
in 1633), and he was a son of Gregorio de Lara, cacique of Tejupan in 1581.[13]

Genealogy of Cuilapan (?)

From Nuttall 61. ♂ 3 Vulture "Xipe" meets with ♂ 8 Deer "Tiger Claw" of Tilantongo, IInd dynasty, 2nd ruler. *Year:* 7 House, A.D. 1045.
Place: Twisted Hill with Tree–Feather Carpet–Quetzals.

♂ 4 Dog "Tame Coyote," a son of ♂ 8 Deer, is the 1st ruler in the IInd dynasty of Teozacoalco.

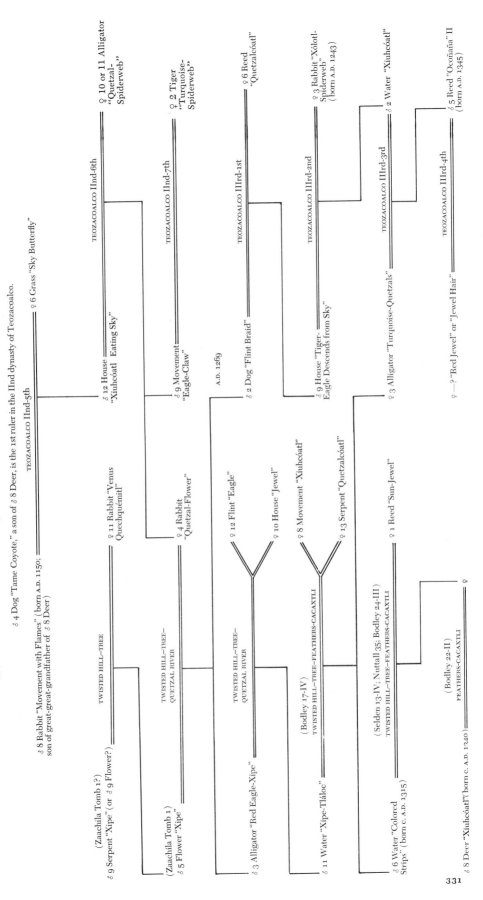

Genealogy of Feathers-Arrow Beak (*Yanhuitlan*)

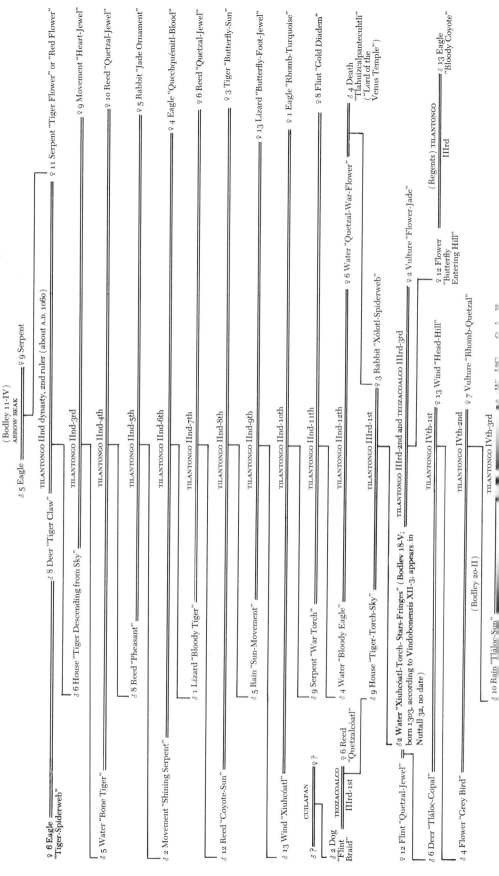

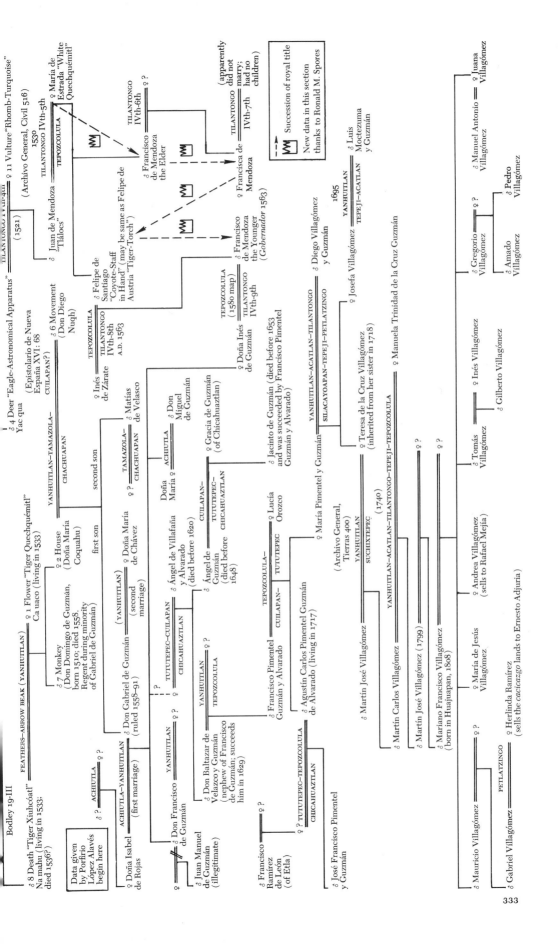

Bodley 19-III

TILANTONGO IVth-4th
(1521)

♂ 8 Death "Tiger Xiuhcóatl" Na mahu (living in 1533; died 1536?)

♂ 11 Vulture "Rhomb-Turquoise"
(Archivo General, Civil 516)
1530
TILANTONGO IVth-5th

♀ María de Estrada "White Quechquémitl"

♀ 1 Flower "Tiger Quechquémitl" Ca uaco (living in 1533)

FEATHERS–ARROW BEAK (YANHUITLAN)

Data given by Porfirio López Alavés begin here

♂ 7 Monkey (Don Domingo de Guzmán, born 1510; died 1558. Regent during minority of Gabriel de Guzmán)

♂ 2 House (Doña María Coquahu)
first son

♀ Juan de Mendoza "Tlálocs"

TILANTONGO IVth-6th

♂ Francisco de Mendoza the Elder

TILANTONGO IVth-7th

(apparently did not marry; had no children)

♂ 6 Movement (Don Diego Nuqh)

YANHUITLAN–TAMAZOLA– CHACHUAPAN

second son

♂ Felipe de Santiago "Coyote-Staff in Hand" (may be same as Felipe de Austria "Tiger-Torch")

♂ Francisco de Mendoza the Younger (Gobernador 1563)

♀ Francisca de Mendoza

Succession of royal title

New data in this section thanks to Ronald M. Spores

ACHUTLA
♂ ? ♀ ?

♀ Doña Isabel de Rojas

ACHUTLA–YANHUITLAN (first marriage)

♂ Don Gabriel de Guzmán (YANHUITLAN) (ruled 1558-91)

♀ Doña María de Chávez (second marriage)

♀ Inés de Zárate

TEPOZCOLULA
TILANTONGO IVth-8th
A.D. 1563

♀ ?

TAMAZOLA– CHACHUAPAN

♂ Matías de Velasco

Doña María ♀

ACHUTLA

♂ Don Miguel de Guzmán

♀ Gracia de Guzmán (of Chicahuaztlan)

♀ Doña Inés de Guzmán

TEPOZCOLULA (1580 map)
TILANTONGO IVth-9th

♂ Don Francisco de Guzmán

YANHUITLAN
♀ ?

♂ Don Baltazar de Velazco y Guzmán (nephew of Francisco de Guzmán; succeeds him in 1629)

YANHUITLAN TEPOZCOLULA

♂ Ángel de Villafaña y Alvarado (died before 1620)

♂ Ángel de Guzmán (died before 1648)

CUILAPAN– TUTUTEPEC– CHICAHUAZTLAN

♂ Jacinto de Guzmán (died before 1653 and was succeeded by Francisco Pimentel Guzmán y Alvarado)

♂ Juan Manuel de Guzmán (illegitimate)

TUTUTEPEC–CUILAPAN ♀ ?
CHICAHUAZTLAN

♀ Lucia Orozco

♂ Francisco Pimentel Guzmán y Alvarado

CUILAPAN– TUTUTEPEC

♂ Agustín Carlos Pimentel Guzmán de Alvarado (living in 1717)

♀ María Pimentel y Guzmán

(Archivo General, Tierras 400)

YANHUITLAN–ACATLAN–TILANTONGO– SILACAYOAPAN–TEPEJI–PETLATZINGO

♂ Diego Villagómez y Guzmán

1695
YANHUITLAN
TEPEJI–ACATLAN

♂ Luis Moctezuma y Guzmán

♀ Josefa Villagómez

♀ Teresa de la Cruz Villagómez (inherited from her sister in 1718)

♀ Manuela Trinidad de la Cruz Guzmán

♂ Gregorio Villagómez

♀ ?

♂ Manuel Antonio Villagómez

♀ Juana Villagómez

♂ Amado Villagómez

♂ Pedro Villagómez

♂ Francisco Ramírez de León (of Etla)

♀ ?

♂ José Francisco Pimentel y Guzmán

♂ Francisco Ramírez de León (of Etla)
♀ ?

♂ ? TUTUTEPEC–TEPOZCOLULA ♀ ?
CHICAHUAZTLAN

YANHUITLAN–ACATLAN–TILANTONGO–TEPEJI–TEPOZCOLULA

1740
YANHUITLAN
SUCHIXTEPEC

♂ Martín José Villagómez

♂ Martín Carlos Villagómez

♂ Martín José Villagómez (1799)

♂ Mariano Francisco Villagómez (born in Huajuapan, 1808)

♀ María de Jesús Villagómez

♂ Tomás Villagómez

♀ Andrea Villagómez (sells to Rafael Mejía)

♀ Inés Villagómez

♂ Gilberto Villagómez

♂ Mauricio Villagómez

♀ ?

♀ Herlinda Ramírez (sells the cacicazgo lands to Ernesto Adjuria)

PETLATZINGO

♂ Gabriel Villagómez

333

Juana de Lara had a sister, whose name we do not know, who married a man named Ramírez de León; their children were Francisco Ramírez de León, cacique of Etla, and Isabel Ramírez de León, who inherited the cacicazgo of Cuilapan and wished to pass it on to her adopted son, Miguel de los Ángeles y Lara. This was opposed by her brother, Francisco Ramírez de León (who is also mentioned as having a daughter who married Agustín Carlos Pimentel Guzmán y Lara, cacique of Tututepec and Teposcolula). But apparently his opposition was unsuccessful, since Miguel de los Ángeles y Lara appears in the documents as cacique of Cuilapan in 1723.

From this point on, we find only sporadic mentions of the cacicazgo of Cuilapan. For example, we know that Inés de Velasco of Cuilapan married Juan de Zárate of Xoxocotlan. Juan de Velasco of Cuilapan married María Álvarez. These Velascos probably are collateral descendants of José Félix de Velasco. A man named Manuel de Chávez appears as cacique of Cuilapan in 1712.[14]

Further information about the cacicazgo of Yanhuitlan is to be found in a document that I examined in a copy given me by Barbro Dahlgren. The author is the priest of Juxtlahuaca, Porfirio López Alavés; but he says he took the facts from a loose page written "by Father Uriel Villagómez Amador, a descendant of the Villagómez family, descended from Ocoñaña, a family that was established in the town of Suchixtepec, of the ex-District of Huajuapan de León, Oaxaca." I have studied the information supplied by Villagómez very carefully, and I find that in general it agrees with the facts presented in the documents in the archives. I therefore think that we may accept it provisionally, and if so, we have the wherewithal to trace the descendants of the Yanhuitlan caciques down to modern times.

The discovery of the Zaachila tombs has made it possible for us to arrive at what probably was the place glyph for Cuilapan, and to connect Cuilapan both with the prehispanic codices and with documents from the National Archives and other sources dealing with the Mixteca and the Valley of Oaxaca. In this way the historical value of the Mixtec codices has been further strengthened: not only do the codex chronicles now form a continuous line with those written about the Mixteca during colonial times, but they are supported by archeological discoveries.

NOTES

1. Archivo General de la Nación, Ramo Civil, Vol. DXVI, Expediente sin número.
2. Francisco del Paso y Troncoso, *Epistolario de Nueva España* (México, 1942), XVI, 68.
3. Alfonso Caso, *Interpretation of the Codex Bodley 2858* (México, 1960), p. 48.
4. Archivo General de la Nación, Civil DXVI.
5. Francisco del Paso y Troncoso, *Papeles de Nueva España* (Madrid, 1905), IV, 73.

6. Wigberto Jiménez Moreno and Salvador Mateos Higuera, *Códice de Yanhuitlan* (México, 1940), Plate XVI.

7. *Ibid.*

8. Roberto Gallegos, "Zaachila: The First Season's Work," *Archaeology,* XVI (1963), 226–33; and "Exploraciones en Zaachila, Oaxaca," *Boletín* INAH No. 8 (June 1962), pp. 6–8.

9. Francisco de Burgoa, *Geográfica descripción* . . . , Archivo General de la Nación, Publicación No. XXV (México, 1934), I, 387, 391.

10. Robert H. Barlow, "Dos relaciones antiguas del pueblo de Cuilapan, Estado de Oaxaca," *Tlalocan,* II (1945), 18–28. Also published in English under the title "Relaciones of Oaxaca of the 16th and 18th Centuries," *Boletín de Estudios Oaxaqueños,* No. 23 (Mitla, 1962).

11. Francisco del Paso y Troncoso, *Papeles,* IV, 190–95. For a conflicting interpretation found in the Cuilapan *Relación* rather than the Teozapotlan *Relación,* see Paddock, this volume, p. 377.

12. Burgoa, I, 395.

13. Archivo General de la Nación, Ramo de Tierras, Vol. XXXIV, Expedientes 1 and 3.

14. *Ibid.,* Vol. XLVI, Expediente 2.

Tomb 30 at Yagul and the Zaachila Tombs

CHARLES R. WICKE

Tomb 30 was unearthed at Yagul during the first months of 1960 by students participating in a field session sponsored by Mexico City College and carried out under my direction.[1] Although architectonically the tomb is the most elaborate yet uncovered at Yagul, we found it thoroughly sacked, and my description of it will necessarily be incomplete. It is situated within Patio 4, which is surrounded by four pyramidal mounds, one of which is the largest such mound at Yagul: this was an important part of the town. In the center of the patio is a low platform, a so-called "adoratorio."[2]

When Yagul was first surveyed in 1954, a ravaged tomb, Tomb 3, was recorded at the western edge of the adoratorio. It was noted during the subsequent exploration of the site that in many cases two or three tombs would open onto a common rectangular area, and since this seemed to be a recurring feature, the region in front of Tomb 3 was tested when erosion revealed what looked like a portion of another façade.[3] The result was the discovery of Tombs 29 and 30, which flanked Tomb 3 at right angles (Figure 1). In addition, a flight of stairs was found leading down to the area onto which they faced.

Tomb 29 had a ground plan in the shape of a T. The tomb had been entered from the roof and sacked. However, the arms of the T had been overlooked by the looters, and yielded pottery vessels all classifiable as Mixtec fine grey ware. The façade, of veneer masonry, showed a small, cursorily carved head projecting at one side of the doorway (Figure 2). Similar sculptures adorn the Zaachila tombs,[4] but there are better examples from both Yagul and Mitla.[5] Tomb 12 of Yagul, located only a few steps west of Tomb 29, had two such heads (Figure 4). Another exists in the enormous and otherwise beautifully made cruciform tomb at Xaaga, Mitla (Figures 5–7).

Facing the façade of Tomb 29 to the north is the front of Tomb 30, with which this paper deals (Figure 3). It, too, had been entered from above. All the slabs that had once formed its roof and walls had been carried away except for a doorjamb, which was still in position, and one wall slab, which was lying face down on the floor (Figure 1). From these two remaining stones it was assumed that the interior had been decorated throughout with greca designs in relief, as in the cruciform tombs at Mitla, Guirun, and Xaaga (Figure 9). Although the walls had been removed, the original stucco floor was in good condition, and by tracing its upturned edges we were able to determine a ground plan: like Tomb 29 and many other Yagul tombs of the same period, Tomb 30 was T-shaped. The monolithic doorjamb, the only interior stone remaining in place, gave us the original height of the chamber. These two data allowed accurate reconstruction (Figure 10): the wall was raised to the height of the jamb, following the outline of the floor plan, and a flat roof was fabricated of reinforced concrete slabs. (Had the roof been angular it would have projected above the floor of Patio 4.)

Working from above and inside, the looters of Tomb 30 had ignored its façade and even its door. The façade is remarkably similar to those of the Mitla palaces (and of course to those of the Yagul palaces as well). The proportions of its panel-and-slope architecture, the greca designs within the panels (originally stucco-covered, the grecas were painted white with a red background), and the stone heads tenoned into the wall were features shared with the palaces of Mitla and Yagul (Figure 8).

As yet I have been unable to identify the personages represented in the sculpture. The head with the goggle-eyes cannot be a rain deity because it shows neither fangs nor a bifid tongue; but it could perhaps be a monkey, monkeys being depicted in the codices with rings around their eyes.

Upon raising the fallen wall slab within the west arm of the T, we discovered a disorderly mass of bones (Figure 1). We were able to distinguish nine crania among many long bones; of these nine, only one appeared to have been articulated with the body at the time the slab fell. From this we may infer that before the looting took place, the tomb floor was completely covered with bones (as has been the case in several smaller Yagul tombs of the same period that were found intact). After the tomb was built, corpses were placed in it at intervals over a long period (thus the need for steps). Articulated bones of the earlier deposits would thus have been scattered by later burial parties.

Alternatively, it could be argued that the looters, not later burial parties, were responsible for the disorder of the bones: that, fearing retribution from the spirits they had disturbed, they swept the bones together and deliberately laid the slab over them. I do not favor this hypothesis because among the bones were fragments of valuable polychrome vessels, which the robbers would probably have removed (Plate 30).

The polychrome fragments are from three vessels. The design on one of

Text continued on p. 343

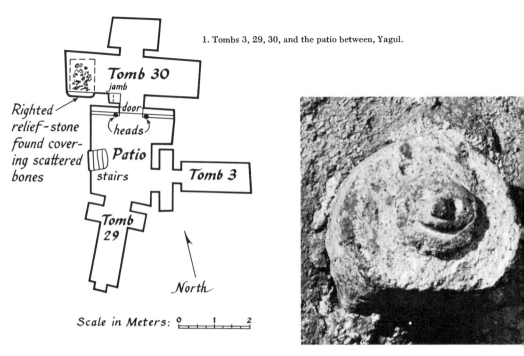

1. Tombs 3, 29, 30, and the patio between, Yagul.

Tomb 30

jamb

door

(heads)

Patio

stairs

Tomb 3

Righted
relief-stone
found cover-
ing scattered
bones

Tomb
29

North

Scale in Meters: 0   1   2

2. *Below:* façade of Tomb 29, Yagul. *Above:* close-up of stone head to right of door, Tomb 29.

3. View across the interior of Tomb 30, with façade of Tomb 29 in background.

Façade of Tomb 12, Yagul.

5. Interior of the cruciform tomb at Xaaga, looking south from the center of the cross.
The crude stone head shown below in Figure 7 is the small projection at top left.
Greca designs are not mosaic, but carved into large stones.

7. Close-up of stone head, Xaaga. This carving is no more incongruous than the crude dishes found in Yagul tombs among fine grey and polychrome pottery offerings of utmost sophistication. It is still the custom in parts of Oaxaca for relatives of the deceased—necessarily amateurs in most cases—to make dishes for funeral offerings.

6. The center and entrance of the Xaaga tomb, seen from the rear or east end. The west (entrance) arm is the narrowest of the four; Figure 5 shows the arm around the corner to the left. Except for Tomb 30 of Yagul, the Mitla area tombs and palaces, besides the most exquisite stone carving and mosaic, were "adorned" with little inset effigies (Figures 2, 4, 7) that can only be the work of amateurs. The recessed background of the carved grecas was left rough and painted red; the grecas were surfaced with polished white plaster.

Façade of Tomb 30, Yagul.

Interior of Tomb 30 during reconstruction. At upper left are the stairs from Patio 4
wn to the antechamber or patio of Tombs 3, 29, and 30.

10. Roofing of Tomb 30.

11. Codex Nuttall, p. 75. The codex here tells of an expedition carried out by ♂ 8 Deer "Tiger Claw" and his ally ♂ 4 Tiger against a hill that rises from a river or lake. In the water we see an alligator (*cipactli*), a fish that has the head of a bird, a large snail, a feathered serpent, and a bivalve. There are five caves on the island, whose name may be Hill of the Máxtlatl (breechclout). On the left shore is a red and black column (Tlillan-Tlapallan?) that holds up the sky. Besides ♂ 8 Deer and ♂ 4 Tiger, a man named ♂ 9 Water "Sun Band" appears in a white canoe. He is not mentioned in other codices, and he may appear here as a momentary ally in the conquest of the island. The event takes place during the three consecutive days of 10 Serpent, 11 Death, and 12 Deer of the year 8 Rabbit, A.D. 1046. (*Note by Alfonso Caso.*)

them is of the same greca type as appears on the tomb façade. This design, by the way, is painted on the interior walls of a tomb recently found in the Chinantec region at Yolox, Oaxaca.[6] Another vessel depicts the human figure in the same manner as the Mixtec codices. The stance, the proportion of head to body, the way the breechclout falls, and the way in which the hand extends holding a banner are the same as shown in the Mixtec books. In front of one figure is a skull, and in front of the other a crocodile with spines and spots— just as in the famous scene of an attack on an island on page 75 in Codex Nuttall (Figure 11). I would guess that the potter copied the design from a book, and that the skull and the crocodile are the day names of the two figures without their numerical coefficients, which made no sense to the illiterate potter and therefore were not copied.

In addition to the pottery, our sifting of the earth just above the tomb floor yielded a plain copper finger ring. This brings another element into the association of traits. This complex, even though it consists of bits and pieces, is significant. We have noted the following elements that are common to Tomb 30 and the Zaachila tombs:

(1) exterior and interior antechambers;
(2) façades at right angles to each other;
(3) steps leading down to exterior antechambers;
(4) a large number of bodies within a single tomb;
(5) polychrome pottery showing designs used in the Mitla mosaics and in codices from the Mixteca Alta;
(6) façades having panels of grecas; and
(7) use of metal.

Why the Yagul complex was rifled when the Zaachila one remained undisturbed may be explained, I think, by the fact that just after the Spanish conquest the inhabitants of Yagul were moved out of their fortified hilltop city by the Spanish and concentrated at Tlacolula in a flat, grid-patterned town a mile or two away (Figure 12). (Before Ignacio Bernal asked local men for another name and was given that of Yagul, the archeological town was known in the region as Pueblo Viejo de Tlacolula, or Old Tlacolula.[7]) Then as today, it was easier to unearth tombs that were out of public view, since people entering tombs were always likely to arouse censure that could burst into violence (as happened in Zaachila when Caso was forced to flee in 1947 and Bernal in 1953; Gallegos worked there in 1962 under armed guard).

The missing wall slabs suggest that Tomb 30 may have been sacked just after the Conquest, when intensive building activities required such dressed stones. During these same years it is known that certain Conquistadores enjoyed a special license to loot prehispanic tombs for gold; and an elaborate gold necklace in the American Museum of Natural History, New York, is said to have come from Tlacolula, probably meaning Yagul.[8]

Our thesis then is simple: because of the similarity of Tomb 30 at Yagul

12. Greca stone built into the church in Tlacolula.

and the Zaachila tombs, we conclude that the same culture is represented in both. In these two examples the stylistic features of the associated artifacts point to the Mixtec culture. Historical data, which are presented in this volume (pp. 367–85) by Paddock, and further archeological materials, discussed by Bernal (pp. 345–66), reinforce such a conclusion.

NOTES

1. See *Mexico City Collegian*, May 19, 1960, pp. 4–5, and Richard T. Owens, "A Descriptive Analysis of Three Tombs at Yagul, Oaxaca" (unpublished Master's thesis, Mexico City College, 1961).

2. John Paddock, "The First Three Seasons at Yagul," *Mesoamerican Notes* No. 4 (1955), pp. 41–44; "The 1956 Season at Yagul," *ibid.*, No. 5 (1957), pp. 21–25.

3. Tombs 1–2, 15–16, and 23–24 form such pairs; Tombs 25–26–27 are a trio of this kind. See also Bernal's reference to these, this volume, p. 356.

4. Roberto Gallegos, "Zaachila: The First Season's Work," *Archaeology*, XVI (1963), 226–33; and "Exploraciones en Zaachila, Oaxaca, *Boletín* INAH No. 8 (June 1962), pp. 6–8. Considerable further material on the Zaachila tombs is presented by Caso, pp. 313–35 above.

5. *Mesoamerican Notes* No. 4, Figure 26; Marshall H. Saville, "The Cruciform Tombs of Mitla and Vicinity," *Putnam Anniversary Volume* (New York, 1909), p. 174 and Plate II; Constantine G. Richards, *The Ruins of Mexico*, Vol. I (London, 1910), figure facing p. 97.

6. Agustín Delgado, "Polychrome Zapotec Tomb Paintings," *Current Anthropology*, II (1961), 269; and his "Investigaciones antropológicas," *Boletín* INAH No. 2 (October 1960) pp. 7–9.

7. Anonymous, *Mesoamerican Notes* No. 4 (1955), p. 68.

8. José Pijoán, *Summa Artis* (Madrid, 1946), Vol. X, p. 223, Figure 358, "Collar de oro procedente de Tlacolula (Oaxaca)." A very similar necklace was found in Tomb 7 at Monte Albán. The Tlacolula example has 34 rectangular beads, each with four tiny loops at the bottom; a miniature bell hangs from one of the loops on each bead.

The Mixtecs in the Archeology of the Valley of Oaxaca

IGNACIO BERNAL

My aim here is to bring together the archeological data referring to the occupation of the Valley of Oaxaca by a people or peoples of Mixtec or similar culture during the final centuries before the Conquest. I shall not deal with the Mixtec region itself, for this is not an examination of Mixtec culture in general but only of its reflection in the Valley of Oaxaca.

THE HISTORY OF THE DISCOVERIES

As a result of accidental finds and small-scale excavations during the nineteenth century and the first thirty years of the twentieth, we have known of the presence of the Mixtec culture in the Valley of Oaxaca for some time. However, it was not at first recognized as Mixtec culture, and only in 1932, when Alfonso Caso identified the offering of Tomb 7 at Monte Albán as Mixtec, did the first clear definition of the problem appear.[1]

In 1935, thanks to continuing exploration of Monte Albán, Caso and Jorge R. Acosta were able to define the last period as seen in the ceramics of the site—a period that represents the establishment of Mixtecs or Mixtec influence in the Valley of Oaxaca.[2] This period was not found at Monte Albán in the stratigraphy as usually conceived, but many data indicate that it is the last occupation of the city.

During 1934 and 1935, Caso and Daniel F. Rubín de la Borbolla excavated in Mitla.[3] The pottery they found beneath the patios of the palaces belongs to this same period (although not all Mitla antiquities are so late), which proves that the palaces could not have been built before Monte Albán V. In 1961, I found another tomb there; those of Xaaga and Guiroo were already known.[4]

Early in 1954, following up the statement of the historical sources that Cuilapan had been the Mixtec capital in the Valley, I undertook some explorations there, even though Saville had worked in the area previously (1904).[5] The results were not very conclusive with respect to what interests us here, but there were some interesting discoveries, and Cuilapan should undoubtedly be explored further.

Immediately after the Cuilapan work I began excavations (in 1954) at Yagul. My visit there in late 1953 had been the first investigation of the place since Bandelier's visit and brief description in 1881. Yagul contained at least one building resembling those of Mitla, a fact that aroused immediate interest. Work has gone on there intermittently until the present. Although it is far from finished, it has already provided important results.

In 1958, Lorenzo Gamio and I started to carry out a survey of the archeological sites in the Valley. Here we shall deal only with the Mixtec sites that we found. Early in 1962, Roberto Gallegos discovered the two tombs in Zaachila that so greatly clarified the late history of that site.[6] It is impossible to discuss all these discoveries here, and so I shall select those that seem most relevant to certain points I consider fundamental.

THE EASTERN AREA

We shall first take up the east side of the Valley, and then the west. In the eastern division there are two important sites for our purposes: Mitla and Yagul. The architecture of Mitla is too well-known to need description here (Figures 1–4). However, I should like to emphasize that as I understand it, this architecture is not a completely new phenomenon in the area; rather it combines elements of an older style, Zapotec, with new elements that we may tentatively call Mixtec. The principal new elements are the elaborate decoration of stone mosaic, the use of enormous monoliths, and the general arrangement of rooms. This last has no direct antecedents in Monte Albán or other Valley cities.

For our present purpose, the most interesting construction groups in Mitla are those known as the Group of the Columns, the Church Group, and the South Group.[7] The first two, as we have already noted, show only one period: that is, their stratigraphy consists of a single level. They are therefore considered to belong to the last period before the Spanish conquest, and they are later than the *last* constructions of the South Group, which shows a stratigraphy of several construction periods. In the Group of the Columns and the Church Group, excavations in the patios revealed some Monte Albán V pottery, but there was no polychrome pottery or metal. We do not know what the two great cruciform tombs of these patios may have contained, but some objects recovered by Saville and never published suggest Monte Albán V.

The South Group, by contrast, provides a long sequence. Burial 1,[8] clearly of Monte Albán IIIa, was placed before the first floor of the patio was laid down. Burial 2[9] is of period IV, but earlier than Tomb 7[10] of Mitla. After Burial 1 the stucco floor of the patio was laid, and clearly at this time the buildings

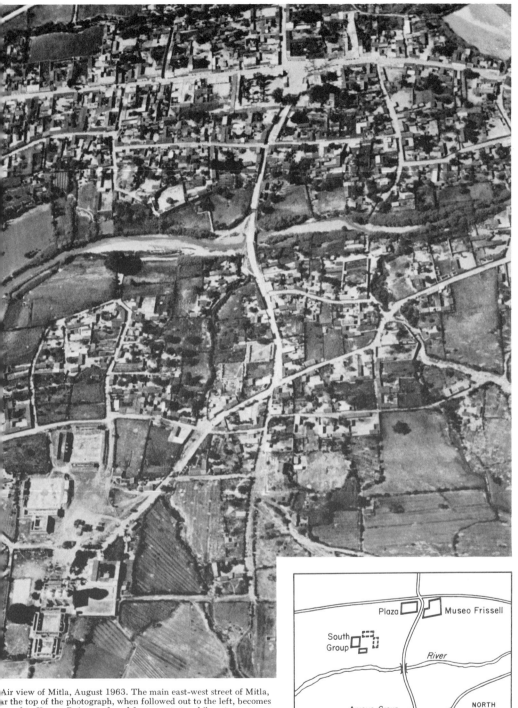

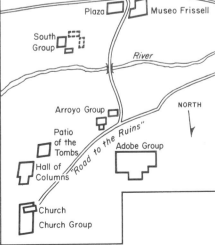

Air view of Mitla, August 1963. The main east-west street of Mitla,
at the top of the photograph, when followed out to the left, becomes
the road to Xaaga. Ruins are found from one to two kilometers
beyond the present limits of the town in all directions. The distance
from the church to the Plaza is about one kilometer.
Drawing by David J. Pauly.

Plaza

Museo Frissell

South
Group

River

Arroyo Group

NORTH

Patio
of the
Tombs

"Road to the Ruins"

Adobe Group

Hall of
Columns

Church

Church Group

Façade of the Hall of Columns, showing remains of the "Adoratorio" in the center of the patio. ntil the Batres-Saville work of 1901, this patio was filled with debris.

, Interior of the Hall of Columns, seen from the southeast corner. he doorway at the right leads to the interior courtyard.

349

which surround the patio were also put up. Tomb 7 is later than the patio floor, since the floor was broken in order to install it; the offerings in the tomb included Monte Albán V pottery, but no polychrome or metal. Its construction, however, is Zapotec, as can be seen from the angular roof and the carved stone at the rear. A last building on the east side of the patio is later than the tomb.

On the north side I found Tomb 3c (Figures 5 and 6). It had been partially dismantled, but plainly was very similar to—although smaller than—the two great tombs in the Group of the Columns. It was lined with stone mosaic, and the small amount of pottery still in place was Mixtec: miniature vessels exactly like those of Mound B at Monte Albán, of Cuilapan, and of Yagul. We do not know whether it had ever contained polychrome pottery or metal objects. It was associated with a building in the style of those of the Columns. Perhaps it was the first tomb of this style to be built in Mitla. Over it—and this may have been the cause of its destruction—the north building of the South Group had been constructed and reconstructed several times, always in Zapotec style.

It appears, then, that there was a patio here, datable according to Burial 1 as Monte Albán IIIa, and, I assume, surrounded by the usual buildings. Another patio was built over this one in period IV, and Burial 2 is contemporary with these new works; Tomb 3c probably is also of that time, and it was below a palace like those of the Columns or the Church. Later the patio floor was cut to build Tomb 7 in Zapotec style, and over it the east pyramid. At the same

5. View from north to south across Tomb 3c, South Group, Mitla.
Remains of original plaster are visible on the column and the floor.

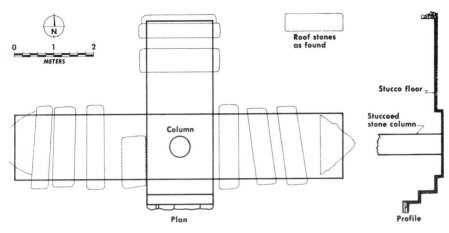

Roof stones
as found

Stucco floor

Stuccoed
stone column

Column

Plan

Profile

6. Plan of Tomb 3c, South Group, Mitla.

time Tomb 3c was destroyed. Over its ruins and those of the palace that covered it, a new pyramidal mound was built, apparently in Zapotec style.

This point has been treated at some length because I think the cultural sequence of the South Group is especially illuminating. First it was occupied by Zapotecs of period IIIa; then by the Zapotecs of period IV who deposited Burial 2; then by the Mixtecs who built Tomb 3c, and then *again by the Zapotecs,* now having a mixed culture including Mixtec elements such as those found in Tomb 7 of Mitla. Does this mean that in the last years before the Conquest Mitla was becoming less Mixtec? Or, more precisely, that the process occurring there would have produced a mixed Mixtec-Zapotec culture if it had not been interrupted?[11] Now let us turn to Yagul. Of all the ancient sites I know, Yagul is the one that most resembles Mitla.[12] (A third one, Matatlan, is still unexplored but apparently similar.) Although the Yagul explorations have been relatively extensive (Figures 7, 8, and 9), we can treat here only one building complex: the Palace of Six Patios. This group has given the best stratigraphies at Yagul, particularly in Patio F, the southeasternmost of the group. Because of its placement with respect to the slope of the hill (Figure 10), this patio has over 5.5 meters of superposed structures. Cutting down through these, I found a series of stucco floors (Figure 11). Below floor 5 I found no pottery fragments certainly identifiable as Mixtec, and therefore we shall not deal here with the lowest levels. Below floor 4, which apparently is a Zapotec construction, there were a few sherds of the Mixtec hemispherical grey bowl, although the long, thin supports ending in animal heads that are so common in the Mixteca were absent. Below floor 2 were two polychrome pottery fragments, as well as abundant examples of nearly all the Valley Mixtec types shown in Figure 12.[13]

It was not possible to determine the forms of the buildings in the lower

Text continued on p. 356

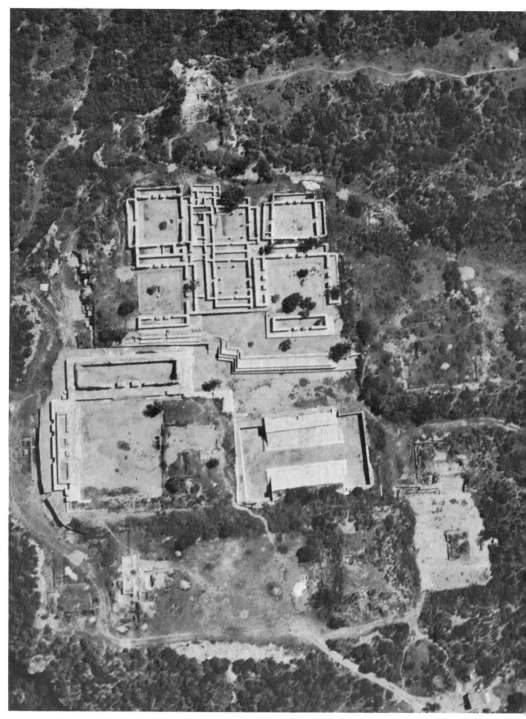

7. Air view of the central buildings of the Acropolis at Yagul, August 1963.
Since that time some minor extension of the excavations has been done,
as indicated in Figure 8. All the unexcavated areas are densely filled
with constructions, in some cases including superpositions laid down
over many centuries. Outside the central area, small houses have been found
wherever excavations have been made on the hill.

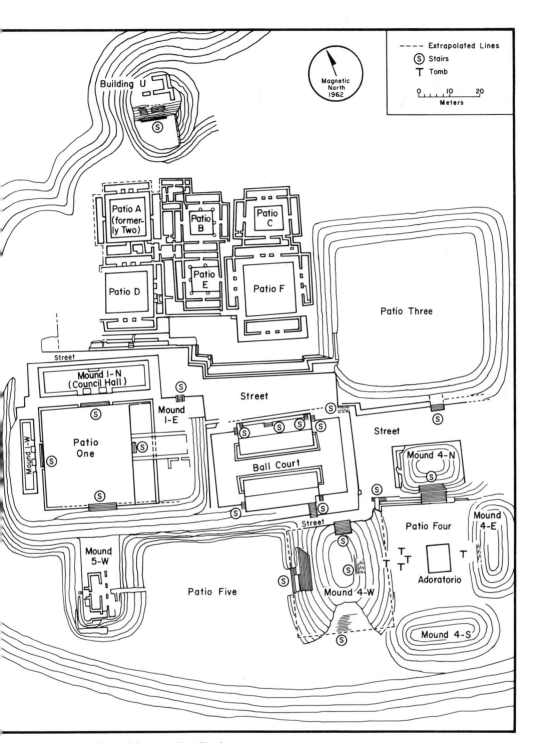

. Plan of the central buildings of the Acropolis at Yagul.
ased on a 1962 survey by Leobardo de la Luz Merino, by permission
f the INAH, the plan includes results of later excavations
s noted by John Paddock in September 1965.

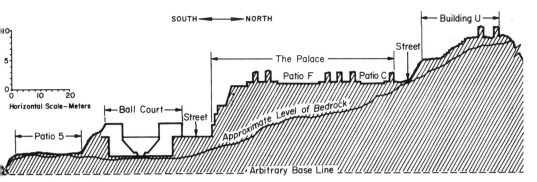

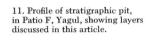

10. North-south profile of the central buildings at Yagul; vertical scale doubled.

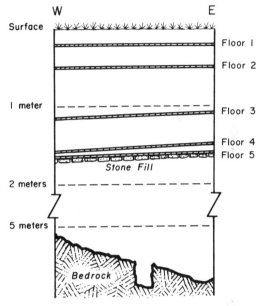

11. Profile of stratigraphic pit, in Patio F, Yagul, showing layers discussed in this article.

12. Mixtec traits in the Valley of Oaxaca. The following traits were found in addition to those shown in the chart: double or triple tombs at Yagul; façades or interiors with stone mosaic at Yagul, Mitla, and Zaachila; carved bone in the Monte Albán and Zaachila tombs; and gold in the tombs at Yagul, Mitla, and Monte Albán.

					Miniatures								Light and Dark Grey Rims		Graphite on Red-Orange	Poly-chrome	Penates	Copper
Yagul Tombs		x		x			x		x	x	x	x		x	x	x		x	x
Yagul Burials and Offerings	x	x	x	x	x	x		x	x	x	x	x		x		x	x	x	x
Mitla Tombs		x		x			x							x	x	x	?		x
Mitla Burials and Offerings	x		x	x										x			?		
Monte Albán Tombs		?	x	x	x		x		x	x	x								x
Monte Albán Burials	x	x	x	x	?	x		x	x	x	x			x			x		x
Monte Albán Offerings	x		x	x	x			x	x	x				x			x		x
Cuilapan			x	x				x	x	x				x				x	x
Zaachila Tombs	x		x		x			x		x				x		x	x		x

355

levels, although they were clearly very different from the later buildings and everything suggests that they were in customary Zapotec style; the pottery was of Monte Albán IIIb-IV. In contrast, the first three floors (starting from the surface) belong to superimposed patios, all of them without doubt in the style of the last one (floor 1), which is a part of the building we repaired and recorded in Figure 7. Thus both the pottery and the architecture show that over older Zapotec buildings had been placed three successive structures in a different style, the first two practically the same as the last. They are obviously very similar to the Mitla palaces, where polychrome pottery also appears very late.

The pits in the other patios, like the many offerings, all indicate the same thing. In every case, polychrome pottery appears only in the last buildings (or, in the case of Patio F, in the last two layers of buildings). In these final levels, long, grey pot-legs were very abundant, as were small jars with open spouts and appliqué decoration. Less common were perforated incense burners and the thin griddles (*comales*) that are characteristic of Coixtlahuaca in the Mixteca Alta (Plates 31–40). Although no gold was found, in these last two layers there were many necklaces of jade or greenstone, associated with small greenstone idols or *penates* (Plate 33), and long copper needles with eyes, like those of the Mixteca.[14]

One out of every five tombs in Yagul has a façade decorated with stone mosaic arranged in simple *xicalcoliuhqui* (step-fret) motifs, or parts of such patterns. With the exception of one (Tomb 17) that was found empty, all the tombs having this façade decoration contained offerings of the pottery we have classified as Mixtec. However, the architecture of the tombs in general seems to be only a variant of the style found in the Zapotec tombs at Monte Albán and other sites. The *xicalcoliuhqui*, of course, occurs in the Valley beginning with Monte Albán II.

One trait peculiar to Yagul is the placement of tombs with their façades joined at right angles to each other. There are at Yagul at least three units of this kind with two tombs each, and two units of three each. Such a triple grouping is also known in Coixtlahúaca, the only other place where it has been found. Since this trait is certainly not a Monte Albán or Zapotec custom, we may consider it a Mixtec form. We shall return later to the question of attributing the tombs to the Mixtecs.

All these Yagul tombs in pairs and trios contained Mixtec pottery. Tomb 30 (see pp. 336–44 above), by far the most sumptuous of them, had as a door a large stone carved in "false mosaic" that was exactly like the decoration on the walls of the great cruciform tombs of Mitla; it had more "false mosaic" on its façade, but in other motifs. It is joined with Tombs 3 and 29 to make one of the trios. Tomb 30 had also a small stone head in high relief at each side of its doorway, as did the nearby Tomb 12; Tomb 29 had one such head.[15] (Tomb 12 also contained an offering of Mixtec pottery.) The small stone heads occurred also on some Mitla tombs, and perhaps on other buildings there.

3. A small part of the rear wall, Building 1-N, Yagul, as left consolidated after excavations. The entire panel of greca mosaic was over 40 meters long.

14. Greca mosaic on rear wall of Building 1-N (the small area at left in Figure 13), as first uncovered.

15. Full length of the rear wall, Building 1-N, Yagul, as seen from west to east.
Note how the hump in the bedrock of the hill, although it interfered with the greca panel
in the center of the wall, was not cut away but incorporated unchanged into the building.

16. Detail of the façade, Hall of Columns, Mitla.

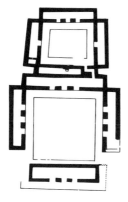
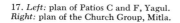
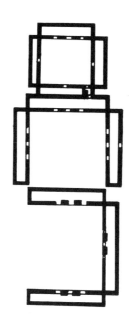

17. *Left:* plan of Patios C and F, Yagul.
Right: plan of the Church Group, Mitla.

The use at Yagul of stone mosaic in Mitla style was not limited to tomb façades. There were panels of this decoration on the front of the Council Hall (Building 1-N); those on the rear of the building, recently uncovered, were still partially in place along the south side of the street that separates this hall from the Palace of the Six Patios. They formed a single panel over 40 meters long, made with two motifs that occur also in the Group of the Columns at Mitla (Figures 13–16). The small platform in Patio 4 (Building 4-C) also has a very simple form of mosaic.[16]

Finally, the resemblances in the arrangement of rooms between Mitla and Yagul are extraordinary. Patios C and F of Yagul and the Church Group in Mitla have an identical distribution of rooms, orientation, number of doors, and connection between the two patios; they even share the trait of having one room with its doors facing away from the patio (Figure 17). In Mitla this occurred because the room in question lies between two patios and opens on only one of them; the arrangement in Yagul suggests that other rooms were to have been built, but the platform was not large enough for them.

These, then, are the data bearing on our topic for Mitla and Yagul, the two cities I consider to be the principal centers built by the Eastern Mixtecs of the Valley of Oaxaca.[17] We can now turn to the Western Mixtecs, whose chief centers are Monte Albán and Cuilapan.

THE WESTERN AREA

At Monte Albán, there is no ordinary stratigraphic evidence of period V occupation. The seven tombs (4 per cent of the total), 17 burials, and 21 offerings there that are assigned to this period are so placed because of their style and their obviously late locations. All the tombs of this period have flat roofs. In some of them, as in some Yagul examples of the period, the side walls come

slightly closer together as they ascend toward the roof.[18] The flat roof is nothing new, having occurred since Monte Albán I; and the inward-sloping walls
may not be a clearly defined trait. A small molding or banquette is also typical
of these tombs; and the niches in them are placed higher than they were in
previous periods. Nevertheless, the Monte Albán tombs that contain period
V pottery could not have been distinguished as a group on an architectural
basis; only the presence of the Mixtec offerings revealed them as forming a
group.

Mound B has some Mixtec architectural traits, such as the use of large flat-
faced stones, placed upright and alternating with groups of small stones, laid
so that their smallest face is visible.[19] We know so little of the architecture of
the Mixtec region that it is not possible now to establish a valid parallel by
comparing other traits. Many Mixtec objects were found in Mound B.

Pottery of the last period at Monte Albán is clearly Mixtec, but the near-
absence of polychrome suggests a period contemporary with that of the Yagul
tombs or Tomb 3c of Mitla.[20] Tomb 7 of Monte Albán, which had been used
twice, contained no pottery dating from its second utilization except some
spindle whorls. It seems to be later, as we shall see when we come to examine
Zaachila. None of the other six period V tombs at Monte Albán contained
polychrome, bowls with long thin legs (with one possible exception in Tomb
93), tripod jars, or spindle whorls (except, as noted, Tomb 7), or two-legged
perforated censers. That is, except for Tomb 93, these seven do not contain
the most typical Mixtec ceramic elements. In addition, their architecture has
little relation to that of the Yagul tombs.[21] Perhaps, then, these are Zapotec
tombs, made in the period when Mixtec influence was being felt; or they might
be the tombs of Mixtecs who were buried before most elements of Mixtec culture were being produced in the Valley. It is possible then that—except for
Tomb 93—they may be earlier than the tombs of Yagul, Zaachila, Tomb 7 of
Monte Albán, and the large cruciform tombs (Tombs 1 and 2) of Mitla, but
contemporary with Tombs 3c and 7 of Mitla and perhaps also with the South
Group of that city. I think they might be placed with the *first* of the three Mixtec palaces under the Palace of Six Patios at Yagul, when there still was no
polychrome pottery there. There is no building at Monte Albán in the style
of the Mitla and Yagul palaces. Thus, except for the splendid Tomb 7, Monte
Albán is not a good site at which to attempt a definition of period V.

Because of its chronological value, I may mention just one find at the large
site of Cuilapan. When Mound III was already falling into ruins, a small "symbolic" tomb (No. 8) was placed at one side of it, using the stucco platform
around it as a floor (Figure 18). This tomb had an offering of Mixtec pottery,
including polished grey ware and miniature *cajetes* or bowls; there were also
two penates.[22] The pyramid is of Monte Albán IIIb or IV.

The two tombs recently found at Zaachila (Plates 13–29, and pp. 319–29,
this volume) have façade decoration of stone mosaic in the Yagul style. Their

18. Doorway and fragment of wall (right)—seen from inside—that make up
the "symbolic" Tomb 8, Cuilapan.

rich offerings include all the pottery forms listed in Figure 12: abundant
polychrome pottery, gold objects, carved bones, and turquoise mosaics.[23] This
is the first association of polychrome and gold to be discovered in the Valley.
Since, as we have seen, polychrome is late in period V, the gold objects must
be too. This I believe enables us to date Tomb 7 of Monte Albán, for the
techniques of both bone carving and goldwork show that it is very close in
time to the Zaachila tombs. Turquoise mosaics, such as those of Tombs 1 and
2 in Zaachila and Tomb 7 in Monte Albán, are a Mixtec trait, as I have shown
earlier.[24] At least one of the Zaachila tombs was used more than once.

In the center of the Valley, Lorenzo Gamio recently explored a tomb, very
similar to the Yagul tombs, at Tlalistac de Cabrera (Figure 19). Unfortunately
we know nothing of its offerings, since it had been sacked before he found it.

SCATTERED SITES

Further data are available from the still unfinished survey of the Valley of Oaxaca that I began some time ago. Up to now over two hundred sites have been
briefly checked, and surface pottery was gathered at almost all of them. Study
of this material shows that Mixtec pottery occurs in two principal areas
(Map 1). One occupies the northwest part of the Valley; the other is in the
east, with an extension along the north that almost connects with the western

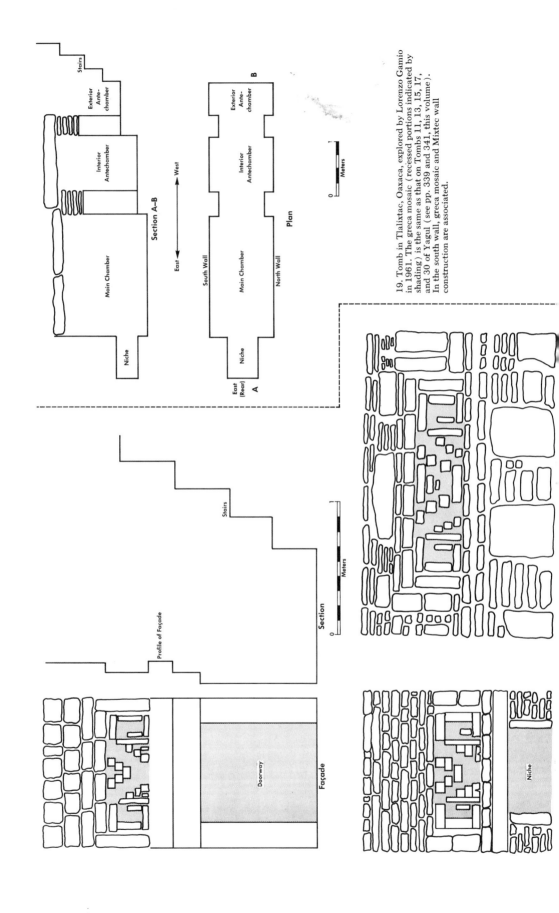

Section A–B

Stairs

Exterior Ante-
chamber

Interior Antechamber

Main Chamber

Niche

West ← → East

Plan

B

Exterior Ante-
chamber

Interior Antechamber

South Wall

Main Chamber

North Wall

Niche

East
(Rear)

A

0   Meters

Stairs

Profile of Façade

Section

0   Meters

Doorway

Façade

Niche

19. Tomb in Tlalixtac, Oaxaca, explored by Lorenzo Gamio in 1961. The greca mosaic (recessed portions indicated by shading) is the same as that on Tombs 11, 13, 15, 17, and 30 of Yagul (see pp. 339 and 341, this volume). In the south wall, greca mosaic and Mixtec wall construction are associated.

group. These two areas seem to correspond more or less with those of the Eastern and Western Mixtecs as distinguished above. The scattered occurrences in other places do not, in my opinion, indicate that the Mixtec culture had taken over the entire Valley, but merely that the Zapotecs had accepted some traits of Mixtec origin, and that these traits were being incorporated into their culture. Obviously the absence of this pottery at other sites means relatively little, since the samples are small; but it is at least suggestive. Older Zapotec remains occur at all the places where Mixtec pottery is found.

We have not mentioned the south end of the Valley. Though I have not yet surveyed it, I am convinced that in the extreme south there is a concentration of Mixtec traits; this may be related to the presence of a Mixtec kingdom with its capital at Tututepec on the Pacific coast.

The following points, then, are presented more as hypotheses than as conclusions.

Two different Mixtec-influenced groups exist in the Valley. Those I have called the Western Mixtecs are concentrated principally in Monte Albán, Cuilapan, and finally Zaachila. Their characteristics are practically the same as those we find in the Mixteca Alta. For this group we have historical as well as archeological information. The Eastern Mixtecs, whose chief sites are Mitla and Yagul, share some of these traits, but present us also with others, which up to now have not been found in the Mixtec region itself.

Neither of the two groups shows all the traits that characterize the Mixtecs in their own Mixteca Alta. Two conspicuous missing elements are the red-on-cream *cajete*, a bowl of cream clay with red-brown paint, and stamped designs in the bottom of the grey tripod *cajete*. Further, whereas the religious buildings of the Western Mixtecs in the Valley are in the Mesoamerican tradition, outweighing the importance of the civil buildings, the contrary is true among the Eastern Mixtecs, whose temples are much less grand than their palaces.

At no site in the Mixtec region proper (in the period we are concerned with) have we found true tombs. As Alfonso Caso has pointed out, tombs are the most prominent feature of Zapotec architecture. Yet among both the Eastern and the Western Mixtecs of the Valley there are many tombs having offerings of period V. These tombs, I think, may be:

1. Zapotec constructions, either (a) re-used by the Mixtecs, or (b) containing burials of partially acculturated Zapotecs (therefore the frequent mixing in them of Monte Albán IV and V objects); or

2. Mixtec constructions, showing that the Mixtecs were being acculturated by the people they had conquered.

Almost all the architecture of the tombs is Zapotec; the Mixtecs have added only a few details, such as the façades decorated with panels of greca mosaics. Tombs of this type are found among both the Western Mixtecs (Zaachila and

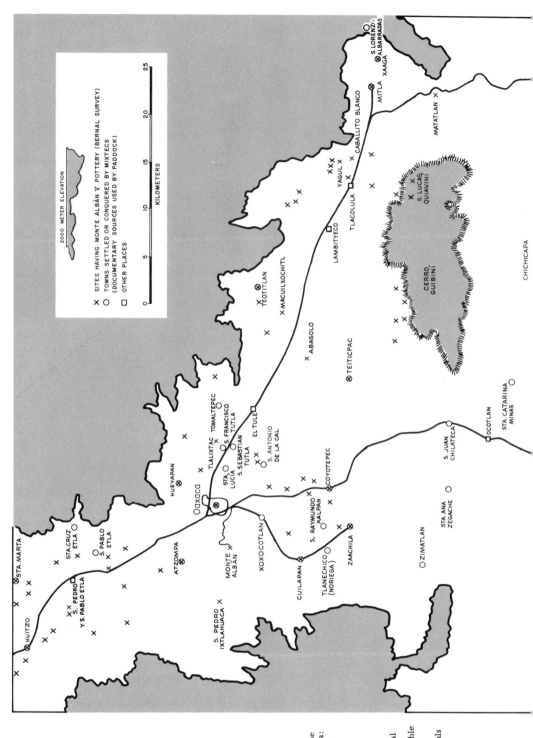

Map 1. Mixtec invasion of the Valleys of Etla and Tlacolula: comparison of archeological and documentary evidence. Neither Bernal's survey results nor Paddock's study of documentary sources can be considered complete. In so densely settled an area, not all the archeological sites can be located, and it has not yet been possible to utilize unpublished data from the several archives containing abundant materials on this area.

Tlalistac) and the Eastern Mixtecs (Yagul and Mitla). The only example I know of outside the Valley is in the Chinantla, although there the greca decoration is painted rather than being carved in stone or made of mosaic.[25]

We may propose two phases of Mixtec influence or dominance. The earlier one brought only some pottery types, the most notable of which is the hemispherical fine grey bowl with lighter or darker rim. Others are grey jars with an open pouring spout in the rim and appliqué decoration; and grey vessels of compound silhouette. Other events of this phase are the introduction of stone mosaic decoration, the Cuilapan tomb, the first new-style buildings of Yagul and Mitla, and almost all the period V tombs of Monte Albán.

The second phase, which seems to represent a much larger Mixtec population, brings all the remaining pottery types, most notably the polychrome; gold objects, carved bones, turquoise mosaics, and long pot-legs often ending in animal heads; and the last and largest buildings at Mitla and Yagul, as well as Tombs 1 and 2 at Zaachila and the contents (not the construction) of Tomb 7 at Monte Albán. The elements of the first phase continued in the second.

If this proposal of two phases is correct, it obliges us to push our dates back. I formerly had thought that Mixtec influence in the Valley began only about A.D. 1350, and that it could be distinguished archeologically only after about 1400. I think now that this is correct as regards the second phase, which, as marked by the presence (not abundance) of polychrome pottery and other traits, perhaps began as late as 1450. Nevertheless, the first Mixtec phase in the Valley—which we might then call Monte Albán Va—may have to be extended back to the middle of the thirteenth century.[26]

From a broader point of view, I believe that the end of Toltec control (in about 1160) was the event which allowed the Mixtecs to expand. This expansion took the Mixtecs into several areas, one of which was the Valley of Oaxaca.

NOTES

1. For Alfonso Caso's articles on Tomb 7, see general Bibliography to this volume.

2. Caso, *Las exploraciones en Monte Albán, Temporada 1934–1935*, Instituto Panamericano de Geografía e Historia, Publicación No. 18 (México, 1935).

3. Caso and Daniel F. Rubín de la Borbolla, *Exploraciones en Mitla, 1934–1935*, Instituto Panamericano de Geografía e Historia, Publicación No. 21 (México, 1936).

4. Ignacio Bernal, "Otra tumba cruciforme de Mitla," *Estudios de Cultura Nahuatl*, IV (1964), 223–32; Marshall H. Saville, "The Cruciform Structures of Mitla and Vicinity," *Putnam Anniversary Volume* (New York, 1909); John Paddock, "Current Research," *American Antiquity*, XXIX (July 1964), 406 (note on Mitla Adobe Group). William G. Bittler has found, in excavations at the Mitla Fortress in 1964 and 1965, that Monte Albán V pottery occurs under the floors of the buildings there also (verbal information, August 28, 1965).

5. Ignacio Bernal, *Exploraciones en Cuilapam de Guerrero, 1902–1954* (México, 1958).

6. Roberto Gallegos, "Exploraciones en Zaachila, Oaxaca, *Boletín* INAH No. 8 (June

1962), pp. 6–8; and his "Zaachila: The First Season's Work," *Archaeology*, XVI (1963), 226–33. See also the articles by Wicke, Caso, and Paddock in this volume.

7. William H. Holmes, *Archeological Studies among the Ancient Cities of Mexico*, Field Columbian Museum, Anthropological Series, Vol. I, Part II (Chicago, 1897), pp. 227–88. Sigvald Linné, *Zapotecan Antiquities* (Stockholm, 1938), pp. 41–54. James P. Oliver, "Architectural Similarities of Mitla and Yagul," *Mesoamerican Notes* No. 4 (1955), pp. 49–67.

8. Caso and Borbolla, *Exploraciones*, pp. 13–15.

9. *Ibid.*, pp. 15–16.

10. *Ibid.*, pp. 11–12.

11. Jorge Fernando Iturribarría, "Yagul: Mestizo Product of Mixtecs and Zapotecs," *Boletín de Estudios Oaxaqueños* No. 17 (Mitla, Oaxaca, 1960); Paddock, "Some Observations," *Mesoamerican Notes* No. 4 (1955), pp. 80–83; and his "Clarifications and Suggestions," *Boletín de Estudios Oaxaqueños* No. 8 (México, 1958), p. 11.

12. Oliver, "Architectural Similarities."

13. See also the table of ceramic materials and forms from Coixtlahuaca in Bernal, "Exploraciones en Coixtlahuaca, Oaxaca," *Revista Mexicana de Estudios Antropológicos*, Vol. X (1949), following p. 40.

14. Anonymous, *Mesoamerican Notes*, No. 4 (1955), p. 68; and Bernal, "El Palacio de Yagul y sus implicaciones socio-políticas," *Actes* du VI⁰ Congrès International des Sciences Anthropologiques et Ethnologiques (Paris, 1960), Tome II, Vol. I, pp. 345–49.

15. Paddock, "The First Three Seasons at Yagul," *Mesoamerican Notes* No. 4 (1955), Figure 26, p. 44. Saville records a similar one from Mitla (Saville, "The Cruciform Structures," p. 174 and Figure 8).

16. Paddock, "The 1956 Season at Yagul," *Mesoamerican Notes* No. 5 (1957), pp. 23–24.

17. Both Mitla and Yagul seem to have been occupied more or less continuously beginning with Monte Albán I, and possibly long before that; obviously the Mixtec construction mentioned here refers only to Period V. —Editor.

18. Tomb 1 at Lambityeco (late Monte Albán IIIb or early IV) has this trait.—Editor.

19. The trait occurs at sites in the Mixteca, and at Mitla and Yagul.—Editor.

20. It would also be possible to explain the available data by proposing that polychrome was too costly for the people of the Yagul tombs other than Tomb 30. —Editor.

21. All the period V tombs at Monte Albán are poorer in construction than any but the poorest at Yagul. Another point of contrast is that several peaked roofs occur in period V at Yagul.—Editor.

22. Bernal, "Exploraciones en Cuilapam," p. 74.

23. See n. 6 above.

24. Bernal, "Archeology of the Mixteca," *Boletín de Estudios Oaxaqueños* No. 7 (México, 1958), p. 8; and his "Exploraciones en Coixtlahuaca," pp. 65–66.

25. Agustín Delgado, "Investigaciones antropológicas," *Boletín* INAH No. 2 (October 1960), pp. 7–9; and his "Polychrome Zapotec Tomb Paintings," *Current Anthropology*, II (1961), 269. The note in the *Boletín* is illustrated. Since the find was made in the Chinantec region, the use of the term Zapotec is puzzling.

26. See Paddock's discussion of the date of the Mixtec invasion, this volume, p. 377.

Mixtec Ethnohistory and Monte Albán V

JOHN PADDOCK

With understandable skepticism, archeologists in the past have been disinclined to base their conclusions upon data found among the abundant contradictions, the serious errors, and the outright fantasies so common in some colonial documents. The prehispanic traditions, with the important exception of the historical codices, very often lack a sense of chronology and tend to mix history with myth.[1] Monte Albán, for example, is obviously very much more important than Teotitlan del Valle or Zaachila, but the oral traditions written down by the early colonial chroniclers mention only the two towns, quite overlooking the metropolis.[2] Our documentary sources, then, are indispensable both for giving us leads worth investigating and for enabling us to interpret archeological data more fully; but none of them standing alone can be accepted as establishing adequately the facts it sets forth.

Mesoamerican archeology has provided us by now with a good number of fixed points, and in the documentary sources there are useful data which, combined with this established archeological framework, have a respectable validity. In the case of period V of Monte Albán and the surrounding valleys, the archeological data seem to combine especially well with the information given in the historical sources.

At some risk of falling into pedantry, I should like to explain rather carefully the three terms used in the title of this essay. The word "ethnohistory" is used here in a very broad sense—so broad, in fact, that I should have preferred to find a substitute. However, there seems to be no customary term for a case like this, a study in what might be described as documentary archeology. I have not limited myself, like a strict ethnohistorian, to documents written by the peoples themselves—the Zapotecs and Mixtecs—whose late prehispanic contacts are the events to be considered.

With the name of "Mixtec" I have designated here, as elsewhere, not only the people who spoke (and, of course, still speak) the Mixtec language proper, but also some of their neighbors.[3] Like Covarrubias, I have included under this term certain peoples who spoke (and speak) rather closely related languages and who lived in very similar ways: the Chocho-Popolocas, Mazatecs, Ichcatecs, Chinantecs, Cuicatecs, Triques, and Amusgos.[4] The Zapotecs and Chatinos, although neighboring and also related, are excluded; this is a classification based on historical roles rather than on linguistic or other relationships. Since we are unable for the present to distinguish the respective roles of the peoples forming the Mixtec group, we must gather them into this uncomfortably vague category. But we should remember that in earlier times, according to the linguists, they were more closely related than they are today, and that for very ancient times such a grouping is inescapable.[5] Thus, although not everyone will agree with my treatment of the problem, the grouping is not entirely an arbitrary one. Actually, I think I am employing the term Mixtec in a perfectly usual way. The English people—designated with adequate precision simply as the English—have an English culture, of which one aspect is the English language; and the language is referred to simply as English without causing confusion. The same may be said for the Eskimos, the Polynesians, and other peoples. Within Mesoamerica, the Mayas have long been called by their own name without our confusing the language with the people or the way of life.

As for "Monte Albán V," I wish to make clear the geographical extension that will be given to the phrase here. It refers to a cultural phenomenon that Caso and Acosta distinguished early in their explorations of Monte Albán, and which they designated with the last of a series of numbers because it appears to be the last of a series of cultural stages as reflected in material remains, primarily ceramic. But Monte Albán forms a part—often a dominant one—of a phenomenon that is extended in space. Thus the Valley of Oaxaca constitutes the scene for a series of cultural events; and although we could invent a sequence of different names for the periods as they occur in each little village of the Valley, the fact is that the periods defined for Monte Albán itself tend to occur throughout the Valley, or most of it. It would be an excess of pedantry to insist on changing the long-used names for these periods to Valley of Oaxaca I, II, III, IV, and V. We shall say, then, that Monte Albán V is the period that begins with the arrival at any community in the Valley of Oaxaca of the culture brought by the Mixtecs to Monte Albán in the final centuries of preconquest times.

One last preliminary point deserves attention. The Mixtec invasion of the Valley of Oaxaca cannot be considered a recent discovery; it was mentioned in several colonial sources, in the nineteenth-century histories, and in the works of Caso and others beginning some thirty years ago. (Caso's paper in this volume seems to show that there is even a prehispanic mention of it.)

The invasion is not, then, a conclusion or hypothesis arrived at in the 1950's after the Yagul excavations began. Caso and Barlow had treated it as an established fact years before, and their works seem to have been most unjustly ignored. Since they are obviously fundamental in this field, we have recently published English versions of them.[6]

The Mixtec invasions in the Valley of Oaxaca, then, are treated here as one of the fixed points making up the tested framework from which we are gradually extending our understanding by means of hypotheses, research, and conclusions. Lest this attitude strike the reader as arbitrary, let me review briefly some of the documentary evidence that years ago led such excellent investigators as Caso and Barlow to conceive of the Mixtec conquests first as a hypothesis and then as a conclusion. It will be possible to add some new material, but the principal aim here is to bring together and interpret from the viewpoint of today's archeological knowledge the sources already known.

Those who are familiar with the present disastrous economic, geographic, and demographic conditions of the Mixteca Norte and the relative richness of the group of three valleys that we call the Valley of Oaxaca may easily doubt the ability of the Mixtecs to take from the Zapotecs the valleys of Etla and Tlacolula (and, although we still know little about it, perhaps also parts of the valley of Zimatlan).[7] But the present catastrophic erosion of the Mixteca Norte, although it began many centuries ago, has advanced incredibly in recent times: even fifty years ago the region was clearly less poor,[8] and in early colonial times large parts of it were often said to be rich.

At the time of the Conquest two Spaniards, reporting on their scouting trip to one of Moctezuma's gold mines near Sosola (a town in the Mixteca not far from Etla), told Hernán Cortés that they had seen "very beautiful land with many towns and cities, and a great number of other settlements, with buildings so numerous and fine that . . . even in Spain they could not be better . . . a lodging house and fortress which is larger and stronger than the Castle of Burgos; and the people of these provinces, called Tamazulapa, were better dressed than any others we have seen."[9]

Bishop Alburquerque, writing in about 1570, believed that "three or four towns [of Spaniards] could be founded in this bishopric [of Oaxaca]. . . . In the province of the Misteca . . . another good town could be started, near the towns called Tecomatlavaca [Tecomastlahuaca] and Ciguistlaguaca [Juxtlahuaca]. It is land with a good climate, and rich in maize; it produces wheat very well, and all the fruits of Spain and of this land. There is plenty of water, good lumber, firewood, stone, and lime. Next to it is the province of the South Sea, which is good land, and the Mixteca Baja, which also is good, and the Alta, which is better."[10]

Somewhat before 1630, Vázquez de Espinosa said that the Bishopric of Oaxaca "has the provinces called the Mixteca Alta . . . and Mixteca Baja. . . ."

[The people] "grow and work . . . much fine silk; they produce abundant maize and other grains and fruits of this land [and?] of Spain; there are plantations of peanuts, and some mills producing quantities of syrup and sugar; they have marvelous melons; they breed all sorts of livestock, including hogs and very good mules."[11]

Fray Bernabé Cobo, at the end of his trip from Peru in 1630, wrote from Mexico to a friend in Lima that he had seen in "the Mixteca Alta and Baja some of the best lands in New Spain . . . extremely fertile."[12]

In 1648 another firsthand chronicler, Thomas Gage, published an account of his New World travels in which he said he had seen "the mountains called La Misteca, which abound with many rich and great towns, and do trade with the best silk that is in all that country. Here is also great store of wax and honey; and Indians live there who traffic to Mexico and about the country with twenty or thirty mules of their own, chopping and changing, buying and selling commodities . . . [they have] rich churches, well built, and better furnished within with lamps, candlesticks, crowns of silver for the several statues of saints; and all the way we did observe a very fruitful soil for both Indian and Spanish wheat [maize and wheat], much sugar, much cotton-wool, honey, and here and there some cochineal, and of plantains and other sweet and luscious fruit great store; but above all great abundance of cattle, where hides are one of the greatest commodities that from these parts are sent to Spain. . . . From here we came to the city of Oaxaca. . . . And so joyfully we went on, and the first place [where we stopped was] at a great town called Antequera. . . . The next to Antequera in that road is Nixapa."[13]

Finally, Fray Francisco de Burgoa, who spent almost his entire life in Oaxaca, spoke both Mixtec and Zapotec, and knew thoroughly both the Mixteca and the Valley of Oaxaca during the seventeenth century, wrote many times that the Mixteca in general was a fertile province.[14]

On the population of the region, Bishop Alburquerque is again worth quoting. He said that his bishopric had "many provinces of different languages . . . the province of the Misteca . . . is the largest. . . . The largest settlement of this Mixtec province is Cuilapa: . . . it must have about six thousand Indian family heads who pay tribute."[15] Since each tributary was a family head (they also were referred to as *casados* or married men), in a stable population a tributary would have to represent somewhat more than four persons: himself, his wife, and more than two children (more than two in order to ensure replacement of the two parents in the next generation). In the middle of the present century, with the population growing, the average number of persons per family in Oaxaca was 4.55.[16] However, since during the early colonial period there was a frightful decline—literally a decimation—of the Indian population by European diseases, one tributary in 1570 might have represented fewer than four persons in the total population. Cuilapan, for example, with 6,000 tributaries, would have had a population of from 20,000 to 25,000 persons.[17]

Alburquerque gives a list of towns with the number of *tributarios* or family heads in each; the largest Zapotec town in the Valley of Oaxaca at the time was Etla, with 2,200; Teozapotlan (present-day Zaachila) had 1,300. And as we shall see, some part of the population of each of them was not Zapotec, but Mixtec. According to this and another list, both dating from about 1570, the Zapotecs in all the towns of the Valley of Oaxaca totaled 18,000 *tributarios* at a time when there were 6,000 tributarios in Mixtec Cuilapan.[18] Later, when there were 12,100 Zapotec tributarios in the Valley, there were 5,000 Mixtec *tributarios* in Cuilapan. In these two lists, Etla, Zaachila, and Huitzo are counted as Zapotec towns even though they and some others had *barrios* (wards) or subject villages of Mixtecs. Burgoa says, "writing this as I find myself priest of this town of Theozapotlan [Zaachila], I have in it a Mixtec barrio."[19] He added that "the Mixtecs still hold the lands and towns they conquered as the principal evidence of their deeds. Even within the [Zapotec] capital at Theozapotlan in which I am writing, they had a stronghold, and they still occupy it as a barrio of this town, not to mention other places that they founded around it."[20]

Burgoa also had firsthand knowledge of the situation in Huitzo (formerly Cuauhxilotitlan, and often mistakenly called Guaxolotitlan, Huaxolotitlan, or Quauhxolotitlan), where he had served as parish priest. He informs us that "the town of Guaxolotitlan . . . has Mixtecs and Zapotecs in its jurisdiction."[21] Other chroniclers—none having the long personal experience Burgoa had in Huitzo—give no indication of this double ethnic origin, some calling it a Zapotec-speaking town and some a Mixtec one. For instance, in 1586 that tireless traveler Fray Alonso Ponce spent a night in Huitzo on his way from Tehuacan to Guatemala, and again on his return; his companions recorded that "he came before sunset to a good town called Quauhxolotitlan, of Zapoteca or Chapoteca [the Nahuatl is correctly Tsapotécatl] Indians. . . . From that town to Tehuantepec this language is spoken . . . he left the monastery and town very early in the morning . . . he arrived at the city of Oaxaca at sunrise . . . after having dinner . . . he left that city . . . he arrived after nightfall at Tlacuchahuaya . . . he left . . . very early . . . he arrived after daylight at . . . San Lucas [Quiaviní] . . . he passed it by . . . he arrived at another attractive town called San Dionisio [Ocotepec] . . . he said Mass for them . . . they gave the Padre Comisario a dinner . . . he left very early in the morning . . . he arrived at sunrise at a little town called Totolapa." And, on the return, "at two in the afternoon the Padre Comisario left Totolapa . . . he arrived before nightfall at San Dionisio . . . he left . . . a little early . . . he arrived before dinnertime at Tlacuchahuaya . . . he left at one in the afternoon . . . he arrived early at the city of Oaxaca . . . he stayed there until the next day . . . he left Oaxaca . . . at two in the afternoon . . . he arrived at Quauhxolotitlan . . . he left that town at three in the morning."[22]

The chronicler Eutimio Pérez, by contrast, says flatly that according to ecclesiastical archives, Huitzo in 1802 was a Mixtec-speaking town.[23] Burgoa tells us that Fray Diego de Acevedo, a *lengua zapoteca* or speaker of Zapotec, was priest at Huitzo for six years—surely an indication that Zapotec, too, was spoken there.[24] Both Pérez and Ponce treated Huitzo as a unit; in fact, it was a group of half a dozen scattered barrios (some of which today are independent towns). In one or more of them Zapotec was spoken, and in others Mixtec.[25]

For Etla, too, there are contradictory data. Although most of its subject towns and barrios have probably been Zapotec at least since the congregation of the Mixtecs in Cuilapan shortly after the Spanish conquest, Helen Miller Bailey was informed by an old man of Santa Cruz Etla in 1944 that in his village nobody spoke Zapotec because the people there were of Mixtec descent.[26] (Of course in at least some of the many other Etlas the people do speak Zapotec now.) Eutimio Pérez says Etla is Zapotec; but we have seen that his data seem to refer only to the majority, or perhaps to the *cabecera*, or seat, of each parish. Burgoa assures us that at least some of the group of villages called Etla were Zapotec, because Zapotec-speaking friars were sent there, as they were to Huitzo.[27]

In 1930–31 Elsie Clews Parsons worked in many Valley towns, although principally in Mitla, and those who have occasion to corroborate her work frequently testify that her accuracy is extraordinary. She does not always tell us how she obtained her information, but she cites the following as Mixtec settlements in the Valley: the hacienda of Xaaga in the municipality of Mitla; San Lorenzo Albarradas, behind the mountain Guirún on the road to the Sierra Mixe; a band of towns crossing the valley of Zimatlan, consisting of Atzompa, Cuilapan, Zimatlan, and Coyotepec; and, at the south end of the valley, Miahuatlan. Further, in speaking of Mitla itself, she refers to "the 'Castellanos,' probably hispanicized Mixtecas, who came to live around the monastery" [which later became the hacienda of Xaaga].[28]

Although Schmieder worked in several archives including that of Mitla, he does not specify the source of his data when he asserts that, "The village of San Lorenzo Alvarradas in the mountains close to the eastern end of the valley of Tlacolula, on territory originally belonging to Mitla, is [like Analco] another exceptional case of a settlement founded by the Spanish. In these mountains there are some small and isolated stands of tree palms. The weaving of the palm leaves into baskets and *petates* (mats) was unknown among the Tzapotec of the valley and surrounding mountains. They bought such products either from the Tehuantepec Tzapotec or from the Mixtec. The Dominicans, in order to take full advantage of the palm stands, imported skilled Mixtec workers and their families. This settlement prospered and its inhabitants carry on their ancient craft. Lost within an alien neighborhood, they have given up their own language and speak Spanish."[29]

It is Villaseñor, writing as Cosmographer of the Realm in 1748, who is most helpful of all. He knew the Valley of Oaxaca at first hand, for as he says of one of the Oaxaca churches, "I admired it many times."[30] In his day, eighteen settlements, grouped into ten pueblos, formed a *partido* that was subject to Cuilapan. In this partido, he said, "the Mexican [Nahuatl] tongue is very little spoken because Mysteco is the language of all the pueblos that make it up."[31] The settlements he cites as making up the *partido* of Cuilapan are, besides the seat: Xoxocotlan, San Lucas Tlanechico, San Raymundo Xalpa, San Agustín de la Cal, San Andrés Huayapa, Santa Lucía, San Sebastián Tutla, Santo Domingo Tomaltepec, Santa Ana Zegache, San Juan Chilateca, San Pedro Guegorese, Santa Catarina Minas, Santa Marta, San Martín Yachila [Lachiláa?], San Martín de las Peras, San Pablo de las Peras, Santa María Atzompa, and San Pablo Etla.[32]

Villaseñor here mentions the "Mexican tongue" because in the *partido* of the Marquisate of the Valley, today almost completely incorporated in the city of Oaxaca, there were a number of Nahua families, and he had been discussing the Marquisate partido in the section that immediately precedes his account of Cuilapan. The settlements he lists as belonging to Cuilapan are almost the same as the list of towns subject to it in the *Relación* of 1580, and considerably longer than that in the *Relación* of 1777–78.[33] We note that Santa Ana Zegache, where Burgoa says there was a rather considerable Zapotec element, is included here by Villaseñor without comment; but Burgoa surely knew the place better. Villaseñor's list agrees with Parsons's claim that Atzompa was Mixtec, and explains Bailey's statement that Santa Cruz Etla was also. Santa Cruz is a village that split off from San Pablo Etla only recently—apparently in the Díaz period, around the beginning of this century.[34]

Many of the villages once subject to Cuilapan, and probably so administered precisely because they all were Mixtec-speaking, have by now been placed within political units defined on a territorial basis. Thus, the old linguistic grouping of villages scattered all over the Valley was later divided among many *municipios* (townships), almost all of them having a majority of Zapotec villages.

Besides all these indications of a Mixtec population in the Valley, we have the demographic data from Cuilapan. Bishop Alburquerque, who assures us that Cuilapan had a population of some 20,000 persons in 1570, is not our only source here. Burgoa says of Cuilapan that "this well-prepared community came to have 14,000 and more married men, with their wives according to their custom, and families."[35] If this figure refers to the early years of the sixteenth century, before the great epidemics, it might easily represent a population of more than 70,000 persons; if it refers to later times, when the average family was smaller, it still would mean 40,000 to 50,000 persons.

How did Cuilapan come to be at least four times as populous as its neighbor Zaachila, the former capital of the Zapotec kingdoms? The answer obviously is the resettlement mentioned in the *Relación* of Chichicapa: "The Marqués

1. The Lápida de Cuilapan, built into a wall of the unfinished monastery at Cuilapan. The year 10 Reed is indicated at upper left of the left panel, and the equivalent of A.D. 1555 is clumsily added—perhaps by the same masterful hand that carved the Mixtec dates. The year 10 Flint, upper left in the right panel, is 1568. The bundle at the bottom of each panel may be the sign for month. An obsidian-edged club goes with it in the left panel, and a flag

[Cortés] congregated the Mixtecs in the town of Cuilapan, which now is theirs."[36] If to all this population we add the Mixtecs who for whatever reason remained in Huitzo, Zaachila, and other towns not subject to Cuilapan, we see that the Mixtecs of the Valley, even if they were a minority, numbered many thousands. The Mixtec invasion of the Valley clearly was not a family affair; nor was their conquest of the Valley the incredible exploit of a handful of men.

We still have not described the conquests that brought so many Mixtecs into the Valley, and there are documentary sources on that subject also. It appears that at the time of the Spanish conquest the Mixtecs were attacking the town of Chichicapa.[37] This suggests that they had by then already driven across the entire center of the Valley—the richest, amplest, and most strategic part, the area where the valleys of Etla, Zimatlan, and Tlacolula come together. If they were installed in Huitzo, Etla, Atzompa, and Cuilapan, they probably controlled all of the valley of Etla. And if, as the archeological evidence strongly suggests, they were living in Yagul, Mitla, and Matatlan, it is very probable that they were also lords of the valley of Tlacolula.[38]

According to the Mixtecs of Cuilapan in 1580, their forebears "had subjugated almost all the Çapotecs of the valleys of Guaxaca, who paid them tribute; and it is clear that if Mitla and Titicpan [Teiticpac] and other important places paid it, the less important ones must have paid it too."[39] The *Relación* of Macuilxóchitl takes us a little further, saying that the people of Macuilxóchitl "were at war with Miquitla [Mitla] and with other towns as the lord of Teoçapotlan [Zaachila] ordered them."[40] That is, the ruler of Mitla was an enemy of the Zapotec king of Zaachila, and Mitla was therefore probably a Mixtec town (unless Zaachila was already in Mixtec hands). The *Relación* of neighboring Teotitlan del Valle is even more revealing. It says that the people of Teotitlan "had as their lord the *cacique* of a town of this bishopric called Teoçapotlan . . . and afterwards another lord, of the town of Teguantepec . . . and later they served and paid tribute to the town of Cuilapa, which is Misteco."[41] Here we learn much: that Teotitlan was subject first to the Zapotec king of Zaachila; that later it paid tribute to someone in Tehuantepec, almost certainly the Zapotec ruler who had fled there; and finally that the Mixtecs took power over Teotitlan. This, essentially, is the interpretation published by Caso thirty years ago.[42]

Not all the Zapotecs of Teotitlan would necessarily have abandoned the town, although the local *cacique* may have done so; but at least the Mixtecs, by then well fortified in Yagul, could demand tribute of the people of Teotitlan. With regard to the flight to Tehuantepec, the *Relación* of Cuilapan says that "finally these [Mixtecs] had a war with the people of Teoçapotlan, who, recognizing that they were at a disadvantage, fled to the land of Teguantepec."[43]

Something further may be inferred from the *Relación* of Huitzo, in which we are told that the local people "were at war with . . . Coatlam, Myaguatlam, Chichicapa, and Nijapa; those of this town fought beside those of Guaxaca, Cuylapa, and Etla."[44] Huitzo, then, was allied with Cuilapan, which we know was Mixtec; and the allies fought against Chichicapa, which we know was Zapotec and was being attacked by the Mixtecs. With slightly less certainty, we might conclude that Oaxaca and Etla (probably one of the several Etlas) also were Mixtec towns because they too were allied with Cuilapan. The mention of Etla in the Huitzo *Relación* coincides with Bailey's evidence gathered in 1944. It appears also that Coatlan and Miahuatlan, far to the south in the valley of Zimatlan, had been attacked, if not conquered, by the Mixtecs. Bernal says that a ceramic sample taken from a pit in the atrium of the Cathedral of Oaxaca appears to confirm the occupation of that place by the Mixtecs; and although his surface survey of the Valley of Oaxaca has not reached the southern end, he has noticed concentrations of distinctive Mixtec pottery types in that region.[45]

Burgoa, too, provides something about the area around the city of Oaxaca: when the Spanish came to the Valley, he says, they found "all the flat lands that are occupied by the city of Oaxaca, and the surrounding area, occupied by Mixtec hamlets."[46] The historian Padre Gay tells us that at the time he was writing (about 1870) the Mixtec language still was spoken in that area.[47] This is as we should expect if we accept Burgoa's statement that "the Mixtecs spread out and founded the town of Xoxocotlan . . . [and] went on to found Huayapa, San Francisco, San Sebastián, and Santa Lucía."[48] These towns are respectively south, north, northeast, and east of the city of Oaxaca, and all are within about an hour's walk from it.

As stated at the outset, we are using the single term Mixtec to signify not only the Mixtecs themselves but several neighboring and closely related peoples as well. Among these peoples, only the Mixtecs proper and the Cuicatecs occupy regions bordering on the Valley of Oaxaca. It is interesting that the Cuicatecs are also the closest linguistic relatives of the Mixtecs proper.

According to Paul Kirchhoff, in prehispanic times the Cuicatecs regarded themselves as closely linked to the Mixtecs.[49] This closeness of kinship was noted also in the sixteenth century, when the *Relación* of Papaloticpac said that "the language spoken in this and nearby towns is called Cuycateca . . . and it appears to be somewhat corrupted with Misteca."[50] Modern linguists agree, although their terminology is different. Both those who work in lexicostatistics and those using only other criteria find this close relationship. Morris Swadesh (working with lexicostatistics) gives 25 centuries as the minimum time needed to achieve the differentiation that today separates Cuicatec from the *remotest* dialect of Mixtec.[51]

Suggestions are advanced from time to time to the effect that the Cuicatecs, or other such peoples, may have taken part in the "Mixtec" invasion of the

Valley of Oaxaca.[52] The *Relación* of the Cuicatec town of Tepeucila says that the town had several subject hamlets, among them one whose name in Nahuatl was Tlacolula—the same as that of the modern town near Mitla. We know that in Mitla Zapotec the Tlacolula of the Valley is called Bahk, a name without meaning for the Zapotecs of today.[53] No attempt has been made to find a Mixtec equivalent. In our Tlacolula, the Valley town, the people have given the name of Pueblo Viejo or Old Town to some ruins that stand on a nearby hill. This hill, they say, is the prehispanic site of their town. They also call it Yagul.[54]

The *Relación* of Tepeucila, speaking of its dependent hamlet, says that "it is called Tlacolula, and in their tongue, which is Cuycateca, it is named Yagu."[55]

A complaint was uttered at the beginning of this essay about the casual attitude toward the time dimension that so weakens the documentary sources. Fundamental as dates are in history, there are few of them in our written materials. The *Relación* of the Zapotec capital, Zaachila, says that the Mixtecs "came more than three hundred years ago," that is before 1280; and it goes on to add that at this time only a few of them arrived, in connection with a marriage. Many more came shortly before the Spanish conquest, it says, the occasion being another marriage. Of course much is left out in this version— an official Zapotec history of Zaachila. A Mixtec lord from Yanhuitlan was a party to the second marriage, his bride being the sister of the Zaachila ruler's wife; and the Zapotec ruler "gave" him the town of Cuilapan to live in.[56]

From the prehispanic codices (in which dates are frequently supplied), we are familiar with the circumstances of such marriages. Often the wife was the widow of some ruler who had just lost a battle; and the new husband in these cases might well have just sacrificed the man he replaced. The Mixtec conqueror 8 Deer "Tiger Claw" (1011–63) married several times in this way to consolidate his conquests; once he even took as a wife the mother of a captain he had just beaten and slain. Of course the survivors among his victims "gave" him towns to rule.[57]

In contradiction to the *Relación* of Zaachila, the *Relación* of Cuilapan (of the same date) says firmly that the Mixtecs arrived in large numbers with the first royal marriage: "On account of certain marriages that took place at different times more than three hundred years ago, these Indians arrived in large numbers."[58] This, of course, is another official history. Zaachila and Cuilapan were involved in a dispute over the land rights of the local Mixtecs. They agree that the first Mixtecs arrived before 1280, but they are clearly as much concerned with presenting a point of view as with presenting the facts. Burgoa seems to have been as disconcerted as we when he observes that "we do not know the beginning of the Mixtec settlements in the Valley, nor why they have held some high points since ancient times."[59]

Since there are no absolute proofs in modern science, perhaps we should consider the possibility that, in spite of all the indications, there never was a Mixtec invasion of the Valley of Oaxaca. We might propose that the Monte Albán V culture resulted not from a physical invasion by Mixtecs, but from a diffusion of ideas and a trade in objects from the Mixteca—ideas and objects accepted among an always Zapotec population. A Zapotec acceptance of outside ideas would be quite contrary to what we know of Zapotec attitudes in such matters during Monte Albán IIIb–IV; but peoples do change. As for the Mixtec speakers noted by a number of authors in the sixteenth, seventeenth, eighteenth, nineteenth, and twentieth centuries, we may explain them away as an invention of the authors cited; or perhaps they were Zapotecs who learned Mixtec for some reason.

For some time now, those who command the largest number of facts about the ethnic situation of the Valley of Oaxaca in late preconquest times have balked at the difficulties introduced by the hypothesis just mentioned. The opinions of Caso and Barlow were cited above. Bernal said in 1950 that the pottery found in his excavations in the Mixteca Alta was identical to that of Monte Albán V; he explained this by proposing that "the Mixtecs, already installed [in the Valley], enter now more forcefully and form the phase Monte Albán V, which is only a provincial extension of the culture of the Mixteca Alta."[60] Bernal and the others were influenced also by the documentary evidence offered here, although until now we may never have felt its full weight because it has remained scattered in so many sources.

If there was in fact a Mixtec invasion, there should be two different kinds of cultural remains in the Valley during late preconquest times, one corresponding to the Zapotecs and the other to the Mixtecs. In fact, this is what we find: Monte Albán IV and Monte Albán V are two quite distinct cultures as seen archeologically, just as the documents suggest they ought to be. Two different peoples lived in the Valley at the same time, and the discrepancies in their tastes and traditions were accentuated by their hostile relations. The inevitable acculturation was much delayed, therefore, because (in a way now known from every corner of the world) the in-group customs became a symbol of the in-group itself, creating a prehispanic situation of nativism.

Even in 1580—after over three centuries of close coexistence—the *Relación* of Cuilapan could say that "the other Indians of this Zapotec region (where this town is settled) are very different from these [Mixtec] Indians for many reasons"; and it goes on to list some details of the differences.[61] The *Relación* of Chichicapa confirms that for the Valley Indians, or at least for contemporary Spanish observers of them, there were two contrasting groups: it speaks of the Zapotec Indians by name, and goes on to say that "the Mixtec Indians [have] another language and lineage of their own."[62]

Today, however, there remain few traces of such cultural differences. The Mixtec language is no longer spoken in the Valley; in 1957 a linguistic inquiry in Cuilapan had to be abandoned because there were not enough people there who knew more than a few words of Mixtec.[63] The moieties of Zaachila, whose social function would seem to be the expression of a mortal hostility for each other, may be the descendants of the ancient Mixtec and Zapotec parts of the town. (In 1846 Juan B. Carriedo said that "one of the barrios [of Zaachila] . . . even today is called the barrio of Mixtecs.")[64] But apparently today the Zapotec language is completely dominant in Zaachila. The potters of Coyotepec, who nowadays speak Zapotec, follow with astonishing fidelity some of the Mixtec ceramic traditions of Monte Albán V.

There are several possible explanations for the disappearance of the Mixtec language from the Valley of Oaxaca. One is that the congregation of the Mixtecs in Cuilapan, carried out by Cortés, reduced or extinguished the Mixtec element in many towns. Another explanation is intermarriage,[65] a natural consequence of which would have been the rapid loss of the minority language—especially in a region of long Zapotec tradition—once the Mixtecs had ceded their dominion to the Spanish.[66] There is still another explanation in the social situation created by the conquests. As Ralph Linton says, "It is characteristic of aristocrats the world over that they are reluctant to take care of their own children. . . . This arduous business is turned over to slaves or servants from the conquered group, which means that the child is exposed to the culture of this group during its most formative period. It learns the language of the conquered before it learns its own."[67] Naturally this tendency could not operate in settlements made up entirely of Mixtecs, but only in those of conquered Zapotecs; perhaps the Mixtec barrio of Zaachila would be an example. The social relations between Mixtecs and Zapotecs may be inferred from the *Relación* of Cuilapan: "These [Mixtecs] are people who hold themselves higher."[68] Kirchhoff has dealt with a similar situation on the opposite frontier of the Mixtec region—that is, in the state of Puebla—where there was contact and interaction among Mixtecs, Chocho-Popolocas, Mazatecs, and Nahuas.[69]

We have treated the late culture with which the Mixtecs invaded the Valley of Oaxaca as if it were a magical creation having no earlier history. Its roots and development have been described—within the severe limitations imposed by our relative lack of data about it—in Part II above. Perhaps we can place the present essay in better perspective if we list a few of the more urgent pending problems in Mixtec culture history, roughly in chronological order. They deal with:

1. The peoples of the Oto-Zapotecan or Otomangue or Macro-Mixtecan linguistic group and the period of incipient agriculture in the region from Tehuacan (in the south of the state of Puebla) to Tecomavaca (in the adjoining northern part of Oaxaca).[70]

2. The Mixtecs and the "Olmecs" or Tenocelome of La Venta.[71]

3. The Mixtecs and Monte Albán I and II.[72]

4. Teotihuacan. Several writers consider it to have been a polyglot metropolis with a significant Mixtec-speaking component.[73]

5. The Classic roots of Postclassic Mixtec or Mixteca-Puebla culture. Was there a definable Mixtec culture in the Classic?[74]

6. Cholula. Was it a great Mixtec capital of the Classic? Did the Mixtec dominion there last until the fall of Tula?[75]

7. Tula. Did the Toltec-Chichimecs have the cultural equipment needed to found a new civilization after the collapse of the Classic? Would it be more sensible to think of the Mixtecs as the artisan-Toltecs of the Postclassic? Did the Mixtecs constitute a part of the population of Tula, at least until the flight of Ce Ácatl Topiltzin Quetzalcóatl and his followers? Was it in fact these Tula Mixtecs who came as "Toltec" refugees to the Mixteca?[76]

8. Xochicalco. Indications have been found more than once that some of the Mixtecs played an important part at this center, either by their physical presence or indirectly.[77]

9. Guasave, Sinaloa. The role of Mixtec culture in this region remains unexplained beyond what Gordon Ekholm proposed long ago.[78]

10. The south. Were there Mixtec colonies in central Chiapas? What contacts were there with Central America and South America?[79]

I do not mean to suggest that our continuing lamentable ignorance of Mixtec culture history reflects some lack of ability or industry on the part of my colleagues; we are few, and Mesoamerica is enormous. I have attempted, rather, to encourage what already appears to be a great awakening of professional interest in the Mixtec people, culture, and region.

NOTES

1. See Alfonso Caso, "The Historical Value of the Mixtec Codices," *Boletín de Estudios Oaxaqueños*, No. 16 (Mitla, 1960); and Ignacio Bernal, "Archaeology and Written Sources," *Akten* des 34. Internationalen Amerikanistenkongresses (Vienna, 1960), pp. 219–25.

2. Alfonso Caso, *The Mixtec and Zapotec Cultures, Boletín de Estudios Oaxaqueños*, Nos. 21–23 (Mitla, 1962), p. 5.

3. John Paddock, *Mesoamerican Notes*, No. 3 (1953), pp. 2–7; *ibid.*, No. 4 (1955), pp. 80–86; *Boletín de Estudios Oaxaqueños*, No. 8 (México, 1958), p. 13. The name "Tetla-mixteca" has now been proposed for this grouping (see pp. 200–210 above). Miguel Covarrubias, *Indian Art of Mexico and Central America* (New York, 1957), map on p. 2.

4. Wigberto Jiménez Moreno, "Diversidad interna del mixteco y su afiliación al Macro-Otomangue," in Francisco de Alvarado, *Vocabulario en lengua mixteca* (facsimile edition, México, 1962), pp. 40–85. Morris Swadesh, *La lingüística como instrumento de la prehistoria* (México, 1960) (the original English publication used different illustrations, not applicable here); his "Ochenta lenguas autóctonas," in Carmen Cook de Leonard, ed., *Esplendor del México Antiguo* (Mexico, 1959), I, 85–96; and his "The Oto-Manguean Hypothesis and Macro-Mixtecan," *International Journal of American Linguistics*, XXVI (1960), 79–111. Robert J. Weitlaner, "Los pueblos no nahuas de la historia tolteca y el

grupo lingüístico Macro-Oto-Mangue," *Revista Mexicana de Estudios Antropológicos,* V (1941), 249–69.

5. See, for example, the works cited in n. 4 above; also Eric Wolf, *Sons of the Shaking Earth* (Chicago, 1959), pp. 36–41.

6. *Boletín de Estudios Oaxaqueños,* Nos. 21–23 (Mitla, 1962). Bulletin 21 is *The Mixtec and Zapotec Cultures: The Zapotecs,* and Bulletin 22 is *The Mixtec and Zapotec Cultures: The Mixtecs.* Bulletin 23 is a translation of Robert H. Barlow's annotated edition of two *Relaciones* (1580 and 1777–78) of Cuilapan and one (1579) of Oaxaca.

See also Alfonso Caso, *Las estelas zapotecas* (México, 1928), pp. 9–12; "La tumba 7 de Monte Albán es mixteca," *Universidad de México,* IV (1932), 117–50; his "Reading the Riddle of Ancient Jewels," *Natural History,* XXXII (1932), 464–80; "*Las exploraciones en Monte Albán, temporada 1934–1935* (México, 1935), pp. 23–25, 30; *Exploraciones en Mitla, 1934–1935* (with Daniel F. Rubín de la Borbolla, México, 1936), pp. 4–10, 17; *Exploraciones en Oaxaca, Quinta y Sexta Temporadas 1936–1937* (México, 1938), pp. 34–39.

Finally, see Robert H. Barlow, "Dos relaciones antiguas del pueblo de Cuilapa, Estado de Oaxaca," *Tlalocan,* Vol. II, No. 1 (1945), original version of the English edition cited above; and his *The Extent of the Empire of The Culhua Mexica,* Ibero-Americana: 28 (Berkeley, Calif., 1949), pp. 118–25.

7. On present conditions in the Mixteca Norte, see Moisés T. de la Peña, *Problemas sociales y económicos de las Mixtecas* (México, 1950); and Sherburne F. Cook, *Soil Erosion and Population in Central Mexico,* Ibero-Americana: 34 (Berkeley, Calif., 1949), pp. 2–32.

8. The data on changes during the past fifty years have been obtained by Paddock, chiefly from informants native to the Coixtlahuaca area. For the customary interpretation, see Ignacio Bernal, "Archaeology of the Mixteca," *Boletín de Estudios Oaxaqueños* No. 7 (México, 1958), p. 5; also Wigberto Jiménez Moreno, this volume, p. 61.

9. Hernán Cortés, *Cartas y relaciones* (Buenos Aires, 1946), Segunda Carta-relación, p. 170.

10. Luis García Pimentel, *Relación de los Obispados de Tlaxcala, Michoacan, Oaxaca, y otros lugares en el Siglo XVI* (México, 1904), pp. 62–63. Where it seemed clear, I have retained the original spelling of place names.

11. Antonio Vázquez de Espinosa, *Descripción de la Nueva España en el Siglo XVII* (México, 1944), pp. 150–51.

12. Bernabé Cobo, letter published in Vázquez de Espinosa, p. 201.

13. Thomas Gage, *The English-American His Travail by Sea and Land: or, a New Survey of the West-Indies* (London, 1928, 1946), pp. 119, 123–24.

14. Francisco de Burgoa, *Geográfica descripción* . . . (México, 1934). For descriptions of various Mixtec towns, e.g., Yanhuitlan, see I, 272ff.

15. García Pimentel, *Relación,* p. 64.

16. *Séptimo Censo General de la Población: Estado de Oaxaca* (México, 1953). From 1940 to 1950 the state of Oaxaca underwent a population increase of 19 per cent. According to the census cited here, the total population in 1950 was 1,421,313. There were 31,311 persons living alone, and 305,287 family heads with families of two or more persons. If the persons living alone are not counted in either the number of households or the total population, the average household has 4.55 persons. If persons living alone are included in both the number of households and the total population, the average is 4.22.

17. Sherburne F. Cook and Woodrow Borah, *The Indian Population of Central Mexico, 1531–1610,* Ibero-Americana: 44 (Berkeley, Calif., 1960), pp. 37–38.

18. García Pimentel, pp. 65, 69–76. 19. Burgoa, I, 395.

20. *Ibid.,* II, 348. 21. *Ibid.,* I, 278.

22. *Relación breve y verdadera de algunas cosas de las muchas que sucedieron al Padre Fray Alonso Ponce* . . . *escrita por dos religiosos, sus compañeros* (Madrid, 1875), I, 271–73; *ibid.,* I, 495–96.

23. Eutimio Pérez, *Recuerdos históricos del Obispado de Oaxaca* (Oaxaca, 1888), table of all the parishes of Oaxaca indicating the language spoken in each in 1802. This table uses

the same approach for several towns in the Mixteca in which there is good reason to believe more than one language was spoken. Pérez thus says that in Tejupan and Coixtlahuaca the language was Chocho, and fails to mention Mixtec; and he says that Tamazulapan was Mixtec, and does not mention Chocho.

24. Francisco de Burgoa, *Palestra historial* . . . (México, 1934), pp. 406–7.

25. Telixtlahuaca and Suchilquitongo, now independent, thus were barrios of Huitzo; but they are relatively far from the center, while Tenexpa, close in, remains a recognized part of Huitzo.

26. Helen Miller Bailey, *Santa Cruz of the Etla Hills* (Gainesville, Fla., 1958), p. 9.

27. Burgoa, *Geográfica descripción*, I, 267. Note that Caso (p. 334 above) records an apparently Mixtec *cacique* of Etla in the eighteenth century.

28. Elsie Clews Parsons, *Mitla, Town of the Souls* (Chicago, 1936). The individual Mixtec settlements are treated on the following pages: Xaaga, pp. 53–54; San Lorenzo Albarradas, p. 376; Atzompa, p. 61, p. 250 n. 20, p. 569; Cuilapan, pp. 122–23, p. 142 n. 189; Zimatlan, p. 250 n. 20; Coyotepec, p. 569; Miahuatlan, p. 541.

29. Oscar Schmieder, *The Settlements of the Tzapotec and Mije Indians, State of Oaxaca, Mexico* (Berkeley, Calif., 1930), pp. 23–24.

30. Joseph Antonio de Villa-Señor y Sánchez, *Theatro Americano* . . . (facsimile edition, México, 1952), II, 114.

31. *Ibid.,* II, 121.

32. *Ibid.,* II, 119–21. See n. 37 below for a mention of Lachiláa.

33. See Barlow, works cited in n. 6 above.

34. Bailey, Chap. 1.

35. Burgoa, *Geográfica descripción*, I, 396.

36. Francisco del Paso y Troncoso, *Papeles de Nueva España*, 2d series (Madrid, 1905), IV, 117.

37. Burgoa, *Geográfica descripción,* I, 394. Burgoa may disagree with the *Relación* of Chichicapa (Paso y Troncoso, p. 116), for he says that the Mixtecs had conquered Zaachila and were attacking "the mines of Chichicapa" at the time of the Spanish conquest, whereas the *Relación* says that Chichicapa recognized its subjection to the ruler of Zaachila, and that at the time of the Conquest the Mixtecs were engaged in a struggle with him. Villa-señor apparently agrees with Burgoa, since he says Santa Catarina Minas was a Mixtec town in the eighteenth century. (Santa Catarina Minas and Chichicapa are, in fact, separate although close together.) Zapotec sources suggest that the Mixtecs had not yet won either Chichicapa or Zaachila at the time the Spanish arrived, but the Zaachila tombs discovered in 1962 (see Caso's paper in this volume, pp. 319–28) are a rather conclusive proof that they had won the war and been settled there long enough to have buried some important personages in the center of Zaachila before the Spanish took over.

Burgoa, though he mentions more than once having consulted Indian histories and traditions recorded on paper and skins, seems at times to be aware of the contradictions: "We must go on following their movements, as far as we can; the tradition of both, Mixtecs and Zapotecs" (pp. 393–94); and he says that the Mixtecs "came out to attack the fields of the Zapotecs, and conquered more and more towns and lands until they arrived at the mines of Chichicapa on the east, and in the south they got as far as San Martín Lachiláa" (p. 395).

38. On the archeological evidence, see Bernal's paper in this volume, pp. 345–66.

39. *Relación* cited in n. 6 above.

40. Paso y Troncoso, p. 102.

41. *Ibid.,* pp. 105–6.

42. Caso and Borbolla, *Exploraciones en Mitla*, p. 17: "In the *Relaciones* of Macuilxóchitl and Tlacolula we are told that these two towns were subject to the Lord of Teozapotlan (Zaachila) and that they were at war with the town of Mitla. The reason that these subject towns fought with Mitla is that Mitla must have been conquered by the Mixtecs, as happened in the neighboring town of Teotitlan del Valle which, according to its *Relación*, paid tribute to the Mixtecs of Cuilapan."

43. *Relación* cited in n. 6 above.

44. Paso y Troncoso, p. 199.

45. Verbal communication, August 1962. See also p. 363 above. Although it may be true, as is so often said, that one cannot tell who made a pot by examining ancient fragments, one may, nevertheless, observe a statistically valid association of a particular way of doing things—such as making pots—with a particular human group. Some of the more daring even think this is a normal part of the over-all anthropological task, and call it ethnography when it is applied to recent peoples.

46. Burgoa, *Geográfica descripción*, I, 397.

47. José Antonio Gay, *Historia de Oaxaca*, 3d ed. (México, 1950), I, 337.

48. Burgoa, *Geográfica descripción*, I, 395.

49. Paul Kirchhoff, "Los pueblos de la *Historia Tolteca-Chichimeca*: sus migraciones y parentesco," *Revista Mexicana de Estudios Antropológicos*, IV (1940), 87.

50. Paso y Troncoso, p. 90.

51. For the Swadesh school, see the works by Swadesh cited in n. 4 above; also the works of his students cited in Jiménez Moreno, "Diversidad." For a more traditional approach, see Jiménez Moreno, *ibid.*, and Weitlaner, "Los pueblos."

52. "We think that in future studies we will find, either in the Mixteca Alta or the region to the east of it, a ceramic complex that will be so similar to that of Yagul as to show that it was from there that the Yagul population of Monte Albán V had come." John Paddock, "Exploración en Yagul, Oaxaca," *Revista Mexicana de Estudios Antropológicos*, XVI (1957), 94.
Bernal seems to suggest the same idea both in the last paragraphs of the article he prepared in 1961 for inclusion in Robert Wauchope, ed., *Handbook of Middle American Indians*, Vol. III (in press), and in his paper in the present volume; and he says it specifically in "Archeology of the Mixteca," *Boletín de Estudios Oaxaqueños*, No. 7 (México, 1958), pp. 11–12. See also the works cited in n. 3 above.

53. Several anonymous authors, "Place names," *Mesoamerican Notes* No. 4 (1955), pp. 68–69.

54. Yagul does not mean Old Town; if it is a Zapotec word it is equivalent to Old Tree. But we are suggesting here the possibility that it might *not* be a Zapotec word.

55. Paso y Troncoso, p. 94.

56. *Ibid.*, pp. 190–91. See also Caso's paper in this volume, pp. 313–35. The present essay was written before I had any knowledge of even the title or general theme of Caso's paper.

57. For accounts of such conquests, see Caso, *Interpretation of the Codex Bodley 2858* (México, 1959), and his *Interpretation of the Codex Selden 3135 (A.2)* (México, 1964).

58. *Relación* cited in n. 6 above.

59. Burgoa, *Geográfica descripción*, I, 392.

60. Ignacio Bernal, *Compendio de arte mesoamericano* (México, 1950), p. 47. Jorge R. Acosta, speaking at the Oaxaca symposium of the XXXV International Congress of Americanists to which these papers were presented, made clear his agreement with this interpretation.

61. *Relación* cited in n. 6 above.

62. Paso y Troncoso, p. 116.

63. Bernal, "Archeology of the Mixteca," p. 10.

64. Juan B. Carriedo, *Estudios históricos y estadísticos del Estado Libre, de Oaxaca*, 2d ed. (México, 1949), I, 107.

65. Jorge Fernando Iturribarría, "Yagul: Mestizo Product of Mixtecs and Zapotecs," *Boletín de Estudios Oaxaqueños* No. 17 (Mitla, 1960).

66. Burgoa provides an example. "This town of Santa Ana . . . because in the times of the Grant it was subject to the great Cuilapan, and because its lands were the best ones the Mixtec chiefs had gotten from the King of Zaachila in open battle . . . taking over the lands . . . they did not take the lives of the inhabitants, so that they might profit from the knowledge and experience of the conquered . . . the survival of both groups . . . has taken place in this town of Santa Ana. The Mixtecs, who won the land with bow and arrow, and the Zapotecs, who although defeated continue enjoying the fertility of these truly produc-

tive lands, so much so that the town has more than four hundred family heads, of both nations, one living on the east side of the town and the other on the west, divided, although they mix through marriages, and now are very much interrelated." Burgoa, *Geográfica descripción*, II, 59–60. (The translation here is as literal as possible, preserving Burgoa's unique syntax.)

67. Ralph Linton, *The Study of Man* (New York, 1936), p. 246.

68. *Relación* cited in n. 6 above.

69. Kirchhoff, "Los pueblos" (n. 49 above).

70. The important paper on this topic by Harvey became known to me only in 1964, upon publication in Vol. II, pp. 525–32, of the *Actas* of the XXXV International Congress of Americanists; it has been cited in Part II of this volume (p. 237). The several volumes of MacNeish's final report on the Tehuacan Valley excavations have not yet appeared. Some useful preliminary reports by MacNeish summarize the work: *First Annual Report of the Tehuacan Archaeological-Botanical Project* (Andover, Mass., 1961); *Second Annual Report . . .* (Andover, Mass., 1962); "Ancient Mesoamerican Civilization," *Science*, Feb. 7, 1964; and "The Origins of New World Civilization," *Scientific American*, November 1964.

See also Paul C. Mangelsdorf, Richard S. MacNeish, and Walton C. Galinat, "Domestication of Corn," *Science*, Feb. 7, 1964; C. Earle Smith, Jr., and Richard S. MacNeish, "Antiquity of American Polyploid Cotton," *Science*, Feb. 14, 1964; and Michael D. Coe and Kent V. Flannery, "Microenvironments and Mesoamerican Prehistory," *Science*, Feb. 14, 1964. Jiménez Moreno has something to say about this and the other problems listed here in Part I of the present volume.

71. See Covarrubias, *Indian Art*, p. 77 n. 2; also Wigberto Jiménez Moreno, "El enigma de los olmecas," *Cuadernos Americanos*, Año I, No. 5 (1942), and his essay in this volume. "El enigma" is extensively cited in English in Covarrubias, *Mexico South* (New York, 1946), pp. 122–41, and refers to "Olmecs" of all horizons.

72. See Alfonso Caso, "Resumen del informe de las exploraciones en Oaxaca, durante la 7ᵃ y 8ᵃ temporadas 1937–38 y 1938–39," *Actas*, XXVII Congreso Internacional de Americanistas (1942), II, 183; also Evangelina Arana Osnaya, "Relaciones internas del Mixteco-Trique," *Anales* del Instituto Nacional de Antropología e Historia, XII (1960), 265 (where she proposes that the Mixtecs proper may have inhabited Monte Negro, and the Amusgos Monte Albán in period I); Chadwick's paper in the present volume, pp. 245–55; and René Millon and Robert E. Longacre, "Proto-Mixtecan and Proto-Amuzgo-Mixtecan Vocabularies, a Preliminary Cultural Analysis," *Anthropological Linguistics*, Vol. III, No. 4 (April 1961), pp. 1–44 (written in 1957).

73. Jiménez Moreno has expressed this view for some years, although recently he seems to have decided that the Mixtecs and their relatives were a minority, and the Nahuas the majority. His works cited above, as well as Part I of this volume, all bear on the question. Meanwhile, others including linguists of both the pro- and the anti-Swadesh persuasions often agree that the Nahua peoples arrived too late in central Mexico to see Teotihuacan as anything but a ruin. The relevant linguistic works are also cited in n. 4 above. Further support for the argument comes from Robert E. L. Chadwick, "The Olmeca-Xicallanca of Teotihuacan: A Preliminary Study" (unpublished Master's thesis, Mexico City College, 1962).

74. Since this essay was presented, I have prepared a preliminary statement about what one such culture might be (pp. 174–200 above).

75. Jiménez Moreno, p. 65 above, refers to Cholula and Teotihuacan as "great twin centers." Paul Tolstoy, citing Eduard Seler and Sigvald Linné, suggests that the "center of gravity" of Teotihuacan culture was in the Puebla-Tlaxcala valley. See *Surface Survey of the Northern Valley of Mexico: The Classic and Post-Classic Periods*, Transactions of the American Philosophical Society XLVIII (Philadelphia, 1958), p. 67. See also Jiménez Moreno's paper "El enigma," in which several other authors who have dealt with Cholula are cited, especially Caso and Noguera.

76. See Wigberto Jiménez Moreno, "Síntesis de la historia precolonial del Valle de México," *Revista Mexicana de Estudios Antropológicos*, Vol. XIV, Part 1, p. 224; Weitlaner,

"Los pueblos"; and Barbro Dahlgren de Jordán, *La Mixteca: su cultura e historia prehispánicas* (México, 1954), pp. 54–56.

77. For example, pottery fragments that I was asked to identify "blind," and that seemed to me identical with a type common in the offerings of the Yagul Mixtec tombs, had been found in a stone crypt with a stela at Xochicalco. See César A. Sáenz, "Tres estelas en Xochicalco," *Revista Mexicana de Estudios Antropológicos*, XVII (1961); and Alfonso Caso, "Calendario y escritura en Xochicalco," *ibid.*, XVIII (1962).

78. Gordon Ekholm, *Excavations at Guasave, Sinaloa, Mexico*, American Museum of Natural History, Anthropological Papers XXXVIII (New York, 1942).

79. Large quantities of ordinary Mixteca Alta household pottery have been found in excavations at Chiapa de Corzo, Chiapas (verbal information, Carlos Navarrete, 1964). See Bernal Díaz del Castillo, *Historia verdadera de la conquista de la Nueva España* (México, 1942), Chapter 166; Jiménez Moreno, this volume, p. 65; Barbro Dahlgren de Jordán, "Un petroglifo mixteca en la Guayana Británica," *Homenaje a Alfonso Caso* (México, 1951); Covarrubias, *Indian Art*, color plate between pp. 196 and 197; Eduard Seler, *Gesammelte Abhandlungen*, 1900), III, 532; Samuel K. Lothrop, "South America as seen from Middle America," in Clarence L. Hay *et al.*, eds., *The Maya and Their Neighbors* (New York, 1940), p. 426; and Thomas A. Joyce, *Mexican Archaeology* (London, 1914), Figure 41.

Bibliography

The following abbreviations are used:

AA	*American Antiquity*
Actas	*Actas y Memorias del XXXV Congreso Internacional de Americanistas,* México, 1962
ADV	Akademische Druck- u. Verlagsanstalt, Graz, Austria
BBAA	*Boletín Bibliográfico de Antropología Americana*
BEO	*Boletín de Estudios Oaxaqueños*
CA	*Cuadernos Americanos*
CIW	Carnegie Institution of Washington, Washington, D.C.
HMAI	*Handbook of Middle American Indians,* University of Texas Press, Austin
IA	Ibero-Americana, University of California Press, Berkeley
INAH	Instituto Nacional de Antropología e Historia, México
MCC	Mexico City College, México (now University of the Americas)
MN	*Mesoamerican Notes*
RMEA	*Revista Mexicana de Estudios Antropológicos*
SMA	Sociedad Mexicana de Antropología, México
UNAM	Universidad Nacional Autónoma de México

Ackerman, Phyllis
    1950   "The Dawn of Religions." *In* Ferm 1950.

Acosta, Jorge R.
    1941   "Los últimos descubrimientos arqueológicos en Tula, Hidalgo, 1941," *RMEA,* V:2–3, 239–48.
    1947   "Informe de la XVI temporada de exploraciones arqueológicas en la zona de Monte Albán, Oaxaca," unpublished report in Archivos Técnicos, INAH.
    1949   "El pectoral de jade de Monte Albán," *Anales del INAH,* III, 17–26.
    1965   "Preclassic and Classic Architecture of Oaxaca," *HMAI,* III, 814–36.

Agrinier, Pierre
    1960   "The Carved Human Femurs from Tomb 1, Chiapa de Corzo, Chiapas, Mexico," *Papers of the New World Archaeological Foundation,* No. 6. Orinda, Calif.

Aguilar, J.
    1883   "Jefatura política del Distrito de Teotitlán del Camino." *In* Martínez Gracida 1883.

Aguirre Beltrán, Gonzalo
  n.d.   "Pobladores del Papaloapan." Ms. Cited in Villa Rojas 1955.
Alcina Franch, José
  1956   "Fuentes indígenas de Méjico: ensayo de sistematización bibliográ-
              fica," *Revista de Indias*, XV, 421–521. Also published separately.
              Madrid: no publisher.
Alvarado, Fray Francisco de
  1593   Vocabulario en lengua mixteca. México: facsimile edition by Insti-
              tuto Nacional Indigenista and INAH, 1962.
Anderson, Arthur J. O., and Charles Dibble. *See* Florentine Codex.
Anonymous
  1955   "Place Names," *MN* 4, 68–69.
Anonymous
  1961   "Yagul Brasero C14 Date," *Katunob*, II:2, 7–8. *See* Paddock 1961.
Arana Osnaya, Evangelina
  1960   "Relaciones internas del Mixteco-Trique," *Anales del INAH*, XII,
              219–73.
Arana Osnaya, Evangelina, and Mauricio [Morris] Swadesh
  1965   Los elementos del mixteco antiguo. México: Instituto Nacional In-
              digenista and INAH.
Armillas, Pedro
  1945   "Oztuma, Gro., fortaleza de los mexicanos en la frontera de Michoa-
              cán," *RMEA*, VI:3, 165–75.
  1946   "Los Olmeca–Xicalanca y los sitios arqueológicos del Suroeste de
              Tlaxcala," *RMEA*, VIII, 137–45.
  1948   "A Sequence of Cultural Development in Meso-America." *In* Bennett
              1948, 105–11.
  1950a   "Teotihuacán, Tula y los Toltecas. Las culturas post-arcáicas y pre-
              aztecas del Centro de México. Excavaciones y estudios, 1922–1950,"
              RUNA (Buenos Aires), III, 37–70.
  1950b   "Visita a Copán," *CA*, IX:4.
  1951   "Tecnología, formaciones socio-económicas y religión en Mesoamé-
              rica." *In* Tax 1951, I, 19–30.
  1956   "Cronología y periodificación de la historia de América precolom-
              bina," *Cuadernos de Historia Mundial* (Neuchâtel), III:2. Also pub-
              lished as a special supplement to the review *Tlatoani* (México:
              Escuela Nacional de Antropología e Historia), 1957.
  1957   Programa de historia de la América indígena. Washington, D.C.:
              Unión Panamericana. In English: Washington, D.C.: Social Science
              Monographs, II. Pan American Union, 1958.
Bailey, Helen Miller
  1958   Santa Cruz of the Etla Hills. Gainesville: University of Florida Press.
Barba de Piña Chán, Beatriz
  1956   Tlapacoya, un sitio preclásico de transición. Acta Anthropologica,
              época 2, I:1. México: Escuela Nacional de Antropología e Historia.
Barlow, R. H.
  1944   Review of Tompkins 1942, in *Tlalocan*, I, 383–84.
  1945   "Dos relaciones antiguas del pueblo de Cuilapan, Estado de Oaxaca,"
              Tlalocan, II, 18–28 (intro. and notes by Barlow). In English: *BEO*,
              No. 23 (Mitla, Museo Frissell). Trans. Douglas S. Butterworth.
  1947   "Bibliografía de Robert H. Barlow," *BBAA*, X, 278–82.

1949   The Extent of the Empire of the Culhua Mexica. IA: 28.

Barrera Vásquez, Alfredo, and Sylvanus Griswold Morley
1949   "The Maya Chronicles," *Contributions to American Anthropology and History*, 48. CIW.

Batres, Leopoldo
1902   Exploraciones de Monte Albán. México: Casa Editorial Gante.
1903   Visita a los monumentos arqueológicos de "La Quemada," Zacatecas. México.

Bauer, Wilhelm
1908   "Heidentum und Aberglaube unter den Maçateca-Indianern," *Zeitschrift für Ethnologie*, XL (Heft VI), 857–65.

Belmar, Francisco
1892   Ligero estudio sobre la lengua Mazateca. Oaxaca.

Bennett, Wendell C., ed.
1948   A Reappraisal of Peruvian Archaeology. Memoirs of the Society for American Archaeology, No. 4.

Bernal, Ignacio
1946   La cerámica preclásica de Monte Albán. Unpublished Master's thesis, Escuela Nacional de Antropología e Historia, México.
1949a   "La cerámica grabada de Monte Albán," *Anales del INAH*, III, 59–77.
1949b   La cerámica de Monte Albán III A. Unpublished doctoral thesis, UNAM.
1949c   "Distribución geográfica de las culturas de Monte Albán," *El México Antiguo*, VII, 209–16.
1949d   "Exploraciones en Coixtlahuaca, Oax.," *RMEA*, X, 5–76.
1950a   Compendio de arte mesoamericano. Enciclopedia Mexicana de Arte, 7. México: Ediciones Mexicanas.
1950b   "The 'Q Complex' as Seen from Monte Albán," *MN* 2.
1951a   "Bibliografía de Robert H. Barlow," *BBAA*, XIII:2, 249–51.
1951b   "Robert H. Barlow" (obituary), *BBAA*, XIII:1, 301–4.
1953   Mesoamérica: período indígena. Programa de Historia de América. México: Instituto Panamericano de Geografía e Historia, Comisión de Historia.
1957   Monte Albán–Mitla: Guía oficial. INAH.
1958a   "Archeology of the Mixteca," *BEO*, No. 7. MCC.
1958b   Exploraciones en Cuilapan de Guerrero, 1902–1954. INAH.
1958c   "Monte Albán and the Zapotecs," *BEO*, No. 1. MCC.
1959   "Evolución y alcance de las culturas mesoamericanas." *In* Cook de Leonard, ed., 1959, I, 97–124.
1960   "El Palacio de Yagul y sus implicaciones socio-políticas," *Actes du VIe Congrès International des Sciences Anthropologiques et Ethnologiques*, Paris, Tome II (1er volume), 345–49.
1962a   "Archeology and Written Sources," *Akten des 34. Internationalen Amerikanistenkongresses*, Vienna, 219–25.
1962b   Bibliografía de arqueología y etnografía de Mesoamérica y el Norte de México. INAH.
1963   "Otra tumba cruciforme de Mitla," *Estudios de Cultura Nahuatl*, IV, 223–32. UNAM.
1964   "Arqueología mixteca del Valle de Oaxaca," *Actas*, I, 453–60.

1965a   "Teotihuacan: Nuevas fechas de radiocarbono y su posible significado," *Anales de Antropología*, II, 27–35. UNAM.

1965b   "Archaeological Synthesis of Oaxaca," *HMAI*, III, 788–813.

1965c   "Architecture in Oaxaca after the End of Monte Albán," *HMAI*, III, 837–48.

Bernal, Ignacio, and Eusebio Dávalos Hurtado, eds.

1953   Huastecos, totonacos, y sus vecinos: la V Mesa Redonda de la Sociedad Mexicana de Antropología, Xalapa, 1951. Published as *RMEA*, XIII:2–3.

Boas, Franz

1913a   "Anezo [sic] al informe del Presidente de la Junta Directiva," Escuela de Arqueología y Etnología Americanas. Año escolar de 1911 a 1912." México.

1913b   "Informe del Presidente de la Junta Directiva. Escuela Internacional de Arqueología y Etnología Americanas. Año escolar de 1911 a 1912." México.

Boos, Frank H.

1964   Las urnas zapotecas en el Real Museo de Ontario. Corpus Antiquitatum Americanensium, I. INAH. Text in both Spanish and English; Spanish version by Fernando Horcasitas. Sponsored by the Union Académique Internationale, Consejo Internacional de la Filosofía y de las Ciencias Humanísticas, and UNESCO.

n.d.   Las urnas zapotecas de las Colecciones Frissell y Leigh del Museo Frissell de Arte Zapoteca, Mitla, Oaxaca. Corpus Antiquitatum Americanensium, II–III. INAH. In press.

Borah, Woodrow, and Sherburne F. Cook

1960   The Population of Central Mexico in 1548. An Analysis of the *Suma de visitas de pueblos*. IA:43.

1963   The Aboriginal Population of Central Mexico on the Eve of the Spanish Conquest. IA:45.

Boulding, Kenneth

1964   The Meaning of the Twentieth Century. World Perspectives 34. New York: Harper.

Brainerd, George W.

1951   "Early Ceramic Horizons in Yucatan." *In* Tax 1951, I, 72–78.

Brinton, Daniel G.

1892   "On the Mazatec Language of Mexico and Its Affinities," *Proceedings of the American Philosophical Society*, XXX, 31–39. Reprinted in Brinton, Studies in South American Native Languages from MSS. and Rare Printed Sources. Philadelphia, 1892.

Brockington, Donald L.

1965   The Archaeological Sequence from Sipolite, Oaxaca, Mexico. Unpublished doctoral thesis, University of Wisconsin, Madison.

Burgoa, Fray Francisco de

1670   Palestra historial de virtudes y ejemplares apostólicos. Fundada del celo de insignes héroes de la Sagrada Orden de Predicadores en este Nuevo Mundo de la América en las Indias Occidentales . . . México. New edition, México: Publicaciones del Archivo General de la Nación, XXIV, 1934.

1674   Geográfica descripción de la parte septentrional, del polo ártico de la América, y nueva iglesia de las Indias Occidentales, y sitio astronómico de esta Provincia de Predicadores de Antequera Valle de

Oaxaca . . . México, 2 vols. New edition, México: Publicaciones del Archivo General de la Nación, XXV, 1934. 2 vols.

Burland, Cottie A.

1947   "A 360-day Count in a Mexican Codex," *Man*, XLVII, 106–8.

1948   "Some Descriptive Notes on MS. Laud. Misc. 678, a Pre-Columbian Mexican Document in the Bodleian Library of the University of Oxford," *Actes du XXVIII Congrès International des Américanistes*, 371–76. Paris.

1957   "Some Errata in the Published Edition of Codex Nuttall," *Boletín del Centro de Investigaciones Antropológicas de México*, III, 11–13.

1958   "Eclipse Data from a Mixtec Codex [Nuttall]," *BEO*, No. 9. MCC.

1965   Commentary on Codex Egerton 2895 (q.v.).

1966   *See* Codex Laud.

n.d.   Commentary on a new edition of Codex Nuttall. ADV. In preparation.

Cámara B., Fernando

1961   "Mixtecos y zapotecos: antiguos y modernos." *In* Genovés 1961.

Canby, Joel S.

1951   "Possible Chronological Implications of the Long Ceramic Sequence Recovered at Yarumela, Spanish Honduras." *In* Tax 1951, I, 79–85.

Carrasco, Pedro

1950   Los otomíes. UNAM.

Carrera Stampa, Manuel

1959   "Fuentes para el estudio de la historia indígena." *In* Cook de Leonard, ed., 1959.

Carriedo, Juan B.

1847   Estudios históricos y estadísticos del Estado Libre, de Oaxaca. 2d ed., México: Biblioteca de Autores y de Asuntos Oaxaqueños, 1949. 2 vols.

Carrillo y Gariel, Abelardo

1946   Técnica de la pintura de Nueva España. México.

Caso, Alfonso

1927   "Las ruinas de Tizatlán, Tlaxcala," *Revista Mexicana de Estudios Históricos*, I:4, 139–72. (Beginning with Vol. III, this series became *RMEA*.)

1928   Las estelas zapotecas. México: Secretaría de Educación Pública.

1929   "Informe preliminar de las exploraciones realizadas en Michoacán," *Anales del Museo Nacional de Arqueología, Historia y Etnografía*, 4a época, VI, 446–52.

1932a   "Monte Albán, Richest Archeological Find in America," *National Geographic Magazine* (October 1932), 487–512.

1932b   "Reading the Riddle of Ancient Jewels," *Natural History*, XXXII, 464–80. Translation of Caso 1932c by Suzannah B. Vaillant and George C. Vaillant, with a foreword by George Vaillant.

1932c   "La tumba 7 de Monte Albán es mixteca," *Universidad de México*, IV:20, 117–50.

1935   Las exploraciones en Monte Albán, temporada 1934–1945. México: Instituto Panamericano de Geografía e Historia.

1938   Exploraciones en Oaxaca, quinta y sexta temporadas 1936–1937. México: Instituto Panamericano de Geografía e Historia.

1939a   Culturas mixteca y zapoteca. México: Ediciones Encuadernables de El Nacional. In English: *BEO*, Nos. 21–22 (Mitla, Museo Frissell), translated and annotated by John Paddock.

1939b   "¿Tenían los teotihuacanos conocimiento del Tonalpohualli?," *El*

México Antiguo, IV, 131–44. Also in *Memorias de la Sociedad Científica Antonio Alzate,* LV, 237–47.

1942   "Resumen del informe de las exploraciones en Oaxaca, durante la 7a y la 8a temporadas, 1937–1938 y 1938–1939," *Actas del XXVII Congreso Internacional de Americanistas, México, 1939,* II, 159–87.

1947   "Calendario y escritura de las antiguas culturas de Monte Albán," chapter contributed in honor of Mendizábal for Vol. I of Obras completas de Miguel Othón de Mendizábal. México.

1949   "El Mapa de Teozacoalco," *CA,* VII:5, 3–40. Special offprint dedicated to the XXIX International Congress of Americanists, New York.

1951   "Explicación del reverso del Códice Vindobonensis," *Memorias de El Colegio Nacional,* V:5. México.

1953   "New World Culture History: Middle America," in A. L. Kroeber, ed., Anthropology Today. Chicago: University of Chicago Press.

1956a   "El calendario mixteco," *Historia Mexicana,* V:4, 481–97.

1956b   "La cruz de Topiltepec, Tepozcolula, Oaxaca," in Dávalos and Bernal 1956, 171–82.

1958   "El Mapa de Xochitepec," *Proceedings of the XXXII International Congress of Americanists, Copenhagen, 1956,* 458–66.

1960a   Interpretation of the Codex Bodley 2858, trans. Ruth Morales and John Paddock, with a facsimile of the Codex. SMA.

1960b   "Valor histórico de los códices mixtecos," *CA,* XIX:2, 139–47. In English: *BEO,* No. 16 (Mitla, Museo Frissell), trans. Charles R. Wicke.

1961   "Los lienzos mixtecos de Ihuitlán y Antonio de León." *In* Genovés 1961.

1962   "Vocabulario sacado del 'Arte en lengua mixteca' de Fray Antonio de los Reyes." *In* Alvarado 1593.

1963   "Calendario y escritura en Xochicalco," *RMEA,* XVIII, 49–79.

1964a   Interpretation of the Codex Selden 3135 (A.2), trans. Jacinto Quirarte and John Paddock, with a facsimile of the Codex. SMA.

1964b   "Relations between the Old and New Worlds: A Note on Methodology," *Actas* I, 55–71. Trans. John Paddock. In Spanish: "Relaciones entre el Viejo y el Nuevo Mundo. Una observación metodológica," *CA,* XXI:6, 1962, 160–75.

1964c   "Los señores de Yanhuitlán," *Actas,* I, 437–48.

1965a   "¿Existió un imperio olmeca?," *Memorias de El Colegio Nacional,* V:3, 11–60.

1965b   "Sculpture and Mural Painting of Oaxaca," *HMAI,* III, 849–70.

1965c   "Lapidary Work, Goldwork, and Copperwork from Oaxaca," *HMAI,* III, 896–930.

1965d   "Zapotec Writing and Calendar," *HMAI,* III, 931–47.

1965e   "Mixtec Writing and Calendar," *HMAI,* III, 948–61.

Caso, Alfonso, and Ignacio Bernal

1952   Urnas de Oaxaca. INAH.

1965   "Ceramics of Oaxaca," *HMAI,* III, 871–95.

Caso, Alfonso, and Daniel F. Rubín de la Borbolla

1936   Exploraciones en Mitla, 1934–1935. México: Instituto Panamericano de Geografía e Historia.

Caso, Alfonso, and Mary Elizabeth Smith

n.d.   Codex Colombino: facsimile edition, with interpretation of the glyphic content by Caso and of the glosses in Mixtec by Smith. SMA. In press.

Castañeda, Carlos E., and Jack Autrey Dabbs
1939   Guide to the Latin American Manuscripts in the University of Texas Library. Cambridge, Mass.: Harvard University Press.

Chadwick, Robert E. L.
1962   The Olmeca-Xicallanca of Teotihuacan: A Preliminary Study. Unpublished Master's thesis, MCC.

Cline, Howard F.
1956   "The Chinantla of Northeastern Oaxaca, Mexico: Bio-Bibliographical Notes on Modern Investigations," in Dávalos and Bernal 1956, 635–56.
1957   "Problems of Mexican Ethnohistory: The Ancient Chinantla, a Case Study," Hispanic American Historical Review, XXXVII, 273–95.
1959   "A Preliminary Report on Chinantec Archeology: Excavations in Oaxaca, Mexico, 1951," Actas del XXXIII Congreso Internacional de Americanistas, San José de Costa Rica, 1958, II, 158–70.
1961   "Mapas and Lienzos of the Colonial Chinantec Indians, Oaxaca, Mexico." In A William Cameron Townsend . . . México: Instituto Lingüístico de Verano.
1964   "Lienzos y comunidades mazatecos [sic] de la época colonial, Oaxaca, México," Actas, I, 397–424. Trans. John Paddock and Arturo Souto.

Cobo, Fray Bernabé
1944   Letter published in Vázquez de Espinosa 1944, 195–214.

Codex Bodley. See Caso 1960a.

Codex Borgia. Eine altmexikanische Bilderschrift der Bibliothek der Congregatio de Propaganda Fide Herausgegeben auf Kosten Seiner Excellenz des Herzogs von Loubat, erläutert von Dr. Eduard Seler. 3 vols. in 1. Berlin, 1904–9. See Códice Borgia.

Codex Colombino. See Caso and Smith.

Codex Egerton 2895 (Codex Waecker Gotter). Commentary by Cottie A. Burland. ADV, 1965.

Codex Fejérváry-Mayer. An Old Mexican Picture Manuscript in the Liverpool Free Public Museum, 12014/M, Published at the Expense of His Excellency the Duke of Loubat, Elucidated by Dr. Eduard Seler; trans. A. H. Keane. Berlin and London, 1901–2.

Codex Laud. Facsimile edition in color, with introduction by Cottie A. Burland. ADV, 1966.

Codex Nuttall. Facsimile of an Ancient Mexican Codex Belonging to Lord Zouche of Harynworth, England, with an Introduction by Zelia Nuttall. Cambridge, Mass., 1902.

Codex Nuttall. Facsimile edition of Codex Nuttall, with commentary by Cottie A. Burland. ADV, in preparation.

Codex Selden II. See Caso 1964.

Codex Vaticanus No. 3773 (Codex Vaticanus B). An Old Mexican Pictorial Manuscript in the Vatican Library Published at the Expense of His Excellency the Duke of Loubat, Elucidated by Dr. Eduard Seler; trans. A. H. Keane. Berlin and London, 1902–3.

Codex Vindobonensis Mexicanus I, Faksimileausgabe der mexikanischen Bilderhandschrift der National-bibliothek in Wien. Walter Lehmann and Ottakar Smital, eds. Vienna, 1929.

Codex Vindobonensis Mexicanus I, facsimile edition. Otto Adelhofer, ed. ADV, 1963.
Códice Borgia. Facsimile edition, with commentary by Eduard Seler; Spanish trans. Mariana Frenk. México: Fondo de Cultura Económica, 1963. 3 vols.
Códice Laud. Photographic edition in black and white, annotated by Carlos Martínez Marín. INAH, 1961. *See also* Codex Laud.
Códice de Yanhuitlan. *See* Jiménez Moreno and Mateos Higuera.
Coe, Michael D.
    1962   "An Olmec Design on an Early Peruvian Vessel," *AA*, XXVII, 579–80. *See* Lanning 1963.
    1963a   "Cultural Development in Southeastern Mesoamerica." *In* Meggers and Evans 1963.
    1963b   "Olmec and Chavín: Rejoinder to Lanning," *AA*, XXIX, 101–4.
    1965   The Jaguar's Children: Pre-Classic Central Mexico. New York: The Graphic Society, for the Museum of Primitive Art.
    1966a   "The Olmec Style and Its Distributions," *HMAI*, III, 739–75.
    1966b   "An Archaeological Synthesis of Southern Veracruz–Tabasco," *HMAI*, III, 679–715.
Coe, Michael D., and Kent V. Flannery
    1964   "Microenvironments and Mesoamerican Prehistory," *Science*, CXLIII, No. 3607, 650–54.
Coe, William R.
    1965   "Tikal, Guatemala, and Emergent Maya Civilization," *Science*, CXLVII, No. 3664, 1401–19.
Comas, Juan
    1950   "Bosquejo histórico de la antropología en México," *RMEA*, XI, 97–192.
Comas, Juan, *et al.*, eds.
    1951   Homenaje al Doctor Alfonso Caso. INAH.
Cook, Sherburne F.
    1949   Soil Erosion and Population in Central Mexico. IA:34.
    1958   Santa María Ixcatlán: Habitat, Population, Subsistence. IA:41.
Cook, Sherburne F., and Woodrow Borah
    1960   The Indian Population of Central Mexico, 1531–1610. IA:44.
Cook, Sherburne F., and Lesley Byrd Simpson
    1948   The Population of Central Mexico in the Sixteenth Century. IA:31.
Cook de Leonard, Carmen
    1953   "Los popolocas de Puebla." *In* Bernal and Dávalos 1953, 423–45.
    1961   "Calli-Akbal y la décima trecena en el Hacha de Yucuquimi," *El México Antiguo*, IX, 325–78.
Cook de Leonard, Carmen, ed.
    1959   Esplendor del México antiguo. México: Centro de Investigaciones Antropológicas de México. 2 vols.
Córdova, Fray Juan de
    1578   Arte en lengua zapoteca. 2d ed., with foreword by Nicolás León, Morelia, Michoacán, 1886.
    1578   Vocabulario en lengua Çapoteca. Facsimile edition titled Vocabulario castellano-zapoteca, with foreword by Wigberto Jiménez Moreno, INAH: 1942.
Corona Núñez, José, and Eduardo Noguera
    1955   La tumba de El Arenal, Etzatlán, Jalisco. INAH.

Cortés, Hernán
  1522–26   Cartas y relaciones. Buenos Aires: Emecé Editores, 1946.
Covarrubias, Miguel
  1943   "Tlatilco, Archaic Mexican Art and Culture," *Dyn*, Nos. 4–5, 40–46.
  1946   Mexico South: The Isthmus of Tehuantepec. New York: Knopf.
  1950   "Tlatilco: el arte y la cultura del Valle de México," *CA*, IX:3, 149–62.
  1957   Indian Art of Mexico and Central America. New York: Knopf.
Cowan, George M.
  1948   "Mazateco Whistle Speech," *Language*, XXIV, 280–86.
  1953   "El motivo 'mariposa' en la cultura mazateca contemporánea," *Yan*,
            II, 92–94. México: Centro de Investigaciones Antropológicas de
            México.
Cowan, George M., and Florence Cowan
  1947   Mazateco: Locational and Directional Morphemes," *Aboriginal Lin-
            guistics*, I, 3–9.
Cubillos, Julio César
  1955   Tumaco, notas arqueológicas. Bogotá: Ministerio de Educación.
"Le Culte rendu au Soleil (Tonatiuh)," in Eugène Boban, Documents pour servir à
            l'histoire du Mexique, I, 329–48. Paris, 1891.
Dahlgren de Jordán, Barbro
  1951   "Un petroglifo mixteca en la Guayana Británica." *In* Comas *et al.*,
            eds., 1951, 127–32.
  1954   La Mixteca: Su cultura e historia prehispánicas. UNAM.
Dávalos Hurtado, Eusebio
  1951   "Una interpretación de los Danzantes de Monte Albán," in Comas
            et al., eds., 1951, 133–41.
Dávalos Hurtado, Eusebio, and Ignacio Bernal, eds.
  1956   Estudios antropológicos publicados en homenaje al Doctor Manuel
            Gamio. SMA.
DeCicco, Gabriel, and Donald L. Brockington
  1956   Reconocimiento arqueológico en el Suroeste de Oaxaca. INAH. Trans.
            Eduardo Noguera.
De la Peña, Moisés T.
  1950   Problemas sociales y económicos de las Mixtecas. México: Instituto
            Nacional Indigenista, *Memorias*, II:1.
Del Paso y Troncoso, Francisco, ed.
  1905   Papeles de Nueva España. Segunda serie: Geografía y estadística.
            Madrid: Sucesores de Rivadeneyra. 7 vols.
  1939–42 Epistolario de Nueva España 1505–1818. México: Antigua Librería
            Robredo. 16 vols.
Delgado, Agustín
  1960   "Investigaciones antropológicas," *Boletín del INAH*, No. 2, 7–9.
  1961   "Polychrome Zapotec Tomb Paintings," *Current Anthropology*, II,
            269.
  1965   "Archeological Reconnaissance in the Region of Tehuantepec,
            Oaxaca, Mexico," *Papers of the New World Archaeological Founda-
            tion*, No. 18. Provo, Utah: Brigham Young University. Revised by
            Gareth W. Lowe.
Descripción del Códice Cospiano manuscrito pictórico de los antiguos Náuas que
            se conserva en la Biblioteca de la Universidad de Bolonia reprodu-

cido en fotocromografía a expensas de S.E. el Duque de Loubat. Rome, 1898.

Díaz del Castillo, Bernal
1962   Historia verdadera de la conquista de la Nueva España. México: Editorial Porrúa.

Dibble, Charles E.
1951   "Robert H. Barlow" (obituary), *AA*, XVI:4, 347.

Dibble, Charles E., and Arthur J. O. Anderson. *See* Florentine Codex.

Dixon, Keith
1958   "Two Masterpieces of Middle American Bone Sculpture," *AA*, XXIV: 1, 57–61.
1959   "Two Carved Human Bones from Chiapas," *Archaeology*, XII:2, 106–9.

Drucker, Philip
1943a   Ceramic Sequence at Tres Zapotes, Veracruz, Mexico. Washington, D.C.: Smithsonian Institution, Bureau of American Ethnology Bulletin 140.
1943b   Ceramic Stratigraphy at Cerro de las Mesas, Veracruz, Mexico. Washington, D.C.: Smithsonian Institution, Bureau of American Ethnology Bulletin 141.
1952   La Venta, Tabasco: A Study of Olmec Ceramics and Art. Washington, D.C.: Smithsonian Institution, Bureau of American Ethnology Bulletin 153.

Drucker, Philip, Robert F. Heizer, and Robert J. Squier
1959   Excavations at La Venta, Tabasco. Washington, D.C.: Smithsonian Institution, Bureau of American Ethnology Bulletin 170.

Dutton, Bertha
1955   "Tula of the Toltecs," *El Palacio*, LXII:6–7, 193–251.

Easby, Dudley T., Jr.
1963   "Una nota tecnológica sobre el pectoral de Zaachila," *RMEA*, XIX, 37–40.

Ekholm, Gordon F.
1942   Excavations at Guasave, Sinaloa, Mexico. New York: Anthropological Papers of the American Museum of Natural His'ory, XXXVIII:II.
1944   Excavations at Tampico and Pánuco in the Huasteca, Mexico. New York: Anthropological Papers of the American Museum of Natural History, XXXVIII:V.

Escalona Ramos, Alberto
1953   "Xochicalco en la cronología de la América Media," in Bernal and Dávalos, eds., 1953, 351–68.

Espinosa, Mariano
1910(?)   Apuntes históricos de las tribus chinantecas, matzatecas y popolucas.
1961   New edition of Espinosa 1910, with notes by Howard F. Cline. Papeles de la Chinantla, No. 3. México: Museo Nacional de Antropología, Serie Científica, No. 7.

Ferm, Virgilius, ed.
1950   Ancient Religions. New York: Philosophical Library.

Fernández de Miranda, María Teresa
1961   "Toponimia popoloca." *In* A William Cameron Townsend . . . México: Instituto Lingüístico de Verano.

Florentine Codex. General History of the Things of New Spain, by Fray Bernardino de Sahagún. Translated from the Aztec into English and annotated by Arthur J. O. Anderson and Charles E. Dibble. Parallel Nahuatl and English versions of the 12 Books of Sahagún, of which all but Book 6 and the planned Index (both in press) have appeared at intervals beginning in 1950. Santa Fe, N.M.: The School of American Research (Museum of New Mexico and University of Utah).

Ford, James A.
1954   "On the Concept of Types: The Type Concept Revisited," *American Anthropologist*, LVI:42–54.

Franco C., José Luis
1959   "La escritura y los códices." *In* Cook de Leonard, ed., 1959, I, 361–78.

Frankfort, Henri
1948   Kingship and the Gods, a Study of Ancient Near Eastern Religion as the Integration of Society and Nature. Chicago: University of Chicago Press.
1956   The Birth of Civilization in the Near East. New York: Anchor.

Gage, Thomas
1648   The English-American His Travail by Sea and Land: Or, A New Survey of the West-Indias. New edition, London: Routledge, 1928.

Gallegos, Roberto
1962   "Exploraciones en Zaachila, Oax.," *Boletín del INAH*, No. 8, 6–8.
1963   "Zaachila: the First Season's Work," in *Archaeology*, XVI:4, 226–33. Trans. Dudley T. Easby, Jr.

Gann, Thomas, and J. Eric S. Thompson
1931   The History of the Maya. New York: Scribner's.

García Payón, José
1941   "La cerámica del Valle de Toluca," *RMEA*, V:2–3, 209–38.
1950   "Restos de una cultura prehistórica encontrados en la region de Zempoala, Veracruz," *Uni-Ver*, Universidad Veracruzana, Xalapa. Vol. II, No. 15, pp. 90–130.
1966   Prehistoria de Mesoamérica. Excavaciones en Trapiche y Chalahuite, Veracruz, México, 1942, 1951 y 1959. Xalapa: Universidad Veracruzana.

García Pimentel, Luis
1904   Relación de los Obispados de Tlaxcala, Michoacán, Oaxaca, y otros lugares en el Siglo XVI. Méjico: en casa del editor.

Gay, José Antonio
1882   Historia de Oaxaca. México: Biblioteca de Autores y de Asuntos Oaxaqueños, 3d edition, 1950. 4 vols.

Genovés, Santiago, ed.
1961   Homenaje a Don Pablo Martínez del Río. Published jointly by UNAM, INAH, MCC, and SMA.

Gillow, Eulogio G., Bishop of Oaxaca
1889   Apuntes históricos. México: Imprenta del Sagrado Corazón de Jesús.

Glass, John B.
1964   Catálogo de la colección de códices [del Museo Nacional de Antropología]. México: Museo Nacional de Antropología.

González de Cossío, Francisco, ed.
1952   El libro de las tasaciones de pueblos de la Nueva España: Siglo XVI. México: Archivo General de la Nación.

Gudschinsky, Sarah C.
1958   "Native Reactions to Tones and Words in Mazatec," *Word*, XIV, 338–45.
1959a   "Discourse Analysis of a Mazatec Text," *International Journal of American Linguistics*, XXV, 139–46.
1959b   "Mazatec Kernel Constructions and Transformations," *International Journal of American Linguistics*, XXV, 81–89.
d'Harcourt, Raoul
1951   "Robert H. Barlow" (obituary), *Journal de la Société des Américanistes*, XL, 245.
Harvey, Herbert R.
1964   "Cultural Continuity in Central Mexico: A Case for Otomangue," *Actas*, II, 525–32.
Hay, Clarence L., *et al.*, eds.
1940   The Maya and Their Neighbors. New York: Appleton-Century. Reprinted, Salt Lake City: University of Utah Press, 1960.
Hendrichs, P. R.
1940   "¿Es el arco de Oztuma de construcción Azteca?," *El México Antiguo*, V:3–5.
Hirtzel, J. S. Harry
1928   "Nôtes sur le classement des manuscrits anciens du Mexique," *Bulletin de la Société des Américanistes du Belgique*, I, 66–70.
Holland, William R., and Robert J. Weitlaner
1960   "Modern Cuicatec Use of Prehistoric Sacrificial Knives," *AA*, XXV: 392–96. In Spanish: "El uso actual de cuchillos prehispánicos de sacrificios humanos entre los cuicatecos," *Anales del INAH*, XII, 75–83.
Holmes, William H.
1897   Archeological Studies among the Ancient Cities of Mexico. Chicago: Field Columbian Museum.
Iturribarría, Jorge Fernando
1960   "Yagul: Mestizo Product of Mixtecs and Zapotecs," *BEO*, No. 17 (Mitla, Museo Frissell).
Jennings, Jesse D., and Edward Norbeck, eds.
1964   Prehistoric Man in the New World. Chicago: University of Chicago Press.
Jiménez Moreno, Wigberto
1939   "Origen y significación del nombre 'Otomí,'" *RMEA*, III:1, 62–69.
1941   "Tula y los Toltecas según las fuentes históricas," *RMEA*, V:2–3, 79–83.
1942   "El enigma de los Olmecas," *CA*, I:5, 113–45. Paraphrased at length by Covarrubias (1946) in English.
1945   "Introducción" a la Guía arqueológica de Tula (by Alberto Ruz Lhuillier). INAH.
1953   "Cronología de la historia de Veracruz." *In* Bernal and Dávalos, eds., 1953, 311–13.
1956   "Síntesis de la historia precolonial del Valle de México," *RMEA*, XIV:1, 219–36.
1959   "Síntesis de la historia pretolteca de Mesoamérica." *In* Cook de Leonard, ed., 1959, II, 1019–1108.
1962a   "Bibliografía selecta sobre el idioma Mixteco." *In* Alvarado 1593.
1962b   "Etimología de toponímicos Mixtecos." *In* Alvarado 1593.

1962c   "Diversidad interna del Mixteco y su afiliación al Macro-Otomangue."
          In Alvarado 1593.
1962d   "Los dominicos en la Mixteca y el Vocabulario de Alvarado." *In*
          Alvarado 1593.
Jiménez Moreno, Wigberto, and Salvador Mateos Higuera
1940   Códice de Yanhuitlan. INAH.
Johnson, Frederick
1940   "The Linguistic Map of Mexico and Central America." *In* Hay *et al.*,
          eds., 1940. *See also* Mason 1940.
Johnson, Irmgard Weitlaner, and Jean Bassett Johnson
1939   "Un cuento mazateco-popoloca," *RMEA*, III:3, 217–26.
Johnson, Jean Bassett
1939   "Some Notes on the Mazatec," *RMEA*, III:2, 142–56.
Joyce, Thomas A.
1914   Mexican Archaeology. London.
Kelley, David H.
1962   "Glyphic Evidence for a Dynastic Sequence at Quiriguá, Guatemala,"
          AA, XXVII:3, 323–35.
Kelly, Isabel
1938   Excavations at Chiametla, Sinaloa. IA:14.
1944   "West Mexico and the Hohokam," in El Norte de México y el Sur de
          Estados Unidos: Tercera Reunión de Mesa Redonda. SMA, 206–22.
1945   Excavations at Culiacán, Sinaloa. IA:25.
1947   Excavations at Apatzingán, Michoacán. Viking Fund Publications in
          Anthropology, No. 7. New York.
1948   "Ceramic Provinces of Northwest Mexico," in El Occidente de
          México: Cuarta Reunión de Mesa Redonda. SMA, 55–71.
1949   The Archaeology of the Autlán-Tuxcacuesco Area of Jalisco. II: The
          Tuxcacuesco-Zapotitlán Zone. IA:27.
Kidder, Alfred V., Jesse D. Jennings, and Edwin M. Shook
1946   Excavations at Kaminaljuyú, Guatemala. CIW, Publication No. 561.
King, Edward, Lord Kingsborough
1831–48   Antiquities of Mexico: Comprising Fac-similes of Ancient Mexican
          Paintings and Hieroglyphs. London. 9 vols.
Kirchhoff, Paul
1940   "Los pueblos de la Historia Tolteca-Chichimeca: sus migraciones y
          parentesco," *RMEA*, IV:1–2, 77–104.
Krickeberg, Walter
1956   Altmexikanische Kulturen. Berlin: Safari Verlag. In Spanish: Las
          antiguas culturas mexicanas. Trans. Sita Garst and Jazmín Reuter.
          México: Fondo de Cultura Económica, 1961.
Lanning, Edward P.
1963   "Olmec and Chavín: Reply to Michael D. Coe," *AA*, XXIX, 99–101.
Lehmann, Walter
1905   "Les peintures Mixtéco-Zapotèques et quelques documents appa-
          rentés," *Journal de la Société des Américanistes de Paris*, II, 241–80.
1920   Zentral Amerika. Berlin.
Lehmann, Walter, and Ottakar Smital. *See* Codex Vindobonensis.
Leigh, Howard
1958a   "Further Discussion of Oaxaca Archeology: A Reply to Mr. Pad-
          dock," *BEO*, No. 8 (MCC).

1958b   "An Identification of Zapotec Day Signs," *BEO*, No. 6 (MCC).
1958c   "Zapotec Glyphs," *BEO*, No. 2 (MCC).
León, Nicolás
1906a   Entre los indios mazatecas. Exploración de los monumentos arqueo-
         lógicos del Cerro de Motecuhzoma y de la Gruta de Nindondahe en
         San Antonio Eloxochitlán (Estado de Oaxaca). Álbum fotográfico.
1906b   "Informe sobre las ruinas del cerro de Moctezuma y la gruta de
         Eloxochitlán," *Boletín de Instrucción Pública*, VI, 645–50.
Leonard, Carmen Cook de. *See* Cook de Leonard, Carmen.
Libby, Willard F.
1955   Radiocarbon Dating. 2d ed. Chicago: University of Chicago Press.
Linné, Sigvald
1938   Zapotecan Antiquities and the Paulson Collection in the Ethnographi-
         cal Museum of Sweden. Stockholm: Bokforlags Aktiebolaget Thule.
1965   Explorations at San Juan Viejo or Diquiyú. *See* Martí, Samuel.
Linton, Ralph
1936   The Study of Man. New York: Appleton-Century.
Lister, Robert H.
1941   "Cerro Oztuma, Guerrero," *El México Antiguo*, V:7–10.
Lizardi Ramos, César
1951   "En memoria de tres miembros de nuestra Sociedad (Robert H. Bar-
         low, Pedro Hendrichs, Mateo Saldaña)," *RMEA*, XII, 187–88.
1955   "Paradero del Códice Fernández Leal," *BBAA*, XVII:1, 234–35.
Longacre, Robert E., and René Millon
1957   "Proto-Mixtecan and Proto-Macro-Mixtecan Vocabularies: a Prelimi-
         nary Cultural Analysis." *Primera Semana Lingüística, México, 1957.*
         In Gloto-Cronología y las lenguas Otomangues. UNAM, 1957. *See*
         Millon and Longacre 1961 *for later version.*
Lorenzo, José Luis
1965   Tlatilco: los artefactos. INAH.
Lorenzo, José Luis, and Miguel Messmacher
1963   "Hallazgo de horizontes culturales precerámicos en el Valle de
         Oaxaca," in Genovés, Santiago, ed., A Pedro Bosch-Gimpera. INAH
         and UNAM, 289–301.
Lothrop, Samuel K.
1926   Pottery of Costa Rica and Nicaragua. New York: Museum of the
         American Indian. 2 vols.
1936   Zacualpa: A Study of Ancient Quiché Artifacts. CIW Publication
         No. 472.
1940   "South America as Seen from Middle America." *In* Hay *et al.*, eds.,
         1940, 417–29 and Plate XX.
Lowe, Gareth W., ed.
1957   Summary Notes, No. 1; New World Archaeological Foundation,
         Publication No. 2. Orinda, Calif. *See* Mason, ed., 1959–
Lowe, Gareth W., and Pierre Agrinier
1960   "Mound 1, Chiapa de Corzo, Chiapas, Mexico," *Papers of the New
         World Archaeological Foundation*, No. 8. Provo, Utah: Brigham
         Young University.
MacNeish, Richard S.
1954   An Early Archaeological Site near Pánuco, Veracruz. Transactions of
         the American Philosophical Society, XLIV:5. Philadelphia.

1958   Preliminary Archaeological Investigations in the Sierra de Tamauli-
          pas, Mexico. Transactions of the American Philosophical Society,
          XLVIII:6. Philadelphia.
1960   "Agricultural Origins in Middle America and Their Diffusion into
          North America," *Katunob*, I:2.
1961a   First Annual Report of the Tehuacan Archaeological-Botanical Proj-
          ect. Andover, Mass.: Peabody Foundation, Phillips Academy.
1961b   "Recent Finds Concerned With the Incipient Agriculture Stage in
          Prehistoric Mesoamerica." *In* Genovés 1961.
1961c   Restos precerámicos de la Cueva de Coxcatlán en el sur de Puebla.
          INAH.
1962   Second Annual Report of the Tehuacan Archaeological-Botanical
          Project. Andover, Mass.: Peabody Foundation, Phillips Academy.
1964a   "Ancient Mesoamerican Civilization," *Science*, Vol. CXLIII, No. 3606,
          531–37.
1964b   "The Food-Gathering and Incipient Agriculture Stage of Prehistoric
          Middle America," *HMAI*, Vol. I.
1964c   "The Origins of New World Civilization," *Scientific American*, CCXI:
          5, 29–37.

MacNeish, Richard S., and Fredrick A. Peterson
1962   "The Santa Marta Rock Shelter near Ocozocuautla, Chiapas, Mexico,"
          Papers of the New World Archaeological Foundation, No. 14. Provo,
          Utah: Brigham Young University.

McQuown, Norman R.
1951   "Robert H. Barlow" (obituary), *American Anthropologist*, LIII, 543.

Mangelsdorf, Paul C., Richard S. MacNeish, and Walton C. Galinat
1964   "Domestication of Corn," *Science*, CXLIII, No. 3606, 538–45.

Mangelsdorf, Paul C., Richard S. MacNeish, and Gordon R. Willey
1964   "Origins of Agriculture in Middle America," *HMAI*, Vol. I.

Il manoscritto messicano Borgiano del Museo etnografico della S. Congregazione di
          Propaganda Fide; riprodotto in fotocromografia a spese di S.E. il
          Duca di Loubat a cura della Biblioteca Vaticana. Rome, 1898.

Il manoscritto messicano Vaticano 3773; riprodotto in fotocromografia a spese di
          S.E. il Duca di Loubat a cura della Biblioteca Vaticana. Rome, 1896.

Marquina, Ignacio
1951   Arquitectura prehispánica. INAH. 2d ed., 1964.

Martí, Samuel
1965a   "¿Ciudad perdida de los mixtecos? Nueva zona arqueológica en la
          Mixteca Alta: Acrópolis de las ruinas de Diquiyú, Oaxaca," *CA*,
          XXIV:1.
1965b   "Diquiyú: Un señorío zapoteco-mixteco ignoto," *CA*, XXIV:2.
1965c   "Un ignoto señorío en la Mixteca Alta, Oaxaca: Diquiyú," *Novedades*,
          16 de mayo de 1965.

Martínez del Río, Pablo
1946   "México, Egipto y Mesopotamia." *In* México prehispánico.
1956   "R. H. Barlow" (obituary), *Tlatelolco a Través de los Tiempos*,
          Memorias de la Academia Mexicana de la Historia, XII, 109–10.

Martínez Gracida, Manuel, ed.
1883   Colección de cuadros sinópticos de los pueblos, haciendas, y ranchos
          del Estado libre y soberano de Oaxaca. Anexo No. 50 a la Memoria
          Administrativa . . . 17 de septiembre de 1883. Oaxaca.

Martínez Marín, Carlos
  1961   Introducción y notas publicadas con la reproducción fotográfica en
          blanco y negro del Códice Laud. INAH.
Martínez Ríos, Jorge
  1961   Bibliografía antropológica y sociológica del Estado de Oaxaca.
          UNAM.
Mason, J. Alden
  1929   "Zapotec Funerary Urns from Mexico," *The Museum Journal*, XX:2,
          176–201. Philadelphia: University of Pennsylvania.
  1940   "The Native Languages of Middle America." *In* Hay *et al.*, eds.,
          1940. *See also* Frederick Johnson 1940.
  1943   "The American Collections of the University Museum. The Ancient
          Civilizations of Middle America," *University Museum Bulletin*, X:
          1–2. Philadelphia.
Mason, J. Alden, ed.
  1959–   Papers of the New World Archaeological Foundation, Nos. 1–18
          (correspond to old series, Publications Nos. 3–13). Papers Nos. 1–7
          (Publications Nos. 3–6, 1959–60) from New World Archaeological
          Foundation, Orinda, Calif. Papers Nos. 8–18 (Publications Nos. 7–
          13, 1960–65) from Provo, Utah: Brigham Young University.
Medellín Zenil, Alfonso
  1955   "Desarrollo de la cultura prehispánica central veracruzana," *Anales
          del INAH*, VII.
Meggers, Betty J., and Clifford Evans, eds.
  1963   Aboriginal Cultural Development in Latin America: An Interpreta-
          tive Review. Washington, D.C.: Smithsonian Miscellaneous Collec-
          tions, CXLVI:1. Papers presented at the XXXV Congreso Interna-
          cional de Americanistas, México, 1962.
Meiss, Millard, *et al.*, eds.
  1963   *Studies in Western Art: Acts of the Twentieth International Congress
          of the History of Art.* Vol. III: Latin American Art and the Baroque
          Period in Europe. Princeton, N.J.: Princeton University Press.
Mejía, Demetrio
  1888   "Informe que el suscrito presenta a la Secretaría de Justicia e Instruc-
          ción Pública, relativo a la exploración de las ruinas del Cerro de Ten-
          guiengajo, en la municipalidad de San Cristóbal Mazatlán," *Anales
          del Museo Nacional*, IV, 17–23 (Entrega 2, 1888). México.
México prehispánico: culturas, deidades y monumentos. Selección hecha por Jorge
          A. Vivó de artículos publicados entre 1935 y 1946 en *Esta Semana—
          This Week*. México: Editorial Emma Hurtado. México, 1946.
Middendorf, Anne. *See* Sosnkowski, Anne Middendorf.
Millon, René, and Robert E. Longacre
  1961   "Proto-Mixtecan and Proto-Amuzgo-Mixtecan Vocabularies, a Pre-
          liminary Cultural Analysis," *Anthropological Linguistics*, III:4, 1–44.
          See Longacre and Millon 1957 *for original form.*
Moedano, Hugo
  1942   "Estudio general sobre la situación de la Fortaleza de Oztuma," *Actas
          del XXVII Congreso Internacional de Americanistas, México, 1939,*
          I, 557–63.
  1946   "La cerámica de Zinapécuaro, Michoacán," *Anales del Museo Micho-
          acano*, 2a época, No. 4, 39–49.

1948   "Breve noticia sobre la zona de Oztotitlán, Guerrero." *In* El Occidente de México: Cuarta Reunión de Mesa Redonda. SMA, 105–6.

Morelli, Giovanni

1890–93 Kunstkritische Studien über italienische Malerei. By Ivan Lermolieff (pseudonym). Leipzig. 2 vols.

Morley, Sylvanus G., and George Brainerd

1956   The Ancient Maya. 3d ed. Stanford, Calif.: Stanford University Press.

Müller, Florencia

1948   Chimalacatlán. Acta Anthropologica, III:1.

Neely, James A.

1965   Irrigation in the Tehuacan Valley. *See* Woodbury 1965.

New World Archaeological Foundation. *See* Lowe, ed. 1957, and Mason, ed. 1959–.

Nicholson, Henry B.

1955   "The Temalácatl of Tehuacán," *El México Antiguo*, VIII, 95–134.

1960a   "The Mixteca-Puebla Concept in Mesoamerican Archeology: A Re-Examination." *In* Wallace 1960, 612–17.

1960b   "News and Notes," *AA*, XXVI:1.

Noguera, Eduardo

1931   "Excavaciones arqueológicas en las regiones de Zamora y Pátzcuaro, Estado de Michoacán," *Anales del Museo Nacional de Arqueología, Historia y Etnografía*, 4a época, VII.

1940   "Excavations at Tehuacan." *In* Hay et al., eds., 1940, 306–19. Translated and condensed by Suzannah B. Vaillant. In Spanish: Noguera 1945a.

1944   "Exploraciones en Jiquilpan," *Anales del Museo Michoacano*, 2a época, No. 3, 37–52.

1945a   "Excavaciones en Tehuacan," *Anales del INAH*, I:49–74. México. In English: Noguera 1940.

1945b   "Excavaciones en Xochicalco," *CA*, IV:1, 1–39.

1946a   "El auge cultural de Monte Albán." *In* México prehispánico.

1946b   "Cultura mixteca." *In* México prehispánico.

1946c   "Cultura zapoteca." *In* México prehispánico.

1947   "Cerámica de Xochicalco," *El México Antiguo*, VI:9–12, 273–98.

1954   La cerámica arqueológica de Cholula. México: Editorial Guarania.

Nowotny, Karl Anton

1961   Tlacuilolli: Die mexikanischen Bilderhandschriften, Stil und Inhalt, mit einem Katalog der Codex-Borgia-Gruppe. Monumenta Americana, III. Berlin.

Nuttall, Zelia. *See* Codex Nuttall.

Olivé Negrete, Julio César

1958   Estructura y dinámica de Mesoamérica. Ensayo sobre sus problemas conceptuales integrativos y evolutivos. Acta Anthropologica, época 2, I:3. México: Escuela Nacional de Antropología e Historia.

Oliver, James P.

1955   "Architectural Similarities of Mitla and Yagul," *MN* 4, 49–67.

Olivera de V., Mercedes, and Blanca Sánchez

1965   Distribución actual de las lenguas indígenas de México. INAH.

O'Neill, John

1893–97 The Night of the Gods: An Inquiry into Cosmic and Cosmogonic Mythology and Symbolism. London: Quaritch.

Orozco y Berra, Manuel
    1864   Geografía de las lenguas y carta etnográfica de México. México.
Owens, Richard T.
    1961   A Descriptive Analysis of Three Tombs at Yagul, Oaxaca. Unpublished Master's thesis, MCC.
Paddock, John
    1953   *MN* 3.
    1955a   "The First Three Seasons at Yagul," *MN* 4, 25–47.
    1955b   "Some Observations," *MN* 4, 80–90.
    1957   "The 1956 Season at Yagul," *MN* 5, 13–36.
    1958a   "Comments on Some Problems of Oaxaca Archeology," *BEO*, No. 4 (MCC).
    1958b   "Further Discussion of Oaxaca Archeology: Clarifications and Suggestions," *BEO*, No. 8 (MCC).
    1959   "Tomorrow in Ancient Mesoamerica," *Texas Quarterly*, II:1, 78–98.
    1960   "Exploración en Yagul, Oaxaca," VII Mesa Redonda de la Sociedad Mexicana de Antropología, 1957. *RMEA*, XVI, 91–96.
    1961   "Yagul Brasero C-14 Date (cont'd)," *Katunob*, II:4, 7–13. Reply to Anonymous 1961.
    1964a   "Current Research: Western Mesoamerica," *AA*, XXIX:3, 406.
    1964b   "Current Research: Western Mesoamerica," *AA*, XXX:1, 132–34.
    1964c   "La etnohistoria mixteca y Monte Albán V," *Actas*, I, 461–78.
    1965   "Current Research: Western Mesoamerica," *AA*, XXXI:1, 133–36.
Palerm, Ángel
    1955   "La secuencia de la evolución cultural de Mesoamérica (del Arcáico a fines del Clásico)," *Ciencias Sociales*, VI, No. 36, 343–70. Also in *BBAA*, XVII:1, 205–33.
Parmenter, Ross
    1961   "20th Century Adventures of a 16th Century Sheet: The Literature on the Mixtec Lienzo in the Royal Ontario Museum," *BEO*, No. 20 (Mitla, Museo Frissell).
    1964   Week in Yanhuitlan. Albuquerque: University of New Mexico Press.
Parsons, Elsie Clews
    1936   Mitla, Town of the Souls. Chicago: University of Chicago Press.
Paso y Troncoso, Francisco del. *See* Del Paso y Troncoso.
Peña, Moisés T. de la. *See* De la Peña.
Peñafiel, Antonio
    1895   Códice Fernández Leal. México.
Pérez, Eutimio
    1888   Recuerdos históricos del Obispado de Oaxaca. Oaxaca.
Peterson, Fredrick A.
    1959   Ancient Mexico. London: Allen & Unwin.
Phillips, Philip, and Gordon R. Willey
    1953   "Method and Theory in American Archaeology: An Operational Basis for Culture-Historical Integration," *American Anthropologist*, LV, 615–33.
Pijoán, José
    1946   Summa Artis. Madrid: Espasa-Calpe.
Pike, Eunice V.
    1954   "Phonetic Rank and Subordination in Consonant Patterning and Historical Changes," Le Maître Phonétique, supplement of Miscellanea Phonetica, II, 25–41.

1956   "Tonally Differentiated Allomorphs in Soyaltepec Mazatec," *International Journal of American Linguistics*, XXII, 57–71.

1957   Vocabulario Mazateco. México: Instituto Lingüístico de Verano.

Pike, Kenneth L., and Eunice V. Pike

1947   "Immediate Constituents of Mazatec Syllables," *International Journal of American Linguistics*, XIII, 78–91.

Piña Chán, Román

1955a   Chalcatzingo, Morelos. INAH.

1955b   Las culturas preclásicas de la Cuenca de México. México: Fondo de Cultura Económica.

1958a   "Excavaciones arqueológicas en el Estado de Morelos," *RMEA*, XIV:2, 121–24.

1958b   Tlatilco. INAH. 2 vols.

1963   "Cultural Development in Central Mesoamerica." *In* Meggers and Evans 1963.

Piña Chán, Román, and Luis Covarrubias

1964   El pueblo del jaguar. México: Museo Nacional de Antropología.

"Place Names," *MN* 4. *See* Anonymous 1955.

Ponce, Fray Alonso. *See* Relación breve . . .

Porrúa, José e Hijos

1964   Diccionario Porrúa de historia, biografía, y geografía de México. México.

Porter, Muriel Noé

1956   Excavations at Chupícuaro, Guanajuato, Mexico. Transactions of the American Philosophical Society, XLVI:5. Philadelphia.

Proskouriakoff, Tatiana

1960   "Historical Implications of a Pattern of Dates at Piedras Negras, Guatemala," *AA*, XXV:4, 454–75.

1963   An Album of Maya Architecture. 2d ed. Norman: University of Oklahoma Press.

Ralph, Elizabeth K.

1965   "Review of Radiocarbon Dates from Tikal and the Maya Calendar Correlation Problem," *AA*, XXX:4, 421–27.

Reed, Nelson

1964   The Caste War of Yucatan. Stanford, Calif.: Stanford University Press.

Relación breve y verdedera de algunas cosas de las muchas que sucedieron al Padre Fray Alonso Ponce . . . escrita por dos religiosos, sus compañeros. Madrid: Imprenta de la Viuda de Calero, 1875. 2 vols.

Reyes, Fray Antonio de los

1593   Arte en lengua mixteca. México.

Rickards, Constantine George

1910   The Ruins of Mexico. Vol. I [the only one published]. London: Shrimpton.

Robertson, Donald

1959   "The Relaciones Geográficas of Mexico," *Actas del XXXIII Congreso Internacional de Americanistas, San José de Costa Rica, 1958*, II, 540–47.

1963   "The Style of the Borgia Group of Mexican Pre-Conquest Manuscripts." *In* Millard Meiss *et al.*, eds., 1963, 148–64 and Plates XLIX–LII.

1964   "Los manuscritos religiosos mixtecos," *Actas,* I, 425–35. Trans. Arturo
          Souto and John Paddock.

Romero, Javier
  1958   Mutilaciones dentarias prehispánicas de México y América en ge-
          neral. México: INAH.

Rubín de la Borbolla, Daniel F.
  1948a   "Arqueología Tarasca," in El Occidente de México: Cuarta Reunión
          de Mesa Redonda. SMA.
  1948b   "Problemas de la arqueología de Chupícuaro," in El Occidente de
          México: Cuarta Reunión de Mesa Redonda. SMA.

Ruz Lhuillier, Alberto
  1945a   Campeche en la arqueología maya. Acta Anthropologica I:2–3.
          México: Escuela Nacional de Antropología e Historia.
  1945b   Guía arqueológica de Tula. INAH.

Sáenz, César A.
  1962a   "Exploraciones en Xochicalco, Morelos," *Boletín del INAH,* No. 7,
          1–2.
  1962b   "Tres estelas en Xochicalco," *RMEA,* XVII, 39–65.
  1962c   Xochicalco, temporada 1960. INAH.

Sahagún, Fray Bernardino de
  1938   Historia general de las cosas de Nueva España. México: Editorial
          Pedro Robredo. Foreword by Wigberto Jiménez Moreno. 5 vols. *See*
          Florentine Codex *for English edition.*

Satterthwaite, Linton F., and Elizabeth K. Ralph
  1960   "New Radiocarbon Dates and the Maya Correlation Problem," *AA,*
          XXVI:2, 165–84.

Saville, Marshall H.
  1909   The Cruciform Structures of Mitla and Vicinity. New York: author's
          edition; reprint of an article included in the Putnam Anniversary
          Volume.

Schmieder, Oscar
  1930   The Settlements of the Tzapotec and Mije Indians, State of Oaxaca,
          Mexico. Berkeley: University of California Publications in Geogra-
          phy, No. 4.

Séjourné, Laurette
  1960   "El simbolismo de los rituales funerarios en Monte Albán," VII Mesa
          Redonda de la Sociedad Mexicana de Antropología, 1957. *RMEA,*
          XVI, 77–90.

Seler, Eduard
  1901–2   Codex Fejérváry-Mayer. *See* Codex Fejérváry-Mayer.
  1902–23   Gesammelte Abhandlungen zur amerikanischen Sprach- und Alter-
          tumskunde. Berlin. Reprinted in facsimile, ADV, 1960–61.
  1902–3   Codex Vaticanus 3773 (Vaticanus B). *See* Codex Vaticanus No. 3773.
  1904–9   Codex Borgia. *See* Codex Borgia and Códice Borgia.

Séptimo censo general de la población: *Estado de Oaxaca.* México: Secretaría de
          Economía, Dirección General de Estadística, 1953.

Sexto censo de población: 1940, tomo *Oaxaca.* México: Secretaría de la Economía
          Nacional, Dirección General de Estadística, 1948.

Shook, Edwin M.
  1960   "Tikal Stela 29," *Expedition* (Philadelphia: The University Mu-
          seum), Winter 1960, 29–35.

Shook, Edwin M., William R. Coe, Vivian L. Broman, and Linton Satterthwaite
1958 "Tikal Reports," Nos. 1–4, *Museum Monographs* (Philadelphia: The University Museum).

Shook, Edwin M., and Alfred V. Kidder
1952 "Mound E-III-3, Kaminaljuyú, Guatemala," *Contributions to American Anthropology and History*, CIW, XI:52–53.

Simpson, Lesley Byrd
1952 Exploitation of Land in Central Mexico in the Sixteenth Century. IA:36.

Smisor, George T.
1952 "R. H. Barlow and *Tlalocan*," *Tlalocan*, III, 97–102.

Smith, C. Earle, Jr., and Richard S. MacNeish
1964 "Antiquity of American Polyploid Cotton," *Science*, CXLIII, No. 3607, 675–76.

Smith, Mary Elizabeth
1963 "The Codex Colombino, a Document of the South Coast of Oaxaca," *Tlalocan*, IV:3, 276–88.

Smith, Robert E.
1955 Ceramic Sequence at Uaxactún, Guatemala. Middle American Research Institute, Publication No. 20. New Orleans: Tulane University. 2 vols.
1958 "The Place of Fine Orange Pottery in Mesoamerican Archaeology," *AA*, XXIV:2, 151–60.

Sosnkowski, Anne Middendorf
1957 An Area Study of the Distribution of Tombs in Mesoamerica. Unpublished Master's thesis, MCC.

Spinden, Herbert Joseph
1911 "An Ancient Sepulcher at Placeres del Oro, State of Guerrero, Mexico," *American Anthropologist*, n.s., XIII, 29–55.

Spores, Ronald M.
1964a Cultural Continuity and Native Rule in the Mixteca Alta: 1500–1600. Unpublished doctoral thesis, Harvard University.
1964b "The Genealogy of Tlazultepec: a Sixteenth Century Mixtec Manuscript," *Southwestern Journal of Anthropology*, XX:1, 15–31.
1965 "The Zapotec and Mixtec at Spanish Contact," *HMAI*, III, 962–90.

Starr, Frederick
1900 "Notes upon the Ethnography of Southern Mexico. Part I." Davenport, Iowa; author's edition, reprinted from *Proceedings of the Davenport Academy of Natural Sciences*, VII.
[1903–4?] "Mexican Literary Curiosities." Chicago.
1908 In Indian Mexico: a Narrative of Travel and Labor. Chicago.

Steward, Julian H.
1948 "A Functional-Developmental Classification of American High Cultures." *In* Bennett, ed., 1948, 103–4.
1949 "Cultural Causality and Law: A Trial Formulation of the Development of Early Civilizations," *American Anthropologist*, LI, 1–27. Also in Steward 1955b, 178–209.

Steward, Julian H., ed.
1955a Irrigation Civilizations: a Comparative Study. Washington, D.C.: Pan American Union, Social Science Monographs, No. 1.
1955b Theory of Culture Change. Urbana: University of Illinois Press.

Stirling, Matthew W.
   1966   "Monumental Sculpture of Southern Veracruz and Tabasco," *HMAI*,
             III, 716–38.
Strebel, Hermann
   1885–89   Alt Mexiko. Archäologische Beitrage zur Kulturgeschichte seiner Be-
             wohner. Hamburg and Leipzig. 2 vols.
Suma de visitas de pueblos por orden alfabético: Manuscrito 2,800 de la Biblioteca
             Nacional de Madrid. Anónimo de la mitad del siglo XVI. This is Del
             Paso y Troncoso 1905, Vol. I. *See also* Borah and Cook 1960.
Swadesh, Morris [Mauricio]
   1959   "Ochenta lenguas autóctonas," in Cook de Leonard, ed., 1959, I,
             85–96.
   1960a   La lingüística como instrumento de la prehistoria. INAH. Trans.
             Leonardo Manrique. Also in Acta Anthropologica, época 2a, II:2,
             93–127. First published in English as "Linguistics as an Instrument
             of Prehistory," *Southwestern Journal of Anthropology*, XV:1, 20–35;
             but the illustrative material used there was not Oaxacan.
   1960b   "The Oto-Manguean Hypothesis and Macro-Mixtecan," *International
             Journal of American Linguistics*, XXVI:2, 79–111.
Tax, Sol, ed.
   1951   The Civilizations of Ancient America. Selected Papers of the XXIX
             International Congress of Americanists, Vol. I. Chicago: University
             of Chicago Press.
Tello, Fray Antonio
   1891   Libro Segundo de la Crónica miscelánea . . . de la Santa Provincia de
             Xalisco. Guadalajara.
Tello, Julio C.
   1953   "Discovery of the Chavín Culture in Peru," *AA*, XIX, 135–60.
Thompson, J. Eric S.
   1948   An Archaeological Reconnaissance in the Cotzumalhuapa Region,
             Escuintla, Guatemala. Contributions to American Anthropology and
             History, No. 44. CIW.
   1954   The Rise and Fall of Maya Civilization. Norman: University of Okla-
             homa Press. Revised edition in press.
Tolstoy, Paul
   1958   Surface Survey of the Northern Valley of Mexico: the Classic and
             Post-Classic Periods. *Transactions of the American Philosophical So-
             ciety*, XLVIII:5.
Tompkins, John B.
   1942   "Codex Fernández Leal," *Pacific Art Review*, II, 39–59.
Torquemada, Fray Juan de
   1723   Los veinte y un. libros rituales y monarchia indiana . . . Madrid. Fac-
             simile edition, México: Editorial Salvador Chávez Hayhoe, 1943.
             3 vols.
Vaillant, George C.
   1930   Excavations at Zacatenco. Anthropological Papers of the American
             Museum of Natural History, XXXII:1. New York.
   1931   Excavations at Ticomán. Anthropological Papers of the American
             Museum of Natural History, XXXII:2. New York.

1941　The Aztecs of Mexico: Origin, Rise, and Fall of the Aztec Nation. New York: Doubleday. New edition, revised and annotated by Suzannah B. Vaillant, 1962.

Valenzuela, Juan
1938　"Las exploraciones efectuadas en los Tuxtlas, Veracruz," *Anales del Museo Nacional de Arqueología, Historia y Etnografía,* 5a época, III, 83–108.
1942　"Informe preliminar de las exploraciones efectuadas en Los Tuxtlas, Veracruz," *Actas del XXVII Congreso Internacional de Americanistas, México, 1939,* II, 113–30.
1945　"La segunda temporada de exploraciones en la región de Los Tuxtlas, Estado de Veracruz," *Anales del INAH,* I, 81–94.

Vázquez de Espinosa, Fray Antonio
1944　Descripción de la Nueva España en el siglo XVII. México: Editorial Patria. An English version of the whole book (Compendio y descripción de las Indias del Perú y Nueva España) of which this is a part was published in a translation by Charles Upson Clark, who discovered the original in the Vatican Library. Washington, D.C.: Smithsonian Institution, Miscellaneous Collections, 102, 1942.

Venturi, Lionello
1936　History of Art Criticism. New York: Dutton. Trans. Charles Marriott.

Villa Rojas, Alfonso
1955　Los mazatecos y el problema indígena de la Cuenca del Papaloapan. Memorias del Instituto Nacional Indigenista, VII. México.

Villagra, Agustín
1942　" 'Los Danzantes,' piedras grabadas del Montículo 'L,' Monte Albán, Oaxaca," *Actas del XXVII Congreso Internacional de Americanistas, México, 1939,* II, 143–58.

Villa-Señor y Sánchez, Joseph Antonio de
1746–48 Theatro americano . . . México: facsimile edition by Editora Nacional, 1952. 2 vols.

Wallace, Anthony F. C., ed.
1960　Men and Cultures: Selected Papers of the Fifth International Congress of Anthropological and Ethnological Sciences, Philadelphia, 1956. Philadelphia: University of Pennsylvania Press.

Wauchope, Robert
1948　Excavations at Zacualpa, Guatemala. New Orleans: Middle American Research Institute, Tulane University.
1950　"A Tentative Sequence of Pre-Classic Ceramics in Middle America," *Middle American Research Records,* I:15, 211–50. Issued individually, 1950; in collection, 1951. New Orleans: Middle American Research Institute, Tulane University.
1954　"Implications of Radiocarbon Dates from Middle and South America," *Middle American Research Records,* II:2, 17–39. Issued individually, 1954; in collection, 1961. New Orleans: Middle American Research Institute, Tulane University. In Spanish: "Las fechas del carbón radiactivo y la arqueología americana," *Ciencias Sociales,* VI, No. 33 (1955), 161–79. Washington, D.C.: Pan American Union.

Weitlaner, Robert J.
  1941   "Los pueblos no nahuas de la historia tolteca y el grupo lingüístico
          Macro-Oto-Mangue," *RMEA*, V:2–3, 249–69.
  1948   "Exploración arqueológica en Guerrero," in El Occidente de México:
          Cuarta Reunión de Mesa Redonda. SMA.
  1961   "The Guatinicamame." *In* A William Cameron Townsend . . . Méxi-
          co: Instituto Lingüístico de Verano.
Weyerstall, Albert
  1932   Some Observations on Indian Mounds, Idols and Pottery in the
          Lower Papaloapan Basin, Veracruz, Mexico. *Middle American Pa-
          pers*, Middle American Research Series Publication 4, pp. 27–69.
          New Orleans: Middle American Research Institute, Tulane Uni-
          versity.
Wheeler, Sir Mortimer
  1954   Rome beyond the Imperial Frontiers. London: Penguin.
Whitaker, T., M. Cutler, and R. MacNeish
  1957   "Cucurbit Materials from Three Caves near Ocampo, Tamaulipas,"
          AA, XXII:4, 352–58.
Wicke, Charles R.
  1964   "La tumba 30 de Yagul. Comparación con las tumbas de Zaachila,"
          Actas, I, 449–52. Trans. Arturo Souto.
  1965   Olmec: An Early Art Style of Precolumbian Mexico. Unpublished
          doctoral thesis, University of Arizona. Revised version in press, Tuc-
          son: University of Arizona Press.
Williams, Howel, and Robert F. Heizer
  1965   "Geological Notes on the Ruins of Mitla and Other Oaxaca Sites,
          Mexico." *In* Contributions of the University of California Archeologi-
          cal Research Facility, No. 1, 41–54. Berkeley: University of Cali-
          fornia, Department of Anthropology.
Willey, Gordon R., and Philip Phillips
  1955   "Method and Theory in American Archaeology. II: Historical-De-
          velopmental Interpretation," *American Anthropologist*, LXII, 723–
          819. *See* Phillips and Willey 1953.
  1958   Method and Theory in American Archaeology. Chicago: University
          of Chicago Press.
Wolf, Eric R.
  1959   Sons of the Shaking Earth. Chicago: University of Chicago Press.
Woodbury, Richard B.
  1965   Report on irrigation in Tehuacan Valley. *In* Paddock 1965.

Index